Praise for *The ... Model of Tragedy*

"Thought-provoking, insightful and compelling ... extremely engaging and impossible to put down." –CAROL CARTER, *NJ DRAMA AUSTRALIA JOURNAL*

"A vision that has been a long time coming ... a fresh, distinctive method for analyzing and staging tragedies ... valuable for scholars, directors, and playwrights." –JAYETTA SLAWSON, *THEATRE HISTORY STUDIES*

"An insightful and compelling read ... Through the art of reinterpretation, Wong manages to present a bold, inventive new model of theatre through the lens of risk." –KERRIE NICHOLSON, *BROADWAY WORLD UK*

"The author's diagnosis and remedy for the current state of theater are imaginative and quite persuasive ... An ambitious, thought-provoking critique of tragedy in the 21st century." –*KIRKUS*

"Beautifully written, original, and compelling ... an Aristotle for the 21st century." –DAVID KONSTAN, BROWN UNIVERSITY

"The idea of tragedy was wrapped in the mystique of motivations and nobility and flaws that put it out of reach for me as a playwright. This book strips away the mystique and makes the form available to me." –two-time Academy Award nominee DONALD CONNOLLY, *GOODREADS*

"If you love literature—theater, film, novels, history, biography, opera, whatever—you need to read this extraordinary work ... Read it—twice. You will never read another work of literature the same way." –CHARLIE EUCHNER, COLUMBIA UNIVERSITY

"If you like Taleb or Nietzsche, and have a liking for the arts, check it out! It has some of the punchy and mentally adventurous qualities of Taleb." –PHILO, *AMAZON*

"Making the case for risk theory as a new definition for tragic theater, *The Risk Theatre Model of Tragedy* is a piquant, far-reaching study of tragedy as an art form." –HO LIN, *FOREWORD*

"Be sure to read the footnotes which are chock full of good stuff from Wild Bill Hickok anecdotes to the link between tragedy and goats! Tragedy will rise again!!" –ALAN THURSTON, *BARNES & NOBLE*

"As I turned the pages his theory grew on me and I found myself both convinced and gripped by this new perspective on tragedy ... A remarkable book in every way. A must for every serious dramatist to read, ponder over and act upon." –DAVID DUNCAN, *GOODREADS*

"*The Risk Theatre Model of Tragedy* offers a fresh perspective not only of the classical theater but more importantly of how we can restructure the old paradigms in a way that speaks to modern audiences." –MIKE, *AMAZON*

"A most excellent and original work regarding tragedy from the perspective of risks and consequences and how it intersects and reflects within our rapidly evolving world. A book of insights that will be invaluable to theatregoers, writers, directors, actors or as an engaging college text. Highly recommended!" –STEVE ROMAGNOLI, *GOODREADS*

"A wonderful, lucid read—erudite, nimble, and approachable. I read the whole book in two days. The author's goal is to clarify ideas and not muddy them, and in this he succeeds. A rare and refreshing thing in today's universe of bizarro literary criticism." –KENNY JAY, *FACEBOOK*

"Wong has written a masterpiece ... His risk theatre model captures the reader's imagination and is presented in a way that appeals to the academic and the layperson." –ESTHER, *GOODREADS*

"Wong presents an original theory of tragedy that resonates with our modern age." –JOY HUEBERT, *ISLAND WRITER*

"Wong's risk theatre is a well thought out and flexible structure built with the intention of reviving the tragic theatre of the past using modern allegories and scenarios." –MIKE ROUTLIFFE, *GOODREADS*

"Wong constructs his risk theatre model with clarity and with a passion for the subject matter that is infectious. A fascinating read." –VISHESH ABEYRATNE, *FACEBOOK*

"Theatre analyzed in terms of risk!—what a clever way of looking at things." –*WISHING SHELF*

WHEN LIFE
GIVES YOU
RISK
MAKE RISK THEATRE

Three Tragedies and
Six Essays

by Edwin Wong, Gabriel Jason Dean,
Nicholas Dunn, and Emily McClain

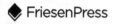 FriesenPress

One Printers Way
Altona, MB R0G 0B0
Canada

www.friesenpress.com

ISBN
978-1-03-913510-9 (Hardcover)
978-1-03-913509-3 (Paperback)
978-1-03-913511-6 (eBook)

1. Performing Arts, Theater
2. Drama, American
3. Literary Criticism, Drama

Distributed to the trade by The Ingram Book Company

For those who lived to win,
but were born to lose

Table of Contents

Foreword

For the past thirty years I have been fortunate enough to be an editor of academic prose—first as a co-editor of the *Ben Jonson Journal*, then as a main editor for nearly fifty volumes about literature published by Salem Press, and then as chief editor of the *BJJ*. In these capacities, I have had the privilege of reading lots of fine work by scores and scores of academic writers—most of them tenured professors, some of them independent scholars. Rarely, however, have I been as intrigued and excited by anyone's writing as I have been by the works I've read by Edwin Wong. I cannot remember precisely how we first made contact, but I do remember reading that first essay and thinking "this man can write" and also "this man has lots of extremely interesting things to say."

After finishing that first essay, I decided that I would try to include Edwin's work in as many different future projects as possible, and I have not been disappointed by that decision. Each new essay Edwin has submitted has helped develop his larger project, which has been to argue that elements of pure chance are extremely relevant in works of dramatic literature, including not only tragedies but also comedies as well. Whereas most academic writings about drama tend to emphasize deep underlying issues of meaningful cause and effect (such as pride being the inevitable cause of tragedy), Edwin argues that things are rarely ever that simple. He contends that chance, bad luck, and what he sometimes calls "black swan events" pay a much more significant role in literature and life than we like to assume.

I have now read and admired numerous essays by Edwin on this general topic, and never have I read an essay by him that was not very engagingly written and extremely thought-provoking. Moreover, although Edwin is definitely advancing a larger argument, his individual essays always offer something new, something unexpected. He is immensely well-read, and his reading encompasses not only the whole range of western literature (from the classics to the present day, with a special emphasis on drama); it also involves an impressive grasp of various secondary scholarship from numerous fields. Often people who write about literature cite other studies of literature. Sometimes they draw on historical scholarship as well. Occasionally they venture into psychology, sociology, and/or philosophy. Edwin draws on all these kinds of fields, but he also seems familiar with scholarship in fields far beyond the usual sorts, such as mathematics, probability theory, arcane economic thought, and so on. Reading Edwin's work has always been, at least for me, a true source of education and stimulation. I always look forward to reading his writing and learning new things from him. And I predict that you will have the very same reaction. It is a pleasure to see so much of his work now published between the covers of a single book.

ROBERT C. EVANS

Preface

In 2018, I picked up a book on web design and purchased a domain. I named the domain *risktheatre.com* and wrote the following words on the homepage:

The Premise of Risk Theatre

There's an undercurrent of interest in risk and uncertainty for theatre to capitalize on. We live in an increasingly complex world where unintended consequences abound. More than ever, we have a moral imperative to understand risk. What is risk? What could go wrong? The best place to simulate risk is on the tragic stage. This belief informs risk theatre, which is based on the following premises:

1) Tragedy consists of a gambling act in which protagonists wager all-in.

2) By wagering all-in, protagonists expose themselves to unexpected and catastrophic low-probability, high-consequence events.

3) As the dramatization of a gambling act, the emotional reaction of risk theatre is anticipation and apprehension: anticipation for what the protagonist wagers and apprehension for the price the protagonist, the

xviii | *When Life Gives You Risk, Make Risk Theatre*

protagonist's friends and family, and the community must pay.

Examples of Risk Theatre

In the risk theatre interpretation of *Macbeth*, Macbeth wagers the milk of human kindness for the crown and is struck down by a low-probability event: Birnam Wood. In *Oedipus rex*, Oedipus bets against the gods and does quite well. Until the Corinthian messenger comes out of nowhere. In *Death of a Salesman*, Loman stakes his dignity on the American Dream, only to find that he is worth more dead than alive. And in *The Cincinnati Kid*, the Kid is on the verge of defeating the Man. But then the Man makes "the wrong move at the right time." Audiences emerge from risk theatre with a heightened awareness of how low-probability, high-consequence events impact us, both in life and on the stage. We had thought it was an error or a tragic flaw but, really, it's chance. Just like how Pablo finds out in Sartre's *The Wall*.

The Risk Theatre Modern Tragedy Playwriting Competition was born. Its goal is to make risk sing again, like it did in the days when tragedy was the greatest show on earth.

The World's Largest Competition for the Writing of Tragedy

In its first year, the competition offered dramatists an $8,000 grand prize and four $500 finalist prizes to play with risk. The winning playwright would be invited to Victoria, Canada, for a workshop which would culminate in a staged reading.

To keep the playing field level, scripts were judged by an international team of jurors in a double-blind process: not only were scripts read blind, the jurors remained anonymous to the public and one another until the winners were announced. I was surprised by the tremendous artistic burst the call unleashed. Initial projections ranged from sixty entries at the low end to one hundred at the high end. Sixty entries would make a competition. If eighty entries came in, well, that would be cause for celebration. The upper limit of possibility was a hundred entries; tragedy, after all, is a specialized art, and one out of vogue. What happened, however, was astounding: 182 entries came in from eleven countries, including former Soviet republics. Who would have thought that risk could skew so far to the upside?

The first year of the competition coincided with the publication of my first book, *The Risk Theatre Model of Tragedy: Gambling, Drama, and the Unexpected*. It hit the shelves in February 2019 and set loose a truly unique theory of tragedy, the first in a long time. In risk theatre, risk is the dramatic fulcrum of the action. Tragedy dramatizes downside risk. Downside risk happens when a low-probability, high-consequence event strikes the hero down. Birnam Wood coming to Dunsinane Hill in Shakespeare's *Macbeth* provided a captivating visual analogy of the risk theatre concept: the probability of the wood advancing on Inverness was low, but, when it happened, the consequences were high. Tragedy happens when more things happen than what we think will happen happens. Tragedy is the art of chance, uncertainty, and the unexpected.

That the highly improbable cuts down the hero's best-laid plans led to a critical insight: tragedy is really a *valuing* mechanism. It shows how much, in human terms, we are willing to sacrifice for the objects of our ambition. To use the example from *Macbeth*, the Scottish crown is worth so many dollars, depending on the price per ounce of gold. But this does not tell you its real value because it is not for sale. Its true value is what Macbeth gives up to obtain it, which is compassion, or the milk of human kindness. Risk theatre's insight is that the economic market values things in dollars and cents while the tragic market values things in terms of the human cost. Tragedy is, at bottom, a valuing mechanism ascribing value to the human. The hero-gambler, by staking the milk of human kindness, friendship, love, honour, dignity, reputation, life, limb, or family on the object of ambition, establishes, through the opportunity cost concept, what the object of ambition is worth, in human terms. Then, when chance rears up in the form of the low-probability, high-consequence event, all is lost. In that moment, the audience realizes not only the fragility of want, will, and intention, but also the human price of all our hopes, dreams, and ambitions.

Not only does risk theatre identify tragedy as a valuing mechanism, it also identifies the hero's wager as the mechanism that allows tragedy to function as a valuing mechanism. Risk theatre is to literary theory what natural selection is to evolution. Although the process of evolution was conjectured prior to Darwin, Darwin identified natural selection as the mechanism which drove evolution. Similarly, although it was long conjectured, prior to risk theatre, that tragedy ennobles, risk theatre identified the process by which tragedy ennobles: by making big bets, heroes drive up the perceived value of life.

Theatre and the Scientific Method

Risk theatre's core concepts—that tragedy dramatizes downside risk and acts as a valuing mechanism—presents the boldest advance in tragic theory since Aristotle's *Poetics* was written some twenty-four centuries ago. By exploding staid and respectable literary theory with probability theory and the random element, risk theatre connects the theory of tragedy with the present age of uncertainty, an age marked by increasing volatility driven by fringe movements, pandemics, artificial intelligence, gene editing, globalization, the decline of Westphalian sovereignty, the revolt against colonialism, resource depletion, income inequality, and climate change. The presses, however, disagreed. University presses deemed the book fit for trade presses. Trade presses deemed the book fit for university presses. All the presses deemed it unfit for publication. At least they could agree on something.

I was at a loss. Here I had a manuscript, thirteen years in the writing, without an outlet. It would have been a shame, however, for risk theatre to remain in the dark. Even if the gatekeepers were unconvinced, risk theatre, to me, was the most convinced. Friends suggested I look into self-publishing. The age of the gig economy and the days of eBay and Etsy were upon us. People were taking control by driving Ubers, renting out Airbnbs, or delivering DoorDash. While the gatekeepers were looking for the keys, everything was becoming possible.

As luck would have it, the self-publishing arm of Friesens Corporation—a major international press—was located in Victoria, Canada. I walked into their office in the summer of 2018 and asked for a quote. For $1,799, they would provide cover art, typesetting, design, and distribution to over fifty thousand booksellers. Without so much as batting an eye, I signed the contract and walked out an author. The distribution channel itself was worth the price of admission. Not only did self-publishing allow my book to become available, it also made it accessible. Traditional academic titles cost north of a hundred dollars. My paperback would cost under twenty and the audiobook and eBook under ten. Thanks to self-publishing, risk theatre is available *and* accessible.

One problem was solved—the gate was now open—but in solving the first issue, another arose: who would read a self-published book on dramatic literary theory by a writer outside academia, and one who laboured as a plumber? Instead of lecturing in classrooms and auditoriums, I could more often be found plumbing restrooms and installing heating systems. Traditional presses drive interest in their titles through advertising campaigns and marketing networks. I would create my own network by founding and funding an international playwriting competition, one based on my risk theatre theory of tragedy. It was a longshot, but one befitting one who writes on risk. By founding the competition, I bet all-in on risk theatre. Having talked the talk, I would walk the walk.

In ways that I had not intended, the one-two combination of the book release with the competition was not only fortuitous, it also struck a contemporary chord. Today's world is an interdisciplinary one where the arts and sciences interact more frequently and with greater intensity. Today's playwrights, students, and scholars expect literary theory to be informed by science. Gone are the wild days of theory driven by invisible processes and speculative faculties based on bogus assumptions on human nature. In the new model, laid out by biologist and two-time Pulitzer Prize winner E. O. Wilson, first in his 1978 book, *On Human Nature*, and again in his 1998 book, *Consilience*, art would take its cue from developments in the social sciences, which would themselves be influenced by the hard sciences in a trickle-down of information. Art would, in turn, modify the direction of science because art is, fundamentally, a form of experiment.

Some things work in art and on the stage; some do not. The scientific method is at work in art. This was the insight of Angus Fletcher, a neuroscientist turned English professor. In his 2021 book, *Wonderworks*, he argues that living art, and especially live theatre, undergoes a scientific process: what works on the stage is reinforced and what fails on the stage is falsified. In my first book, I presented the hypothesis that tragedy achieves its effect by dramatizing low-probability, high-consequence risk events. There was only one way to find out whether this hypothesis was true, and that was by inviting dramatists to write risk theatre plays. If audiences enjoyed their plays, risk theatre would achieve proof of concept. If not, it would be falsified and thrown into history's great dumpster of failed ideas.

Imagine where science would be without the experimentalists—the Eddingtons and the Cavendishes—to test the theories of the Einsteins and the Newtons. Science would be full of wacko theory. Today is a great day because literary theory must prove itself in the real world, in the world of the experimentalists. The dark age rife with groundless speculation dawns into a new day. Today is a day of celebration: the competition will test the hypothesis of risk theatre. Risk theatre is an honest theory of tragedy because it takes theory from page to stage.

Three Risk Theatre Plays

This collection starts off with three tragedies where risk works. The three tragedies are alike in that they showcase uncertainty, the unknown, and the empire of chance in its meridian times. These are the plays where dynamos overcome the smallness of their existence with the greatness of their daring. Each play is unique, however, in showcasing a different face of risk. Each time risk breaks out, it breaks out in its own unique way.

The risk theatre tragedies begin with the 2019 winner: Gabriel Jason Dean's *In Bloom*. In the play, journalist Aaron Freeman arrives at Cambridge to accept the prestigious Sommerville Prize for his work to end the *bacha bazi* subculture of child prostitution in Afghanistan. There are flashes of Arthur Miller here: for Miller, as well as Dean, the past is never far behind. With great dexterity, Dean weaves the past that took place in Badakhshan Province, Afghanistan, into the present of a Cambridge auditorium. In an explosive finale, the past crests and consumes the present. It is a delight to relate the magic of *In Bloom* through a story, a true story from the night of the risk theatre staged reading. A friend had come to see the show. She said, "After the intermission, I have to run home to put the kids to bed." At the end of the show, I looked around. She was there. She smiled and said, "I *had* to see what happened." These moments capture the magic of live theatre and showcase *In Bloom*'s power to move. Risk captivates, holding audiences in thrall.

While *In Bloom* is set far away, the next risk theatre tragedy and winner of the 2020 competition, Nicholas Dunn's *The Value*, is set closer to home. It is set in a motel room, any of the ones that line the interstate highways. As its title suggests, the play examines worth, exchange, and commerce. As an examination of capitalism, *The Value* is the next great American tragedy. It brings to life the story of a trio of petty thieves who have little idea of the precariousness of what they have stolen: a painting fittingly called *Summum bonum*, Latin for "the highest good." The only thing they know about the painting is that it is in crate thirty-two. As the thieves work through the process of price discovery, they ask themselves what their own highest good is, and the price they will pay for it. In *The Value*, one of the thieves has a line he repeats like a mantra: "This is what happens," he says. The line captures risk's allure. While workshopping the play, actor

Anthony Gaskins put an emphasis on *this*, separating the initial word from the rest of the sentence with a subtle pause. Dunn encouraged us to associate the line with basketball superstar LeBron James's iconic chalk toss ritual: something magic is in the air. Watching risk theatre is like going into game seven of the NBA finals—when *everything* is on the line, *anything* can happen.

Emily McClain's *Children of Combs and Watch Chains*, a finalist in the 2020 competition, rounds out the selection of the risk theatre tragedies. The pacing of this intensely personal tragedy is like no other. A vitality and forward-striving helter-skelter intensity reminiscent of Shakespeare drives *Children of Combs and Watch Chains* straight to the finish line. McClain's play brings to life the dream of a couple who work out elaborate and labyrinthine strategies to become parents. In the complexity of their individual arrangements, they lose sight of the forest for the trees. As husband and wife dare to pursue their mutual yet contradictory paths to parenthood, life's grand jest plays out: they are at their highest the moment before the fall. In eleven accelerating scenes, McClain emphatically demonstrates that, on the stage, risk equals speed. Risk drives the action onwards, inexorably. In driving the action forwards in as few words as necessary, risk theatre resonates with today's audiences familiar with Twitter character limits and the wonderful brevity of texting. Pity and fear are too wordy. Risk, being brisk, is the new pity and fear.

Each of these plays, while showcasing a different face of risk, also springboards into a discussion of today's critical issues. The Youngs' domestic tragedy in *Children of Combs and Watch Chains* segues into the silences, secrets, and communication breakdowns between couples that take place behind closed doors. While some work on unlocking the mysteries of nature and the cosmos, McClain's play reminds us of how great a mystery lies in the dynamics between a husband and a wife, and of how so much goodness can be so quickly unwound. Dunn's play, on the other hand, dramatizes the opportunity cost of decision. *The Value* sets on the stage life's heartbreaking either/or propositions. Finally, Dean's character Aaron brings to mind disgraced cyclist Lance Armstrong and other do-gooders with questionable backgrounds. Armstrong, like Aaron with his philanthropic Bloom Project, also worked great good through his Livestrong Foundation (supporting cancer patients). But, also like Aaron, he has worked great harm. *In Bloom* is a springboard into a larger question of legacies. As a new *Beeldenstorm* breaks out where the statues of colonialism's saints are hurled from the altars, how shall we redefine all the broken legacies? The answers are written in risk theatre.

The Youngs are your neighbours living across the street. Close by, further away, across the tracks, in the darkness on the edge of the town small-time thieves look for the immaculate score so high and wild that it sets them free. You have seen them, hooded shadows. On your television screens and your social media feeds, every day another podcast talks about a new Aaron. These plays are great because they are relevant to life. They capture the faces of risk. They are the vanguard of a coming age of grand theatre, the theatre of low-probability, high-consequence events.

Risk Theatre's Critical Reception

Many an author's first book goes through the first book blues. Looking back, I find my first book repetitive, uneven in tempo, and rigid, like the words were cut from the marble of Michelangelo's quarry. Pre-publication, I thought critics would call out my repetitiveness and the liberties I took in creating risk theatre's foundational myth, the myth of the price you pay. My repetitiveness was due to my fear of being misunderstood: risk theatre was too new, too different. As for the myth of the price you pay—the myth of how tragedy arose as a revolt against the monetization of human values—that was my power play to bring together the arts and the social sciences in a new consilience. The economic basis of risk theatre roots it into the social sciences and differentiates it from the teleological basis of Aristotle, the mechanical-ethical basis of Hegel, and the musical basis of Nietzsche. Post-publication, it turns out that I had been mistaken, in large part, on how risk theatre would be received. Critics identified three general points of contention, only one of which I anticipated.

A recurring criticism of *The Risk Theatre Model of Tragedy* was that risk is too broad a phenomenon to usefully apply to tragedy. "Everything is risk," said the critics. I agree. I see the ubiquity of risk, however, as being fruitfully ambiguous rather than a limitation. The most successful theories of tragedy are also built from the most general concepts: Hegel's theory sees tragedy as the collision between ethical forces, and Nietzsche's theory sees tragedy as the collision between the mental forces of the rational and irrational mind. One could as easily say to Hegel or Nietzsche, "Everything is a collision." One, however, seldom does. Their theories are appreciated precisely because they are fruitfully ambiguous. Playwrights experimenting with Hegel and Nietzsche's theories—from Hebbel to Strindberg and O'Neill—appreciate precisely this ambiguity. It gives them room to stretch their thoughts. Too definitive of a definition would be to the playwright what the bed of Procrustes is to the traveler.

By basing the risk theatre theory of tragedy around a fruitfully ambiguous term—risk can refer to the probability of loss, the appetite for danger, the degree of deviation from an expected outcome, or exposure to loss—I wanted to give creators, innovators, and theatremakers a vast intellectual expanse. Far from being a Procrustes's bed, risk theatre is rather a California king. Risk today commands the same interest as ethics did in Hegel's time or the subconscious did in Nietzsche's time. I have been, however, working on a solution for the critics who say that risk is too broad a phenomenon: I now argue that because there are two forms of risk—downside risk, where low-probability, high-consequence events harm and upside risk, where low-probability, high-consequence events help—there are two forms of drama. While tragedy dramatizes downside risk, comedy dramatizes upside risk. With this new observation, an even bolder insight emerges: risk can be the basis of a grand unified theory of drama. At higher dramatic energies, risk binds together tragedy and comedy, each of which once was thought to have constituted a distinct force. They are really both different aspects of risk.

Another criticism of *The Risk Theatre Model of Tragedy* is that it is overfull of Wall Street and the jargon of the markets. It is true that many of the terms I used to describe tragedy—risk, value, opportunity cost, price discovery, free lunch, monetization, the shadow market—were influenced by the language of economics and finance. Some thought I was an MBA. Others, put off by the parallels between theatre and finance, and, wanting to call me the dirtiest word they could think of, called me—for having adorned art with the language of finance—a businessman. In a way, however, the critics were correct in identifying ties between risk theatre and the world of finance. Like many ideas, risk theatre began from one insight. That insight was that, in tragedy, low-probability, high-consequence events trigger the hero's fall. It is chance, not hubris. This curious revelation came to me, of all places, while browsing books in the business section of Borders Books in Providence Place Mall.

It was the end of 2006. I was at Brown finishing my dissertation. I was working on a theory of tragedy. It looked nothing like risk theatre. It was based on the conflict between the hero who claims to have suffered woes "greater than that mortal man has ever borne" and the consoler, who says to the hero: "not to you alone has this suffering come." This consolation is a commonplace in ancient tragedy. Echoes of it can be seen later, for example, in *Hamlet* ("You are not the only son who has lost a father, Hamlet") or *Othello* ("You are not the only husband who has been cuckolded, Othello"). My take was that tragedy functions by dissolving the hero's suffering into the universal ocean of human tears. Tragedy had a civic function to democratize suffering: individual suffering is projected onto kings, heroes, and even the gods. Back then, I believed art had to perform some kind of social function. The dissertation was well underway. It would be successful. But it felt strained. Something was amiss.

On the weekends, I loved to walk the aisles of the big Borders bookstore. There, one evening, a book dazzled me. As a recreation from disserting, I had been reading books on finance and economics. Recently, I had discovered Princeton economist Burton Malkiel's 1973 classic: *A Random Walk Down Wall Street*. He argued that, because a stock's current price reflects everything that can be known about the business, the price movement of any given stock follows a random pattern. That randomness was built into the market on a fundamental level flew in the face of everything I knew. That was my first encounter with the empire of chance. While browsing through the business section one evening, another book would catch my eye and acquaint me further with chance and uncertainty. That book was mathematician, trader, and philosopher Nassim Nicholas Taleb's groundbreaking work from 2004 called *Fooled by Randomness: The Hidden Role of Chance in Life and in the Markets.*

In *Fooled by Randomness*, Taleb argues that we are disproportionately affected by the highly improbable because we expect likely outcomes. Thanks to Malkiel, I was already tuned into randomness and uncertainty. I had not, however, connected the random element with tragedy. As I flipped through *Fooled by Randomness*, I saw story after story of how the high and mighty, from Nobel winners to celebrated economists, would be cast down by unexpected chance events. Then, in a singular flash, it occurred to me that this is precisely what happens in tragedy: heroes—like Taleb's Nobel laureates and celebrated economists—were being struck down by low-probability, high-consequence events. They were being struck down by chance. This singular insight transfigured me. If ever I knew anything, I knew right then and there that I had the basis of a *real* theory of tragedy. It was so good, it would write itself.

All those years, I had been working on a dead-end theory. It was, by that time, too late to rewrite my thesis. I started, however, exploring economics in earnest. I read John Kenneth Galbraith's *A Short History of Financial Euphoria* on stock market bubbles: Tulipomania, Banque Royale, the South Sea Bubble, and the Great Depression. I explored the history of ideas, reading Ian Hacking's *The Emergence of Probability*. During this time, I was going through the dramatic canon making notes on chance and coming up with forgettable names for my new theory: "Ludic Theatre," "Theatre of Chance," "The Theatre of the Uncertain," and "Aleatory Theatre," were some of the blah candidates. Eventually, I discovered that the economists had a term for what happens when more things happen than what you think will happen happens. They called it *risk* and there was a large body of literature devoted to it. By now, it was 2008 and the Great Recession was roiling through the markets like a dark wave, sucking under jobs, homes, and dreams. Suddenly, risk was the "it" word on the television screens and the airwaves. Risk was breaking the internet. Movie after movie replaying the irrational exuberance of the markets rolled out: Charles Ferguson's *Inside Job* (2010), Curtis Hanson's *Too Big to Fail* (2011), J. C. Chandor's *Margin Call* (2011), Nicholas Jarecki's *Arbitrage* (2012), Martin Scorsese's *The Wolf of Wall Street* (2013), and Adam McKay's *The Big Short* (2015).

Only one name was now possible: Risk Theatre. It was perfect. Risk is memorable. It is contemporary. It is inherently dramatic. Not only did it check off all the boxes, it also memorializes how risk theatre is the first theory of tragedy to be born from an economic crisis. It was the Great Recession that convinced me that the world needed a risk theatre, a stage upon which to simulate, explore, and understand risk. We simulate risk on stage to model it in life, as life without theatre is like a show without a dress rehearsal.

The risk theatre theory of tragedy expresses itself through the jargon of the markets because it was inspired by economists from Adam Smith to John Maynard Keynes and from Frank Knight to James M. Buchanan. As an homage to its roots, this text is set in Berling, the same typeface I saw in *Fooled by Randomness*. It makes me smile when I think how risk theatre found its form through the very process it describes: were it not for the fortunate accident of seeing that book that night, the idea of a dramatic theory based on risk would never have occurred to me. Sometimes, to affect change, you have to bring together opposites, bring together Main Street and Wall Street. Progress is a ceremony of opposites. But are they even that different? Economics is the dismal science. Tragedy is a dismal art. It is a match made in heaven.

The third criticism of *The Risk Theatre Model of Tragedy* was that— either by reluctance or inability—I had failed to engage with competing theories. It is true that, besides an observation that theories of tragedy have been products of their age—Aristotle focused on the final effect of tragedy upon audiences in a time fascinated with teleology, Hegel focused on a mechanistic collision in a time fascinated with Newtonian mechanics, and Nietzsche focused on the irrational in a time grappling with an incipient understanding of the subconscious mind—I engaged but tangentially with the richness of the critical tradition of tragic theory, the volume of which is, to this day, exceeded only by biblical exegesis. There I was, interpreting scripture without paying homage to Augustine. It was modern heresy.

Even without engaging in the critical tradition, *The Risk Theatre Model of Tragedy* came in at 373 pages. To have engaged with the critical tradition would have easily doubled its size. This would have created an undue demand on readers and was not the goal. Instead, I wanted for my readers a delightful book that would be fast, exciting, and, above all, readable. I wanted people to enjoy my book, to want to read it. One of my favourite comments was from a reviewer who said: "I read the book in two days." To me, that is how literary theory should be: immediately accessible, not something requiring a lifetime of study and multiple degrees. One of my favourite philosophers revolutionized speech acts by talking about cats on mats and smashing champagne bottles across ships' bows. Though fun, slender, and accessible, it is also full of the profoundest insights. J. L. Austin's *How to Do Things with Word* is great precisely because it presents novel arguments while declining to dive into the history of linguistic theory. Austin, rather than Hegel, is the new model of how to write theory.

What is more, as the critics themselves have pointed out, there are already many books commenting on, summarizing, and questioning the critical tradition. Every decade, a new one comes out. Many are good. They summarize the different approaches of explaining why the sad tales of tragedy have captivated generations of audiences. Some are great. Walter Kaufmann's *Tragedy and Philosophy* is a work of art itself, written with a deep love and fine understanding of tragedy's nuances. Because I was setting out to create a new theory of tragedy from whole cloth, one that says that tragedy engages us because we are fascinated with gamblers and gambling, with accident and the unexpected, I had little reason to engage with the critical tradition. In hindsight this was, perhaps, in error.

It surprises me how, in both dramatic theory and the art of playwriting, Aristotle is still that mountain that playwrights and critics have to climb. When today's scientists discover new elements, or describe the motions of the earth, the planets, and the sun in greater detail, how many critics would ask them to relate their new discoveries with the theories of Democritus, Ptolemy, or Lucretius? Since the heliocentric model of the solar system overcame the Ptolemaic earth-centred model, how many today would resort to a geocentric model to calculate the position of the planets? In the arts, however, the *Poetics* is still the gold standard. It surprises me how so much of the world has advanced, and how, in literary and dramatic theory, time has stood still. After all these years, so many flat-earthers still see the stage as a place full of pity and fear.

To confess, I never felt pity and fear while watching tragedy, did not even know what it meant to feel pity and fear. For me, the emotions were always anticipation and apprehension: anticipation for the magnitude of what the hero wagers and apprehension for the oncoming trainwreck of the low-probability, high-consequence event. Likewise, the idea of the tragic flaw, or hamartia, was also alien to me. Melpomene, tragedy's Muse, spoke to me instead of how chance waylays heroes' acts of derring-do by shooting their bulletproof plans into smithereens. Because it was so clear that it was chance rather than error, it was surprising that critics expected me not only to discuss Aristotle, but also to merge risk theatre with his *Poetics*. "Could pity and fear," they asked, "be merged with anticipation and apprehension?" As competing theories, they are incompatible. My Dionysus is not the Dionysus of Aristotle, Hegel, and Nietzsche. When Copernicus developed his sun-centred cosmology, he did away with Ptolemy's epicycles, equants, and deferents. Who would have asked the astronomers to explain the workings of the Copernican cosmos through the barbaric relics of the Ptolemaic theory? The proposition itself is laughable. In science, there is no turning back. But in dramatic and literary theory, an endless atavism arrests art from being what it must become.

I wrote risk theatre to root out, and to pull down, and to destroy, and to throw down, to build and to plant. With this theory of mine, I wanted to say things never said before in theory, the things that Aeschylus, Shakespeare, and Miller experienced while they were writing. With risk theatre, there is no going back. No more regressions nor atavism. No more new wine in old wineskins. No more theories like chimaeras, patchwork creations grafted together from lions, goats, serpents, and whatever haphazard beast happens to be available. Risk theatre resets the theory of tragedy—it is daybreak.

Six Risk Theatre Essays

Having showcased the practice of risk theatre in the first half, the second half of this volume turns to the theory of risk theatre. Between the first book and today, I have been working on a series of essays reexamining the relationship between risk and literature. These essays have been published separately, in different volumes. But, as they are united in their focus on chance, probability, and the random element, they belong together. They contain many second thoughts and are collected together for you here.

Despite wanting to go ever forwards and never back, the critics calling me out for failing to address Aristotle were many. I needed to make it clearer that risk theatre is a new theory, not a further reworking of Hegel, Nietzsche, or Aristotle. In the first essay of this volume, "Faces of Chance in Shakespeare's Tragedies: Othello's Handkerchief and Macbeth's Moving Grove," I argue that the legacy of Aristotle's concept of hamartia is that it has persuaded generations of critics to come up with simplistic, misleading, quarrelsome, trivial, and irrelevant explanations (error, hubris, confidence, etc.,) of how the hero could have sidestepped tragedy. This is wrong because the hero is brought down by chance, not error. What is more, in the closing section of this essay, I draw attention to a fundamental point of departure between risk theatre and the *Poetics*: the former is rooted in the improbable while the latter is rooted in the probable. While the *Poetics* talks of probability and learning from heroes' errors, risk theatre talks of improbability, chance, and the thrill of the unknown.

The second essay, "Greek Tragedy, Black Swans, and the Coronavirus: The Consolation of Theatre," was written in the tumultuous and uncertain months of February to March 2020 when the threat of COVID-19 became daily more tangible. In this essay, I highlight how we live in a world of low-probability, high-consequence events. To understand these events, we need to simulate them. By simulating what happens when what we did not think would happen happens, we become better prepared. Using Euripides's *Bacchae*, Sophocles's *Oedipus the King*, and Aeschylus's *Seven against Thebes*, I argue that tragedy has always been a risk simulator dramatizing the impact of the highly improbable. By simulating risk and uncertainty, tragedy is our Muse in times of crisis. Looking back, there is something special in how this essay was written in medias res, as the pandemic unfolded.

The third essay, "The Price of Patriotism: Opportunity Cost and the American Dream in Arthur Miller's *All My Sons*," considers tragedy's role as a valuing mechanism. *All My Sons*, I argue, presents a master class in opportunity cost, the idea that there is a negative component of choice: when one chooses, one loses the opportunity to have realized the next best choice. The forsaken choice reminds us of how there is no free lunch. For everything that we do, say, want, and achieve, there is a price to be paid. When we forget, tragedy is there to remind us.

The fourth essay, "Aeschylus's *Seven against Thebes*: A Patriot's Portrait of a Patriot," is a personal milestone (patriotism is the theme again because both the third and fourth essays were originally commissioned for a volume on patriotism). *Seven against Thebes* is the tragedy that inspired the risk theatre concept. It could be said, in my two decades exploring this play, that I invented risk theatre to solve *Seven*. It is a play in which fortune turns on a thin dime. This essay illustrates how the best of the tragedians suppresses what must happen so that when it does happen, the characters and the audience let out a gasp of surprise. Drama is a magic trick involving a certain sleight of hand, a certain deception. This essay has been presented over the years at the University of Victoria, the University of Calgary, and at annual general meetings hosted by the Society of Classical Studies and the Classical Association of the Middle West and South. To finally bring home, in one place, the feedback and suggestions from so many enthusiastic panelists and audiences has been a pleasure and an honour.

The fifth essay, "But Who Does Caesar Render Unto? Three Faces of Risk in Shakespeare's *Julius Caesar*" provides an in-depth look at risk in all its guises: first, as danger; second, as exposure to danger; and third, as the trigger of cataclysmic yet entertaining low-probability, high-consequence black swan events. Risk is truly as polysemous, motley, and colourful a term as the best and most celebrated literary terms of literary theory: catharsis, Dionysian, *Verfremdungseffekt*, and many others. Written half a year after the *Othello* and *Macbeth* essays, the *Julius Caesar* essay continues differentiating—and with growing conviction—risk theatre from the *Poetics*.

The sixth essay, "Tragedy, Comedy, and Chance in Hardy's *Far from the Madding Crowd*," responds to a question Columbia professor Charlie Euchner asked in a 2019 interview: "What happens when you bring risk theatre to the novel?" Thomas Hardy's *Far from the Madding Crowd*, a most theatrical novel full of both comedy and tragedy, provides an ideal testing ground. This concluding essay points the way forward for risk theatre in more ways than one: in this essay, not only do I take risk theatre to the novel, I begin outlining the shape of a risk theatre theory of comedy. Because there are two types of risk, there are two forms of drama: tragedy to dramatize downside risk and comedy to dramatize upside risk. The grand day of a unified theory of drama dawns. What the sirens were to Odysseus is what a unified theory of drama will be to theatre. Stay tuned.

The Grand Day of Risk

Risk theatre is gaining momentum. A year after the 2019 release of *The Risk Theatre Model of Tragedy*, Findaway Voices released an audiobook version narrated by *Coronation Street* star Greg Patmore. In two-and-a-half years, the book, eBook, and audiobook have sold thousands of copies. It is available around the world from the Russian State Library in Moscow, the Bibliothèque nationale in Paris, the Universitätsbibliothek der Eberhard Karls in Tübingen, and the Senate House Library in London to the City University of New York, the Public Library in Indianapolis, and the libraries right here in my hometown. Not bad for a book that was almost orphaned.

Universities are beginning to include risk theatre in their curricula. Students, seeing how risk is opening up doorways of interpretation, are applying to graduate programs with the intention of exploring risk not only in playwriting, but in acting as well. Dramaturgs dramaturge new works with risk theatre and directors apply risk theatre to classic plays. When life gives us risk, let us make risk theatre.

The Risk Theatre Modern Tragedy Playwriting Competition—a joint venture between myself and playwrights across the world to model risk—is kicking off the fourth annual competition for 2022. Together, we are unmasking uncertainty. Over the years, the finalist prizes have gone from four at $500 to five at $600. The grand prize has grown from $8,000 to $10,200 and will continue to grow. As I write this, the jurors are reading the 2021 entries. They will nominate a new winner in August. To date, playwrights from fifteen countries have responded to the challenge of risk theatre. Whether full gas or full-load amps, we are driving into the unknown, and with many friends.

People are noticing this tremendous playwriting opportunity. They are coming from all walks of life. Some are young playwrights, showing mastery in their first strokes. Others are established masters who hear tragedy calling. Some are husband and wife teams who have created popular soap operas, adored by the masses. Others are scholars in universities adapting classic plays. Some are students exploring tomorrow's emerging themes. Some are big-shot executives who wear a suit by day and write tragedy by night. Others are scientists cracking the code of nature by day and the code of tragedy by night. Some are veterans who fought in the wars and others are inmates who fought in the streets. Some of you write of Marlene Dietrich while others write of Jean-Claude van Damme. Some of you are writers who code by day and write theatre by night. Wherever you come from and whatever you write about, welcome to risk theatre. Join me on this journey to make risk sing a new song. The pieces are in place so that, on the day after tomorrow, whoever says "tragedy" will say "risk." Today, a stillness hangs in the theatres and on the stages. It is the stillness of the hour before the winds of criticism rise again, blowing out the old books and bringing in the new.

EDWIN WONG
Victoria, Canada
May 2021

THE TOWER.

PART I

The Risk Theatre Tragedies

CHAPTER 1

THE TOWER.

An Introduction to *In Bloom* by the Playwright

Before I get into the "big why" for *In Bloom*, I am compelled to acknowledge the people and organizations that helped midwife this play into the world. Without these folx, the script you're about to read would not exist. First and foremost, I'm deeply indebted to my friend and collaborator Humaira Ghilzai for her many, many hours of dramaturgy, cultural consultation, and translation/literation work. Humaira was, quite literally, the perfect dramaturg for this play and I consider myself the luckiest playwright on the planet to have found her. And in addition to Humaira, I'm equally indebted to "Z," as he called himself, a former *bacha bazi* dancer who escaped from Afghanistan. I was privileged to interview him in Paris in 2010. My eternal gratitude to Steven Dietz, Suzan Zeder, and Octavio Solis for mentoring me and this play while I was writing it as a graduate student at the University of Texas at Austin; to Jim Nicola and Linda Chapman at New York Theatre Workshop for giving me a coveted amount of time and space and envious artistic talent to develop the script; to Broadway Producer Ken Davenport for making me see my play's value; to my-ride-or-die director pal Lucie Tiberghien; to Doug Hughes and Manhattan Theatre Club; Amanda Watkins at The Araca Group; and Jonathan Berry and PJ Papparelli (RIP) at the American Theatre Company (also RIP) in Chicago; the scores of dedicated actors who've left their marks on these roles as I've developed the script; and finally, of course, to

Edwin Wong and the Risk Theatre Modern Tragedy Competition for giving *In Bloom* an international platform.

And now…why this play? The roots for *In Bloom* planted themselves in 2006 when I found myself midst a real-life, epic tragedy. My brother-in-law, Nolan, was dating a young woman whose father was a civilian contractor building schools in Afghanistan. Since his contract was for two years and didn't allow travel between home and Afghanistan, in the summer of 2006, the father arranged for his entire family—Nolan's girlfriend, her sister, and her mother—to visit him. Their transport helicopter crashed north of Kandahar and no one survived. The Taliban claimed responsibility.

I was one of the first people Nolan saw after he found out his girlfriend and her entire family had ostensibly been killed by the Taliban. I didn't know what to say to him. I felt immobile. Stupid. I knew that the U.S. had sent troops to Afghanistan as a counter to 9/11. But that was the extent of my knowledge. My ignorance in that crucial moment motivated me to learn as much as I possibly could. I started reading anything and everything about Afghanistan, hoping that I'd have something to say to Nolan that would bring him some peace. All these years later, and a huge amount of research, to the point of obsession, and I still don't know what to say to him about that tragic moment in his early life. But I do know a lot more about Afghanistan and its relationship with the U.S.

It turned out that the helicopter was not taken down by the Taliban, but actually crashed because of poor maintenance. When this tragedy spurred me to start reading about Afghanistan, I had no intention of ever writing plays set there. Flash forward three years later and I'm in grad school in Texas studying playwriting.

As an introduction to the community, my cohort was to write an evening of short plays inspired by the music of the Ramones. I drew "Blitzkrieg Bop" as my song of inspiration. Listening to the lyrics, I thought of the paradox of war and dance, beauty among the rubble. I did a google search for "war and dance" and not too far down the page, I encountered Ghaith Abdul-Ahad's article in the

Guardian, "The Dancing Boys of Afghanistan." Given my obsession with Afghanistan, I clicked.

The article described the subculture practice of *bacha bazi* in Afghanistan. Pre-pubescent boys dress in feminine attire and dance for wealthy warlords at parties. Afterwards, they are prostituted to the highest bidder. I was struck by how one of the young dancers in the article spoke to Abdul-Ahad about himself and his dance with such confidence. I personally identified with this veneer. It's the mask you feel you have to wear to survive. Although this boy was half a world away living in a very different culture, I felt like I understood this part of him. And so, Hafiz was born. Not long after, he was followed by Aaron, the do-gooder documentary filmmaker who relentlessly wants to see behind Hafiz's protective veil.

To be honest, this play scared the hell out of me. I tried my best not to write it. I became paralyzed by the idea that I had no business writing a play about a young queer Afghan boy. But Hafiz wouldn't let me go. He insisted on being seen. On being loved. As much as *In Bloom* is a political tale deeply critical of U.S. imperialism, now, with years of perspective on the process of writing the play, as a survivor of male-to-male sexual abuse myself, I understand that, more than anything, *In Bloom* is a personal play for me.

My strong advice to stalwart producers of this play: find the joy in the tragedy (the beauty in the rubble), immerse your audience in the experience, don't overplay the language, and hire age appropriate and culturally appropriate actors. And don't pass on this play because you think you can't cast it. The actors are out there. Look for them. Or contact me for recommendations. I have a long list.

As I write this, the United States is pulling out of Afghanistan, leaving Afghans, particularly women and young men like Hafiz, in desperate fear for their futures under Taliban rule. The great irony, of course, is that the Taliban themselves are one of the many global by-products of American Imperialism. Though the 2021 regime is a different generation, the original Taliban fighters were former members of the Mujahideen, the late 1980s/early 1990s American-funded resistance fighters to Russia. The United States supplied the weapons and trained these men that eventually became the original Taliban. And now we are walking away from a problem of our own making. My character Aaron does the same thing. In the last moment of the play, after a public humiliation at a global conference, Aaron walks offstage mumbling his soft-spoken apology. His humiliation is certainly hard to watch, but nonetheless the true consequences of Aaron's relentless pursuit to "do good" lethally landed on a queer Afghan boy called Hafiz. For me, the most upsetting tragedy of my play isn't Hafiz's death. It's the fact that Aaron gets to walk away without consequence.

Allegorically, Aaron is America and Hafiz is Afghanistan. As is the privilege of the Empire, we walk away while the ones we vowed to protect suffer under an enemy we created. In many ways, *In Bloom* feels more relevant to this moment now than it did when I finished the first draft in 2011. I truly hope that it will become an irrelevant play in the future. But the abusive supremacist stripe deeply woven into the American identity suggests *In Bloom* will remain current for a long while. At least until we have the courage to rip supremacy from the cloth of the American fabric.

GABRIEL JASON DEAN

About Gabriel Jason Dean

Dubbed "feisty as hell" by the *New Yorker* and "a great modern American playwright" by *Broadway World*, Gabriel Jason Dean is an award-winning playwright and screenwriter whose critically acclaimed plays for children and adults include *In Bloom* (Risk Theatre Modern Tragedy Playwriting Competition Prize, Kennedy Center Paula Vogel Award, Laurents/Hatcher Award Finalist, Princess Grace Award Runner-Up); *Qualities of Starlight* (Broadway Blacklist, Kesselring Nomination, Essential Theatre New Play Prize, B. Iden Payne Awards for Outstanding Comedy & Best Original Script); *Terminus* (James Tait Black Prize Finalist, B. Iden Payne Awards for Outstanding Drama & Best Original Script, Austin Critic's Table Award Best Production, PlayPenn); *Heartland* (National New Play Network Rolling World Premiere, InterAct 20/20 Commission,

Austin Critic's Table David Mark Cohen New Play Award, B. Iden Payne Award for Best Original Script, PlayPenn), *Entangled* (co-written with Charly Evon Simpson, New York Innovative Theatre Award Nomination Best Full-Length Script); *The Transition of Doodle Pequeño* (American Alliance for Theatre & Education Distinguished Play Award, Kennedy Center TYA Award, New England Theatre Conference Aurand Harris Award); and others. He has written the books and lyrics for the musicals *Mario & the Comet* (NYU Plays for Young Audiences) and *Our New Town* (Civilians R&D Group). Screenplays include *Get Gomez* with Cranium Entertainment, *Pigskin*, and *D'Angelico*. TV Pilots include *We Belong* (Humanitas New Television Writer Award Finalist), *Deplorable*, *Rabble*, and the animated series *Tenderfoot*. His plays have been produced or developed at places such as New York Theatre Workshop, Manhattan Theatre Club, McCarter Theatre, The Cherry Lane Theatre, Araca Group, The Lark, The Flea, The Civilians, Oregon Shakespeare, The Kennedy Center, The Amoralists, Geva Theatre Center, PlayPenn, Interact, The Playwrights' Center, Davenport Theatrical, Stage Left, The VORTEX, Theatre [502], Aurora Theatre, Seattle Children's Theatre, Dallas Children's Theatre, People's Light and Theatre, Dad's Garage Theatre, Actor's Express, Horizon Theatre, Source Festival, Essential Theatre, and the Illinois Shakespeare Festival. Gabriel received the Hodder Fellowship from Princeton University, Dramatist's Guild Fellowship, and the Sallie B. Goodman/McCarter Theatre Fellowship. His scripts are published through Samuel French, Dramatic Publishing, and Playscripts. He is on faculty for Spalding University's Brief-Residency MFA Program, is a Visiting Writer in Residence, and Assistant Professor of Theatre at Muhlenberg College, an alum of The Civilians R&D Group, and Affiliated Writer at the Playwrights' Center, an Associate Artist with Monk Parrots and a Usual Suspect at New York Theatre Workshop. Current commissions with Geva Theatre and the Alley Theatre. MFA: UT-Austin Michener Center for Writers. He grew up in Chatsworth, GA, a mill town in the foothills of the Appalachian Mountains. He currently lives in Brooklyn, NY.

In Bloom

by Gabriel Jason Dean

Dari transliterations by Humaira Ghilzai
Music by David Dabbon

The touch which does not understand is the touch which corrupts.
The touch which does not understand that which it touches is the
touch which corrupts that which it touches and which corrupts itself.
  –from *Homebody/Kabul* by Tony Kushner

In Bloom, a Risk Theatre Tragedy, was named the *Winner* of the 2019
Risk Theatre Modern Tragedy Playwriting Competition by an international panel of jurors:

Yvette Nolan (Canada)
Armen Pandola (USA)
Sally Stott (UK)

Permissions Contact:
A3 Artists Agency
Sara Barkan & Max Grossman
Empire State Building
350 Fifth Avenue, 38th Floor
New York, NY 10118, USA
646-486-4600
sara.barkan@abramsartistsagency.com
max.grossman@abramsartistsagency.com

Risk Theatre Staged Reading

On October 20, 2019, Edwin Wong and Langham Court Theatre produced a Risk Theatre staged reading of *In Bloom* in Victoria, Canada. Michael Armstrong directed in collaboration with Gabriel Jason Dean. Stage management by Michelle Buck. Musical accompaniment by Arian Aminalroaya. Cast as follows:

Characters

AARON FREEMAN	Late 20's / early 30's, an American documentary filmmaker (Jason Vikse)
NAWEED	30's, a fixer (Wayne Yercha)
HAFIZ	a teenage dancer (Steven Piazza)
MUNIR	50's, a businessman (Cam Culham)
THE SWISS	Early 20's, one of Shabah's men (Douglas Peerless)
BOY / RASHEED	younger than Hafiz, an orphan, a singer (Gene Sargent)
DR. KASHI JONES	30's, a professor at Cambridge, British-Indian (Rahat Saini)
SHABAH / COLIN / MAN	50's, a feared opium distributor / sound technician / Afghan man (Gabriel Jason Dean)
SALIM / MAN	30's, one of Shabah's men / Afghan man (Michael Armstrong)

Ideally, casts will include at least two additional men for the party scenes, but it's not crucial. These additional actors or those playing Salim and Shabah will ideally be able to provide drumming during some musical moments.

Setting

A lecture hall at the University of Cambridge, 2009
Badakhshan Province, Northern Afghanistan, 2006

Punctuation Notes

/   indicates interruption
< >   indicates a slight pause, a beat for the actor
—   at the end of a line of dialogue, indicates the next
                  line should flow without pause
[Silence.]   space, opportunity for the unspoken

In spotlight, KASHI sits in a chair in her office in Cambridge. She finishes the last page of Bloom: A Shock Tourist's Account of Afghanistan. *She puts the book down on the table, sips her tea.*

KASHI. Hunh. Very interesting.

She picks the book back up, examines it and lights shift, revealing an Afghan MAN. He begins to sing the azaan. This should incorporate all the actors except those playing AARON, HAFIZ and RASHEED. The man is joined by others, each in his own spotlight. The voices clash with each other, filling the space with a big, beautiful cacophonous sound. This is Afghanistan. Lights fade on KASHI in Cambridge.

VOICES.   *Ash-hadu an-lā ilāha illā allāh*
            Ash-hadu an-lā ilāha illā allāh
            Ash-hadu anna Mohamadan-Rasulullāh
            Ash-hadu anna Mohamadan-Rasulullāh

A strong, charged silence as the Afghans look into the eyes of the audience. As they disperse, lights reveal a field of poppies, tight in the bud, aching to bloom. The sky is a deep and singular blue. Bone-dry mountains are projected against an upstage scrim.

PROJECTION: BADAKHSHAN PROVINCE, NORTHERN AFGHANISTAN, 2006

NAWEED stands behind a camera on a tripod and holds a boom mic aloft. AARON is in front of the camera.

AARON. Come on, Naweed, let's go! We've got like two minutes left in this light. Chop, chop.

NAWEED. I go as fast as possible. [*fidgets with camera*] OK. It's ready.

AARON. Are you actually recording this time?

NAWEED. I believe us to be recording.

AARON. Do you see my face on the monitor?

NAWEED. All the tiny hairs.

AARON. And the green light?

NAWEED. Check, boss.

AARON. OK, so you say, "rolling."

NAWEED. I know to say it.

AARON. Then say it.

NAWEED. < > Rolling.

AARON. Thank you. < > July fourteen 2006. Day 22. Possible intro footage. Take nine. [*tousles his hair, readies himself for…*] The fall of the Taliban—

Distracted, NAWEED lowers the boom into the frame.

AARON. Naweed! Come on…keep the boom out of the frame!

NAWEED. My arm is tired. We do many times. [*He raises the boom.*]

NAWEED. Rolling.

AARON. I know we're rolling, you don't need to…oh my god. OK. Possible intro footage. Take ten. [*consummate professional*] The fall of the Taliban has created a new problem for Afghanistan. Opium. A booming business was reborn on the Silk Road. Opium has an export value of about $4 billion, close to 60% of the reported 2005 Afghanistan GDP. And everybody here wants a piece of that pie. One man, known only as Shabah, a former Taliban warlord, is allegedly the largest poppy grower here in the Badakhshan Province. Possibly in the entire country. In English, Shabah translates as the *Ghost*. He is known as the *Ghost* because, according to locals, no one has ever seen his face. I'm documentary filmmaker, Aaron Freeman, and I'm here to change that. I want to see the face of the man who makes the poppies bloom. < > Cut. How was that?

NAWEED. Very professional. Anderson Cooper.

As AARON plays back the footage on the monitor, NAWEED lights a smoke.

AARON. Don't forget to download this one to the laptop when we get back.

NAWEED. Yes, boss.

AARON. Is that cigarette good?

NAWEED offers it.

AARON. No. No. Staying strong. < > You know what I'm beginning to think?

NAWEED. You should hire more help?

AARON. You know it's not safe to have a crew following me around.

NAWEED. It was joke.

AARON. Oh. OK. Anyway, I'm starting to think that Shabah isn't real. Like, it's just a bunch of smoke and mirrors.

NAWEED. Smoke and mirror?

AARON. Yeah, a fear myth. What you can't see is more frightening than anything you can.

NAWEED. Perhaps for you the unseen is more scary, but I see enough.

AARON. I'm just saying, we've talked to what, thirty farmers? And not a single one can definitively say they've laid eyes on Shabah.

NAWEED. Even in Kunduz, I hear of boys he steal to swim opium across the Pyanj into Tajikistan. I knew one...son of a friend of a friend. When they find him, his body was...the man only know his son by his prayer beads. When you live in place for so long where war is way of life, there is no truth. There is no lie. We do not need to see evil to know it exist. < > We got footage. We go. Chop, chop.

Lights shift as KASHI enters and NAWEED exits.

KASHI. Go ahead. Try it now.

AARON. Hmm?

KASHI. Try the mic?

PROJECTION: CAMBRIDGE, ENGLAND, 2009

AARON. Oh, um, testing testing, one two—

KASHI [*shouting to the booth*]. Colin, the level's a bit hot, don't you think?

KASHI adjusts AARON's lapel mic. COLIN speaks from the booth, is never seen.

COLIN. Try it again.

AARON. Testing testing, one two.

COLIN. Keep speaking.

AARON. One two. Test. Test. One two three…four?

COLIN. Speak naturally. Give us a joke or something.

AARON. Oh gosh, I'm not very funny. < > Wait, there was one on the plane, the guy next to me, he said, "Lad, why do you think Americans go to war so much?" And I shrugged, not wanting to blow my cover, you know. And he smiled and said, "How else would they learn geography?"

KASHI. < > Right.

AARON. I didn't really think it was funny either.

KASHI. Oh, it's very funny. Colin, are we set?

COLIN. Set.

KASHI. Great.

AARON. How many are you expecting?

KASHI. Your book is required reading for first year seminar, so we should be filled to the brim. But most of them probably haven't read it.

AARON. At Cambridge?

KASHI. What was your phrase? "The inherent apathy of Millennials?"

AARON. Good memory.

KASHI. You accept the prize tomorrow night?

AARON. Yes. < > And there's a cocktail reception.

KASHI. Well, well, the Sommerville Committee knows how to treat a winner.

AARON. You wanna be my plus one?

KASHI. / Oh, Mr. Freeman—

AARON. I don't really know anyone here and I figure I should thank you somehow.

KASHI. For what?

AARON. Arranging this. It's my first international audience. Well, I guess I should count Canada.

KASHI. I'm afraid your gratitude is misplaced. My colleague, Professor Campbell, he's on the Sommerville Committee. He put your book forward for the prize. He's on sabbatical in China and thought I might be the best person to moderate in his absence. No one told you?

AARON. No.

KASHI. Ah, well. No harm. No foul. I'm not in Literature. I'm a social anthropologist. I did my field work with women in Kabul.

AARON. I know. I read your bio.

KASHI. And I read your book. I found it to be…compelling.

AARON. Thank you. But?

KASHI. Pardon?

AARON. That pregnant pause. You found it…compelling, but?

KASHI. Ohhhh…let's not do this.

AARON. I've probably heard much worse.

KASHI. I'd rather not.

AARON. Come on, I'm a big boy. I can take it.

KASHI. Honestly?

AARON. Always.

KASHI [*KASHI chooses diplomacy*]. I suppose I'm a just a bit… jealous of your success. People are actually reading what you wrote. Your book is inspiring change in Afghanistan. I'm lucky if five mealy-mouthed graduate students download my research for free from the university website. I'm already sorry I said it. Your book is beautiful and important.

AARON. So is your work.

KASHI. How would you know? You haven't read it.

AARON. I will download it ASAP. [*Awkward silence. Looking out at the audience*] Wow. That's gonna be a lot of people. I'm a little nervous.

KASHI. Don't be. They're just children. They rarely bite.

NAWEED [*entering*]. Grand news, brother! Grand news!

KASHI exits as lights reveal a cot, a table and some duffels: AARON's rented room in Afghanistan.

NAWEED. I had the meeting.

AARON. Great.

NAWEED. You will be happy.

AARON. I'll be happier if you tell me the grand news.

NAWEED. Tomorrow night, we go to party. [*NAWEED does a little dance.*]

AARON. I thought you were meeting with the lead?

NAWEED. Yes. We go to his party.

AARON. OK—

NAWEED. The man is called Munir. And…he is…eh…exotic?

AARON. What do you mean?

NAWEED. He is…exotic. That's how I say it, exotic.

AARON. Fine. Exotic. And?

NAWEED. Eh, our contact did not have the best information. Munir is not, eh…he is not smuggler for Shabah. He is…*morda gow*.

AARON. What?

NAWEED. *Morda gow*. Um, eh…playboy…like Tom Cruise in *Risky Business*.

AARON. What?

NAWEED. He sell…the sex?

AARON. You mean a pimp?

NAWEED. Yes. Pimp! Pimp! That is the word.

AARON. How is a pimp supposed to get me closer to Shabah?

NAWEED. Well…eh…Munir associate with some of Shabah's men at the party.

AARON. He told you that?

NAWEED. Yes. So, you see, if we go to party, we are close to Shabah. *AARON high fives NAWEED.*

AARON. What's the occasion?

NAWEED. < > Ah, yes…Munir is pimp for *bacha bazi*. < > How to explain? It translate…boy play? < > Uh…there will be boys? And, eh…they wear costume? To be like girl. And they dance. Maybe sing. And then they are…eh…rented. That is not / best word, eh…

AARON. / Wow.

NAWEED. Yes. The *bacha bazi* is, eh…[*defensive*] Not Afghan. From the Greeks. Alexander, you see? Not Afghan. A boy is not man until he has beard. And so man and boy together…ehhh…it is not… it is not same as man and man. It not considered…eh…

AARON. Homosexual?

NAWEED. Yes. It is considered…not that. Something different.

AARON. That's… / that's…

NAWEED. Also, he wants Motówn.

AARON. What?

NAWEED. Motówn….music. Munir say, "Jackson Five, Diane Ross…"

AARON. He wants Motown Motown?

NAWEED. Records. He collect.

AARON. The pimp wants vinyl Motown? How the hell am I supposed to get vinyl anything here?

NAWEED. It is possible. Very difficult. But possible.

AARON. When is the party?

NAWEED. Tomorrow night.

AARON. What?! That's ridiculous! I can't find Motown records in one day.

NAWEED. I know of musician in Fayzabad who collect.

AARON. You do?

NAWEED initiates a fist bump. AARON bumps it.

NAWEED. You see? I am very valuable. Munir is even happy for camera.

AARON. He's cool with me filming?

NAWEED. Yes. Yes…yes.

AARON. Naweed, what exactly did you tell him?

A man enters from the flowers, his face obscured by his lungee.

NAWEED. You say to me, "Make this count, Naweed." So I make it count, Boss. The pimp believe you to be rich American…pornographer.

Lights shift and projection photo reveals an eager moon peeking over the mountains.

MUNIR [*revealing his face dramatically*]. "Let us sit on ground and tell the sad stories of the death of kings." Shakespeare. *Richard Two.*

NAWEED. *Beradaar* Munir, you not tell me you speak English.

MUNIR. I have many surprise. English profitable, yes? Language of Shakespeare and Wall Street.

AARON. Uh, *Khosh…shodam…az…didanetan.* [It is…pleasurable…to meet…you.]

MUNIR. The pleasure is all for me, Brother America.

AARON. Aaron.

MUNIR. Aaron? < > My father was scholar. Study at Oxford. Teach English at university in Kabul. Before Russians, he read for me Ustad Shakespeare. I am in love for Othello. You know it?

AARON. Of course.

MUNIR. I hear Othello and I know how the Christian hate the Muslim. I think, you are Western, you love Ustad Shakespeare.

AARON. Shakespeare's OK.

MUNIR. OK? Ha! Ustad Shakespeare is poet. And a poet speak to Afghan heart. You hear of the poet Jalal ud-Din Muhammad Rumi?

AARON. Rumi…of course. He wrote love poems.

MUNIR. Americans always know Rumi. [*clears his throat and prepares*:]

> Welcome, embrace them all.
> Even if he is crowd with sorrows
> And clean your house
> Empty of furniture.
> Still, still treat him with honor.
> He may be cleaning you out for new delight.

Awkward silence.

AARON. Um, here…I have gifts for you. [*AARON offers MUNIR an LP, still in its cover.*]

MUNIR. *Amrikaei hoshiar.* [Ahh, clever American.]

NAWEED. *Bale.*

MUNIR. < > Lesley Goré? I not know.

AARON [*singing softly*]. It's my party and I'll cry if I want to, cry if I want to…

MUNIR. Cry as I want to, Cry as I…yes! Not Motówn. I say to your man, I want Motówn.

AARON offers another record.

MUNIR. "You Don't Own Me?" Is same Lesley Goré. Not Motówn.

AARON. It's what I could get on short notice. We were lucky to find these. Two records instead of one.

NAWEED. *Beradaar*, we did not sleep last night because we were going through Fayzabad to find these records for you.

MUNIR. Not Motówn.

AARON. This song? It's a classic. Who doesn't love Lesley?

NAWEED. Who doesn't?

MUNIR. Who doesn't you say. How is it, eh…"the man who has no music…bah, bah, bah…let no such man be trusted." *Merchant of Venice*. You know of it?

AARON. I saw the movie with Al Pacino.

NAWEED. Yes, Pacino.

MUNIR. Scarface… bang bang bang! Gangster jihad! < > Very good, my friends. I take Lesley. [*sniffs the records*] Records, sound of childhood. One year ago, Taliban will crush Munir for hearing this music. I love for American rock n' roll. Classics as you say. Motówn is best. Munir's secret. Taliban is not sharing this love with Munir. But you send Taliban in the mountains! [*his best Elvis*] You ain't a nothing but the hound dog! Ha! Freedom sound like Elvis Presley. < > I hear secret from you.

AARON. < > I don't have a secret.

MUNIR. Then you are not a man. < > Eh, you no understand. Eh, you wish for to see my party, I needs must have something…eh… something…*mana ast?*

NAWEED. Forbid.

MUNIR. Ah…yes… forbid, as he say.

AARON. Well, you already know I'm a…pornographer.

MUNIR. More.

AARON. How 'bout we skip all this and you just name your price instead?

MUNIR. Americans. Always wanting to pay. < > You are…you seem *shawqee*…

NAWEED. Eager.

MUNIR. Yes. The pornogeraafer is eager to see my boys?

AARON. Yes.

MUNIR. Four thousand Afghanis.

NAWEED. Is eighty dollars.

AARON. Will Shabah's men be there?

MUNIR. You fear of them?

AARON. Well…I don't suppose they like Americans very much.

MUNIR. Do not fear of the uglies. Brother, you earn a man's trust when indulge in his…sins. Four thousand Afghanis. Please…I am paid now.

AARON pays. MUNIR counts the money.

MUNIR. No…fortee thousand Afghanis. Fortee.

NAWEED. Eight hundred.

AARON. Yeah, I got it. But I heard you say twenty thousand Afghanis.

MUNIR [*laughing*]. Ahhhh, no, no, I say thirty thousand Afghanis.

AARON. Twenty.

MUNIR. Twenty-five.

AARON pays. MUNIR covers their faces with their lungees and as they exit, MEN crowd into a dark room with a few large, patterned rugs. The MEN, some with knobby cudgels, sit upon small red cushions around the rugs. BOY bursts into the group of MEN, chasing a battered soccer ball. Note: whenever AARON is not present onstage, the Afghan characters speak in unaccented fluent English.

BOY. He picks up the pass…rushes toward the goal…he's past the center-back…he shoots…

BOY kicks the ball. SALIM catches it. BOY hesitates, then…

BOY. GOOOOAAAAL! The people are on their feet. The stadium roars! Ahhhhhhhhhh!

BOY does his victory dance. SALIM laughs.

SALIM. It's easy to score if your goal is imaginary.

BOY. Hey, give me back my ball!

SALIM. It's my ball now. What are you gonna do to get it back?

BOY. I don't know. I can sing for it?

SALIM. OK, then, sing. [*SALIM begins to walk away with the ball…*]

BOY [*sings Lullaby*].   Our big red rooster crows night and noon,
        The big red rooster is so confused.
        He struts and preens and puffs his chest.
        Soon we will eat him.

Too bad for the rooster.

The MEN laugh and SALIM pulls out some money, shows it to BOY.

SALIM. You want this money?

BOY goes for the money.

SALIM. Ah, ah, ah…you gotta earn it.

MUNIR enters, AARON and NAWEED following behind, their faces still covered. MUNIR snatches the money from SALIM.

MUNIR. O *khirs, e bacha ba e kar amada nist. Sar waqt as!* [You bear! This boy isn't ready for you. Behave. In time.]

AARON. Is that one of the boys?

MUNIR. No, no, this boy not ready for dance. *Biadara! Salaam, Salaam! Beshiened. Beshiened. Beshiened.* [Brothers! Hello, hello! Sit. Sit. Sit.] Make friends. Christian, Muslim, we all sleep under same stars in eyes of Allah. Remember, what uglies do to enemies now, they do to friends tomorrow. < > You not laugh. It is comedy.

AARON. Do they understand English?

MUNIR [*massaging Aaron's shoulders*]. Do not worry of the uglies. They have no English. [*loudly*] *Biadara, een biadara mohtaramem ast, Mohammad.* [Brothers, this is my esteemed friend, Mohammad.] *The MEN laugh.*

NAWEED. He introduces you as Mohammad.

MUNIR. We are all Mohammad for *bacha bazi. O injast ke far-hanga e ma ra yad begira, rasmo rewaje ma ra maza kona.* [He is here to learn our tradition, to taste our custom.]

NAWEED. *Ma hamchinan…Mohammad Hastom.* [And I am also called…Mohammad.]

The MEN laugh again. MUNIR raises a bottle of vodka.

MUNIR. *Ba salamatee!* [Cheers!]

MEN. *Salaamatee!*

MUNIR drinks and passes the vodka to AARON. He drinks, passes it along. The MEN drink. MUNIR cues the musicians. HAFIZ's song begins. A dancer enters the room, donning a red dress and tumban, small bells tied to hands and feet, face obscured with a red silk scarf. The bells chime, the skirt floats past the men who reach their hands to touch it.

The dancer glides, spinning faster and faster until finally the scarf drops revealing...HAFIZ. He speaks as he dances.

HAFIZ. *Naam e ma Haafez ast.*

AARON. Translate, please.

NAWEED. My name is Hafiz.

MUNIR throws money, inciting the other MEN to throw. SALIM dances sexually around HAFIZ.

HAFIZ. *Beradaar Salim ma emshab tana raqas astom.*

NAWEED. Brother Salim, I am only dancer tonight.

HAFIZ. *Loftan, ejaza betin Ustad ra.*

NAWEED. Allow the professional, please.

SALIM sits.

HAFIZ. *E lezat baray mo ast ke ba shoma beragsam.*

NAWEED. It is my duty to dance for you.

HAFIZ. No, no...I say pleasure. Not duty.

The MEN jeer and throw paper money. HAFIZ dances around AARON.

HAFIZ [*to Aaron*]. Munir say you the special one. I make poem for you:

> When I spin, our divided world mend.
> When I spin, muscle in mountain go soft.
> I am one of few flowers in this dry valley.
> Come to know me and know the Beloved.
> Let us dance with fullness of blood.
> For you, Beloved, I dance to the edge of desire.
> Behold my face and skinny fingers,
> My soft skin stretches for you, Beloved.
> I am the cobra. A beautiful [*suddenly stopping*] danger.

SALIM. *Chob Bash! Beraqs!* [No talk! More dance!]

HAFIZ continues dancing. MUNIR and the MEN throw money and jeer. BOY collects the money as it lands, brings it to MUNIR. HAFIZ gives all his attention to AARON, trying to coax money from him. AARON hesitantly throws money, but not much. HAFIZ moves to SALIM. The song swells and during the rise, AARON approaches MUNIR.

AARON [*over the music*]. How much for your boy?

MUNIR. *Chee?* [What?]

AARON [*louder*]. The boy! How much?

HAFIZ stops dancing.

MEN. *Bishtar, bishtar!* [More, more!]

NAWEED. What are you doing?

AARON. How much for the boy? That's the way this works, right?

MUNIR. Ahh, *Beradaar* Mohammad, too *shawqee.* Uglies wish for more dance.

AARON. I've seen what I need to see. I want to buy the boy.

MUNIR. Very expensive. Premium.

MEN [*agitated*]. *Bishtar, bishtar!* [More, more!]

NAWEED pulls AARON aside as the music and dancing continues.

NAWEED. We were not to buy the boy.

AARON. Munir says if you want to earn a man's trust, indulge in his sins. If I buy him, I buy their trust.

NAWEED. No, you buy him, you make them angry.

AARON. This kid has valuable intel on these men. Maybe even Shabah.

NAWEED. He is boy in dress.

AARON. Who hears a lot of pillow talk.

NAWEED. Pillow talk?

AARON. Information. Secrets are currency here. Trust me. I know what I'm doing.

AARON breaks away, gives MUNIR money.

AARON. This should cover it.

MUNIR. You insult. Hafiz is more. Much more.

AARON gives more. Much more.

MUNIR. Americans! "Oh the brave new world with such people in it!"

MEN. *Bishtar, bishtar!* [More, more!]

MUNIR silences the musicians.

SALIM. *Monir ejaza e shart ra bitay!* [Allow the bid, Munir!]

MEN. *Bale, bale!* [Yes, yes!]

The MEN throw money.

AARON. What'd they say?

NAWEED. They want him to allow bidding.

AARON. Wait! I already paid you—

MUNIR. We are bidding! *Panj hazaar.* [Five thousand.]

NAWEED. I told you this was not good idea.

AARON. I just paid him. What is he doing?

NAWEED. I believe the word is…hoodwinked?

MAN. *Shash?* [Six?]

MUNIR. *Shash!* [Six!]

SALIM. *Haft.* [Seven.]

MUNIR. *Haft.* [Seven.]

AARON. Wait, what's the bid?

MUNIR. Seven thousand. Hafiz much more than seven thousand.

AARON. Ten thousand.

NAWEED. Brother Munir, please, uh, he not understand the custom.

AARON. I understand perfectly. I said ten thousand.

MUNIR. *Dah hazaar.* [Ten thousand.]

SALIM. *Panzdah.* [Fifteen.]

MUNIR. *Panzdah!* [Fifteen!]

MAN. *Beest.* [Twenty.]

MUNIR. *Beest!* [Twenty!]

SALIM. *Si!* [Thirty!]

MAN. *Si o panj!* [Thirty-five!]

MUNIR. *Si o panj!* [Thirty-five!]

AARON. What's the bid?

MUNIR. Fifty thousand.

NAWEED. The bid is thirty-five!

MUNIR. Ha, the game's afoot! You think I give boy for free?

AARON. Fifty thousand. That's what, one thousand American?

NAWEED. You are driving price too high. We should make friends here, not enemies.

AARON. Fifty thousand!

MUNIR. *Panj a hazaar? Panj a hazaar?* [*taking Aaron's money*] Uglies always lose to Americans. Brother Mohammad, Hafiz is yours for the night.

MUNIR points HAFIZ in the direction of AARON. The MEN are loudly disappointed. A man, dressed as an Afghan militant, enters and stands just outside the light. HAFIZ goes to AARON, taking his hand with a flourish.

SWISS [*from the darkness*]. Mohammad! O oqadar Mohammad ast ke ma Eisah astom! [Mohammad! He is no more a Mohammad than I am a Jesus Christ!]

AARON. What'd he say?

SWISS. I say you are no more Mohammad than I Jesus Christ.

AARON. I thought they didn't speak English.

SWISS. I learn the language of conqueror. Show the face. Or Americans think you are important and shoot you. [*SWISS unveils AARON*] Ahhh, if he pay top price, even Jesus can experience paradise. What is your name?

AARON. < > Mohammad.

SWISS. You are far from home, Mohammad.

MUNIR. *Ma entizari shoma ra nadashtam. E yak rewaj ast ke bayad anjam shawa.* [I was not expecting you tonight. There is custom to keep.]

SWISS. *Ma wa to kharij azin rasmo o rewaj hastim.* [You and I are beyond custom.]

HAFIZ comes to SWISS's side.

SWISS. Forgive, brothers. I am called the Swiss, Swiss for short.

AARON. Swiss?

SWISS. I am Nooristani, so when I was boy, I have the blonde hair. The name follow me. Are you soldier, Mohammad?

AARON. No.

SWISS. Then what are you?

AARON. I am…curious.

SWISS [*SWISS laughs*]. Curious Mohammad. [*SWISS suddenly embraces AARON, kisses him on the cheeks*] Munir, a drink to celebrate curiosity!

MUNIR. I have only vodka.

SWISS. I will not tell Shabah. Will you?

AARON. You work for Shabah?

SWISS [*SWISS gets very close to AARON*]. Boo. [*laughs*] Is the vodka *Tajik?*

MUNIR offers the bottle. SWISS swigs it.

SWISS. *Tajik* taste is so pure. The secret: water from the mountains. To my new friend, Mohammad! *Salamatee!*

ALL. *Salamatee.*

SWISS passes the bottle to NAWEED. KASHI enters another part of the stage.

NAWEED. We should go.

SWISS. Forgive, forgive. Yes. I invade curiosity. You have good taste for boys, Mohammad. Hafiz is name of great poet of Persia. But he is…more than pretty words. He is mine. You are lucky I was not here to take him first.

SWISS takes HAFIZ's hand, kisses it. Rubab plays: "Signed, Sealed, Delivered." All exit except AARON, HAFIZ and NAWEED. Lights rise on Cambridge. AARON moves into the light with KASHI. NAWEED and HAFIZ stay in Afghanistan.

AARON [*reading*]. "The car was gravely quiet. Naweed didn't blast the radio. Didn't light a cigarette. Didn't crack any jokes like usual. He solemnly drove the three of us back toward my rented room, forehead glistening, eyes darting to and from the rearview, checking to be sure we weren't followed. He said—"

NAWEED. Aaron, I do not trust this.

AARON. Hafiz sat silently in the front seat, looking out the window at the lights in the distant countryside. I could smell him, a mixture of adolescent sweat and jasmine. But that man, Swiss, he could be our connection to Shabah, I said.

NAWEED. Or he kidnap us because we take his boy.

Lights fade on NAWEED and HAFIZ.

PROJECTION: CONVERSATION WITH SOMMERVILLE PRIZE WINNER AARON FREEMAN, AUTHOR OF *BLOOM: A SHOCK TOURIST'S ACCOUNT OF AFGHANISTAN*

KASHI. You're leaving us on quite the cliff.

AARON. Well, I wouldn't wanna spoil it for anyone who hasn't read it.

KASHI. Clearly you were in a dangerous situation. I wonder if you would talk about your decision to stay.

AARON. Well...the story was finally breaking open. It was the closest we'd come to seeing Shabah and we had Hafiz, who we could turn into an asset.

KASHI. But your translator was uncomfortable. Didn't that worry you?

AARON. Not really. You see, prior to me Naweed had only worked translation jobs for NGOs. He was never part of a journalistic process. So he didn't understand that when things get dangerous, it's a good sign you're onto something.

KASHI. How did you convince him to stay? You never say in the book.

AARON. I tripled his pay.

KASHI. You were there independently, not affiliated with a large media outlet, which means you funded your own project?

AARON. Yes.

KASHI. You literally paid every penny you had to be in the most dangerous place on Earth.

AARON. That's one way of putting it.

KASHI. That's how you put it in the book.

AARON. Right.

KASHI. As you know, I did my field work with women in Kabul. When the bombings started there, virtually the entire ex-pat community, media included evacuated as soon as possible...why do you risk everything, your life, your financial stability, simply to get a story?

AARON. < > Because...because stories are what makes life worth living...what make us human. You see, I believe in the power of empathy, Doctor Jones. Investing so fully in the state of being of your fellow man that you come to better understand his plight, his joys and fears. And we do that by hearing other people's stories. And if no one tells those stories, no one risks something to get those stories, then what? If empathy disappears, what's left for us then? I don't want to live in that world.

KASHI. That's very inspiring, Mr. Freeman. But one could argue that a Western...a Christian notion of empathy is in fact, its own form of oppression.

AARON. Yes one could argue that. In fact, I talk about it in the book. But, there's a big difference between saying, "I understand you" versus "I want to understand you." That was my biggest epiphany in all this.

KASHI. Hmm. < > Why opium initially?

AARON. Well...after the success of my first film, I wanted to look into—

KASHI. You're talking about *The Dawn?*

AARON. Right.

KASHI. Which was nominated for an Academy Award—

AARON. Yeah. I didn't win though. A documentary about football won that year. Anyway, after *The Dawn*, I wanted—

KASHI. Would you indulge us and briefly tell us about it? For context.

AARON. Well... I was embedded with a group of Iraqi insurgents during the Second Battle of Fallujah for three weeks. A hell of a lot more dangerous than being in a poppy field in Afghanistan. *The Dawn* tells the insurgents' side of the story. And after that experience, I wanted to see if I could find something similar in Afghanistan. Opium fit the bill. It was a big story, a global story that I could tell on a personal level from the viewpoint of the quote unquote "enemy."

KASHI. Creating empathy for the enemy.

AARON. Well, not necessarily. The hope is to be objective, but...I'm a doc filmmaker, part journalist, part artist. Whenever I focus on a subject, there's inevitably a point of view, which left unchecked can become manipulative and destructive. The ultimate goal is to shed light on the truth.

KASHI. Some people would argue that the only way to tell the capital T truth is...well, science. Research. Hard facts.

AARON. Sure that's one kind of truth. But there are many mysteries of the human experience that no amount of research will ever be able to explain, Kashi. The closest we can come is...art. And that's why I love my camera. It doesn't lie.

KASHI. I'm just going to read here, a bit from your preface. I find this part...fascinating.

As KASHI reads, the shadow dancer appears once again behind the scrim. AARON watches.

KASHI [*reading*]. "While English is surprisingly pervasive in Afghanistan, my portrayal of it in this book is not truly representative and parts of this story—names, places, dates—have been changed to protect the innocent. But more than that, in some cases, things have been fictionalized in order to expose a greater truth." < > It's a beautiful idea. And simpatico with proper fiction. But this is memoir.

AARON. Writers have done this since writers existed. You know what they called it before memoir? < > History.

KASHI. But come on, really...as a scholar, I'm perplexed by the notion as it relates to memoir. I mean, I believe it's fair to say the audience expects the truth and this caveat at the beginning of your book...well, doesn't it give you the freedom to sort of make things up?

AARON. It is the license of the artist to invent.

KASHI. < > Forgive my reductive questions. I suppose what I'm trying to understand is actually quite simple. In the narrative, you never distinguish fact from fiction, so how can we actually know what's true and what's not?

AARON. < > There's a quote that I love from Rumi. "The truth is a mirror in the hands of God. It falls and breaks into pieces. I take a piece. You take a piece. We look at it and think we each have the whole truth."

Lights up on AARON's room in Afghanistan.

HAFIZ. Who is to be first? You or translator?

AARON. Please, um, Hafiz...keep your...pants on.

HAFIZ. Not understand.

AARON. I'm not...I don't want...tell him I don't want sex.

HAFIZ. Everyone want for the sex. Especially my sex. You pay. Hafiz is yours.

HAFIZ dances toward AARON, then stops in front of NAWEED. He takes NAWEED's cigarette from his mouth, takes a drag, passes it back to NAWEED, approaches AARON.

HAFIZ. Munir say you are of America.

AARON. That's right.

HAFIZ. I hear it. Your talk has no God in it. No God in American English. [*HAFIZ spots a pair of pants draping the back of a chair.*] From America too?

AARON. Yeah. But probably made in China.

HAFIZ [*HAFIZ drapes the jeans at his waist*]. I never have *patloon e kow boy.*

NAWEED. Blue jeans.

AARON. I got that one, thanks.

HAFIZ. No, no. I say cowboy pants. [to AARON] He no good translator. Pay me. I translate.

AARON. He's gunning for your job, Naweed. Watch out.

HAFIZ. I wear?

AARON. Sure. Try 'em on.

HAFIZ quickly removes his dress. He beckons AARON to assist with unfastening...

HAFIZ. Help?

AARON hesitantly unfastens the dress and then looks away as HAFIZ removes it and slips into the jeans.

HAFIZ. How it is?

AARON. Looks good. You need a shirt.

AARON rifles through a bag and pulls out a t-shirt with a faded yellow Batman logo on the front. He tosses it to HAFIZ, who puts it on.

HAFIZ [*pointing to the logo*]. What does it mean?

AARON. Batman.

HAFIZ. Batmahn?

AARON. Exactly.

HAFIZ. *Ma nafameedom.* [I don't understand.]

NAWEED. The boy is saying *batmahn.* It's...an old word for weight. About three kilograms.

AARON. Oh...no...a bat...Like an ugly blind bird.

HAFIZ. No…

AARON. Surely you have bats here. [*AARON makes a bat face / noise.*]

NAWEED. *Shah parak e charmee?* [Leather butterflies?] [*NAWEED makes the same bat face / noise.*]

HAFIZ. Ah, *Bale!* [*HAFIZ makes the same bat face / noise.*]

AARON. Exactly. So Batman's a comic book character. A super-hero. Like Superman?

HAFIZ. Ah, yes! Superman. Batman fly?

AARON. The character named for a creature that flies can't actually fly himself. Ironic, right? < > Anyway, his powers aren't magical. He uses technology to fight criminals. Plus, he's a badass who knows karate.

HAFIZ. Bad ass?

AARON. Tough guy. Strong.

AARON strikes a strongman pose. HAFIZ mimics him.

AARON. < > Hey, how about this? I'll let you have the Batman if you can keep a secret.

HAFIZ. See-cret?

NAWEED. *Raaz.*

HAFIZ. Keep Batman?

AARON. You keep it, yes.

HAFIZ. < > OK.

AARON. I'm not who you think I am.

NAWEED pulls AARON aside.

NAWEED. What are you doing?

AARON. We need to tell him the truth.

NAWEED. If this boy tell Munir or those men of your intention—

AARON. He won't.

NAWEED. How you know this?

AARON. I'll pay him not to.

NAWEED. If he is not easy to buy?

AARON. He will be.

NAWEED. How you know?

AARON. Because he's a…he's a kid. It shouldn't be that hard to make him feel special. And when he opens up, I'll get some compromising information about the Swiss and before you know it, he'll be talking on camera and leading me to Shabah. [*AARON breaks from NAWEED, approaches HAFIZ.*] I'm not a pornographer, Hafiz.

HAFIZ. Not know this por-no-graaf…

AARON. A little help, Naweed?

NAWEED. < > *Pornograafer.*

HAFIZ. Ah, yes. *Pornograafer.*

AARON. It sounds exactly the same. You just say it with an accent.

NAWEED. Is very different.

AARON. Hafiz, I'm not a [*his best*] *pornogeraafer.* I'm a documentary filmmaker. Like *National Geographic.* I'm shooting a film about opium.

HAFIZ. Opium?

AARON. Yes, but Munir and all the men at the party, I need them to think I made a sexy movie with you. That's why I'm giving you Batman. OK?

HAFIZ. < > OK, cowboy.

AARON. It's very important that you keep that between us.

HAFIZ. You buy me, you my secret.

AARON shoots NAWEED a look: I told you so.

AARON. Those men at the party…how well do you know them?

HAFIZ. I do not talk of the men.

NAWEED shoots AARON a look: I told you so.

AARON. You can say anything you want here. It's just between us.

HAFIZ. No, you buy me, you…see-cret.

AARON. But those men, the Swiss, he'll never know you talked to me.

HAFIZ. I do not—

AARON. This conversation is between us. *Raaz.* Our secret. Is the Swiss your boyfriend?

HAFIZ. Boy-friend?

AARON. He said you were his. Is he your boyfriend?

HAFIZ. Not understand.

AARON. Help me out, Naweed.

NAWEED. There is no good translation for boyfriend.

AARON. OK…well…have you ever seen Shabah at your parties?

HAFIZ [*laughs*]. Shabah? No, no…he no like *bacha bazi*.

AARON. So…why are his men at your parties if he doesn't like it?

HAFIZ doesn't know how to respond.

NAWEED. Boss, America does not have monopoly on hypocrisy.

AARON. Would you mind if we talk on camera? [*AARON begins setting up his camera.*]

HAFIZ. It is better just you and me.

NAWEED. Boss, you wish me to leave?

AARON. < > Do you mind?

NAWEED exits. A charged silence as AARON and HAFIZ regard each other.

HAFIZ. He is very tight. Like a fist.

AARON. Day 24. July 15, no 16, 2006. Interview with Hafiz, a *bacha bee reesh*. [*moving out of the frame*] Hafiz, do you consent to this interview? < > Can I film you? I'll let you keep the cowboy pants too.

HAFIZ. < > OK. *Bale*. But no talk of the men.

AARON. Not about the men. About you.

HAFIZ. Me?

AARON. Yes.

HAFIZ. I am…a fascinating.

AARON [*laughing*]. Yes. You are. [*through the lens*] The camera likes you. Just for the interview, would you mind wearing the dress? I think it'll look better than Batman. The dress tells your story.

HAFIZ. My story?

AARON. Yes.

HAFIZ. You say I keep—

AARON. But just for the camera—

HAFIZ [*rising*]. I not like this…in-ter-view. Translator is gone. Hafiz is yours.

AARON. No, that's not...Here. Maybe you could interview me first to get the hang of it? Stand here? [*AARON offers HAFIZ his spot behind the camera.*] Ask me questions.

HAFIZ [*HAFIZ peers through the lens*]. You are beautiful inside the camera. But you have sadness around the eyes. [*Silence*]

AARON. You're supposed to ask me questions.

HAFIZ. Sorry. You live Hollywood?

AARON. No, I live in New York.

HAFIZ. The towers?

AARON. Yeah.

HAFIZ. Bloom there?

AARON. What do you mean...bloom?

HAFIZ. Ah. You grow to become man in New York?

AARON. No, I grew up in Texas.

HAFIZ. Not / know.

AARON. George Bush, the President is from there. Some of us aren't proud of that though.

HAFIZ. Your parents in Tex-as?

AARON. My parents are deceased. < > They're dead.

HAFIZ. You same as Hafiz. The orphan.

AARON. Yeah. < > Yeah, I guess I am.

HAFIZ. You have the wife?

AARON. No.

HAFIZ. Every man has the wife.

AARON. Not where I come from.

HAFIZ. You cannot take the wife with you. But boy, you take everywhere.

AARON. It doesn't work that way in New York.

HAFIZ. When I marry, I have the beard.

AARON laughs.

HAFIZ. It is not to laugh. When boy grow beard, no longer *bacha bee reesh*.

AARON. I'm sorry...I misunderstood. In my culture, having a beard means—nevermind. Do you have any more questions?

HAFIZ. Why you come here?

AARON. Because I'm making this film.

HAFIZ. This is no film.

AARON. It's not like Hollywood. I make films about real people. Like you.

HAFIZ. The film is about me?

AARON. Like you said, you're fascinating…what you do. Dancing.

HAFIZ. It is film about the dance?

AARON. Right now, it's about a lot of things. Too many things. Opium. Capitalism. Democracy. America and Afghanistan.

HAFIZ. I will not watch this film.

AARON. Yeah. Me neither. How about this? Tonight, while the camera's rolling, this movie is about you. About your life and how you became this way.

HAFIZ. Way?

AARON. A dancer.

HAFIZ. The movie about the dance?

AARON. Yes.

HAFIZ. How you are your way?

AARON. I'm not sure I understand what you mean.

HAFIZ. You make film about my way. I make film about your way.

AARON. Oh, uh…well…my way is, I went to school.

HAFIZ. School?

AARON. Yeah. Well, uh, first, I went to college for journalism. Then to the Peace Corps in South America. Came back stateside. Wrote for newspapers for a minute. When people still read them. And now I make documentary films.

HAFIZ. The film about you?

AARON. My movies aren't about me. They're about other people. I'm not that interesting.

HAFIZ. I think you are interesting. You movie star?

AARON. No, documentary filmmaker.

HAFIZ. But you movie star now. For my film.

AARON. OK, what's your film about?

HAFIZ. A handsome cowboy lose horse, but find love instead.

AARON laughs.

HAFIZ. Blockbuster! I make famous. < > You say you go to school for your way. Schools for this in America?

AARON. Yeah, I went to film school. NYU. New York University.

HAFIZ. No, no…your way. How you come to love boys? This way, you call it.

AARON. Oh…uh…

HAFIZ. You love boys, yes?

AARON. < > My turn to ask the questions. [*AARON breaks away to the camera, seats HAFIZ in front of it.*]

HAFIZ. Go, cowboy.

AARON. How old are you?

HAFIZ. Young.

AARON. I can see that, yes. But do you know your age?

HAFIZ. Sixteen? Seventeen? Eighteen? Not know.

AARON. Well, where are you from?

HAFIZ. Around Fayzabad.

AARON. Do you have any brothers, sisters?

HAFIZ. Sister.

AARON. Where is she?

HAFIZ. No one watch the movie with these question!

AARON. I'm just trying to get to know you.

HAFIZ [*not touching him*]. Better way.

AARON [*sotto voce*]. You are…persistent. How did you meet Munir?

HAFIZ. Bore, bore, bore.

AARON. Come on, answer the question. I gave you Batman. How did you meet Munir?

HAFIZ [*HAFIZ performs a small step, getting close to AARON*]. You not first American.

AARON. Really?

HAFIZ. Other, not talk much. See my dance?

AARON. Does the Swiss ever tell you things? About his business? About opium?

HAFIZ. You are only man who buy me and talk.

AARON. Is he intimate with you?

HAFIZ. See my dance?

AARON. Hafiz, I gave you the shirt. Answer the question. Does Swiss have sex with you?

HAFIZ. I say when you buy me, you are secret. See the dance.

AARON. I don't want to film the dance—

HAFIZ. Is better for film—

AARON. I want to talk about the Swiss. What happens between you and him?

HAFIZ. You wish make sexy film?

AARON. No, I want to hear about you…about what hurts you.

HAFIZ. Hurts?

AARON. Yes, when the Swiss buys you.

HAFIZ. See my dance.

AARON. Answer the question. Does Swiss have sex with you? I need you to say it on camera.

HAFIZ. All men must satisfy urge to bring war on another person's body.

AARON. Sex isn't war.

HAFIZ. If war not same as sex, we would stop making it. They are same thing…games for boys. Now, see my dance.

AARON [*turning the camera away from HAFIZ*]. No more dancing! *HAFIZ stops dancing.*

AARON. < > Hafiz, you're a victim. You do know that, don't you? *Silence.*

AARON. I'm sorry. I shouldn't have said that.

HAFIZ. The lights.

AARON. No, I told you, Hafiz—

HAFIZ. Off the light! I teach dance.

AARON. No, Hafiz, this isn't—

HAFIZ [*HAFIZ turns off the light*]. Is best in dark. You will not be shy. Trust. Good teacher. [*HAFIZ begins to clap out a 7/8 beat*] Stand up straight.

AARON. Hafiz—

HAFIZ. Straight.

AARON stands.

HAFIZ. Rhythm. One two three one two one two. One two three one two one two. Clap it.

AARON and HAFIZ clap / count together.

HAFIZ. Yes. Hear beat—one, two, three—in head. < > Begin in chest. Most think hips. No. Burden of dance live in chest. The heart's cage. Move chest from side to side. Straight. Now you. Dancing means moving.

AARON. I don't want to dance.

HAFIZ. You wish to ask question?

AARON. Yes.

HAFIZ. Dance.

AARON [*AARON poorly imitates HAFIZ*]. I'm no good.

HAFIZ. No. You are not good. But practice. Close the eyes. In the mind, see a line...and on this line, this tight string, your heart walk above the crowd.

AARON tries. He's a little better.

HAFIZ. Good. This is good. Now move the head. The brain. Against the heart—like so. [*HAFIZ demonstrates*] This take...more than you have. But practice and maybe. Hear rhythm. One, two, three one two one two. Feel pull between heart and brain—heart... open like flower in bloom speaking yes yes yes—and brain...a heavy diamond, balancing on the tip, ready to fall, saying no no no, and you catch it just as...you see?

HAFIZ claps. AARON tries.

AARON. I'm so bad at this.

HAFIZ. Do not hear brain—no no no. Hear heart—yes yes yes.

AARON. I feel stupid.

HAFIZ. Then you doing it right! Keep going! Balance the flower and the diamond.

As AARON mucks it up. HAFIZ comes behind him, takes AARON's hands, lifts them. AARON is frozen.

HAFIZ [*whispering into his ear*]. Now the hands. Hands are ears for Allah. Raise them, turn them at the wrist, turn like a question to your maker...you ask...am I worthy? Am I worthy? And Allah whisper—yes yes yes.

AARON breaks away.

HAFIZ. You stop so soon? The dance is a quest to unfold yourself. Not like prayer—when we fold the body. [*Dancing*] Last, feet. Strong to hold head and heart. They spin, left over right. Slow, but then they spin into ground, hard, hard, harder, raise dust, ring bells, say I am here! You will see me! You must see me! And then you lost in spin—over and over—while hands listen for answer and heart walk on line and brain try not to fall.

HAFIZ dances fully. AARON is transfixed. He finishes with a flourish, his beating heart close to AARON. For a moment, they are suspended and something uncoils.

AARON. We should stop.

HAFIZ [*HAFIZ draws closer*]. Now you know the dance, brother Mohammad.

AARON. My name is Aaron.

HAFIZ. Aaron. Now you know its power. Do not say I am victim. *Black out.*

INTERMISSION

In the darkness, we hear a scratchy record blasting Lesley Gore's "You Don't Own Me." Lights reveal BOY and HAFIZ sitting on the floor, on a very large rug, listening to a record player wail Lesley Gore.

HAFIZ. Do you like this music?

BOY. It sounds kinda angry.

HAFIZ. Yeah. [*HAFIZ stops the record. Lampooning*] Dunh-dunh-dunh! Dunh-dunh-dunh! You don't own me! I not just a little boy!

BOY. How do you know so much English?

HAFIZ. Shakespeare.

BOY. Who?

HAFIZ. A stupid American writer. Munir will do it with you too. He's obsessed. You wanna learn some?

BOY. Not really.

HAFIZ. Munir'll be impressed. You're more valuable with English.

BOY. < > OK, I guess.

HAFIZ. This is one of his favorites: "Doubt thou the stars are fire; Doubt that the sun doth move; Doubt truth to be a liar; But never doubt I love."

BOY. What does it mean?

HAFIZ. Well…it's sort of a long way of saying, "No matter what, I love you." Try it. Doubt thou the stars are fire.

BOY. Dowt dow—

HAFIZ. Thou—

BOY. Dow—

HAFIZ. The stars—

BOY. Thuh istars—

HAFIZ. Are fire—

BOY. Are fawyer—

HAFIZ. Doubt thou the stars are fire.

BOY. Dowt dow thuh istar are fawyer. This sucks. Let's do something else.

HAFIZ [*HAFIZ takes a small bag from his pocket, rolls a smoke, lights it, puffs, passes*]. Try this instead.

BOY. What is it?

HAFIZ. You really don't know?

BOY shakes his head.

HAFIZ. Hashish.

BOY. I shouldn't.

HAFIZ. It's no big deal.

BOY takes the joint, hits it hard, coughs uncontrollably. HAFIZ laughs.

HAFIZ [*imitates BOY*]. You are like a fish! Like this. [*HAFIZ hits it lightly to demonstrate, passes it.*]

BOY. It burns my throat.

HAFIZ. Just try again. So you don't look stupid when other boys wanna smoke with you.

BOY takes it, hits it less, still coughs, passes it back to HAFIZ.

BOY. Have you ever done heroin?

HAFIZ. No…it fucks up your brain. Makes you like a zombie.

HAFIZ does a zombie imitation. Hits the hashish, passes. BOY puffs, coughs. MUNIR enters. HAFIZ immediately extinguishes the smoke, stands. BOY is still coughing.

MUNIR. When you are brought to me, Hafiz, I said, "This one will shine like a thousand stars."

HAFIZ. Thanks.

MUNIR. I'm lucky to have seen your light and I will protect it. Even from your own foolishness.

MUNIR holds out his hand. HAFIZ reluctantly places the small bag of hashish, then his rolling papers, then his lighter in it. MUNIR pockets it all.

MUNIR. Who gave this to you? Salim?

HAFIZ. No—

MUNIR. Who? < > Who?

HAFIZ. Swiss.

MUNIR. You gave to the boy?

HAFIZ. < > No.

BOY coughs violently.

HAFIZ. I smoke and he coughs! Very strange.

MUNIR. Come here.

BOY looks to HAFIZ. MUNIR grabs BOY's face.

MUNIR. Blow. < > Blow!

BOY does. MUNIR smells his breath.

MUNIR. It's bad enough that you smoke it, but now you give it to the boy too?

HAFIZ. Only a little—

MUNIR [*MUNIR smacks HAFIZ very hard*]. Do not keep secrets from me, Hafiz. Secrets will kill you, understand?

HAFIZ. Yeah. OK.

MUNIR. All these years, I've protected you.

HAFIZ. Thanks.

MUNIR. You're like a son to me, Hafiz. But I fear for you. I don't want to send you into the world.

HAFIZ. Into the world? What do you mean?

MUNIR gently takes HAFIZ's face into his hands. HAFIZ flinches a bit.

MUNIR. As Allah wishes, you have become a man. You've bloomed, beautiful boy. Your beard breaks the skin.

HAFIZ. I'm still young, Baba Munir.

MUNIR. Look into a mirror. This can't be a surprise.

HAFIZ. How will I dance?

MUNIR. You will not dance. That's how.

HAFIZ. But I—

MUNIR. If you wish to have honor, you can never again speak of the dance. If someone accuses you of dancing with men, look them in eye, call them a liar, and spit at their feet. You have to become someone else.

HAFIZ. I don't want to be someone else!

MUNIR. First you'll find work, then you'll find a wife.

HAFIZ. How am I supposed to be a husband? I don't know how to love a woman.

MUNIR. Allah will show you the way to a woman's…heart. It takes a long time, Hafiz. And practice. Just like the dance.

HAFIZ. How would you know?

MUNIR. < > My father was a good man. He read me Shakespeare.

HAFIZ. You've told me this a million times.

MUNIR. Listen, boy! When I lived with my father, we had a house with a garden, furniture from Europe. But the Russians took everything! < > My parents were murdered by Russian soldiers who fired their AKs in the middle of a market. Target practice. I went to live with an uncle near Fayzabad. I was too young to fight, so my uncle sold me…and I became a dancing boy.

HAFIZ. You?

MUNIR. I was beautiful. Full of grace. A solemn face the men loved. < > But when I bloomed, I traveled far away and became someone else. I became Munir. No one knows this. It's my secret.

HAFIZ. Why didn't you ever tell me this?

MUNIR. For a man to be a dancing boy, Hafiz, it is a disgrace. This is Afghanistan. We go a long distance out of way to come home safely. I trust you'll never tell my secret because I will never tell yours. < > Tomorrow night, we'll have a party for Shabah's men. The boy will make his first dance. And you will make your last.

HAFIZ. Please…I cannot—

MUNIR [*MUNIR smacks HAFIZ again*]. < > I'll sing for you. I never sing for my boys. But I will sing for your last dance. Does that honor you?

HAFIZ. < > Yes, Baba Munir.

MUNIR. Good. [*kisses him on the cheek*] Now, show me what he knows.

HAFIZ. He's a footballer. Not a dancer.

MUNIR. Show me.

HAFIZ [*HAFIZ claps*]. Boy…let's dance. One-two-three. One-two. One-two. Raise your hands. [*HAFIZ raises BOY's hands for him. He elegantly shows BOY a pattern, who repeats it crudely.*] He sucks.

MUNIR. Yeah, because he isn't trained.

HAFIZ. He is too young to learn the dance and what it means.

MUNIR. But old enough for your hashish? What've you been doing with him all this time?

HAFIZ. It is only a few weeks. It takes years to learn to dance like I do.

MUNIR. You have a few hours. Think of something. Also I arranged a meeting for you tonight at Mahgreb.

HAFIZ. No, if I can't dance, I'm not for sale.

MUNIR. We are all for sale, boy. Why should you be different? It's a meeting with the filmmaker.

HAFIZ. Brother Aaron? Yes, yes! I say yes!

MUNIR. I thought so. < > You like the American?

HAFIZ. He's a bad ass. Like Batman.

MUNIR [*MUNIR does not understand*]. < > Three nights together. He pays top price.

HAFIZ. Well, I'm worth it.

MUNIR. You think he's beautiful?

HAFIZ. Not more than you.

MUNIR. You are kind to an old man. "Age with his stealing steps has clawed me in the clutch."

HAFIZ. *King Lear?*

MUNIR [*MUNIR moves in as though to kiss HAFIZ on the lips*]. The clown in *Hamlet*. [*moving away*] Teach the boy a simple Attan. And he can sing. He has a sweet voice. He will never be you, Hafiz. No one will.

MUNIR exits. BOY kicks the ball to HAFIZ. It hits his feet.

BOY. Are you OK?

HAFIZ claps: one two three, etc. Subtitles project.

HAFIZ. I'm fine. Watch me. Don't use your ears to understand me. Use your body. Like this. And this. And this. Do as I do. Move the shoulders. Side side side. Side side side. And spin.

BOY tries.

HAFIZ. Faster. Spin faster! < > No! You are dancing for your life! They will kill you if you dance like this.

BOY. I'm sorry.

HAFIZ. Don't apologize. Never apologize. [*HAFIZ grabs BOY's hips.*] You need to know some things, beautiful boy.

Rubab plays the melody of "Got to Give it Up." AARON and KASHI enter, watching from the darkness.

HAFIZ. Listen:

> They will take you with rough hands.
> They will hold your face to the ground.
> They will push their pain inside you.
> They will try to break you apart.
> But you must not break. Never break!
> Your hips will bruise the worst.
> Bruises in shapes of men's fingers.
> Always in the valley between the ribs and hips.

Lights fade on Afghanistan, rise on Cambridge.

KASHI [*reading*]. Would you drink fine wine as you would water?

> Then treat me not as you do yourself.
> Rather than murder my fruits with compassion,
> Enjoy them, dark and sinful to your tongue.

That's your epigraph, taken from a poem by the Afghan-American poet, and last year's Sommerville winner, Nazrul Sajadi. < > For those who don't know, Mr. Sajadi was keenly upset when Mr. Freeman was named the winner of the Sommerville.

AARON. Yes. Yes he was.

KASHI. I'd like to read a bit from his open letter in the *New York Times*. Would that be all right?

AARON. Oh, why not.

KASHI [*reading*]. "Poets live and die to be quoted. But after reading your book, I did not feel honored. I felt pillaged. I imagine, since you borrowed my language to sanctify your own, that you admire my work. Hopefully, that admiration will make these words carry extra weight. *Bloom* was never your story to tell. Electing yourself spokesperson for another culture is a hallmark of the imperialist values you say you wish to reject, the biggest show of activism on your part would be to turn down the Sommerville altogether. If you accept it, it will be for a book that professes to condemn but ultimately condones American imperialism." And he goes on...but of course we all know you're here to accept the prize, a prize that honors a piece of literature that effects social change. I bring this up because I think the students would benefit from hearing how you're handling the controversy.

AARON. Well...I didn't respond to him.

KASHI. Why not?

AARON. It's not a conversation that interests me. My book is an examination of my own culture's values. I never claim to be a spokesperson for Afghanistan. I plan to have the epigraph removed in the next printing. And also, I'm donating the entirety of the cash prize to The Bloom Project. Which I would've done despite Sajadi's letter. We have a website for those of you who are interested in contributing. It's at...

Projection shows The Bloom Project website.

AARON. Hey, there it is. Thanks, Colin. Yeah, so check it out. Donate if you can. If not, there are other ways to get involved.

KASHI. I don't necessarily agree with the language Mr. Sajadi uses in his letter, but I am curious to hear you speak to his accusation of imperialism.

AARON. The story is written from my perspective. How can I imperialize myself?

KASHI. But what of the Afghans? There are moments in your book when you are not present and you speak for the Afghans.

AARON. I guess you want to have the appropriation conversation?

KASHI. Well, yes. I think it's important to discuss—

AARON. Let's cut to the chase. I've had this conversation before. Are you asking me this because I'm white?

KASHI. No, I'm, no—I'm asking because I think your privilege which is, yes, inextricably linked to the color of your skin and your nationality and your gender, is the only reason you can actually tell this story. Do you disagree?

AARON. I don't disagree with that at all. And that's why it's not my right, Kashi, to tell this story. It's my obligation. Do you think the world would be better off not knowing about Hafiz?

KASHI. I'm not saying that.

AARON. Rather than having to suffer through my white American male version of the story, it's better if we just continue to let these boys be exploited?

KASHI. I'm afraid you're misunderstanding me.

AARON. First world journalists should always check their lens before telling any story about Afghanistan. But we are under no obligation to leave the telling of those stories only to people with blood ties to the country. Unlike Mr. Sajadi, I do not practice identity politics.

KASHI. You don't have to, Mr. Freeman. The dominant identity never does.

AARON. < > No, I don't practice identity politics because they are a form of censorship and a cause of war. Do I have the right to tell this story? As an American citizen engaged in a war with Afghanistan, yes, I have plenty of right to tell this story.

KASHI. But your story isn't about war—

AARON. Kashi, I was there. I risked my life to get the story. And I am very open about my own culpability and what I did as a result of my biases. In my field, that's a huge risk—

KASHI. But that doesn't answer my quest—

AARON. Let's be honest, Sajadi, like other people, is probably jealous of my success. < > Doctor Jones, I gotta be honest, I'm feeling a bit sabotaged up here.

KASHI. I'm sorry, but I hope you'll understand, I can't let your achievements or your confessional book get in the way of asking important questions.

AARON. Are you Hindi?

KASHI. I suppose you mean Hindu.

AARON. OK. Yes, I beg your pardon. Hindu. Are you?

KASHI. I don't see how this is relevant.

AARON. Come on. You read my book. You know everything about me. Are you Hindu?

KASHI. Culturally yes. Spiritually no.

AARON. Are you Muslim?

KASHI. No.

AARON. You're an Indian woman, living and working in Britain, judging by your last name, Doctor Jones, you're probably married to a Brit, which I think means you know a thing or two about imperialism—

KASHI. Mr. Freeman!

AARON. And your work is about women in Afghanistan. What qualifies you to tell their stories? You're not Afghan.

NAWEED enters, sets up the camera on a tripod.

KASHI. I'm not a storyteller. I'm a scholar.

AARON. So academics get a pass?

KASHI. No, that's not what I'm saying—

AARON. Is my perspective on this irrelevant because I'm not brown…enough?

Lights reveal AARON's rented room. AARON is seated staring at footage on his laptop. NAWEED peers over his shoulder, behind him, smoking a cigarette. Projection: footage of HAFIZ dancing plays behind them.

AARON. This footage is amazing. Look at the way he moves.

NAWEED. Hmmm…when is he coming?

AARON. Soon, I hope.

NAWEED. These American Spirits you bring…very smooth. No additive.

AARON. You should quit.

NAWEED. And be miserable like you? No thanks. < > On the phone with daughter, she say she wake last night because she hear dog howling in the house. But we have no dog. She find that it is her mother, crying in quiet hours. Crying because she misses me. When you have wife, brother, you will learn children are important for marriage. They tell when wife cries in middle of night. I cannot think how much more my wife cry if she know I spend nights with boy prostitutes.

AARON. She'll have you back soon enough. And a lot richer.

NAWEED. < > I'm sorry. I have to say this. < > It is mistake to make this movie about Hafiz. Opium was a good project. This film is…it is…it is…

AARON. Where is this coming from all the sudden?

NAWEED. Please, I say it only for your interest. Brother, you are being cheat. And you cannot see because…you are infatuate.

AARON. I'm not infatuated. I'm personally invested.

NAWEED. That boy and the pimp have you wrap around fingers. Three nights? Fists of money? And Hafiz wants me out of / room.

AARON. Yeah, because you make him uncomfortable.

NAWEED. No, he knows I see past the charade. < > What you do together in there for so long?

AARON. I'm working. I'm trying to get him to break on camera.

NAWEED. Break?

AARON. Tell his story.

NAWEED. How difficult is that?

AARON. Victims of pedophilia aren't exactly open books. It takes time and space and, and…nuance. I'm sorry if you don't understand the process of conducting interviews. I shouldn't even have to justify this to you.

NAWEED. I am only thinking for you. I want to help make best film.

AARON. This is the best film. I was getting nowhere with opium. A film about Hafiz, about *bacha bazi*...exposing something like this? It could actually help put a stop to it.

NAWEED [*laughing*]. Good luck with that. The Taliban could not stop it. You make this movie and what? It will have many likes on the Facebook? Thousands will sign online petition—save dancing boys! People will be so upset. For a few hours. Because, my experience, that is the life of repugnance—a few hours. Do you really expect Americans to fly to Afghanistan and steal orphans from warlords?

AARON. That's not / the point—

NAWEED. When people watch this movie about poor Hafiz, you wish them to feel guilt?

AARON. Not guilt. Empathy!

NAWEED. I am willing to bet my entire pay that it is not empathy. It will be superiority they feel.

AARON. There are still good people in the world, Naweed. And they will see this and be inspired to do something. To help Hafiz and other boys like him.

NAWEED. Donate money? Make another NGO?

AARON. Yeah, maybe, I don't know. The point is exposure.

NAWEED. Charity from superiority is like...is like beating slave with gold whip and then offer him the whip as his own. The poor slave take it. What choice he has? Point your camera to me. I tell you everything you need for film about poor Hafiz. People want to survive. And to survive, boys will dance. < > Credits roll. End of movie.

AARON. How can you be so indifferent?

NAWEED. Dancing boys? This is not every day in Afghanistan.

AARON. Yeah, I should hope not.

NAWEED. War: every day. And sacrifice we make because of it. Fear: every day. And I raise my daughter to trust, to love. Regret: every day. And yet I do not know what to change if I could.

AARON. Don't you see, though? Hafiz is all of that. He is Afghanistan. The contradiction of this country is written on his body.

NAWEED. You wish to show my country? Show the face of the humble farmer. Show daughters who love their father and a father who die to feed his children. That is Afghanistan. We are much more than pretty boy in a dress.

AARON. Why are you taking this so personally?

NAWEED. Because I am Afghan! *Bacha bazi* is terrible, yes, but you show this...this dirty, dirty boy play, these perverted *Koonee*—

AARON. I don't know—

NAWEED. These faggots, Aaron! You show these faggots and you will bring shame, great shame to my people!

AARON. I'm sorry, Naweed, but shame is exactly what you should feel.

HAFIZ enters. His face is bruised.

HAFIZ. Aaron?

NAWEED. Your star returns.

AARON. Naweed. Chill out. [*to Hafiz*] Are you OK?

HAFIZ is silent.

AARON [*to Naweed*]. And you don't think a film about his life is important? Look at him, Naweed.

NAWEED. I see one boy. And I see million poppies.

AARON. Take a walk.

NAWEED. What?

AARON. Walk. Get out of here.

NAWEED. Why? You need space for nuance?

AARON. No, because I'm the filmmaker and you're the fixer.

NAWEED [*throws up his hands*]. < > As you say...boss.

NAWEED exits.

AARON. I'm sorry about that.

HAFIZ. Is OK.

AARON. Can we just...can we just...take a minute? [*AARON paces, composes himself and then positions his camera in the direction of HAFIZ.*] What happened to your face?

HAFIZ. You worry for me. I like that.

AARON. Here. [*positioning Hafiz*] Left...a little more. That's great.

HAFIZ. I make new dance for the film.

AARON. I don't want to film dancing this time, Hafiz. I just want to talk. What happened to you?

HAFIZ. It is nothing.

AARON. Almost forgot. [*AARON gives HAFIZ money.*]

HAFIZ. *Tashakor.*

AARON. Did Munir do this to you?

HAFIZ. You are like dog with a wound. You cannot stop.

AARON. This is how I want to spend my time. I'm paying you to answer my questions on camera.

HAFIZ. What good is it if I say things for the camera?

AARON. Because saying it for my camera makes it real. [*AARON approaches HAFIZ, holds him by the shoulders, looks into his eyes.*] Listen, Hafiz, I've got two days left here.

HAFIZ. And then to New York?

AARON. Yes. Now I know it's hard to talk about these things, but I need you to open up, tell me who did this to you. Tell me something about your life, so I can help you.

HAFIZ. I am not needing help.

AARON. You just don't know you do. I know you want to be strong. I understand that more than you know. But until you say these things, the things that no one ever wants to say, the things that have really hurt you, then you'll never truly be strong.

HAFIZ. You think I am beautiful?

AARON. You are a child.

HAFIZ. In America I am child. In Afghanistan, I am luxury.

AARON. How old were you the first time a man took you?

HAFIZ. Please...I not talk of this—

AARON. We've been playing cat and mouse for three days. I've given you a lot of money and all I want in return is your story. Do you understand why I might be frustrated?

HAFIZ. Wish for story?

AARON. Please. And a true one this time.

HAFIZ. Cat and mouse...I have story of lion and lamb.

AARON. No, come on, something real—

HAFIZ. Story is real. My father tell me. Lion and lamb. They belong to rich man. Lion live in cage for he is dangerous and lamb walk free among man's garden because lamb is harmless and pretty. < > For years it is this way until lamb become sheep. And when rich man lose all his gold, he can no feed his animals, so he slaughter sheep to feed to lion. < > Last words my father say: *Shayr wari bash.* Be a lion.

AARON. What happened to your father?

HAFIZ. Gone.

AARON. Where did he go?

HAFIZ. < > Ten. I was ten the first time a man take me. How old for you?

AARON. < > This isn't about me.

HAFIZ. I see sadness in your eyes. The danger between us is not we are different. The danger between us is we are same. How old?

Silence.

AARON. Five. I was five. The first time.

Silence.

HAFIZ. I am special for you.

AARON. You're special for my film.

HAFIZ. For you. [*HAFIZ gently wraps AARON's fingers around his neck.*] Hafiz is much more than a story. When I dance, men know themselves completely. In the night, Swiss is so in love for me, he holds my neck like gold. And when my eyes flash, he release—like snake on fire. I am that power. You can feel that power, Aaron—

AARON. Stop—

HAFIZ. Pretty pearl skin Aaron—

AARON. Hafiz—

HAFIZ. When I dance, muscle in mountain go soft—

AARON. No—

HAFIZ. For you, Beloved, I dance to the edge of desire—

AARON. STOP.

HAFIZ retreats. AARON turns the camera back toward HAFIZ.

AARON. I'm not one of your men.

HAFIZ. I know.

AARON. So please just answer my questions. What happened when you were ten?

HAFIZ. No more question. I cannot know you, you cannot know me.

AARON. This isn't about me. It isn't about us. It's about helping others. If I can show even a glimpse of what happened to you, of who you are, then something more can be done. For other boys.

HAFIZ. Other boys?

AARON. Yes. But you have to talk to me. You have to tell me your story. All of it. Hafiz, you don't see it now, but telling me your story, helping me make this film, it's going to make a difference. Think about it. If you could go back and you could help yourself as that ten-year-old boy, if you could put a stop to this whole thing, save the boy you used to be, wouldn't you do it? I would. You can still be a lion, Hafiz.

HAFIZ. I love for the men, you understand? It is my way.

AARON. I understand that. I do.

HAFIZ. Here, dance is the only way.

AARON. But what they do to you is abuse.

HAFIZ. That is what you wish me to say? When they touch, they do with rough hands? Yes! They hold my face to the dirt and push their pain inside. That is what you wish? < > The only thing I wish is for to be touch by the man who does not want to make me bleed. By someone gentle. By you.

AARON. I can't do that.

HAFIZ. I wish to know your kindness.

AARON. I'm sorry—

HAFIZ. It is only once. And I say my story. All of it. Please.

AARON. Hafiz—

HAFIZ. I say my story because you are good man. I not beg you. You must want it. I see how you look to me. With love-fire in the eyes. I want for you, Aaron. I want everything you are. < > If you do not for want me—

AARON kisses HAFIZ. It is a sweet kiss, filled with promise and sus-picion. AARON pulls away, but HAFIZ brings him back, kissing him with unbridled, beating red passion. A heartbeat bumps on the drum. Beat-beat. Beat-beat. HAFIZ and AARON now stand side by side: AARON reading from his book at Cambridge and HAFIZ mid-interview in Afghanistan.

HAFIZ. My father was a farmer.

AARON. ...he said and I asked, "What happened to him, to your father?"

HAFIZ. Pakistan.

AARON. "Why?" I could feel his silence shattering. I asked again, "Why did he go to Pakistan?"

HAFIZ. Mother and sister...

AARON. He trailed off. His eyes brimmed with tears. "Where are your mother and sister?" I asked.

HAFIZ. Mother was in the courtyard...

AARON. He bit his lip, closed his eyes and took a deep breath. "Hafiz?"

HAFIZ. I find her there. < > She has no head.

AARON. His body shook with this memory. I was afraid to ask about his sister.

HAFIZ. I think the opium men take her. We never find...any of her.

AARON. The opium men?

HAFIZ. My father, farmer for poppies. And he...he use the opium.

AARON. He was an addict?

HAFIZ. He owe opium men much money. He go to Pakistan to free of them.

AARON. "Why didn't he take you with him?" Hafiz seemed nervous. It was clear he had never told this story to anyone before now.

HAFIZ. He needed money for passage.

AARON. I struggled with what question to ask next and then realized..."Your father sold you."

HAFIZ. He say my beautiful face reminds him too much of my mother. Of his mistakes.

AARON. My gut drops with this revelation.

HAFIZ. I cry at first, but then...I learn the dance and realize I am important.

AARON. "What makes you feel important?" I asked.

HAFIZ. The power you have when you are no one. To lay yourself open like a valley to the stranger.

AARON. "What happens when a man buys you?" I ask. He was quiet, afraid to betray his lovers. "Be a lion, Hafiz. Tell me what hurts."

HAFIZ. When he force into you, the body tightens, wanting so much to push him out, but when you squeeze it pull him further inside. < > The body wants to be invaded. The men rip open my body, in hope…in hope that in this gap, a glimpse of God.

AARON. In the middle of his horror Hafiz found something beautiful. He was a true poet, a living contradiction.

HAFIZ. Please…now I dance. You film.

Music begins…

AARON. …he said. And as he moved, the light came back into his eyes, the flush to his cheeks. Once again, his body was his own. As he whirled, I asked, "What would you do if you couldn't dance?"

HAFIZ. If I cannot dance, I will die.

Tight spotlight on MUNIR.

MUNIR [*singing*].   My Beloved is the moon,
                                with his round white face,
                                he will never, never feel the dance.

Lights reveal the MEN and SWISS sitting around MUNIR on small red cushions. MUNIR sings as HAFIZ dances his last dance.

MUNIR.   But I will have it.
                    I will remember the pages of
                    my Beloved's body
                    like a book
                    I am not meant to read.
                    Sick with his love-fire I spin, flinging
                    the weight of my war to the stars.
                    I dare you to see me, Beloved!
                    Hear me, cool, cool prince!
                    Then, under Allah's blessing,
                    unfold yourself finally
                    and meet me in the field

in this valley
under the stars
in the night
among the gentle-savage flowers.
Come for me again
with your white-hot hands!
Come for me!
Take me!
Take me!

The MEN and SWISS erupt in applause, showering HAFIZ with money.

SALIM. Wow. I don't even have words…

SWISS. Take all my money!

SALIM. Come with me tonight, Hafiz!

SWISS. Hafiz is mine, fuckface!

MEN. More dance!

MUNIR. Brothers! Please, I told you before. This was his last dance. His beard has bloomed. There's nothing more to say.

SWISS. You're killing me, Munir. Take my money. No one will know.

MUNIR. Allah knows.

SALIM [*SALIM gets close to MUNIR*]. You have a beautiful voice. Where did you learn to sing like that?

MUNIR [*MUNIR shoves SALIM away*]. I have something special for you all. Come, come! Music! Tonight is a special night. My newest boy will make his debut! Allow me to present: Safia…the little pearl!

BOY—dressed in a blue gown—nervously enters.

SALIM. Beautiful girl!

BOY runs to HAFIZ.

HAFIZ. Go on. Just get it over with.

MUNIR. Don't be shy, Safia. Play! Play! Music, music!

The musicians accompany BOY, who sings…

BOY.   Nobody knows where my Johnny has gone
But Judy left the same time
Why was he holding her hand
When he's supposed to be mine

It's my party and I'll cry if I want to
Cry if I want to
Cry if I want to
You would cry too if it happened to you
Woah – oh – oh
It's my party and I'll cry if I want to
Cry if I want to
Cry if I want to...

BOY finishes unceremoniously and the MEN offer a little applause.

SALIM. Well, he's not Hafiz, or you, but he is beautiful.

MUNIR [*MUNIR brings BOY to the SWISS*]. Brother Swiss, do you like him?

SWISS. He's quite the little songbird.

MUNIR. Safia's yours tonight. You have him first.

SWISS. No—

MUNIR. He is beautiful.

SWISS. He's a child!

MUNIR. Such a very beautiful one—

SWISS. I don't want a child! I want Hafiz.

MUNIR. We cannot question Allah's will. Hafiz has bloomed.

SWISS [*SWISS takes MUNIR aside*]. Please, I'm in love with him, Munir. One last time.

MUNIR. In love with him? This is not the place to be in love. Do you wish to break Allah's law?

SWISS [*SWISS addresses MUNIR and the crowd*]. Do not forget who I am. Who we all are.

MUNIR. < > You're threatening me? Please, tell Shabah of me, what I do. And I do the same, brother. Who you are, what you do, your forbidden desire. Hafiz has bloomed. Take Safia.

SWISS quickly raises his cudgel to MUNIR's chin as lights shift and HAFIZ grabs BOY's hand.

HAFIZ. Run, boy, run!

Lights reveal AARON packing his bags. HAFIZ enters, still wearing his dress.

AARON. Hafiz.

HAFIZ. Aaron.

AARON. What are you doing here?

HAFIZ. I come for you.

AARON. Does Munir know you're here?

HAFIZ. Free of Munir.

AARON. What do you mean?

HAFIZ. Bloom. I am not *bacha bee reesh*.

AARON. Wait, what?

HAFIZ. Tonight was my last dance.

AARON. Wow. So…what are you gonna do?

HAFIZ. Be a movie star. In the film.

AARON laughs.

HAFIZ. You are leaving?

AARON. I have everything I need for the film, so, yeah, I'm going home tomorrow afternoon.

HAFIZ. You go and no goodbye to me?

AARON. I was planning to call Munir to arrange one last meeting.

HAFIZ. There is no need of Munir. I am here now.

AARON. Yes. You are. < > I wanna show you something. [*AARON opens his laptop, plays a clip of HAFIZ dancing.*]

HAFIZ. This is me?

AARON. Yeah. You really are beautiful on the screen.

HAFIZ. And here? I am beautiful here? [*HAFIZ leans to kiss AARON who pulls away, pauses the clip.*] You are suddenly shy?

AARON. Uh, no, I just…

HAFIZ. What? You just what?

AARON. Hafiz…I crossed a line that I shouldn't have crossed.

HAFIZ. You do not desire me? < > I know what I feel from you and it was desire.

AARON. This isn't something that can happen.

HAFIZ. Why deny what you feel?

AARON. Because what I feel is insane, not to mention illegal and—

HAFIZ. But you feel?

AARON. Of course I feel. But I shouldn't.

HAFIZ. I am yours. What is the problem?

AARON. Please stop—

HAFIZ. Do not listen to brain. Hear heart. Yes yes yes.

AARON. This is crazy and all kinds of unethical on my part.

HAFIZ. Crazy good.

AARON. We need to say goodbye to each other.

HAFIZ. No, I will not say goodbye. < > I am love for you, Aaron. What do you say to that? [*It hangs in the air, then HAFIZ kisses AARON.*] You feel?

AARON. Yeah.

HAFIZ. It is good?

AARON. It's very good.

HAFIZ [*HAFIZ dances a bit around AARON*]. I teach you. Now teach me.

AARON. Teach you what?

HAFIZ. The dance.

AARON. You know I'm a shitty dancer. What could I possibly ever teach you?

HAFIZ. It is true you shit dancer. But who else teach me how the boys move in New York? [*HAFIZ claps one-two-three-one-two-one-two.*]

AARON. No, no try this. [*AARON claps one-two-three-four, one-two-three-four.*] You got it?

HAFIZ. I got it. Dance, Batman.

AARON [*AARON attempts to show some moves, fails miserably*]. The thing is…Americans don't always dance alone.

HAFIZ. They dance group?

AARON. No…I mean, sometimes we dance with each other. [*AARON offers his hand.*]

HAFIZ. Boy and boy?

AARON. A man and a man.

HAFIZ takes his hand. They slow dance. Simply and sweetly. After a while, NAWEED enters, carrying a hard camera case. BOY follows behind, still wearing his dress. BOY is about to speak, but NAWEED silences him. They are unnoticed by HAFIZ and AARON.

HAFIZ. Aaron, take me with you tomorrow.

AARON laughs.

HAFIZ. Serious.

AARON. I can't take a child out of this country.

HAFIZ. You know I am no child.

AARON. Well...OK. To my government you are.

HAFIZ. I have no regard for government.

AARON. It's illegal—

HAFIZ. Nothing worth doing in Afghanistan is legal.

AARON laughs.

HAFIZ. It is not to laugh. If you do not take me, where will I go?

AARON tenderly caresses HAFIZ's face.

NAWEED. I download the footage, boss.

HAFIZ and AARON quickly separate.

AARON. Thank you. Thanks, Naweed.

NAWEED. This girl...boy was outside.

AARON. That's the boy with the soccer ball?

NAWEED. Yes.

AARON. Why is he here?

NAWEED. Ask your boy-friend.

AARON. It's not what you think, Naweed—

NAWEED. It is exactly as I think! *Bawaram namiaya.* [I cannot believe this.]

AARON. You don't understand—

NAWEED. *Choochah e sag!* [Child of a dog!] The line between filmmaker and pervert is not a fine line, Aaron. *Choochah e sag!*

AARON. Please, just listen, it's not—

NAWEED. All the time you spend with boy and I think to myself... now I see why it is you are so interest in this. You have no wife, no family. You and this perversion!

AARON. / Hey!

NAWEED. You point your lens but you do not see yourself. You are shock tourist with expensive camera! You keep me here, danger my life, so you can make sex with this boy—

AARON. / No!

NAWEED. *Koonee! Koonee!*

AARON. / Naweed, please—

NAWEED. You dishonor me! [*NAWEED tosses the hard camera case near AARON.*]

BOY. *Maysha ke alay borame? Loootfaaan! Mard az poshte ma miaya!* [Can we please go now? Pleaaaassse! The men will be coming for us!]

NAWEED. Let me translate for you. He says the men will be coming. < > *Baan saag ha yakee dega ra bekhoran.* [Let the dogs eat each other.]

NAWEED spits at their feet, exits. Silence.

AARON. Hafiz, why is this boy here?

HAFIZ. Forgive me, Aaron, I was going to tell you of the boy.

AARON. What is going on?

BOY. *Ma payshay Monir maykhayom borom!* [I want to go back to Munir!]

AARON. What is he saying? Something about Munir?

HAFIZ. They are coming. So we leave now.

AARON. What are you talking about?

HAFIZ. Munir, the Swiss, they come for us.

AARON. Why are they coming? / What did you—

HAFIZ. They will kill me for what I have done.

AARON. What did you do?

HAFIZ. < > I steal the boy. We are running.

AARON. Why would you do that?

HAFIZ. Because you say to me, "Save the boy. Be a lion, Hafiz."

AARON. I didn't mean for you to—

HAFIZ. Aaron, please, we leave together tonight.

AARON. No—

HAFIZ. Take me to New York. Take us both. Tonight.

AARON. That's impossible.

HAFIZ. We go into Tajikistan.

AARON. Two boys travelling across the border with an American? That will never work.

HAFIZ. There are ways.

AARON. I think the only thing we can do is to go back to Munir. I will talk to him.

HAFIZ. Talk?

AARON. I'll tell him the truth about all of this.

HAFIZ. He will not hesitate. You leave me with Munir and I am no more. A boy who runs is dead boy!

AARON. Hafiz, I'm sorry. I can't take you with me. Not like this. It's too dangerous.

HAFIZ. < > I think you are different. I think you are kind. That you love for me. But you are no more than the men who throw money at my feet. Go back to New York! I do not want to see you! I do not want to know you! I wish you never come here!

AARON. Hafiz, calm down—

HAFIZ. I am tired to death of calmness! I want to scream!

AARON. If you calm down, I can help you.

HAFIZ. You help enough.

HAFIZ runs offstage. AARON runs out after him.

AARON [O.S.]. HAFIZ!!! Come back! HAFIZ!!!

BOY. Hafiz? Hafiz!!

AARON re-enters. BOY goes to him.

BOY. America, where Hafiz?

Lights shift, revealing a full white moon hanging over the mountains. The poppies bloom before our eyes. HAFIZ runs to them, stops, out of breath and considers the danger of where his feet have led him.

HAFIZ. Ugly white moon!!

HAFIZ trembles and quakes, spinning and spinning, knocking over the newly bloomed poppies. He roars, full of rage and lust and heartbreak. Blinding headlights interrupt from offstage. Doors from a pick-up truck slam. HAFIZ cowers in the flowers. A man approaches from the shadows, his face unseen.

SWISS. This is a private field.

HAFIZ. I'm sorry. I'll be on my way.

SWISS [*SWISS appears from shadow*]. Hafiz?

HAFIZ. Swiss?

SHABAH [*from the darkness*]. Swiss, do you know this person?

SWISS. I'm sure he's seen me around. I make quite an impression.

SHABAH. Just give a warning. Be quick. And quiet.

HAFIZ. No, please, I'm sorry. I'll be on my way.

SWISS. Only speak in English. He doesn't speak.

A man, face obscured, looms at the edge of the poppies, flanked by two other MEN.

HAFIZ. That's him? That is—

SWISS. Do not say his name. He'll know you recognize him. And you cannot recognize him, you understand?

SHABAH. What's taking so long, Swiss?

SWISS. Why did you run from me tonight?

HAFIZ. Please, I'm sorry…don't send me back to Munir. I'll do anything you want.

SWISS. < > This place…where you are…right now…Allah circled on a map for you.

SHABAH. Are you finished? Let's go!

SWISS. Sir, he speaks English. He could be an asset to us.

HAFIZ. What are you doing?

SWISS. Trust me.

SHABAH steps into the light.

HAFIZ. Please…I mean no harm—

SHABAH. Who's your father?

HAFIZ. Allah is my father.

SHABAH. Stand straight.

HAFIZ. Please—why?

SHABAH. Do not ask why. I say. You obey.

HAFIZ stands straight.

SHABAH. Your dress is pretty. [*SHABAH rips the dress from HAFIZ's body.*] You're thin. Can you swim?

HAFIZ. What?

SHABAH. Swim? I need good swimmers.

HAFIZ. No.

SHABAH. This is a waste of time.

SWISS. Sir, his English will be invaluable at the border.

SHABAH. Ok, let's see her strength. Give her the test.

SWISS holds out his cudgel.

SWISS. Take the stick from me.

HAFIZ. What?

SWISS. Take the stick. To show your strength.

HAFIZ wraps his hand around the cudgel.

SWISS. Yes. Now. Take it.

HAFIZ tugs. SWISS rips it from his hand.

SWISS. If you want something, take it. Don't ask for it. Again.

HAFIZ wraps his hands around it, tugs harder. SWISS easily rips it from him again.

SWISS. You don't want it, Hafiz. This stick is your life. Now take it!

HAFIZ lunges at SWISS, pulling and grunting, with little effort, SWISS forces HAFIZ to the ground.

SWISS. Now you want it. But you don't have the strength to take it. I will teach you strength.

HAFIZ lunges again. SWISS strong arms him, taking the cudgel to his throat. SWISS pins HAFIZ on the ground. HAFIZ reverses the move and pins the SWISS to the ground, screaming incoherently at him, smacking him in the face. SHABAH pulls HAFIZ from the SWISS. SWISS collects himself.

SWISS. You see, sir? This boy is very strong.

SHABAH. Yeah, yeah, I see that. He's yours to train. Give him some pants to wear. If he screws up, it's your ass.

SHABAH disappears into the darkness.

SWISS. Come, Hafiz—

HAFIZ. You let me win! You gave up! Why are you helping me?

SWISS. You and I...there is no word for who we are. Invisible. We can be invisible together. I will make you strong, Hafiz. [*SWISS takes a small lance from his pocket.*] You see this? The razor. [*taking HAFIZ's hand*] Do you know how the farmer harvests the poppy? The opium is harvested just after the poppies bloom. Just before the flowers die. When the petals fall, he cuts small slits in the pod. [*SWISS slices HAFIZ who pulls his hand back quickly.*] After a few days, the flowers bleed the opium. It is sticky. Difficult. He scrapes it off by hand, gently with a razor. [*SWISS slices his own hand.*] I will be your family and your loyalty to me is your life. Will you be loyal to me?

As SWISS offers his hand to HAFIZ, lights shift to reveal MUNIR, sitting alone at the scene of the party. After a while, HAFIZ enters.

MUNIR. I knew you would return to me.

HAFIZ. I'm sorry.

MUNIR [*MUNIR violently grabs Hafiz's face with his hands*]. You never, never run, boy!

HAFIZ slaps his hands away. SWISS and the MEN enter, bearing cudgels. Their faces are covered.

MUNIR. What is this, Hafiz?

SWISS. He is no longer Hafiz. He is Shayr. The lion. [*SWISS reveals himself.*]

MUNIR. Leave this place! All of you! Get out! Get out of here! [*MUNIR goes toward SWISS. MEN restrain him.*] Take your dirty hands off me!

MUNIR is bound. SWISS strikes him with his cudgel.

MUNIR. Why are you doing this, Hafiz?

SWISS. Old man, you are the only person who knows who I really am. Who Shayr really is. And so if we kill you, our secret is safe.

MUNIR. No—

SWISS. Tell him what it is you wish, Shayr.

HAFIZ. < > I want to know true love. I want to work. I want to be a man.

MUNIR. No, you are too beautiful for their world.

SWISS. Shayr, finish it. [*to the cudgel bearers*] Take the old man outside.

MUNIR. No!

SWISS. Make sure his body can be seen.

The MEN begin to drag MUNIR outside.

SWISS. Finish it. Tell the men what to do, Shayr.

HAFIZ. Please, no…I cannot be the one. Munir is like my father.

SWISS. To become Shayr you must forget Hafiz. Tell them what to do.

MUNIR. My beautiful boy of a thousand stars—

SWISS. You must kill everything you were to become who you wish to be. Give the order, Shayr.

MUNIR. He is not Shayr! He is Hafiz!

SWISS strikes MUNIR, taking him down. HAFIZ intercedes.

HAFIZ. Please, don't—

SWISS. What do you want? Say it! < > SAY IT!

HAFIZ. I want to know true love. I want to work. I want to be a man.

SWISS. Again!

HAFIZ [*breaking*]. I want to know true love. I want to work. I want to be a man.

SWISS. Again!

HAFIZ [*broken*]. I want to know true love. I want to work. I want to be a man.

AARON and BOY enter. AARON carries his duffels and equipment, a small camera in hand.

BOY. Hafiz!

BOY moves toward HAFIZ. AARON stops him.

HAFIZ. Aaron, you are not to be here.

AARON. I'm bringing the boy back. Hafiz, what is...what's going on?

SWISS signals one of the MEN to restrain AARON. BOY runs to HAFIZ.

AARON. People know I'm here! Very important people! They'll come for me.

SWISS. Let them come. Americans are everywhere and poppies have never been more plentiful. [*SWISS strikes AARON in the knees with his stick, taking him down. SWISS gags AARON.*]

HAFIZ. Please, no!

MUNIR. *Lotfan Beradaar Swiss. Ma yak padar astom. Lotfaan, raz e shoma payshe ma mahfooz ast.* [I beg you Brother Swiss. I am a father. Please, your secret is safe with me.] Please Hafiz!

SWISS. Now, finish what is begin, Shayr. Give order. Kill the fool.

HAFIZ. I can no be the one!

SWISS [*SWISS raises his cudgel to HAFIZ's chin*]. Do it or you will not live to be a man.

MUNIR. *Ney, ney*...please...beautiful one, there is no choice. It is what must be done. You have my blessing.

HAFIZ cannot look MUNIR in the eye.

MUNIR. Please, Hafiz. I do good for you? Tell me I did.

HAFIZ. Yes, Baba Munir.

SWISS. Give order.

HAFIZ. Do it outside, away from the boy.

The MEN strong-arm MUNIR.

MUNIR. NO! Take your hands from me! "I will die bravely. I will be jovial. Come, come I am a king."

MUNIR walks out, flanked by the MEN with cudgels. The courtyard is silent except for a few birds in the distance and AARON and HAFIZ's mounting breath. SWISS goes to BOY, covers his ears. In the distance, the MEN kill MUNIR.

HAFIZ. Baba Munir! No! Baba Munir! Baba Baba Baba Baba Baba Baba Baba….

The beating continues until it is finished. The cudgels smash. Brutal. Unflinching. The MEN reappear, their cudgels bloodied. SWISS helps HAFIZ to his feet.

SWISS. Now what do we do with Mohammad?

HAFIZ. Please, Swiss, no—

SWISS. *Estadesh sho!* [Stand him up!]

The MEN help AARON stand, take the gag from his mouth.

HAFIZ. Not him. He is good man.

SWISS. You believe him to be good? [*SWISS strikes AARON in the back.*]

AARON. Please! No! I can still help you, Hafiz—

SWISS. With this? [*SWISS picks up the camera, tosses it on the floor in front of AARON.*] This is how you will help him? A camera?

AARON. I'm not a pornographer.

SWISS. We all know what you are. Shayr tell me everything. Journalist. Pornogeraafer. It is the same. [*SWISS crushes the camera with his cudgel.*]

HAFIZ. Swiss, please, we do what we come to do. Let him free.

SWISS. Why you wish to save him?

HAFIZ. He is good man.

SWISS. Hmmm. Mohammad, are you good man?

AARON. I just…I just want to help him.

SWISS. Help Shayr?

AARON. Help Hafiz.

SWISS. < > Then you prove it. I crush boy or I crush you. Which you choose?

AARON. What?

SWISS seizes HAFIZ.

HAFIZ. Swiss—

SWISS. Choose. Which will you help? Boy or Mohammad?

AARON. That doesn't make sense—

SWISS. Not for American, but for me, yes. Now choose.

AARON. I have money. I can buy him from you. Name your price.

SWISS. Not negotiation. Choose.

HAFIZ. Swiss, I am important for you—

SWISS. Choose.

AARON. You're right. This is not negotiation. If you hurt him, I swear to God, I'll find a way to end you and all of this!

SWISS. To God you swear, eh? [*SWISS shoves HAFIZ to the ground, raises the cudgel over him.*]

AARON. No, no!

HAFIZ. Please! Do not do this!

SWISS. Make a choice, Mohammad!

AARON. Please—

SWISS. *Khalasesh ko.* [End him.]

The MEN circle around AARON and raise their cudgels over his head.

AARON. No, no, no! Me! Me! I choose me! I choose myself! Please don't. Please don't. I want to go home. Please.

SWISS. [*SWISS laughs. He breaks up the MEN, helps HAFIZ to his feet*]. You see, Shayr? American is never loyal to his Afghan boy. We do not speak in the same faith. Do with him what you wish. [*SWISS gives HAFIZ the cudgel.*] Now you are a man. *Bia ke beroon borame.* [Let's go outside.] Boy, come with me. There is much to learn.

SWISS exits, taking BOY by the hand as he goes. The MEN follow him. HAFIZ and AARON regard each other. The thing that once uncoiled is now tighter than ever before.

AARON. Hafiz—

HAFIZ. I am Shayr!

AARON. Come with me, Hafiz! We can go right now!

HAFIZ [*HAFIZ strikes AARON*]. Why I go with you? I have power now.

AARON. Hafiz, please—

HAFIZ. You break me apart—

AARON. Stop—

HAFIZ. And I break you apart! [*HAFIZ strikes AARON again.*] You look through the camera, but you do not see! You come here. You show me kindness and I am a fool to believe you. < > But you woke the lion. And he is beautiful, blood red lion. It is a new time in Afghanistan. And I will not be ruled but by lions who roar so strong that all of Asia will shake! And I wait for the pearl-white lamb to sleep. And in the darkest hour, I slaughter you and feast! < > Go home. Find God. And pray. [*raising his cudgel*] GO!

HAFIZ is a lion blooming with a heart on fire. AARON runs out of the light into the lecture hall.

KASHI. The last line of your book, you write, "This is a love story and the end has yet to be written." Can you expand on that a bit?

AARON. Well…on a…an allegorical level, it's meant to signify the relationship between Afghanistan and the United States. Um…we are, all of us in this room, right now, engaged in a war. The end of that story has yet to be written. But, I'm hoping that story becomes one of love.

KASHI. Do you really think it will?

AARON. Barack Obama is President of the United States. I'm feeling pretty optimistic nowadays.

KASHI. I suppose you also mean the love story of you and Hafiz?

AARON. < > Yes.

KASHI. You never say it.

AARON. What?

KASHI. In your book. That you love him. Is it fair to say that you love Hafiz?

AARON. Sure.

KASHI. Sure?

AARON. Yes, it's fair to say that.

KASHI. Do you know where he is now?

Lights fade on HAFIZ.

AARON. No.

KASHI. Have you tried to find him? Through the Bloom Project?

AARON. < > It's virtually impossible to find him.

KASHI. Yes, I suppose it is. But your book is enacting change for other boys. The UN recently cited Bloom as part of an international pledge to end the practice of *bacha bazi* in Afghanistan. That alone is deserving of the Sommerville.

AARON. We're very proud of that. Thank you.

KASHI. Your book very much creates questions of responsibility in the minds of your reader. Who is to blame? How can we remedy this? Not easy answers. Blame is manifold, centuries old. I found myself wondering if this practice would even exist in a country not plagued by fundamentalism and patriarchy, in a culture where the female was honored rather than subjugated.

AARON. That's a very good point. Our causes aren't exclusive of each other. Helping the dancing boys of Afghanistan also means helping the women of Afghanistan. As long as the mentality of "boys are for pleasure" continues then so will the idea that "women are only for child-bearing." Women and boys are both second class citizens in Afghanistan.

KASHI. The difference, of course, is that the practice of *bacha bazi* is a subculture and the mistreatment of women is mainstream. But, of course, both causes are equally important. < > Why write this book instead of making the film as you had originally intended? Surely, a film would reach a wider audience.

AARON. After everything that happened...the idea of exposing Hafiz, of showing his face to the world...I just didn't want to put him in any more danger. He's safer if he is anonymous.

RASHEED [*from the back of the audience*]. Liar!

KASHI. There will be a chance for Q and A in a moment. Just hold your—

RASHEED. He is a liar!

KASHI. Young man, please wait till the appropriate time.

RASHEED—BOY—approaches the stage. He is dressed in blue jeans and a T-shirt and has the shadow of a beard.

KASHI. What is he doing?

AARON. I think he's coming up here.

KASHI. Young man, please return to your seat at once.

AARON. Shouldn't we call security?

KASHI. Colin, call security, please.

RASHEED. A brown boy gets out of his chair to speak out and you call the police?

KASHI. You really should return to your seat.

RASHEED. I want to know why he lies about Hafiz. [*RASHEED is onstage now.*] You do not recognize me?

AARON is silent.

RASHEED. He knows who I am. Do not pretend.

KASHI. Do you know each other?

RASHEED. I am Rasheed, the boy with no name in his book.

KASHI. What is he talking about?

RASHEED. He tells the story of a boy named Hafiz. Of my friend. A boy who ran away with opium smugglers. It is a moving story. But it is not a true story. I was there. I see it all with these eyes. If greater truth is most important, why did you lie?

AARON. They're calling security. You don't want this kind of attention.

RASHEED. No, you don't want this kind of attention.

AARON. Just come backstage with me and we can talk.

RASHEED. Talk talk talk. I sit here with patience, listening and I want only to know why you lie. You cannot answer this question?

KASHI. Young man, what are you talking about?

RASHEED. Hafiz never joined with Shabah.

AARON. Rasheed—

RASHEED. The Swiss took us to see the horrible thing they did. Tell them!

KASHI. Mr. Freeman?

RASHEED. Hafiz never came back to Munir because—

AARON. Please don't do this.

RASHEED. Either you tell the truth or I will.

KASHI. Mr. Freeman, you understand, if you've falsified information—

AARON. I explicitly say the book is fictionalized.

RASHEED. To answer your question, Doctor Jones, he never made the film because he couldn't. He couldn't stand to look into Hafiz's eyes again. Tell the truth! < > I see you are still a coward. You disgrace Hafiz with your lies.

Silence.

KASHI. Colin, there's no need for security. < > Mr. Freeman, I think it might be in your best interest to say something.

AARON. I'm not on trial here.

KASHI. We deserve some explanation, don't you think?

AARON. After Hafiz ran, I took Rasheed back to Munir...just like I say in the book. I took him back and...Swiss was already there... just as I wrote it.

RASHEED. Tell the whole truth!

AARON. Swiss took us all to the poppy field...me, Munir and Rasheed...to show us...to show us what they had done to Hafiz. < > I only recognized him because he was still wearing his dress.

KASHI. Hafiz was killed?

RASHEED. Murdered. And when Munir saw what they did, he tried to rip apart those men with his bare hands, but...but they beat him into the ground...right there beside Hafiz.

Silence and then, in the distance, a single cantor sings the azaan. Lights rise on the poppies. NAWEED enters and begins the ablution.

RASHEED [*to KASHI*]. And then he took my hand and we ran. Like cowards. He, back to America. I to Pakistan. And then to London. [*to AARON*] Hafiz was never the lion. He was the lamb you sent to slaughter.

AARON. No, this isn't my fault. Those men existed long before—

RASHEED. If you had never come to Afghanistan, if you never make Hafiz fall in love—

AARON. I didn't make him fall in love. It happened. To both of us.

RASHEED. If not for you, Hafiz would still be alive! *Baba* Munir would be alive.

AARON. Rasheed, if it weren't for me, you wouldn't be alive. Standing right here. Right now. You would be a dancing boy, not a student at Cambridge.

KASHI. Mr. Freeman, why would you lie about this?

AARON. It's not a lie! Jesus Christ, why is it so hard to understand that truth is more than just facts!?

KASHI. But you lied about the death of a child.

AARON. I didn't lie. I made a myth. There's a difference.

KASHI. A myth? Well, that's quite convenient.

AARON. Hafiz is still alive in this book because as long as he's living, as long as he's out there, then these people will have cause to care. And more can be done to save these boys. There is greater power in hope than in fear.

RASHEED. No, there is greater power in truth!

AARON. < > Hafiz was the only person who has ever meant anything to me, who really saw me. And so I transformed Hafiz's story into something that would matter. And it has. His life has finally mattered. For just a brief moment, the people who read his story, the people in this room right now, they cared about him. They cared about a boy in a dress on the other side of the world.

KASHI. No, they cared about you. Because you put yourself at the center of Hafiz's story. You've made fools of us all. Of these students. Of the Sommerville. We've all been unwittingly cast in your narcissistic melodrama.

AARON looks out at the audience and sees the sea of confused eyes as HAFIZ dances and NAWEED folds his body in prayer toward Mecca. He turns to face the scrim.

KASHI. Mr. Freeman?

Silence.

KASHI. Mr. Freeman?

Silence. A few cameras flash from the audience.

AARON. Excuse me, Kashi. [*AARON removes the lapel mic, begins to exit.*]

KASHI. I suppose you don't have a quote from Rumi to justify this?

AARON [*almost inaudible*]. < > I'm sorry. I'm so sorry. Forgive me.
AARON exits as the azaan rises and the petals fall from the poppies.

END OF PLAY

CHAPTER 2

An Introduction to
The Value by the Playwright

I didn't intend to write a tragedy, not by any definition.

My only intention, really, was to write something for some goddamned adults—or for myself—as I had been writing for a children's theatre company for a few years and really needed a palate cleanser. Also, I didn't want breaks in the action. No scene changes! Everything in real time! Those were my intentions. But I did eventually succumb to an Act break. And to Tragedy.

I started with a character who detests his own reflection, then trapped him in a room surrounded by reflective surfaces. Oh, and this was meant to be funny. Yeah, *The Value* started out as a comedy somewhat in the vein of *It's Always Sunny in Philadelphia*. I had read an internet article about art heists and how in reality they are generally quite mundane affairs, a notion that, again, I thought was funny; art thieves are so often depicted as a kind of high-class criminal, sophisticated and sexy and executing a complicated scheme with James Bond-worthy technology, but the truth is that most cases are more akin to shoplifting in a Walmart. (When Edvard Munch's *The Scream* was stolen in 1994, the thieves left a note thanking the gallery for the poor security. When it was stolen again ten years later, the theft was considered much more sophisticated because the thieves thought to wear masks.) In fact, many pieces of stolen art are never recovered in part because once in their possession, the thieves have no idea what to do with them. For all the heist stories we've seen in popular culture, the real drama might be in what happens *after.*

This fascination laid the groundwork for the play and, at first, provided a lot of mileage. But, like the thieves, I got stuck once I came up against the question of how to capitalize. I utterly stalled at McEvoy's entrance. I walked away from it for a year.

When I came back to it, it looked different. Like Ian looking into the mirror, it seemed to want to be something else. Notions of identity, status, class, our obligations to one another as members of a community peered back at me. I saw that the characters were not merely trapped in a room, they were trapped in a dog-eat-dog world where worth is synonymous with gain, where the intrinsic nature of something—or someone—is irrelevant if it cannot be used, consumed like a fuel. This, I thought, is tragic.

A friend recommended *The Gift* by Lewis Hyde, and it lit the way forward as McEvoy entered the room. I reread *Poetics,* and Arthur Miller's *Tragedy and the Common Man,* and these were helpful returns, and I incorporated some of the classical tragic structure, such as the anagnorisis and the midpoint peripeteia, but I never felt it was a traditional tragedy because my character was not going to fall from grace due to some innate tragic flaw. Ian and Zoey and Victor had never felt grace and the tragedy of their story is inherent to their world and the choices they feel they *have* to make.

All of these broader concepts hovered in the background, because the real challenge remained in keeping the forward momentum while I hubristically maintained that there would be no breaks in the action, no sporadic leaps forward or backward in time. My primary focus was on trying not be boring as hell. There's a natural forward thrust to cause and effect, choice and consequence. The engine of the plot was that the characters were continuously confronted with a decision to make—a risk to take—and not given much time to contemplate the possible outcomes, and the big-picture stuff reflected back more clearly when the characters were active and aggressive.

I read *The Risk Theatre Model of Tragedy* after submitting my play to the competition. Mr. Wong's theory of risk theatre expertly articulated many concepts that I had wrestled with in the writing of *The Value*, and many more that had never occurred to me before fascinated me all the more. Above all, there was an uncanny match between my play and his book's excellent argument of the tragic dramatic form serving as a valuation mechanism for the "all too human," that which cannot be assigned a monetary worth. And a bonus byproduct of the theory of risk theatre is that it demands an active protagonist; a character cannot spend the play in a debate—at some point they *must* act. They must make a choice and they must face the consequences that come as a result. In the end, they *have to* look in the mirror.

NICHOLAS DUNN

About Nicholas Dunn

Nicholas Dunn is a writer, actor, and filmmaker based in Salt Lake City. In the hellscape that was 2020, Nick won the Risk Theatre Modern Tragedy Competition with his play *The Value* and the Marius P. Halford IV Award for his one-act *Temp*. He also wrote the short film script *Editing 2020* for Salt Lake Acting Company. Nick has written several plays for youth, including *The No Girls Allowed Club*, the books and lyrics to the original musical adaptations of Hans Christian Anderson's *The Little Mermaid*, *Thumbelina*, and *Great American Tall Tales*, all of which were presented at Kingsbury Hall by the University of Utah Youth Theatre. His original play, *Viral*, debuted at the Edinburgh Fringe Festival in Scotland in 2011, and his short play *Open* premiered at Wasatch Theatre Company as part of their Page-to-Stage festival. He has also written several short films and commercial campaigns, including the award-winning short *Art* and the award-winning commercial spot "I am Downtown" for the Salt Lake Downtown Alliance. He also works in the film industry as a script coordinator, most notably on HBO's "Mosaic," directed by Steven Soderbergh. Nick holds a BFA in acting from the University of Utah, and an MFA in Playwriting & Screenwriting from Point Park University in Pittsburgh, and was a participant in the Salt Lake Film

Society's Screenwriter's Program, co-sponsored by the Academy of Motion Pictures Arts & Sciences. He is a proud member of the Dramatists Guild.

The Value

by Nicholas Dunn

Modern capitalist societies, however richly endowed, dedicate themselves to the proposition of scarcity…
–Marshall Sahlins

[W]hen the dominant myth is not "to possess is to give" but "the fittest survive," then abundance will lose its motion and gather in isolated pools.
–Lewis Hyde, *The Gift*

The Value, a Risk Theatre Tragedy, was named the *Winner* of the 2020 Risk Theatre Modern Tragedy Playwriting Competition by an international panel of jurors:

Kelli Fox (Canada)
Anthony Giardina (USA)
Anthea Williams (Australia / New Zealand)

Permissions Contact:
Overcranked Pictures
721 South 200 East
Salt Lake City, UT 84111, USA
801-641-7132
nicholas@overcrankedpictures.com

Risk Theatre Staged Reading

On October 18, 2020, Edwin Wong, in collaboration with Anton Brackage and Kara Flanagan at Theatre Carpe Diem, produced a Risk Theatre reading of *The Value*. The production was streamed live by Janet Munsil at A Canadian Play Thing. Wong directed in collaboration with Nicholas Dunn. Narration by Ali Grams. Cast as follows:

Characters

IAN	30's (Anthony Gaskins)
ZOEY	20's / 30's (Leslie Appleton)
VICTOR	Zoey's brother, 20's / 30's (Vishesh Abeyratne)
MCEVOY	40's, 50's, or 60's (Wayne Yercha)

Diverse casting is encouraged.

Setting

Present. An overnight motel room. There are worse motel rooms than this one, but it's nothing that would make a Motel 6 envious.

The room is cramped, dominated by a queen-size bed, above which hangs a generic landscape painting. A bathroom door separates the toilet and shower, but the vanity and its large mirror make up the stage-left wall of the main room. Opposite it on the stage-right wall is a large window overlooking the parking lot outside, and the entrance to the room, equipped with a key-card lock. Downstage is a free-hanging or free-standing rectangle frame representing a full-length mirror.

The large window, the mirrors, and the painting above the bed unify the otherwise unremarkable space, but the effect is unpleasant.

They leer, these rigid rectangle frames, enclosing the room in a maddeningly symmetrical, inescapable way. Each of them—the window, the mirrors, and the piece of art—in some sense of the word, *reflect*.

Punctuation Notes

/   indicates beginning of next line

ACT ONE

A motel room. IAN looks out toward the audience through a narrow rectangle frame, representing a mirror, his eyes locked intently on his own reflection. He does not move for an uncomfortable amount of time.

All around him is dark, but as light begins to spill in through a window, a cheap motel room is revealed. A queen bed dominates the space, an end table at its side with a phone console and an alarm clock glowing the time: 4:08.

A painting hangs above the bed: A landscape in acrylic. It could have been purchased at a farmer's market.

IAN is dressed in soiled work clothes; pants caked in drywall and putty, etc. He turns his head slightly, inspecting his own face like he just tried it on. He leans closer, then back. He raises his clenched fist as though he may strike his own reflection, but then pauses to examine the look of himself poised to strike.

IAN. This is what happens… [*His fist trembles in the air, then relaxes. He pops his knuckles. He straightens up, and his expression morphs. It's now cocky, sly.*] I'm Ian. *Ian.* Hi. Hello…Sorry, these shindigs are always so loud, aren't they? You know the host? Oh. And you are?…I didn't catch that…Katisha? Katisha, I like it. What is that, like Japanese? It sounds Asian. You're not Asian though. What do *I* do? Oh, I'm a… investor. An entrepreneur. I'm a banker. Wall street, you know, stock market bullshit, insider trading, fucking up people's retirement, fraud, hookers, blow, typical American dream stuff…No. [*He begins to undress, discarding his work clothes in a pile.*] I'm a fucking…mafia boss. Pssh. I'm a producer. A big-shot producer. You know that movie that just won all the Oscars? Yeah I made that. Oh, you're an actress? [*He chuckles. He pulls more fashionable clothing from a backpack on the bed and redresses through:*] What was it, Alison? No, something Asian. Katisha, that's right. Let me refresh your drink. [*He looks back at the*

clock, then crosses to the window and looks out, then goes to his backpack, stuffs his work clothes in and withdraws a laptop computer. As the computer boots, he goes back to the mirror and finishes dressing.] Yes. Yes, I got it. Did you think I couldn't? Why? Did you think I was some kind of…Well, now you know. [*He returns to the computer, looks at the screen, fiddles with the mouse-pad. He reaches to the bedside table, and turns on the lamp to read a card that sits beside the phone, referring to it as he types. He sighs, refers back to the card, types again.*] Come on. [*He angles the card under the lamp to read better, which turns his face downstage. The mirror draws his gaze. He stares into it. Beat. He strips a sheet from the bed and takes it to the mirror, tucking the sheet around its edges, covering it. He returns to the bedside table and dials on the phone.*] Yeah, I'm—hello? Hello?…Yeah, I'm trying to get on the internet, and I'm using the passcode that's on the little, uh, the little card that—
Voices are heard on the other side of the door, and the sound of three staccato beeps: A failed attempt with a key card.

ZOEY [O.S.]. Don't hold it like that. You want to get fingerprints all over it?

VICTOR [O.S.]. I'm not doing anything! I'm just / doing this—

IAN [*distracted, into phone*]. What? Hello?…Are you there? / Sorry I—

ZOEY [O.S.]. You should really have worn gloves or something.

VICTOR [O.S.]. I did. I took them off in the van. Shut up. Open the door.
Beep Beep Beep.

IAN. Wait, wait. What? Say that again.

ZOEY [O.S.]. It's / not working.

VICTOR [O.S.]. You're doing it wrong.

ZOEY [O.S.]. There's only one way to do it, dipshit! Is this / the wrong room?

VICTOR [O.S.]. Are you holding the card the right way? Look, if you… / Give it—Ow!

ZOEY [O.S.]. Don't! Seriously, just keep your hands on the—Stop!
A thud, a scratching sound, Beep Beep Beep.

IAN. Goddamn it—I'll call you back in a minute. [*He hangs up.*]

ZOEY [*O.S.*]. They coded / it wrong.

VICTOR [*O.S.*]. Just let me do it!

ZOEY [*O.S.*]. Don't set that on the ground. What's wrong with you?

VICTOR [*O.S.*]. Just open the fucking door!

ZOEY [*O.S.*]. It's a piece of shit! It won't work.

IAN [*yanking the door open*]. Are you both retarded?

ZOEY and her brother VICTOR jump at IAN's rebuke. ZOEY is wearing a cap, gloves, a thick dark sweater and carrying a bag. VICTOR is carrying a rectangular object in a large garbage bag in one arm and a duffle bag in the other. They enter.

VICTOR. You shouldn't say "retarded."

IAN. You shouldn't act "retarded."

VICTOR. Dude, come on.

ZOEY. How long have you been here?

IAN. A while. But I forgot to scream and shout in the parking lot and draw as much attention to myself as possible, so thanks for taking care of that.

ZOEY. Did your key card work?

IAN. First try.

ZOEY. Piece of shit.

VICTOR. It's the user.

ZOEY [*removing, throwing her gloves at VICTOR*]. I'm gonna break your nose, Victor. I swear to God.

VICTOR [*referring to the garbage bag*]. Where should I put this?

IAN. Let me see it.

He hands it across the bed to IAN. IAN pulls back the garbage bag, revealing the edges of a canvas, similar in dimensions to the one hung above the bed. He stares at it for a moment.

IAN. No problems?

VICTOR. Nah, easy. Just: [*He pulls a small crowbar from his bag with a noise and a motion, then drops the crowbar at the foot of the bed.*]

ZOEY. We were in and out in like twenty minutes.

IAN. There was no alarm, right?

ZOEY. You said there wouldn't be.

IAN. I know. And you didn't hear one, right?

ZOEY. No, you were right. No alarm. Why is it so dark in here? [*turning on the overhead light*] Seriously Ian, you should live in a cave.

VICTOR. Wouldn't be any worse than this place. What a shithole. You couldn't splurge for like a Discount Inn or something?

IAN. We're not on vacation.

ZOEY. Write it off as a business expense.

VICTOR. How long do you guess?

IAN. Won't know 'til he calls. Few hours.

VICTOR. Well, that's what the beer is for.

He pulls a case of bottled beer from his bag. He tosses one to IAN, who discards it on the table immediately.

ZOEY. I brought something stronger if you prefer it.

IAN. After.

The soft sound of a small bling. VICTOR pulls a cell phone out of his bag.

IAN. Victor, was that...? Is that your / fuckin' phone?

ZOEY. Vic! Jesus!

VICTOR. What? What?

IAN. Turn it off! Turn your phone off.

VICTOR. It's just a text message!

IAN. Didn't I say—I said no cell phones. We don't want nothin' that can be traced to a, a location or a person. Why do you think we're here? A motel with free phone and internet?

VICTOR. Why—

IAN. None of this stuff's connected to us.

VICTOR. So I can't even send a text?

IAN. No. Nothing. That is the point.

ZOEY. What is it, a drug deal?

VICTOR. Maybe.

IAN. Oh god, what else is in that bag? What, are you selling oxy or something? Here, tonight?

Beat.

VICTOR. No.

IAN looks hard at ZOEY.

ZOEY. What?

IAN. He's *your* brother.

ZOEY. You said to use him.

IAN. If he fucks this up—

VICTOR. Hey! I'm not gonna fuck up anything, okay? Look, look. Phone's off. Won't touch it. Okay? Shit.

IAN. Gonna be a long couple of hours.

ZOEY. Maybe you should have that drink.

VICTOR moves frantically, messing with his bag.

ZOEY. Vic, relax, would ya? All we do now is wait. So chill.

She tosses him the TV remote. VICTOR flops onto the bed and turns on the TV. IAN pulls the garbage bag back over the painting and sets it next to the bed, then returns to the computer.

ZOEY. So?

IAN. So what?

ZOEY. So we got it, we pulled it off. Like, a *heist*! Like the guy in the, um, *The Thomas Crowne Affair*. Have you seen that?

IAN. The old one or the shitty newer one?

ZOEY. There's an old one? Never mind. *So*. What's it worth?

IAN. I don't know.

Pause.

ZOEY. What?

IAN. What?

ZOEY. You don't know?

IAN. No.

Pause.

ZOEY. What do you mean you don't know?

IAN. Do *you* know how much it's worth?

ZOEY. You said—How would I know?

IAN. Well, how would *I* know?

ZOEY. You told us which number to get. You told us right where it was. You don't know what it's worth?

IAN. No. I only know which it is.

ZOEY. Well…What's it called?

IAN. I don't know.

ZOEY. What the f—Ian. What is this? What's going on?

IAN. I'm gonna find out what it's worth. That's what I'm doing. That's why I need the internet. The motel internet. The TV. Victor, find a local news channel.

VICTOR. What?

IAN. Find a local news channel.

VICTOR. But this is *Airplane!*

IAN. I don't give a shit, find a news channel. And keep it there.

ZOEY. Who's doing the news at four in the morning?

VICTOR. Yeah!

IAN. We just need a channel with a news ticker or something like that. A news broadcast will be on in like two hours.

VICTOR. Are you kidding me? We have to hide in this shit motel room all night and we can't even watch TV?

IAN. You *can* watch TV. You can watch the news ticker.

VICTOR. No way, man. That'll make me crazy.

IAN. *You're* making me / crazy.

VICTOR. That's like something a serial killer would do, watch a news ticker in a motel room, and like, you know, like make a list of people to eat.

IAN. Yeah well I'm starting to think I could stomach human flesh. Change it…Change it! [*IAN wrestles him for the remote. He pokes his thumb into VICTOR's eye to make him drop it.*]

VICTOR. Ow! Ouch! Dude! [*to ZOEY*] He put his thumb in my eye! You could have really damaged my eye, man. Ow. God. Don't fuckin'…poke eyes!

IAN shuffles through TV channels.

ZOEY. See, Ian, there's no news channels yet, it's all reruns of yesterday's stuff. Just let him watch whatever, it'll keep him occupied.

IAN [*tossing the remote at VICTOR*]. You're like a child.

VICTOR. Well fuck you.

IAN. Whatever you're watching, you're watching it on mute.

VICTOR. Fine, I don't need sound. I'll watch porn. How 'bout that?

ZOEY. You'll need a credit card for porn channels.

VICTOR. Isn't the room on a credit card?

IAN [*back at the phone*]. Cash.

VICTOR. This is like a prison.

IAN. Yeah well. You would know…[*He dials. A beat*] Yeah, hey, I called a few minutes ago about the password for the internet and I had to hang up on you, sorry…Yeah, the code on the card…Well, it's not working…Okay, can you fix it, I paid for it…I am paying for it. It's rolled into / the room cost.

VICTOR. Tell him to unplug the modem and the router and then turn it on again.

IAN. I need it for work, okay, you understand? I need it…Right, well, could you do that, please? I'm going to keep trying. [*He hangs up. Goes back to the computer.*]

VICTOR. Told you. This place is a shit hole.

ZOEY. I can maybe get the internet on my phone. I mean I don't pay for like data or whatever but—

VICTOR. You don't have internet on your phone?

ZOEY. I do. I mean, I could. I don't pay for it. I'm not like, a fucking Kardashian.

VICTOR. So how would you look it up on your phone?

IAN. We're not looking it up—

ZOEY. I'm just saying I could turn it on and then, I mean, paying for it later shouldn't be a big deal after this is done.

IAN. Zoey, what did I just say?

ZOEY. Don't talk to me like you talk to him. I'm not stupid. I'm not going to Google how much the painting is worth. I'll just like look for news stories about a missing painting or—

IAN. Even that. A phone can be traced. It can be traced right here to where you're standing—

ZOEY. So can a laptop—

IAN. The laptop will be logged on to some motel network, and just left on a news feed all night. That's much less likely—

ZOEY. Why would they trace my phone?

IAN. What if they lift a print or something? You never know—

ZOEY. They won't. We were in and out in like twenty minutes. It was easy / actually—

IAN. Don't use your phone. Nobody uses their phone, they should be off. Okay?

ZOEY. Okay! I was just trying to help. 'Sides, it'll be a while before anyone even finds out it's missing. They don't really seem like they're on top of it down there. No alarm, no surveillance, no security...

IAN. It's a museum. Not a bank. What did you expect, a fuckin' field of laser-beams? This isn't a fucking movie.

ZOEY. Even a pawn shop has security—

IAN. Yeah, probably better security than most museums. You'd be surprised.

ZOEY. They should have cameras or an alarm at least—

IAN. They *do* have an alarm, and it shouldn't be too long / before they know.

ZOEY. What? You said there was no alarm!

VICTOR. Wait—

IAN. I said there was no alarm to worry about. They have a silent alarm—

ZOEY. A silent alarm?

VICTOR. What does that mean?

IAN. Easy!—

ZOEY. You sent us in there / knowing—

VICTOR. Did he set us up? Zoey? / Do they have cameras too?

ZOEY. Why did you do this, Ian? What, is this some kind of way of getting back / at me—

IAN. Hey, hey. Calm down. Would you listen to me? They have a silent—*silent* alarm that is pretty much pointless. It just sends a signal to another part of the museum. It's a glorified baby monitor. There's one security guard who also mans two other civic buildings downtown. He might not even have got the message yet.

ZOEY. Goddamn it. [*Calming herself*] And what then, you think once he does figure it out, they'll put out like a release online or something?

IAN. They'll call the cops. Dust and all that. Then, yes.

ZOEY. Why?

IAN. Because that's all they *can* do. That's why no phones, no web search, no nothing. They have nothing to go on, so they're gonna try *anything*. Online hits, you know, whatever.

VICTOR. They can track all that stuff?

IAN [*back at the computer*]. Yeah guys, come on. They listen to your phone calls, they watch you watch porn. Your provider knows everything there is to know about you and sells it the highest bidder. You're always being tracked.

VICTOR. Plus fucking Facebook. You know? Selling our shit to Russia or whatever.

IAN. We are dark, got it? We'll have the computer sitting on the news page. That's it. And when they publish something then we'll know what we got. [*typing*] If I can ever get the damn thing to log on to this stupid, piece of shit, fucking stone-age dump connection! *Pause. ZOEY puts a hand on his upper back and rubs gently. It seems habitual. IAN sighs, closing his eyes. Her hands move up to his neck and hair. He looks back at her. She stops.*

ZOEY. Well, it sounds like we should at least get comfortable. [*She retrieves her bag.*] You didn't look up anything about the painting before tonight? Like at a library or something? Seems like a ballpark figure would have been—

IAN. I don't know the name of the painting or who painted it. I didn't even know what it looked like until ten minutes ago. I only knew where it was in the museum and that their security makes a Seven-Eleven look like Fort Knox.

ZOEY takes off her cap and puts it in her bag. IAN stares at her. She catches him.

ZOEY. What?

IAN shakes his head, and turns to the phone again. ZOEY turns her back to him. As IAN talks on the phone, his gaze travels back to ZOEY.

IAN. Hey, me again. Still no internet…Uh huh…Have you tried unplugging and plugging back in the modem or the router or whatever?…Have you tried anything?…Could you try it, please?… Thanks. [*hangs up*] Prick.

ZOEY removes her heavy black sweater. IAN stares.

VICTOR. It's late. He's probably trying to sleep.

ZOEY continues to undress, changing into something more business casual.

IAN. What?

VICTOR. Sleep. He's probably trying to sleep. Some of these motels have little rooms off of the office where the night shift person can sleep, you know? They have like a bell that rings when someone comes in for a late check in or someone needs something. Plus the phone. I mean, their job is to be here at night, but they can sleep a bit if—

IAN. Victor, I don't care.

ZOEY turns to the covered mirror. She throws a look at IAN, then back at the mirror.

ZOEY [*to herself*]. Weirdo.

She pulls the sheet off of the mirror. IAN turns away. She continues to redress, fixes her hair.

VICTOR. Zoey, what are you doing?

ZOEY. What do you mean?

VICTOR. What are you getting all dressed for?

ZOEY. For the guy. For Ian's guy.

VICTOR. Why?

ZOEY. Victor, you dumb? Some big shot, like, underground art guy is coming to buy an expensive…like, you know? You're gonna sit there looking like a homeless person and watching porn—

VICTOR. I'm watching *Airplane!*

ZOEY. They're not gonna take you seriously. They're gonna know you're just a trash heap. Me and Ian at least will look like we know what we're doing. And we surely won't be drunk.

VICTOR. I'm not drunk. And don't call me Shirley. Classic.

VICTOR laughs at his stolen joke, then inspects himself as he finishes a beer, and tosses the bottle beside the bed. He opens another, popping the cap off with the edge of the bedside table.

IAN. Victor, would you mind not cracking open your piss-beer over a prestigious work of art?

VICTOR *catches himself with a nervous look at IAN, and moves the bottle away. Beat.*

VICTOR. Prestigious?

IAN. Did we steal it off of some kid's refrigerator?

VICTOR. Uh, whad'ya / mean—

IAN. It was in a museum.

IAN *grabs it, pulls back the garbage bag.* VICTOR *stares at it, then looks at IAN, his expression falling.*

VICTOR. This is a piece of shit!

ZOEY. What?

VICTOR. It looks like a five-year-old's finger painting.

IAN. You're just looking at it now?

VICTOR. It was dark in the museum.

IAN. You weren't curious?

ZOEY. We just yanked it and stuffed it and got out. Let me see.

VICTOR. I had a paint by numbers book as a kid that looked like this. Remember Zoey? That's what this looks like! You think this is worth thousands of dollars?

IAN. Tens of thousands.

VICTOR. You can't even tell what it is? What the fuck is it?

IAN. I don't know! [*looking closer*] An old town and some people looks like. A fire or a sunset, I guess.

VICTOR [*touching it*]. There's people in there?

IAN. Don't touch it.

IAN *sets it on the bed, right beneath the landscape painting hung above it. He steps back. All three of them take it in.*

VICTOR. I can't believe that piece of shit could be worth that much money.

IAN. Well. It's a style, you know?

ZOEY. It's like what Picasso painted, right? They were all weird looking too, but they're like, worth a shit-ton.

VICTOR. Seriously?

IAN. That's art for you.

VICTOR [*referencing the landscape*]. Man. Look. At least with this one, I know what it is. You got, you know, a mountain, you got some trees and grass and shit. Probably like a deer and some rabbits living up in there. [*leaning closer*] Like that. What is that? That's a animal right there, I think.

ZOEY. Where?

VICTOR. Right there, in those trees a bit.

ZOEY. I can't tell. It just looks like blobs of color when you're looking too close. I don't think the painter even knew what it was.

VICTOR. No, look, right there. It's like a cougar or something. A lurking cougar.

ZOEY. What? That's nothing. It's just globs of color.

VICTOR. It's a lurking cougar. See, those are eyes. No, maybe… Yeah, I think it's a coyote. See, Zoey, it's a coyote.

ZOEY. Okay!

She shares a bemused look with IAN. He laughs.

VICTOR. I saw one here in the city the other night. A Coyote. Lurking. They come down out of the mountains when there's not enough food for them. They kill people's dogs.

ZOEY. You didn't see a coyote.

VICTOR. Yes I did! It was just walking down the road at night. It was a coyote, a fucking big one. This guy I knew, his dogs were killed by a coyote. Right in his back yard. There's not enough food for all of 'em. So they come down. Get risky. See, if you paint a coyote I know that's what it's supposed to be.

ZOEY. You said it was a cougar—

VICTOR [*back to the stolen painting*]. But this, I don't even know what this is. I feel like I'm on acid when I look at it.

ZOEY. I don't know. I kind of prefer the weird one to the landscape one.

VICTOR. What? Why? What do you like about it?

ZOEY. I didn't say I like it. I just said I like it better than that one. That one's boring. I didn't even notice it until you pointed it out.

IAN [*amused*]. The real question is do you really care about either of them?

VICTOR & ZOEY. No.

IAN. Then who cares what they look like? But one of them we can sell for thousands and the other we couldn't even pawn if we wanted to. Like I said, that's art.

VICTOR. Thousands. Tonight right?

IAN. That's what we're doing.

VICTOR. Like what? Like, like forty thousand, right?

IAN. Well, I don't really know, Victor. You see, I can't seem to get on the goddamn internet to—

VICTOR. Right, yeah, okay. Okay. But if you have a buyer lined up you must at least know roughly how much—

IAN. Yes, *I* know it's worth *a lot*. Because someone *wants* it. It's worth whatever he's willing to pay to get it. This is how it works. This is what happens. And to make sure you're both with me on this, we're not selling stolen car stereos here, all right? Bring the A-game because we're going Machiavellian on this motherfucker. We're climbing the food chain. Tonight.

ZOEY. I'm with you.

IAN tries the password again. Same result.

ZOEY. No?

IAN. All right. I'm going down to the office and I'm going to make that kid fix this even if I have to take his fingernails.

VICTOR [*seizing upon this*]. Yeah! Make him do it. Watch him. You know, sometimes you just have to restart everything. It's that simple. Sometimes. Just unplug everything and then, and then plug it back in.

IAN goes to the door.

ZOEY. Get him to fix that key card too.

IAN. Don't...do anything stupid.

IAN exits. VICTOR goes to the window and watches IAN leave. Then he goes to his bag and retrieves his phone.

ZOEY. What are you doing?...Vic?

VICTOR. I have to check these texts. I have to. Don't tell Ian.

ZOEY. It's not a deal? What is it then? [*Beat. ZOEY goes after him.*] Get off your phone! Turn it off, dumb-ass. You want to blow this whole thing? [*She tries to wrestle the phone from him.*]

VICTOR [*fighting her off*]. Stop it! Zoey! God...Stop it!...I owe these guys money!

Pause. ZOEY steps back.

VICTOR. I owe them. And they want it tomorrow. [*Beat*]

ZOEY. You're being called in? How much?

VICTOR. Eleven.

ZOEY. God.

VICTOR. I know, but it's not my fault. I mean, okay, it was kinda my fault for trusting fuckin' Sanchez, but I lost their shit when I got busted. It was worth about six then, but the juice was running they said and now...And they're not fucking around. I told them I could pay them tomorrow. I have to pay them tomorrow. That's why I agreed to this.

ZOEY. Ian is going to kill you.

VICTOR. I didn't tell them *how* I was getting their money! They don't know where I am, okay? Don't tell Ian. I've just got to... They...I don't want them to look for me, you know? To go out looking for me because they think I'll skip town or—

ZOEY. Do they know your van?

VICTOR. No. Maybe. I mean, I don't know if they know the license plate or...

Pause. ZOEY takes a plastic cup from the vanity, gets a bottle from her bag and pours a drink.

VICTOR. This guy Ian has coming. What if he doesn't show up?

ZOEY. Why wouldn't he show up? He'll show up.

VICTOR [*VICTOR drains a beer, but it's not helping his anxiety*]. What are you doing with your share?

ZOEY. Well, I've got some debt of my own to pay. No one who's gonna break my knees or anything, you know, but just...get some breathing room, I guess. I don't know. I want to go on a cruise.

VICTOR. A cruise? Are you serious?

ZOEY. What? I never been on a cruise. I never been out of the country. I never seen anywhere else! I could go to, I don't know, like the Bahamas or something.

VICTOR. You've never been on a cruise. You got real problems.

ZOEY. Blow me. You know what I'm talking about, Vic. People should get to, you know, move around a bit. Go somewhere else.

Pause.

VICTOR. What if this shit painting is only worth like, I don't know, like five thousand. Wouldn't surprise me. You'd only get, like, less than two thousand. That's not enough, right?

ZOEY. Whatever it takes.

VICTOR. Wouldn't be enough for me. I don't think they're interested in a payment plan. Would you help me? Loan me or whatever? You could wait to go wherever 'til I pay you back. [*Pause*] Zoey?

ZOEY. It'll be more than that. These paintings are worth a lot. Ian, he knows what he's doing. He said get this one. This number specifically.

VICTOR. He doesn't seem to know what he's doing. He doesn't know what it's worth. He can't even get the internet working.

ZOEY. He will. He finds a way, you know that.

VICTOR. Finds a way. Yeah, finds a way for himself. Fuck everyone else.

ZOEY. It wasn't like that. He's not like that, Victor.

VICTOR. You sure? [*Beat*]

ZOEY. Remember when he gave that money to the Johnson kids, after Derek was found dead.

VICTOR. No.

ZOEY. This was just a few years ago. When Ian was trying to do school. Not long before you were—

VICTOR. Yeah.

ZOEY. You know where that money came from?

VICTOR. No.

ZOEY. Ian's place was broken into and they stole all kinds of stuff, including his ID and checkbook, cards, all that. The thieves—a guy and a girl—this couple—started forging checks all around the city and the police, well they're fucking useless, you know, they didn't help at all. So he tracked the thieves down himself, using the trail they were leaving with the forged checks.

VICTOR. Bullshit. How would / he—

ZOEY. He did. He saw they were forging them in a different police precinct each time. He could see where they hadn't been, where they'd go next. Something like that.

VICTOR. Come on. What'd he do? A citizen's arrest?

ZOEY. No. They were busted, and he got money from the courts and everything. And he gave Derek's kids that money.

VICTOR. So he gave orphans some easy cash. Don't make a, you know, doesn't erase what—

ZOEY. I'm not finished with my story, Vic!

VICTOR. Okay! I'm just saying—

ZOEY. Can I finish my story? [*Beat*] Can I finish it?

VICTOR. Yeah, I'm waiting. Finish it.

ZOEY. The thieves. Well, only the girl went down in the end. The dude that was using Ian's identity, he wore a sling. Like he had a broken arm, so he couldn't sign the checks. She signed everything.

VICTOR. What would that do?

ZOEY. Technically, he wasn't forging checks. He wasn't the one committing fraud. *She* was. She took the heat. And that bothered Ian. A lot, that this dude got basically nothing for it. But now he knew his name. He had seen his face.

Beat.

VICTOR. He...He kill him?

ZOEY. No. He found him though. Put the guy's face through a window.

Pause.

VICTOR. Is your story finished?

ZOEY. Well. Yeah.

VICTOR. So what's the point?

ZOEY. The point is...Ian...He makes it right.

VICTOR. How do you know all this, with the different police zones and stuff. Did he tell you?

ZOEY. I was there.

VICTOR. Was this when you guys were together?

ZOEY. We were never together.

VICTOR. Uh, I'm pretty sure I heard—

ZOEY. We had a thing, yeah. But we were just…screwing around.

VICTOR. Hmmm. [*Pause*]

ZOEY. It was hard. You know how he can be. He's kinda…cold.

VICTOR. Yeah, and you're a freakin' Disney princess.

She gives him a look. Beat. VICTOR's phone blings. He quickly goes to it.

ZOEY. What's it say?

VICTOR. They want to arrange a meet up.

ZOEY. For when? What are you gonna say?

VICTOR begins to type a reply, but the sound of a long beep behind the door stops him, and he shoves the phone into his pocket as IAN returns. IAN goes straight to the computer.

IAN. The stupid kid was like half asleep. Probably has another job in two hours or something. Still… [*IAN types the password into the computer and clicks.*]

ZOEY. So the key card works now?

IAN. There was nothing wrong with the key card.

VICTOR. Told you.

ZOEY. Is the internet working?

IAN. No. I mean, I don't know. It's trying. It's slow.

VICTOR. Shit hole.

ZOEY. Did you type it right?

IAN. There we go! Finally.

ZOEY and VICTOR come to his shoulders.

VICTOR. You got it?

ZOEY. Does it say anything? About…

IAN [*IAN scans the screen. He types, scans again*]. Doesn't look like it. Not yet. [*He turns and checks the clock. Pause*] All right, listen. We keep it on the newspaper website and Channel 2's page. That's it. We just refresh these two pages. We keep our eyes on 'em until they announce what we got.

VICTOR. Yeah, these rich pricks spending all this money on shitty art you can't do nothing with. They'll probably pay more than it's worth, right? I'll bet he would. I'll bet. [*VICTOR retrieves the TV remote and changes the channels, looking for a news broadcast.*] What am I looking for? Like CNN?

IAN. Now he's cooperative.

VICTOR. Like C-Span?

IAN. C-Span? No, something local.

ZOEY. You know why it's called the "News?" It's actually an acronym. North, East, West, South. That's what it stands for.

IAN. Where did you hear that?

ZOEY. It's true. Did you find a station, Vic?

VICTOR. I should probably move the van.

IAN. What do you mean?

VICTOR. Don't you think, just, you know, like as a, a…just to be safe. Move it to a different spot, not outside our room. Or move it down the street maybe.

ZOEY. It's not going to hurt, right?

VICTOR. Yeah, I'll just move it away. Just a block or something. You never know.

IAN. Uh huh.

VICTOR. Then at least the front desk kid can't recognize it. If he wakes up or whatever. You know? Or your buyer, what's his name? Mac…McKinley. That's not it—

IAN. McEvoy.

VICTOR opens the door.

VICTOR. Yeah, then he can't recognize it or describe it neither. Just in case. Okay. I'll just be a minute.

He exits. IAN watches him out the window. We hear the van start up and pull away.

IAN [*over his shoulder to ZOEY*]. He probably shouldn't be driving. [*Still at the window, his gaze moves to his own reflection on the glass. Softly, to himself.*] This is what happens… [*He becomes aware of ZOEY watching him, but remains looking into the window.*] I don't know if it matters that McEvoy sees the van.

ZOEY. You can't cover yourself too much. We're not even touching our phones, it seems consistent.

IAN. Uh huh.

ZOEY. Are you sure of this guy? How do you know he won't go to the cops? [excitedly] Or that he isn't a cop? You know, like undercover.

IAN. I told you, he *wants* it. I mean, he was the one—He approached me. He knew I could get it.

ZOEY. So how do you know that he isn't setting you up, or—

IAN. Zoey, come on, this isn't *The Sting*.

ZOEY. What?

IAN. He's after something we have. We want what he has. So why would he go to the cops? This is a victimless crime. It's just people trying to get what they're after.

ZOEY. Ian?…Ian?

IAN. What?

ZOEY. You're not going to fuck us over, right?

IAN. What? Come on. No.

ZOEY. Ian, look at me.

IAN turns deliberately and locks eyes with her.

ZOEY. You didn't tell me there was a silent alarm. You told me there was *no* alarm.

IAN. Okay. What are you trying to say? You think I—

ZOEY. I just…I know that…I hurt you and I don't know—I don't know if—

IAN. Zoey. Don't… don't worry. It's me.

He sits on the edge of the bed, closer to her. Pause.

ZOEY. I was glad when you asked me. I'm glad that you trusted me to do this. It feels good to do this together. To go all "whatever" on these motherfuckers.

He smirks. Pause. She puts a hand on his face. He leans into her touch, inhaling. Then he gently pushes her hand away.

IAN. Listen, don't touch me…like that.

ZOEY. Okay. [*softly*] God, you're an asshole.

IAN. Come on, I was just sayin'—I didn't mean—I just don't want to be touched. Right now.

ZOEY. What does that even mean? You don't want to be touched? It's nice to be touched. I'm trying to be nice.

IAN. I don't need you to be nice. Okay, that's done. I need you to be—

ZOEY. What? You need me to be what?

IAN. Consistent.

ZOEY. Consistent? How? / What do you—

IAN. Forget it. Let's just stay focused, all right?

ZOEY. I am focused. But we're waiting. Just waiting. We could talk, you know? We could really talk like we used to...You know you act like everything that touches you is poison.

IAN. Yeah well, if something damages you—weakens you, what do *you* call it?

ZOEY. Oh my god, Ian! I fucked up! People fuck up because life is hard, okay? Look at me, look at where I am tonight. What I've just done. What do I have to do prove to / you that—

IAN. Forget it.

ZOEY. I'd fucking love to but it's not so easy to forget. Is it?

IAN. What?

ZOEY. Why did you ask me to do this? To help you. And Victor, you said—

IAN. I couldn't be the one to go into in the museum. Isn't that obvious?

ZOEY. Why us?

IAN. You don't need the money?

ZOEY. You turn up, out of the blue like that. You've got a fuckin' reason. So what is it? What? Like, revenge?

IAN [*laughing*]. Revenge? I don't want—No, this is about...I knew you would help me. I knew you would want a part of this, so—

ZOEY. It's a business transaction.

IAN. If it helps you to think of it that way.

ZOEY. Or is it guilt?

Beat.

IAN. Guilt? Guilt for what?

ZOEY. Why can't you just answer a question? Huh? Why did you come back to me? I need to know—

IAN. Let me get this straight. *You* don't trust *me*? You're the one who's worried about being burned again?

ZOEY. I may have / fucked up.

IAN. Fucking rich.

ZOEY. But you fucking LEFT. [*Beat*]

IAN. Yeah.

ZOEY. You left us! That wasn't an accident. That wasn't a mistake. That was a choice. To abandon.

IAN. Of course I left. Why the fuck would I hang around? I'm not your caretaker, or your / brother's or anyone else—

ZOEY. We depended on you.

IAN. You think I was gonna stay there forever, running dope or some shit my whole fucking life? Live in a hellhole forever a goddamn beggar. You knew me better than that.

ZOEY. You didn't even say anything. You were just gone.

IAN. What should I have said? And I don't know how you coulda been surprised after...I left for me. Okay? Because that's what my gut told me to do. It told me to go. I follow my gut.

ZOEY. Your gut. Right. That's exactly why I'm asking you. Why am I here?

IAN. So what then, you're worried that, that I'm using you? That I'm gonna... [*Beat*] I'm not. [*Pause*]

ZOEY. We were family.

IAN. Family? You and I did some pretty sick shit if we're family.

ZOEY. Family means more than that and you know it. Where you come from, who your people are, what you have to do to make it. Those bonds are...they're sacred.

IAN [*smirking*]. Save that for your biography.

ZOEY. Stop being an asshole.

IAN. I'm not! We're talking, like you wanted. This is good.

ZOEY. Why did you ask me to do this? I want an answer. Open your mouth, say the fucking words. [*Beat*]

IAN. I asked you because I wanted...Look, I needed, or I knew you needed...Fuck, it's an easy job, a chance to make a lot of money with very little risk and I figured you...and, and Vic would, you know, want in on it. And be good for it. Okay?

ZOEY. You suck—sooo bad—at saying what you mean.

IAN. Doesn't matter.

IAN turns away. ZOEY marches to the vanity and pours herself another shot of whiskey.

IAN. You two should slow down on the drinking, don't you think? *She shoots it emphatically. The door knob on the door rattles. Then there's a knocking.*

VICTOR [O.S.]. Hey, I forgot the key card. Let me in.

IAN doesn't move. ZOEY crosses the length of room and opens the door.

VICTOR. I moved it. Just down the street a few yards. It's in the dark now. Anything in the North, East, South, West yet? Wait— North, East, West, South. News. Yeah…Anything yet?

IAN. No.

VICTOR. I don't see anything here on the TV. [*VICTOR goes to the painting.*] It is colorful.

ZOEY exits to the bathroom. VICTOR starts to open another bottle of beer. Realizing he's still standing over the painting, he looks at IAN and takes a deliberate step away, then pops the cap. He drops himself onto the bed, drinking and staring at the TV.

IAN [*to himself*]. Mad bitch.

VICTOR. My sister?

IAN goes back to the computer, acknowledging VICTOR with a glance.

VICTOR. Yeah, sometimes. My grandma was too though, so…

IAN. Your grandma, raising the two of you, she shoulda been sainted.

VICTOR. Well, she *was* a martyr. If you asked her, anyway.

The sound of a flush, and ZOEY comes out of the bathroom. She washes her hands at the vanity. Looking into the mirror, she catches IAN's eye. IAN turns away.

ZOEY [*to VICTOR*]. Give me one of those.

He hands her a bottle. The empties are starting to pile up on the floor and furniture. ZOEY lies on the bed next to VICTOR.

IAN. So are you guys having fun? Huh? Getting pleasantly buzzed? Hey, maybe we should play a drinking game!

ZOEY. Ian, it's dawn. We're not going to hear from anyone for a while yet.

IAN. Yes, and Victor is going to be wasted by the time we do.

ZOEY [*sharply*]. Everyone has their issues.

Beat. IAN takes a beer for himself and goes back to the computer. Still nothing there.

VICTOR [*pushing* ZOEY]. You're crowding me.

The phone rings. IAN and ZOEY exchange a quick look, and IAN goes to the phone.

IAN. No, it's too soon. [*answering*] Yeah?...Yep...Yes...Now? What happened to...Wait, wait! Hold on, you went to the museum? Why? Why would you...Yeah, of course, the cops are there, they— Wait, no, listen there's no—Hello? [*He hangs up.*] Okay...

ZOEY. Was that him?

IAN. Yes.

ZOEY. Is he coming now?

IAN. Yes.

VICTOR. But we still don't know what it's worth.

IAN. I know.

VICTOR. So what are you going to do?

IAN. I don't know.

VICTOR. You don't know?

IAN. Well, I'd like to be thinking, Victor, but I'm having trouble getting started!

ZOEY. How long do we have?

IAN. I don't know. However long it takes him to get here.

VICTOR. Where does he live?

IAN. I don't know!

VICTOR. You don't know?

IAN. No! I don't know. Why would I?

VICTOR. So what are you going to do?

IAN makes a go at VICTOR. VICTOR scampers.

ZOEY. We look it up.

She goes to the computer. IAN changes directions and blocks her.

IAN. No, we don't. What the fuck is wrong with you guys?

ZOEY. We can look up *something*, can't we?

IAN. Nothing they can trace! I'm telling you, they're going to check for hits—

ZOEY. On the name of the painting, which we don't have. And I'll be shocked if they even look for that because they'll probably assume we didn't have to look up the fucking worth of the painting we took on the / fucking internet!

IAN. Stop! We don't want to start some kind of trail or anything that leaves footprints.

VICTOR. Footprints? We've been walking all over—

IAN. Meta-fucking-phorical footprints, Victor. Stop drinking.

VICTOR. Okay!

IAN. We just have to think. All we need to do is get a, a general idea of what the market value of this thing could be.

ZOEY. But the only way we find that is to look it up. And we're not in a library, we're in a motel room.

VICTOR. A shitty motel room.

IAN. Is this not nicer than the state pen?

ZOEY. Come on, Ian, the chances of it getting put on the news before he gets here are pretty slim. If they post it at all.

VICTOR. We don't know the name of the painting or the name of the painter. What are you going to search for?

ZOEY. We just find a way to compare it to something else out there that has a dollar sign attached. If the search is, you know, generic enough it shouldn't matter, right? [*Beat*]

IAN. Like what?

ZOEY. I don't know. We search…"famous paintings?"

IAN. It's not the Mona Lisa. Or the two farmers.

ZOEY. The what?

IAN. The two farmers. Old couple. The pitchfork—

ZOEY. Oh. That one.

VICTOR. Search "expensive shitty finger painting."

ZOEY. Maybe "art auctions"—

IAN. Think about that.

ZOEY. Okay! Um, "colorful…village…people painting"—

IAN. You want to search "village people?"

ZOEY. Ugh! Do we know what like century it was painted?

IAN. No.

VICTOR. "Freaky, abstract town nightmare."

Pause. IAN looks at him.

VICTOR. …on acid.

IAN. Abstract.

ZOEY. Huh?

IAN. Yeah, yeah. Just search "Abstract." It's, you know, vague, but specific.

They all head for the computer. ZOEY wins the race. IAN and VICTOR crowd around her.

IAN. Look out.

ZOEY. I can do it. [*She types*]

IAN. You missed the "S."

VICTOR. "Abtract." That's not a word.

IAN. Now click images.

ZOEY. I know how to do it!

They watch the screen.

ZOEY. Ugh. Looks like a hippy's tie-dyed t-shirt.

IAN [*pointing*]. Try that one.

ZOEY. Where?

IAN. Right there. That one there.

VICTOR. Yeah, that kinda looks like it.

Their eyes scan the screen.

IAN. No, go back.

ZOEY. What about this one?

IAN. Sure.

ZOEY. Doesn't say anything about how much.

IAN reaches over ZOEY's shoulders and messes with the mouse pad.

VICTOR. Wait, right there! What is it?…A hundred and twelve dollars! Are you fucking kidding me? I knew it! One hundred and twelve bucks! Oh that's it! We're fucking dead—

IAN. That's for a print! A print. Calm down. You're making me crazy.

Pause. Still searching.

IAN. Right here. Right here. Let's see…1909 modern expression-ist…blah, blah, blah, at Phillips de Pury, New York…sold to…some asshole for *sixty thousand dollars.* [*Pause*]

VICTOR. Sixty grand?

ZOEY. Sixty.

VICTOR. That's twenty each. Twenty thousand dollars! We can get that? I mean that one looks pretty much just like this one. Like fuckin' unicorn shit. Ian, you think this guy will pay that?…Ian?

IAN. I think sixty sounds…yeah. But we should start higher with him though, you know, because he's going to try to work us down.

VICTOR. So we aim for seventy-five and we get sixty. Maybe sixty-five? That's great. That's perfect. That's great.

ZOEY [*still looking at the computer*]. So the one we have is *modern expressionist?* How's that different from *abstract?*

VICTOR. Holy shit! Sixty grand. For a picture! This guy has that kind of cash?

IAN. He's stuffed up, believe me. And as bad as he wants it, he knows it's gonna cost him.

ZOEY. What if it's worth more than that? It could be, couldn't it? Or what if it's worth less?

VICTOR. Worth less?

IAN. It could be, I don't know. How can you tell with these? But with the risk we took, and what it is, yeah, I think we can make that work.

VICTOR. Oh hell yes. Vic is back mothafuckas.

IAN covers the painting with the garbage bag and takes it into the bath-room. VICTOR goes to the window. With his back to the room, he checks his phone.

ZOEY. What do we do while he's here?

IAN [*coming back to the room*]. Don't do anything. Don't talk. Don't be drunk. Victor, get away from the window.

VICTOR pockets his phone and turns back to the room. IAN gathers bottles and bags into some kind of order.

ZOEY. Don't talk? So you're going to handle everything?

IAN. I arranged it with him, didn't I? He knows *me*. It's just a, a formality now. Are you worried? You'll be here, listening, won't you?

ZOEY. You don't *really* know this guy. He could be dirty. Or he could call the cops, he could have a weapon—

IAN. I really don't think—

ZOEY. You know, there seems to be an awful lot of guesswork in your plan here tonight!

IAN. Right, it's a chance! An opportunity. They're rare, and sudden, and yeah, usually a gamble. But that's how we get ahead. You afraid?

ZOEY shakes her head. IAN turns to VICTOR.

IAN. You?

VICTOR. What—What do you mean, afraid? Afraid of—

He's cut off by a knock at the door. Beat. They stare at each other. IAN crosses to the door and looks through the peep hole. He steps back away from it.

ZOEY [*whispering*]. Is it him?

IAN [*nodding*]. You open it.

ZOEY. Me? Why?

IAN. Just do it.

ZOEY. Vic, you open it.

VICTOR. What, does he have a gun or something?

Another knock on the door.

IAN. Just open it.

ZOEY. Why does it matter who opens it?

IAN. Victor, open it. Let him in.

VICTOR hesitates, then goes to the door, and opens it a crack.

VICTOR. You Mc...Uh.

VICTOR turns back to the others.

ZOEY. Evoy.

VICTOR. Evoy. McEvoy?

Beat. VICTOR looks back at IAN, who nods, and VICTOR opens the door. MCEVOY steps slowly over the threshold. He carries a leather satchel on his shoulder. He is demonstrably uncomfortable. A man out of his element. His eyes travel over VICTOR and ZOEY, and meet IAN's.

VICTOR [*closing the door*]. He's alone. There's no one else.

MCEVOY. I am alone. Shouldn't I be?

VICTOR. Just figured maybe if you had like, muscle or something.

MCEVOY. Had what?

IAN [*gesturing to quiet*]. Victor.

MCEVOY [*softly*]. I thought we...

IAN. What's that?

MCEVOY. I didn't expect, um, other people. I thought—I expected only you, Ian.

IAN. Right, well. This is Zoey, her brother, Victor. I required their help.

ZOEY [*pours a shot*]. Would you like a drink, Mr. McEvoy?

MCEVOY. No.

IAN. You sure? You seem like you could use one.

MCEVOY. I'd prefer not to draw this out.

ZOEY. Suit yourself. [*She shoots it.*]

MCEVOY. You required help?

IAN. To get in and out of the museum, yeah. It wouldn't have been smart for me to be anywhere near the building. And it wasn't smart for you either.

MCEVOY. Well—yes, but I—

IAN. What were you doing?

MCEVOY. I couldn't help it...I, I had to see...I just, I only drove by. There were policemen, and I wondered...well—

IAN. I told you to wait. To call in the morning.

MCEVOY. You said—yes—but you also said it was just you.

IAN. Don't worry, the number of people is on my end. It doesn't change the arrangement.

MCEVOY. The arrangement? *Arrangement*, god, we never even... That's why I called earlier. When I saw the police, I didn't know if, if you had—or if you'd been...You've done it then?

IAN. Yes.

MCEVOY [*breathlessly, sitting down on the bed*]. Oh my god. [*Beat*]

ZOEY [*ZOEY turns to IAN, quietly*]. What's his problem?

MCEVOY. I haven't slept. I watched the clock, all night, wondering, until I couldn't take it anymore. I, I, I wasn't sure how far we'd gone beyond, uh, beyond hypothetical. I half expected to call and get an empty room or, or a stranger—

ZOEY [*to IAN*]. What is he talking about?

IAN. You gave me the crate number.

MCEVOY. I did. I did. Yes. It's just such an extreme thing to do. Of course, I knew that, but, but when, when I drove by—

ZOEY. Have you never done this before?

IAN. Zoey—

MCEVOY. You have it here?

ZOEY. He sounds like he's gonna pass out! What did you say to each other?

MCEVOY. I told him there was a painting arriving, and, and wondered how possible it would be to, to get to it. Without being…We really only discussed what might be possible.

ZOEY. What? / Wait, you—

MCEVOY. I didn't know if you would—I don't know if I believed you / would actually—

ZOEY. Jesus! It sounds like neither of you really agreed to anything! It's like you found each other on craigslist!

IAN. We agreed that—

MCEVOY. Let me see it.

VICTOR. Aren't you an art dealer?

MCEVOY. I'm a curator.

VICTOR. So you don't sell paintings?

MCEVOY. I work at the—I do collect and sometimes I broker a deal—

ZOEY. Hey, just like you, Vic.

VICTOR. Are you trying to be funny?

MCEVOY. But that is hardly—

IAN. Shut your mouths!

All three go quiet.

IAN. Well, not you, McEvoy. Listen. Yes, the things we talked about—speculated on—they have happened. I told you what I could do and it's done. It's done. Let's move on to what happens next. [*Beat*]

MCEVOY. It's here, yes?...Is it here? Now?

IAN. It's here.

MCEVOY. Well where? Where is it?

IAN. You'll see it.

MCEVOY. My god. Are you sure you opened the *right* crate? The right one—

IAN. Yes!

ZOEY. Number / thirty-two.

VICTOR. Thirty-two, yeah. Who painted it?

MCEVOY. And there were no problems? I mean, in terms of being...[*the word sticks in his throat*]...caught?

IAN. There were no problems. I told you the opportunity was perfect.

ZOEY. *We* know what we're doing.

MCEVOY. You had no issues bringing it here? How do you know it's not traced or—

IAN. Security is shit for another week. There's no way of knowing where it is or who has it. And right now, that's me.

MCEVOY. And now that they know it's missing—

IAN. Cops, FBI, they'll do their thing. Eventually the museum will make the insurance claim. Their only hope really is that the thieves fuck up and it resurfaces.

ZOEY. You mean, like, trying to ransom it back?

IAN nods.

MCEVOY. Let me see it.

IAN. First I want—

MCEVOY. Please! Show it to me! Is it damaged? Have you damaged it?

IAN. No.

MCEVOY. I assume you know that these things must be treated—

IAN. It's not damaged.

MCEVOY. You're sure, you're sure that you safely—

ZOEY. It's fine!

MCEVOY. Well, then let me see it!

IAN. We have it covered.

VICTOR. We was real careful with it. You'll / be happy.

ZOEY. Be quiet, Vic. Ian, just / get the—

IAN. Let me handle this.

MCEVOY. Assuming you have the right one—

IAN. We have the right one.

VICTOR. Yeah, it's a piece of shit. [*Beat*]

MCEVOY. Pardon?

IAN. Christ! What is wrong with you two?

VICTOR. No, I mean, I'm saying if it's the right one—

IAN. It *is* the right / one!

VICTOR. Then he'd know it looks like a blind kid's coloring book! Right? You know what I'm talking about? These paintings that are all weird looking and shape-y, we can't believe it could be worth—

IAN grabs VICTOR and pushes him to the corner, forcing him to sit.

IAN. Shut your mouth. And stop drinking.

ZOEY. He's talking about how it's abstract. Or expressionist. He doesn't know shit about art.

VICTOR [*indicating the landscape*]. Oh yeah! McKinley, look at this one here. What do you think this is?

IAN snatches an empty bottle from the nightstand and holds it up threateningly. VICTOR goes silent and back into the corner. MCEVOY's unease is apparent as IAN rounds on him.

MCEVOY. Yes, expressionist. German Expressionist. Let me see it. Let me hold it. Please. If all that has transpired, all we talked about has brought it here, now, then show it to me. I must *see* it.

IAN hesitates, then exits to the bathroom.

VICTOR. You know a lot about art, huh?

MCEVOY. It's what I do. It's who I am.

VICTOR. Look at this then.

VICTOR points to the landscape painting above the bed.

VICTOR. What's that there?

MCEVOY. What?

ZOEY. Oh god.

VICTOR. That there, what is that? What was the painter making?

MCEVOY. Those are…brush strokes?

VICTOR. Right, okay. But the brush strokes represent something, right? Doesn't all art stuff represent stuff?

IAN returns carrying the painting in the garbage bag. He watches from the bathroom doorway.

VICTOR. Look at that, look at it closely and tell me that's not a coyote.

MCEVOY. A...coyote—

VICTOR. A coyote—

IAN. A coyote. They come out of the wild and feed on inferior canines during famine. Apparently.

MCEVOY. That's it?

MCEVOY yanks a pair of cloth gloves from his jacket pocket and pulls them onto his hands. He goes to IAN with his arms extended. IAN hands him the garbage bag. MCEVOY slides the plastic off and rests the painting gently on his fingers and takes it in. Pause. He exhales.

IAN. The right one?

MCEVOY. Yes.

He holds it before himself, studying it, his eyes glistening with wonder. IAN, ZOEY, and VICTOR all exchange an incredulous look.

MCEVOY. Oh. I...I can't believe it. Just how...The color, the looseness, the fluidity of line, the harsh—almost *violent*—application of hues. Vibrant and dark at once. It's the blue...The blue raging against yellow...(*sighs*) No second-guessing. And it's here. My god, it's in this room. [*Beat*]

IAN. Why this one?

MCEVOY. What?

IAN. What is it? What makes it so...I mean, who painted it?

MCEVOY. Kirchner. E. L. Kirchner. German painter.

VICTOR [*referring to the landscape*]. Who painted this?

MCEVOY. This painting was among the earliest pieces of the style. Kirchner and his contemporaries were beginning to reject traditional style in pursuit of a, of a new artistic mode.

VICTOR. You mean they painted this way on purpose?

MCEVOY. Yes. They were painting as an impulsive reaction to life, not...not to capture the picturesque. [*Off of VICTOR's blank stare*]

Not to depict reality, but rather to reflect their deepest inner feelings. This is an art of anxiety, of unease, of...rage. Realism was sacrificed to the benefit of its...its internalized image. [*Beat*]

VICTOR. ....'kay.

IAN. What's it called?

MCEVOY. *Summum bonum.*

VICTOR [*aside, to ZOEY*]. Is that English?

MCEVOY. And here it is. In this dim, dank room. When not so long ago and for decades no one knew if it even existed anymore.

ZOEY. What do you mean?

MCEVOY. This painting, and the others have been lost since the Second World War. They were recently discovered in the apartment of an old man, the son of a German officer. Hundreds of pieces the Nazis had branded degenerate.

ZOEY. Branded *what?*

MCEVOY. Degenerate.

VICTOR. Wait. Nazis painted these?

IAN. No—

MCEVOY. Nazis stole them. From the painters, from the galleries. From their owners. They destroyed, uh, confiscated or sold abroad art they considered a, a threat, in what may be the most severe display of jealousy and spite the modern world has ever known.

Beat. They look at MCEVOY.

MCEVOY. Hitler was a failed painter.

VICTOR [*chuckling*]. What the fuck?

IAN. There was dozens of crates in that shipment. We could have taken any one of 'em. They were all *degenerate* art?

MCEVOY nods.

VICTOR. All degenerate? So they all suck?

MCEVOY. I'm sorry. Suck?

ZOEY. We mean if they're "degenerate" does that make them worth less?

MCEVOY. Worth—if anything it makes them prized all the more, but—

IAN. Why number thirty-two?

ZOEY. And why *only* this one? I mean, you could have had—

MCEVOY. Now wait. Don't, don't mistake me. I'm not interested in just *any* piece. I'm not some criminal art dealer—

ZOEY [*under her breath*]. That's for sure.

IAN. Would you stop? This isn't a fucking movie.

MCEVOY. *This* piece. This is the one, the only one, that...that I would go to such lengths to acquire. Not for any kind of monetary justification or, or, or prestige associated with possession. But for, for reasons that...motivations that I doubt the three of you could comprehend.

ZOEY. What do you / mean by that?

MCEVOY. I wouldn't be here, I wouldn't have thought of doing this for anything off the wall. This is the *only* one I would even think—

IAN. I get that, but why?

MCEVOY. I'm not interested in the price.

IAN. I am.

Pause. IAN holds open the garbage bag. MCEVOY reluctantly places the painting inside.

MCEVOY. We arrive at the crux. Now, we both want—

IAN. We both *want*. This couldn't be simpler.

MCEVOY looks at ZOEY and VICTOR, then back at IAN.

MCEVOY. Yes.

He goes to his satchel. He withdraws a few short stacks of cash, crisp and bound. IAN passes the garbage bag to ZOEY, and accepts the cash as MCEVOY places it in his hands. Pause.

IAN. How much is here?

MCEVOY. That's twenty thousand dollars.

IAN and ZOEY exchange a look. VICTOR stands up from his chair.

MCEVOY. Twenty thousand. [*Pause*]

IAN. Hmm. You know, I gotta say...that seems a bit low for a something that could be the plot of an Indiana Jones movie.

MCEVOY. Low?

IAN. A little low, yes. This is a famous piece of art, and we took it from a museum.

MCEVOY. But, but we never discussed—I mean, we only agreed that—

IAN. We agreed I could get it, and you could pay for it.

MCEVOY. I—Pay you for the *act* of doing it! And when we talked, it was only you. Just you, no one else!

IAN. Yes.

MCEVOY. You said that was on your end. That it doesn't—

IAN. It doesn't. I'm not talking about the number of people, I'm talking about the deal. The exchange. For the painting, prized, prestigious, an appropriate price.

MCEVOY [*getting heated*]. And what do you deem appropriate? You, what? Broke a window? Disabled a security camera?

IAN. I did what you couldn't do. I had the angle. You didn't. I set the price. That's commerce.

MCEVOY. An opportunity, indeed.

MCEVOY goes back to his bag. He pulls another stack of bills out.

MCEVOY. Five thousand. Five thousand *more*.

IAN [*as he expected*]. Ah…

MCEVOY. That's what I have. I'm showing my hand. You understand? The game is played, the cards are all out, you win. That's all I have…Twenty-five thousand dollars is a lot of money.

IAN. But it's not enough.

MCEVOY. Not enough? And what is *enough*? Please, tell me! How do you quantify the cost of this transaction?

IAN. We want what it's worth. [*Beat*]

MCEVOY. What it's *worth*?

IAN. I want seventy thousand.

MCEVOY [*dumbfounded*]. Seventy thousand?!…That's… That's not…I—

IAN. Fuck it. I'll cut you a deal. We know we're going there eventually and I don't want to wait all night for you to finish a sentence. Sixty thousand. I'm not going lower.

MCEVOY. Sixty thousand!

ZOEY. Stop repeating everything he says!

IAN. Why would I let it go for less?

MCEVOY. What use do you have for it? For artwork you don't even understand? It means nothing to you—

ZOEY. We don't give a shit about its meaning!

MCEVOY. You can't do anything with it but, but this! You can't take it to auction, or, or—

IAN. You have no idea what I can or cannot do. Sixty thousand, McEvoy.

MCEVOY. I don't have sixty thousand dollars! I don't have a suitcase full of money. Who—How did you expect / that—

VICTOR. You had a bag of twenty-five grand.

MCEVOY. I don't have it! I don't know why you expect me to have that kind of liquidity but I—

ZOEY. Maybe it was the fancy words!

MCEVOY. I'm telling you, this is all I have. Twenty-five thousand! Here it is, cash. And as you said, everybody gets what they want. Everyone gains. No one loses anything.

IAN. I lose forty thousand dollars.

VICTOR. *We* lose.

MCEVOY. Please! I don't have it. I...I *need* that painting! I can't— And think about this: You've stolen. You've taken from powerful organizations. Do you want to carry that around, looking aimlessly for the right buyer? Is it worth that kind of risk? You could walk away now—richer—having troubled yourself little beyond the cost of a, a cheap motel room and a few cases of beer. There's no guarantee that you'll ever find anyone who can pay what you want for it. If you do find someone like that, rest assured they'll have the ability to *take* it from you. And the longer you have it...

IAN snorts in derision

MCEVOY. I needed your help. I'm trying to pay you for your help. I'm paying you all I can. *All* I can...I'm begging you.

Pause. They all stare at IAN. IAN is looking at MCEVOY, sizing him up. Finally:

IAN. I'm glad you got a good look at it. Because that's all you get.

MCEVOY. No!

IAN. Get out.

MCEVOY. No, please! Listen to me—

IAN tosses the money back to MCEVOY, most of it slapping against him and falling to the floor. MCEVOY struggles to pick it up, as his eyes are on the painting in the garbage bag. VICTOR dives to floor and begins to gather the money stacks.

IAN. Put those back in the bag, Victor.

MCEVOY. Ian! No, listen—

VICTOR kneels, holding the money, and staring at it. ZOEY grabs MC-EVOY's bag and takes the money from VICTOR. She slams the bag into MCEVOY's chest. He fumbles with it as ZOEY pushes him towards the door, stepping over VICTOR.

MCEVOY. Please, just listen to me!

IAN. Good night.

ZOEY opens the door.

MCEVOY [*escaping ZOEY*]. I'll get it! I'll get it!

IAN. Say again?

MCEVOY. Give me some time, I'll get it. Damn it, I'll…I'll get it.

IAN. How much time?

MCEVOY. A couple of days.

VICTOR [*to IAN*]. You said tonight.

IAN. I could be gone in a couple of days.

ZOEY doesn't miss this.

VICTOR. Ian, you said sixty thousand tonight!

IAN. A day.

MCEVOY. A day?

IAN. Twenty-four hours.

VICTOR. Zoey—

ZOEY. Shhh!

MCEVOY. That's not enough—

IAN. Twenty-four hours. Sixty grand. And it's yours.

Pause. MCEVOY stands on the threshold of the open door, looking hard at IAN.

MCEVOY. I thought…thought you were something different.

IAN [*calmly*]. Now you know better. Twenty-four hours.

MCEVOY. I'll come back. I will! Don't…Don't leave.

MCEVOY exits. ZOEY closes the door behind him.

VICTOR [*still on the floor*]. Fuck!

IAN. He'll get it.

VICTOR leans against the bed. He takes his phone out and looks at it. IAN doesn't notice.

ZOEY. What if he doesn't? He said that's all he has.

IAN. But he can get it. He said that too.

ZOEY. How did you know he would?

IAN. Call me an optimist. You can always count on greed.

ZOEY. So what the hell do we do for twenty-four hours?

IAN. Wait. Sleep. Whatever. [*IAN moves to the computer.*]

ZOEY. He really threw me with that Nazi degenerate stuff. Makes it sound like no one would want it.

IAN. That's art.

ZOEY. And you knew he's got more…Or you guessed?

IAN. Went with my gut.

He smirks. She can't decide if she's impressed or pissed off. IAN breaks the moment by picking up the laptop.

ZOEY. We should get some food or something…

She looks at VICTOR, still on the ground, expressionless.

ZOEY. Vic?

IAN [*looking at the computer*]. It's up.

ZOEY. Huh?

IAN. There's a headline.

ZOEY darts over to IAN, reading over his shoulder.

ZOEY. What does it say? They don't have a lead, right? They don't know…

They read silently. Their eyes lock on the screen. Then their heads slowly turn towards each other. They share a look. Black out.

ACT TWO

Light isolates the downstage frame, where IAN stands looking through it. He is dressed in his work clothes. He looks over his shoulder. Then back out.

IAN. I think…I mean I'm pretty sure…I could get to it, without any issues. The new security system isn't live until after the weekend, still the old one 'til then so this is the time. Do you know the crate number—I mean, is there any way to know the exact crate for that one because you know it's just gonna sit there for twenty-four hours to acclimate, just sit there without being opened. Twenty-four hours before anyone even touches the box. So I assume you have some kind of, like, itinerary, a list with the numbers and all that…Yeah, okay, a "manifest," right, then yes. I could. I *could*. And if I *did*, and there were no problems, you *could* just call a hotel room number. You know? Here, listen, we never exchange personal phone numbers, I don't know where you live, you don't know where I live, we just pass in a night. We make a deal, and it's done. We *could*. Depends on you, how bad you want it. And if you know the number of the crate…I'm here again tomorrow doing the wiring, but after that, electrical is done and I'll be done here, you'll never see me again. So tomorrow. If you give me the number of a box, I'll give you the number of a hotel… [*Pause*] …And we'll just…see what happens.

The lights fade and IAN vanishes. The motel room is dim, lit only by the lamp and the light that spills in through the window. The clock glows 8:20. Empty bottles are scattered around the room, some fast food wrappers balled up among them. ZOEY is asleep on the bed. VICTOR is on the floor, a visible mess. He has not slept, and has not stopped drinking. He is damp with sweat, his breathing is heavy, and he sobs and sniffs in intervals. He holds his phone in one hand. The light of it illuminates his tired face, shining in the tears in his eyes. The crowbar rests in his other hand. He stares at the phone. He clumsily moves to his knees and puts the phone on the floor. He raises the crowbar over his head, poised to slam it down on the device, but holds in the position. Pause. He slumps down on the floor again, sobbing, the crowbar clanking on the floor. The sound wakes ZOEY.

ZOEY. What are you doing?

VICTOR [*mumbling*]. I'm fucked, Zoey.

ZOEY. Huh?

VICTOR. I'm fucked! They're gonna fucking kill me.

ZOEY. Wait. Did something happen?

VICTOR. No, nothing happened, and that's the problem! I got nothing. Not a dollar. And Ian is not going to sell the painting. There's just no way. Not now. Even *if* McEvoy comes back.

ZOEY. He's coming back. And we don't know...I mean, if... Did you tell them you just needed a little more time? That you're going to—

VICTOR. Yes! Yes! I tried! I, I texted...They don't give a shit!

ZOEY. Slow down! Did they text back or...? What'd they say?

VICTOR. Nothing. And that's bad, believe me.

ZOEY. We don't know yet—

VICTOR. I'm getting nothing and they're gonna be looking for me. They're looking for me and they're gonna take it out of my fucking blood!

ZOEY. Well, they don't know where you are—

VICTOR. They'll find me! You think they / can't find—

ZOEY. They won't! Not tonight. And we can think of something. We can change the plan. We can...

VICTOR *waits for her to finish, but she never does. He clenches his fists and puts them to his pounding head. He growls.*

ZOEY. What time is it?

VICTOR. What if...What if I turn myself in? To the police—

ZOEY. Turn yourself in?

VICTOR. For stealing the art. Confess, you know.

ZOEY. Why?

VICTOR. Well, they'll arrest me. They'll take me in and, you know, I'll be—

ZOEY. They'll question you. They'll want the painting, Vic! Want to know where you put it. What do you think they'll—

VICTOR. I'll protect you. Both of you. I won't say.

ZOEY. No! You're not turning yourself in. You want Ian coming after you instead? Just...You need to calm down, okay?

VICTOR *goes back to the floor, a pathetic heap. He tries to drink from the closest bottle, but it's dry.*

ZOEY. Where's Ian?

VICTOR. This whole thing is broken. Broken because of a stupid, ugly, stupid shit painting. *Sum...*Something... [*smirking*] *Summon Boner.*

ZOEY [*allowing a smile*]. *Summum bonum.*

VICTOR. Whatever the fuck that means. I can't believe it matters this much. A fucking picture... Just because of Nazis. Why is it always *like the Nazis?* Whenever people are obsessed with something and something bad happens they always say: "That's like Hitler," or "It's like the Nazis." On the internet. If someone's being racist, or an asshole about politics or money or something it always ends up being "like the Nazis."

ZOEY. This wasn't *like* the Nazis. This fucking *was* the Nazis.

VICTOR. These cartel assholes are like Nazis. About their money. They're gonna murder me like the Nazis. [*He coughs, choking on bile.*]

ZOEY. God, Vic. You need water. [*She goes to the vanity sink to fill a plastic cup.*]

VICTOR. I need money.

She brings the cup over to VICTOR. He takes it with both hands and drinks. ZOEY picks his phone up off the floor. She looks at it.

ZOEY. You texted them? Again, I mean, since...Can they track this?

VICTOR. What?

ZOEY. I mean, is there some way to know where you are, or *roughly* where you are because of your phone?

VICTOR. I don't know. How would they? With my phone number?

ZOEY. I don't know. Like Ian said, these days there's no way of being hidden, everything's connected. They're always...you know. The government listening to your phone calls and stuff.

VICTOR. They're not the government. They're the opposite of the government.

ZOEY. I mean—You know what I mean! Have they been calling or messaging you or...?

He shakes his head.

ZOEY. They've gone silent. Maybe turn it off.

VICTOR. Or get rid of it?

ZOEY. Just turn it off. [*She turns off the phone and hands it back to him.*] And drink more water. *VICTOR struggles to his feet, and sets his phone on the desk. He catches his reflection in the long mirror and stares at it. His face clenches as he fights against crying. He wipes his eyes. ZOEY goes to the window and peeks out.*

ZOEY. Where's Ian?...Vic?

VICTOR. Huh?

ZOEY. Where's Ian?

VICTOR. He left. I don't know. I think down to the office. The front desk. Where the hotel kid is. I don't know.

ZOEY. How long ago? Did he take the painting?

VICTOR shrugs.

ZOEY. Where is it?

VICTOR sits on the floor, his head in his hands. She checks the bathroom.

ZOEY. Did you even eat any of this? Have you eaten anything since yesterday?

She handles the food wrappers, scraps of food still unfinished. She looks at VICTOR, but he's not listening to her. She lifts the mattress, checking underneath it.

VICTOR. You remember Lucky?

ZOEY. Lucky? You mean—

VICTOR. Yeah. Lucky.

ZOEY. Your dog? The mangy one you had when we were little?

VICTOR. Yeah yeah.

ZOEY. Sure. What about him?

VICTOR. I don't know. Just...I don't know.

ZOEY. Oh...He was a good dog.

VICTOR. He was a little bastard. Crazy little...He would snarl and bark at people. Chase anything that moved. Tried to bite.

ZOEY. Not at you though.

VICTOR. He was that way because Grandma kept him chained to a rusty pole in the yard.

ZOEY. Oh yeah.

VICTOR. Mean bitch.

ZOEY. Lucky was male, wasn't he? Oh. Grandma.

VICTOR. We should have let him in the house. He coulda slept with me.

ZOEY. Well, I don't know—

VICTOR. They're not supposed to be chained up like that!

ZOEY. But he was wild! He would have bit someone, maybe a little kid.

VICTOR. No, he wouldn't have. I coulda trained him.

ZOEY. Oh yeah right, Victor, you train him?

VICTOR. Yeah? What?

ZOEY. What do you know about training dogs? And I don't think that dog / could be tamed.

VICTOR. Jesus, Zoey, I could train a fucking dog! Why you always talk to me like that? I'm sick of it. I'm not a fucking idiot. I'm sick of everyone talking to me like that, sick of it!

ZOEY. I was just saying—

VICTOR. I'm fuckin' sick of being pushed around.

ZOEY. We all are!

VICTOR. I loved that dog. I coulda taken care of him. Isn't that why we got him? God, I'm not a fucking idiot. Okay, I'm not stupid!

ZOEY. I know—

VICTOR. And I'm not always wrong either! You think I'm wrong about everything—

ZOEY. No / I don't—

VICTOR. But I know some things!

ZOEY. I don't think you're always wrong!

VICTOR [*darting towards the landscape on the wall*]. And that is a fucking coyote!

ZOEY. Okay, okay, it is! God, chill.

VICTOR slumps onto the bed. Pause.

ZOEY. Where's Ian?

VICTOR. I miss that dog.

ZOEY shakes her head at him and turns back to the window. The phone rings. It startles ZOEY, and VICTOR reacts like it's a gunshot.

ZOEY. Shit.

It rings again.

ZOEY. Do we answer it?

VICTOR. Uh—

It continues to ring.

ZOEY. What if it's Ian? From the lobby?

VICTOR. What if it's someone else?

ZOEY. Or McEvoy.

VICTOR. Oh shit.

ZOEY. He didn't say anything about the phone?

VICTOR. Who? McEvoy?

ZOEY. Ian!

VICTOR. No.

ZOEY. If someone calls?

VICTOR. No!

They stare at the phone until it stops ringing.

VICTOR. It stopped.

ZOEY. Well... [*Pause*]

VICTOR. If it rings again...

ZOEY. I'll answer it?

VICTOR. Yeah. [*Pause*]

ZOEY. Fuck. I shoulda answered it.

VICTOR. Yeah. [*Pause*]

ZOEY. Wait, you don't think there's any chance that...

VICTOR. What?

ZOEY. No. There's no way.

VICTOR. What?

ZOEY. Nothing. Just...If it rings again, let me answer it.

The sound of the long BEEP from behind the door, and it swings open, admitting IAN, holding the key card.

ZOEY. Where did you go?

IAN. The lobby. Checked out of the room.

ZOEY. We're leaving?

IAN. We've waited long enough. Help clean this shit up. [*IAN begins to gather his things, and round up the trash and beer bottles.*]

ZOEY. Wait! What about—What about McEvoy?

IAN. What about him?

ZOEY. He's coming back. He expects to finish the deal.

IAN. Fuck him. He used us.

ZOEY. We knew he was using us. That was the point.

IAN. He didn't tell me what the painting was. He made it sound like a smash-and-grab job.

ZOEY. It *was* a smash-and-grab job.

IAN. It's not like we broke into a store or stole a car. In our ignorance—maybe because of it—we stumbled into something…something bigger. Into—I don't know—like a different level.

ZOEY. What?

IAN. We caught a break! We caught that bit of fate, that kind of lucky chance that you can't buy or, or work your way into. We caught it by accident. We have to use it!

ZOEY. Yes, for sixty grand! Tonight! That's pretty damn good, Ian. What else are we going to do? Put it on Ebay?

IAN. I don't know exactly. But I'll figure that out. Everything's different now.

ZOEY. No it's not! Look, McEvoy is coming back, you were sure of that! If he comes back and we're not here, what do think he's gonna do? Call the cops. He knows our faces, our names.

IAN. He also knows he can't say shit without incriminating himself!

ZOEY. That's a big risk to take after you full-on fuck him over! Let's wait. For a bit more.

IAN. It could be hours. And I don't want—

VICTOR. The phone rang! [*Beat*]

IAN. When?

ZOEY. Just before you came in.

IAN. Was it him?

ZOEY. We didn't answer it.

IAN. Why not?

ZOEY. We didn't know if you'd want us to.

IAN. He's the only one who would call. Who else would call?

ZOEY. So he's on his way.

IAN stops gathering his things.

ZOEY. And what about the painting?

IAN. What about it?

ZOEY. You gonna at least talk to him? [*Beat*] You said you didn't want to take it home.

IAN. That was before.

ZOEY. Yes, I know. But McEvoy can't pay more. We've already driven him up as high as he can go. So just take / his money and—

IAN. As high as *he* can go.

ZOEY. What are you going to do then? Hang it on the wall or, or hide it under your mattress? The longer you hang onto it—

IAN. It's been almost twenty-four hours, they've announced that it's missing. They got nothing. It's lost. And last time it disappeared it stayed lost for more than half a century.

ZOEY. Lotta confidence from the guy who banned cell phones and personal computers.

IAN [to VICTOR]. What is her deal? Give her an opioid or something.

ZOEY. Let's be done with it! We got what we set out for. Sell to McEvoy. Everyone gets what they want—

IAN. *I* don't get what I want.

ZOEY. What *do* you want? Do you even know? You're just flailing around, like, improvising until you find something and not paying attention to what you might lose!

IAN. What I set out for—from the beginning—What I *want* is possibility. Opportunity. I been looking for a crack in the door and the fucking thing swung so wide open it fell off its hinges. You understand?

ZOEY. No! Ian, no one understands you when you talk like that! If you're after more money just fucking say it!

IAN. I'm not talking about money! You guys think money is the end of all this, but it's not. It never is! I been hustlin' my whole life and it just gets me to the next one and the next one. This is about *means*. This is about access. About power. About the ability to go up. *Beat. ZOEY looks at VICTOR, who remains shrunken against the wall.*

ZOEY. Did that make any sense to you?

VICTOR doesn't reply. She turns back to IAN.

ZOEY. My turn. And listen how easy this is, to communicate, when the concept is plain and simple. This is about *need*. The three of us need money. And the three of us need each other. Those are the things we need to survive. You know that, don't you? That we need each other? I thought you did know that—finally—but maybe you forgot again when McEvoy told you what we had. But the painting is nothing. It's fucking splotches of color on cloth. Soon, one way or another, it'll be gone. And when it disappears it makes no difference. But I'm here. You're here. And that does make a difference. It doesn't have to disappear. It can stay. This *is* an opportunity. To fix things. To survive together. To maybe get to a place where *having* something is just as good, just as fulfilling as *wanting* it. I came here for you. I did this for you. I risked everything for you. Because we are kin. Now we can sell this useless thing to McEvoy, make his fucking life complete, and walk away with enough money to go somewhere, somewhere different, and start over. I need that. You need that. [*Pause*]

IAN. Zoey…

ZOEY. You need me. The question is, do you know it. Do you finally know it? If you do, you'll sell the painting and we'll be unstuck. If you don't, this is it. This is the last time we see each other. This isn't a hustle, it's the goddamn truth. So *make this right*. There. See how straightforward that is?

There's a soft knock on the door. Beat.

ZOEY. Well? What will you do?

Pause. Another knock.

ZOEY. Ian? [*Beat*]

IAN. I. Can't. Settle.

ZOEY betrays a moment of hurt, then her expression hardens.

ZOEY. We'll be outside.

She grabs VICTOR's phone, and then pulls VICTOR towards the door.

VICTOR. Wha…? What are we—

IAN. What do you mean? Why?

ZOEY opens the door. MCEVOY stands there with his bag clutched tight to his chest. Pulling VICTOR, she slips by MCEVOY at the threshold.

MCEVOY. Thank God. You're still here.

ZOEY. Move.

MCEVOY *steps into the room and ZOEY pulls the door shut as she and VICTOR exit.*

MCEVOY. What's going on?

IAN. They're...I don't know. Forget about them.

MCEVOY *steps toward IAN, removing a bundle of money from his bag and extending it towards him.*

MCEVOY. There. Sixty thousand. There it is. A significant portion of my retirement.

IAN. Your retirement. What a tragedy.

MCEVOY. Take it. Please, take it and give me the Kirchner. Where is it?

IAN [*knowingly*]. What's your rush?

MCEVOY. My *rush* is to, to complete this before we're—it's to part ways, both satisfied, and never have to see or speak to each other again—

IAN. I want you to look at something.

MCEVOY. Take the money. Let's be done with it.

IAN. Put your hand down. Look at this.

IAN *hands the laptop to MCEVOY. He looks at it, confused, then looks back at IAN. IAN gestures to read the screen.*

MCEVOY. I don't—

IAN. Read it.

MCEVOY. It says: "There is no internet connection. You can diagnose the problem by—"

IAN. Goddamn it fucking piece of—Okay, the internet is—This place *is* a shit hole. It worked earlier, and what was there was a *breaking* report. Published on the *Times* site early this morning. [*Pause*] You know what it said?

MCEVOY. What is it? Did they find something? The police? Are they—

IAN. No.

MCEVOY. Then, no. I don't know. What?

IAN. *Summun bonum.* E. L. Kirchner…Twenty-four million dollars. [*Pause*] Twenty-four *million*. And sixty thousand was some kind of outrageous demand.

MCEVOY. I—Yes, and do you know how highly subjective that number is? An artwork's monetary value is determined by comparing it to the artist's other—

IAN. Was it the most expensive one?

MCEVOY. What?

IAN. The Kirchner. Was it the most expensive of the lot in the crates?

MCEVOY. No. I don't know. That never—that doesn't matter to me.

IAN. But you knew. You're the curator, you know what / this thing—

MCEVOY. I knew only as much as anyone could about a piece that, that vanished from sight and memory! That was seen by so few before it disappeared.

IAN. You're telling me you had no idea. You knew all about the artist, the history of the painting but had no clue that it was worth a fortune?

MCEVOY. Well, no…I—

IAN. No?

MCEVOY. What, what it's worth is / not simply—

IAN. Did you fucking know?

MCEVOY. I *knew* only what my grandmother told me. [*Beat*]

IAN. What your?…What?

MCEVOY. I knew about how it was taken. How it was loved, then loathed then altogether lost! [*his voice rising; urgently*] It could have been ashes like so many others, but then by the most unlikely happenstance—a, a miracle, really—it is discovered unscathed.

IAN. What does your grandmother have to do with any of—

MCEVOY. It was hers, as a child in Dresden many years ago—

IAN. Jesus, you have / to be—

MCEVOY. No! Please, listen to me! She could describe it to the very brush stroke, as I asked her to so many times. To her, it was precious as it was, only as it was. It didn't need an appraisal, it didn't need prestige. It was innately beautiful.

IAN. I don't—that doesn't—

MCEVOY. Then the world changed. And the, the fascist machine churned and, and devoured all beauty and humanity within its expanding reach. The men operating the machine feared what that beauty could inspire, so they sought to extinguish it. Or they would use it, leverage it until it was sapped of its virtue. And if that is gone, what are we? Kirchner killed himself. The painting was seized, and my grandmother thought it gone forever, with so much else. [*Beat*]

IAN. Then how did it survive?

MCEVOY. By its own merits. A, an officer—some mid-ranking footnote kept it for himself. Hid it. With others. Was he an art lover, an opportunist, a soldier of fate? Who knows? But those pieces gathered dust in an attic in Austria for decades. And that is, to me, an unfathomable miracle.

IAN. Well, write a book.

IAN resumes packing his stuff.

MCEVOY. Ian, please. The painting is more than, than just pigment and canvas. It is blood. It is...It is feeling. It is hope and despair. It is humanity at its basest and its most glorious. It is Kirchner. It is refugees and prisoners and graves. It is my family. It is mine!

IAN. Why wasn't it returned to you? To your family? Isn't there some way that they, that historians or whoever can—

MCEVOY. These pieces in this exhibit, the, their provenance is undocumented, it's impossible to prove. They will show for a short time while their rightful ownership is contested, and then be auctioned off or, or traded to dignitaries in exchange for favors, stolen again!

IAN. Traded?

MCEVOY. To the rich. The powerful. It may yet be damned as spoils of war. That is why. That is *why* I had to get this exhibit, I had to find a way—

IAN. All right, listen, man—

MCEVOY. Why can't you understand this? The feeling of, of violation, the indignity of being robbed of something that is rightfully yours! The, the impulse to fight for what was taken from you before you ever had it!

Pause. This lands. IAN considers.

IAN [*almost sympathetic*]. You can't prove it though. That it's yours, I mean. Can you? You can't—

MCEVOY [*heated*]. No, no, regretfully, I can't. But justice and fairness failed this story a long time ago, so I won't wait for it. That painting belongs to me. I just needed someone, someone like you. Someone who could, who could—

IAN. Who could get it.

MCEVOY. Yes.

IAN. Without knowing what it was worth. [*Beat*]

MCEVOY. I...I, I am the rightful owner—

IAN. There is no *rightful* owner. There is no *right* to anything. Deep down, you knew that too.

MCEVOY. Meaning?

IAN. You thought you could use me—

MCEVOY. Use you? We, we had made an agreement. Did I need to tell you about World War II for you to know you wanted to make some money?

IAN. Sixty thousand—No, no twenty-five K when the target was worth millions!

MCEVOY. Sixty thousand for the, for, for your services. For your... access. For the act of, of acquiring it. Not for the painting itself. The painting is what *I* am after, not you, and sixty was the price that *you* named! That *you* insisted—

IAN. I had no idea what this was. Its history, its significance! What if I *had* known?

MCEVOY. Known what?

IAN. If I had known what it was. If I had happened to read a certain book about art in Germany. If I had happened to love expressionism or, or...But you looked at me, and you figured this was a safe bet. That twenty thousand dollars would be some kind of unimaginable fortune to me. So long as I had no idea about it.

MCEVOY. You still have no idea! You never will. To you it's a price tag, but you cannot quantify its beauty. And you'll never appreciate it for what it represents, and what it cost—beyond money—the artist who achieved it. You do not know who he was, what he endured. The hours of study and practice, of the pressure required to be the one to create it.

IAN. Okay, great, it's very pretty—

MCEVOY. It was a *gift*. A gift beyond dollar signs, beyond price. But it is lost on a society dominated by greed, driven by, by market exchange. Where one man's offering becomes another man's capital. So no, as long as you fixate over the price, you will never understand what is contained within every masterful stroke on that canvas.

IAN. Did I ask for a fucking art theory lesson? No, I think I asked why the fuck you / didn't tell me—

MCEVOY. And how it went from his hand to *yours* here in this stagnant motel room is an irony beyond your comprehension.

IAN. Beyond my comprehension?

MCEVOY. Yes, yes. Clearly, you have no clue what or, or how—

IAN. Shut up. Here's what I *do* understand. That fucking picture is worth more than anything I have ever touched before—

MCEVOY. It's just a number! / A meaningless—

IAN. It's not just a number to me.

MCEVOY. But still *just* a number. It could be one hundred billion, it could be zero! It's irrelevant. Money is the language we use, the crude word that was given to try to, to simplify, to measure something we cannot otherwise define!

IAN. Says the guy who walked in with an expendable sixty grand in hand.

MCEVOY. It may have fetched millions at auction had its chronicle been different, but money is no longer the currency by which this treasure changes hands. The painting isn't worth twenty-four million. It is priceless! *Priceless.* And if it is priceless, then it is also worthless...

IAN. What?

MCEVOY. You can't auction it, you can't advertise that you have it. You don't know who to look for to sell it illegally. It is now only worth what someone like me can give and what people like you can find.

IAN. People like—

MCEVOY. It won't be millions, I promise you.

IAN. *People like me* don't have the luxury of giving a shit about its history or its beauty or its sentimental value. And really, I don't give a shit about the number. You're right, it's more than that. Its weight on a scale, and its tipped in my favor.

MCEVOY. How? What, *what* can you possibly hope to—

IAN. Fucking something! I'll ransom it back to the insurance company. I'll bide my time, I'll get it to another country and, and find someone—

MCEVOY. That's madness! You don't understand the risks.

IAN. Of course I do! But I will do whatever I can. If you think *people like me* won't try, then you underestimate how desperate we are.

Again, MCEVOY offers the money to IAN, trying to push it into his hands.

MCEVOY. Desperate? Then take the money. Please! This is a lot of money, we can still both come away—

IAN. This is great. Proof of what I'm saying—

MCEVOY. Where is it? Show me!

IAN. Look at you! Look at the way you cower, you plead with me because you covet what I have.

MCEVOY. Does it please you? Do you enjoy it? This is the type of person you are. You take and take. What do you give? I, I *am* begging. I've been looking for that painting my whole life.

IAN. And if I *give*, then what? It hides in closet or a box the *rest* of your life. You hoard it, bury it. It disappears again. It ends! *I* can use it.

MCEVOY. So you will go to a, a black market? That's all you can—

IAN. It's all the black market! Whether its Wall Street, Main Street or a dark alleyway, it's all the same. Someone is trying to get above you!

MCEVOY. To some of us, there's more than that. I'm so sorry for you that you cannot see it—

IAN. Keep your pity, I can't use it—

MCEVOY. But, but some people transcend all that.

IAN. No, you were just born on top of it!...But all of this, that you think you are is nothing.

MCEVOY. No—

IAN. You are not what you feel inside. You are what people see, what people think you are worth.

MCEVOY. You are what you do! What you do. Nothing more. [*Pause*]

IAN. Well then. We're thieves. That's it. And you're a fool, because you thought you were a better one than me. [*Beat. Eyes locked with MCEVOY, IAN inhales deeply.*] There we go. I wanted to see the look in your eye when you realized that. Now we're done. [*IAN crosses to the door.*]

MCEVOY. No...No, no. I'm not leaving—

IAN yanks open the door.

MCEVOY. No. No, please. You have no idea how I worked! I, I begged to get this exhibit. How could I put a number on that? How can anyone—

IAN [*calling out the door*]. Zoey?

MCEVOY [*MCEVOY begins to move around the room, throwing open the bathroom door, pulling up the bed covers...*]. Where is it? Where is it?! [*MCEVOY moves around the room, frantic.*]

IAN. You're wasting your time.

MCEVOY. Where? Tell me where!

IAN. Stop. Listen to me.

MCEVOY. Where are you?

As he moves past him, IAN deftly catches hold of MCEVOY's arm, holding him on the spot. IAN pulls MCEVOY close, their faces inches apart.

IAN. It's gone. [*Beat*] Gone.

MCEVOY. It's not. [*Beat. MCEVOY desperately reads IAN's eyes.*] That's impossible.

IAN [*IAN speaks calmly, neither angry nor sympathetic*]. You thought I was some small-time sucker. That I had no idea what you were after. That it was just a handshake between you and me. It's been gone from the moment you gave me the number.

MCEVOY. No. No. How? What could you have possibly...

IAN. You saw it. You touched it. You got what you needed from it. And I got what I need. And on and on it'll go. And it endures.

Pause. Then IAN lets go of MCEVOY's arm. He makes a show of closing his laptop computer. MCEVOY is frozen on the spot. He can only shake his head. Finally, he finds what's left of his voice.

MCEVOY. I...Who did you...Is it safe? Will it be protected? Regarded with care? God, please, *please* tell me that it will—

IAN [*crossing to the door*]. Worth millions, yeah, sleep easy. Unless you go to the police. And then I promise you, all they'll find is a trail of ashes. [*calling out the door*] Zoey. [*IAN leaves the door open.*]

MCEVOY [*MCEVOY looks down at his empty, shaking hands. He withdraws the cloth gloves from his pocket, and stares at them. Despondent, he turns to the door. But he stops at the threshold and looks back at IAN. He cannot suppress the rage in his voice*]. I don't...understand a person like you. I only told you about a painting and you... you put this all in motion. Why? Why did you do this?

Beat. IAN genuinely ponders the answer. Finally, shrugging:

IAN. Dog will hunt.

With a last hard look, MCEVOY slowly exits, closing the door behind him. Pause. IAN looks up into the vanity mirror. His expression is impossible to read. The sound of three staccato beeps is heard on the other side of the door.

ZOEY [*behind the door*]. I swear to god!

The door bangs as she hits it from the other side. The three staccato beeps deny her again as IAN crosses the room and yanks the door open. ZOEY zips past him at a frantic pace, slapping VICTOR's phone into his hands as he stumbles in after her, leaving the door ajar. She pockets the key card and grabs her bag and starts stuffing her things back into it.

IAN. Zoey. Hey! Listen to me. I—

ZOEY. Get your shit, Victor.

VICTOR starts to gather empty bottles and trash.

IAN. Slow down!

ZOEY. What's he doing? He going to the police?

IAN. Who?

ZOEY. McEvoy.

IAN. No.

ZOEY. How can you know that?

IAN. What's wrong with you?

ZOEY. Vic! What are you doing? Stop with the garbage. Just get your stuff!

VICTOR is out of it. He moves slowly, continuing to hold the bottles.

IAN. Stop moving around!

ZOEY. So where's the painting?

IAN. Why?

ZOEY. You better find it quick.

IAN. Fuck does that mean?

ZOEY [*ZOEY goes to VICTOR and looks him in the eyes. Calmly, clearly*]. We don't need to clean. Forget this shit. Let's move.

She takes a bottle from him and tosses it. He drops the rest on the bed, not realizing that he dropped his phone with them. Moving faster, he goes to his bag and begins to stuff it.

IAN. Zoey, would you stop? Listen to me. I—

VICTOR's phone blings. Beat.

IAN. Why is your phone on?

VICTOR. We...

The energy has changed. IAN looks at ZOEY.

IAN. What did you do?

ZOEY goes to the window and looks out. She turns and looks at IAN. Beat. ZOEY darts to the phone. IAN does too, but he's a second behind her, and she has it only long enough to type two digits and hit send before IAN has wrestled it out of her hands. He looks at it, the screen illuminating his face as he breathes heavily.

IAN. Our room number. [*looking at ZOEY, slowly*] Who is it?...
Who the fuck is it?

ZOEY. Drug dealers. Gang members. A cartel. Whatever the fuck.
Low-lifes. The lowest of the low, and they're owed a lot of money
from us.

IAN. Us?

ZOEY. We made them the bargain of a lifetime. They know what
we have, where we are, and they're minutes away.

IAN. Why did you do this?

ZOEY. Like we were going to let you use us to—

IAN. I wasn't! I wasn't using you!

ZOEY. Oh, you had a whole plan, Ian. You always do! You were
gonna freeze us out—

IAN. You're stupid, Zoey! You are so stupid. You and your stupid
drunk brother have plunged us to the bottom in one stupid move!

ZOEY. Not us. Grab your shit, Victor.

IAN. You're not leaving!

*He goes toward ZOEY. VICTOR jumps up and clumsily grabs IAN,
turning him away from ZOEY. Quickly, IAN rips away from his grip
and shoves VICTOR hard. VICTOR stumbles to the ground. On his
knees, and on the verge of tears, he pleads.*

VICTOR. We gotta go, man! I'm telling you, these people—You
should leave, Ian. Leave the painting here and go, dude.

IAN. I'm not going anywhere.

VICTOR. I owed them money. I'm sorry. I thought I could pay
them. My back was against the wall.

IAN. They can take it up with you, you piece a shit!

ZOEY. Fuck him, Vic! Let's go!

VICTOR [*rising, going to IAN*]. I'm sorry, Ian! I wasn't trying to—I
swear! I, I was just—

*VICTOR is only inches from IAN. As he reaches out toward IAN, IAN
grabs him by the throat. Taken by surprise, VICTOR struggles against
him, and his flailing causes them to fall to the floor. VICTOR begins to
crawl away. On the floor next to IAN lies the crowbar, and he seizes it.*

Before he can do anything with it, ZOEY plunges into the scuffle, raising the empty beer bottle to strike.

ZOEY. Stop it! Leave him!

IAN drops the crowbar and catches her arm before it can fall. He pushes her toward the still open door.

IAN [*in her face*]. You want to leave me? Huh?

ZOEY. Let go of me!

VICTOR [*struggling to stand*]. Zoey!

IAN. Fine. Leave!

IAN shoves her out the door and slams it shut. ZOEY screams from behind it. VICTOR gets to his feet. IAN moves toward him, controlled, and picks up the crowbar. ZOEY screams and pounds the door.

IAN. Really Victor? You're in debt to a bunch of fucking thugs?

VICTOR. Please. Open the door.

IAN. She can wait out there 'til your guests arrive.

VICTOR. Jesus, Ian, this is over. Let's just get out of here before—

VICTOR tries to move past IAN to the door, but IAN is on him, hitting him hard in the stomach. VICTOR crumbles. Outside the door, ZOEY sounds like a trapped rat. The door handle twitches desperately, and then the sound of three staccato beeps.

ZOEY [O.S.]. Ian! Open the door! Let me in! Victor!

IAN drops down to the floor trying to get a hold of VICTOR. They struggle. The sound of incessant beeping continues as ZOEY desperately tries to unlock the door. Every beep is a denial. IAN gets VICTOR on his back, and straddles him. He pins VICTOR's right arm down with his left knee, and takes VICTOR by the throat with his left hand. VICTOR fights for breath, but he has little strength and dexterity remaining. The frantic beeping and screaming behind the door does not stop. His left hand still pinning VICTOR's throat, IAN raises the crowbar in his right hand. Then, slowly, he looks up, and takes in his reflection in the full-length mirror. They are lying right before it, framed perfectly. IAN studies the scene—not surprised by it, but rather, intrigued, as though he intended this struggle to take place before it. He admires the brutality of it. His grip tightens on the crowbar, his arm flexing, the look on his face intensifies as he gazes at it. Then he looks down at VICTOR, and sighs. He lets go of VICTOR's throat. VICTOR gasps, choking.

IAN. Oh Victor. You are the runt. What would this accomplish?

A single long beep is heard from the door as it bursts open. ZOEY flies into the room with the bottle raised high, and just as IAN turns to see her, she brings it down. With a sickening CLINK it connects with his skull, sending him to the ground. He crumbles into a heap, holding his head. ZOEY drops the bottle and goes to her knees beside VICTOR.

ZOEY. Vic, are you okay? Are you all right?

She holds him to her as he sobs. IAN groans, rolling over onto his back.

IAN. Oooh. I thought it would break. The goddamn bottle is supposed to break.

ZOEY. Well, this isn't a fucking movie. [*ZOEY raises herself up to check out the window. Then she helps VICTOR up.*] We're going. Get your stuff…No, leave the bottles!

VICTOR retrieves his bag.

ZOEY [to IAN]. Just give it to them, Ian. Because it doesn't matter. With a shit-load of money or none, you're the same. You're nothing. You're no one.

She drops the key card on the floor and she and VICTOR exit quickly, the door banging shut behind them. Pause. IAN takes a deep breath, and then rises slowly, still holding his head, blinking hard. He goes to the window, and looks out. He crosses to the bed and reveals a wide cut he's made in the top mattress. He pulls the garbage bag containing the Kirchner painting from inside. He gives it a glance, and then drops it on the bed. He moves to the mirror and looks at his forehead, checking the damage. Then he takes in the rest of his face. Disgusted, he jerks his eyes away.

IAN [*under his breath*]. Fuck.

He starts to gather his things, trying to move quickly. He throws his bag over his shoulder, and makes for the door. But before the mirror, he stops suddenly, holding still for a moment, thinking. His eyes turn to his reflection again, taking in his slumped, defeated figure, his cringing face, his dim eyes. And then slowly, methodically, he changes himself. He straightens, seeming to grow taller. His face becomes stern, confident, almost welcoming. His eyes alight, determined. He drinks in his new reflection.

IAN. This is what happens.

He turns and looks at the landscape painting above the bed. Quickly, with a glance out the window, he jumps on the bed and pulls the landscape off the wall. He grabs the garbage bag, and removes the priceless Kirchner painting, and places it carefully on the landscape's vacated hooks. He jumps down and looks at it, and then stuffs the boring landscape painting into the garbage bag. He sits down on the bed, facing the window with the landscape on his knees. It's unclear whether he's looking out the window or at himself reflected. The sound of a car pulling up outside. The lights slowly fade as the beams from the headlight of a car appear through the window, blasting IAN's face. He does not flinch or blink. Black out.

END OF PLAY

CHAPTER 3

THE TOWER.

An Introduction to *Children of Combs and Watch Chains* by the Playwright

One of the most beloved American short stories is O. Henry's (pen name of William Sydney Porter) "The Gift of the Magi." First published in 1905, the story features poor-but-devoted newlyweds Jim and Della expressing their love through selecting a gift for the other that requires something of a personal sacrifice: Jim purchases tortoise shell combs for Della by pawning his cherished pocket watch while Della purchases a gold watch chain for Jim by selling her luxurious hair to a wigmaker. I remember first reading this story in a collection entitled *One-Minute Christmas Stories*, compiled by Shari Lewis (Lamb Chop may have been involved as well, although uncredited). Reading the story as a child, I remember feeling frustrated by Jim and Della's situation. It seemed so unfair but was fascinating for me because it was the first time I'd read a story that didn't have a completely happy ending. As an adult, I'm able to see that, actually, their mutual love and willingness to sacrifice for each other is the true happy ending O. Henry intended but escaped me as a child. The idea of this personal sacrifice for the one you love and the realization that the sacrifice ultimately renders the gift useless by the recipient was the basis for my play, which I nod to in the selection of the items in the title "Combs" and "Watch Chains."

Risk theatre requires the playwright to consider the extremes of human experience and one of the most intense and primal desires that we have as a species is the desire for children. In *Children of Combs and Watch Chains*, my characters Jim and Della both wager something deeply personal and both attempt to keep this sacrifice secret from the other: Jim enters into the criminal underworld of human trafficking to purchase a child (sacrificing his safety, financial security, and personal moral code) while Della engages the services of a radical unlicensed fertility specialist (sacrificing her physical health and mental stability). Both Jim and Della believe that the sacrifice they are making is the *only* way to provide this ultimate happiness to their beloved. This desire is profoundly relatable for most people, especially anyone who has first-hand experience with the challenges of trying to conceive.

Society has placed a code of silence around the deeply personal struggle of infertility, which discourages people from candidly sharing their challenges. We still carry the pressure to not acknowledge infertility or pregnancy loss, as if such a thing could be contagious and the mere fact of speaking about it could bring misfortune to the pregnant or soon-to-be-pregnant. It feels medieval and irrational, but the fear persists and the desire to minimize the discomfort of those around us creates a self-fulfilling prophetic cycle. Feelings of isolation, shame, and paralyzing anxiety often accompany this experience and many suffer as a result. While this stigma is not nearly what it was ten or fifteen years ago, due to more people now being willing to share their experiences publicly, the pressure to keep quiet about infertility or the loss of a pregnancy can lead individuals to feel they are facing insurmountable odds alone. The events in the play take these emotions to their extreme upper limit, which allows us to observe from the relative safety of our theater seats and ask ourselves: "What would I do in this situation?" While few may readily say they would follow the same path as Jim and Della, the exercise of exploring the question for themselves and perhaps discovering empathetic understanding is the true strength of the theatrical form. It's why I love writing and seeing plays performed on stage, and if the global pandemic has taught us nothing else, it's shown us that there is something unique about being in the same physical space with strangers, experiencing the same live performance together.

My hope is that readers and audiences find the play an engaging exploration into the depths of human desires and the point at which the pursuit of those desires leads us into tragedy. An early reader of the play described it as "A Coen Brothers movie wrapped in a relationship drama with some body horror thrown in for fun" and, honestly, I don't mind that assessment. My goal is to continue the grand tradition of theatrical suspense dramas like *Wait Until Dark, Deathtrap,* or *The Perfect Crime,* and the structure of risk theatre is a brilliant foundation for creating the built-in source of tension. These plays are true thrillers rather than mysteries, and I believe modern audiences enjoy the thriller genre even more now than when some of those plays were originally written. Audiences delight in knowing things characters don't, and the dramatic irony of watching characters navigate situations where they have incomplete understanding is catnip for contemporary theatre goers. In a thriller, the audience is shown in no uncertain terms where the danger for the protagonist is and the journey within the play is in how the protagonist navigates the danger. In a mystery, both the protagonist and the audience are not sure where the threat is at any given moment. Audiences walk into a risk theatre tragedy knowing the outcome is likely to be bad; the trick is allowing the *how* to unfold in a way that draws them into the world and entices them to care about the characters enough to hope that maybe, just maybe, the soft-hearted playwright will take pity on them and allow the unlikely positive outcome to occur.

Alas, dear reader, I am not a soft-hearted playwright. Enjoy!

EMILY MCCLAIN

About Emily McClain

Emily McClain is a professional playwright and theatre educator living in Atlanta, Georgia. Emily is a proud member of Working Title Playwrights and the Dramatists Guild, and she is a founding member of Playwrights Thriving and Write Stuff Atlanta. She is an educational associate artist with Essential Theatre and has had the pleasure of serving as their playwriting instructor for the past year. She joins the faculty of the new School of the Arts at Central Gwinnett High School as their acting and playwriting instructor. Her play *Slaying Holofernes* was co-winner of Essential Theatre's New Play Festival and received a world premiere production in 2019. The Pumphouse Players held readings of *My Brother's Secret Keeper* and *Paradise, Stayed*. She was a featured playwright with Elephant Room Productions for her play *Cheek by Jowl*. *Cheek by Jowl* was also featured in Essential Theatre's Bare Essential Reading Series in October 2020. Her full-length comedy, *Julie's Place*, was selected for the JOOKMS Spotlight Series in July 2020 and later went on to be a semifinalist with the New American Voices with The Landing Theatre Company. Her tragedy, *Terminus Andronicus*, was a finalist at the American Shakespeare Center Shakespeare's New Contemporaries competition in 2019. Her risk theatre play, *Children of Combs and Watch Chains*, was named a finalist for the Risk Theatre Modern Tragedy Playwriting Competition in August 2020 and was produced by the Quarantine Players in February 2021. In March 2021, her one-act thriller, *Owl Creek*, was workshopped through Garage Theatre Ensemble. Her historical drama, *Copper Angel*, was performed as an audio drama by Borderless Theatre Company in April 2021. Rutgers University presented her one-act comedy, *180 Days*, in April 2021. Her short plays have been staged at many professional theatres across the country including Mississippi, California, Wisconsin, Indiana, Virginia, New York, and numerous venues in Georgia, with highlights including Snowdance Comedy Festival 2021 (*Tooth or Dare*–3rd place overall), Theatre Oxford (*Secret Family Recipes*–Festival Winner and Audience Choice), Raze the Space (*The Un-Help Desk*–Audience Choice), and Eden Prairie Players (*Ashes to Ashes*–Audience Choice). Emily is extremely grateful for workshop opportunities at Ethel Woolson Land and the Table Series through Working Title Playwrights. She is published through ArtAge, Smith Scripts, and the Next Stage Press. More of her work may be found on New Play Exchange: https://newplayexchange. org/users/27781/emily-mcclain.

Children of Combs and Watch Chains

by Emily McClain

Children of Combs and Watch Chains, a Risk Theatre Tragedy, was named a *Finalist* in the 2020 Risk Theatre Modern Tragedy Playwriting Competition by an international panel of jurors:
Kelli Fox (Canada)
Anthony Giardina (USA)
Anthea Williams (Australia / New Zealand)

Permissions Contact:
Emily McClain
emilymcclain234@gmail.com

Characters

DELLA YOUNG	40's, female
JIM YOUNG	40's, male, married to Della
POLLY AMANTE	30's, female, adoption counselor
ESTHER SALGADO	50's, female, fertility clinic nurse
TRICIA MCDONALD	30's, female
JAMIE BULLARD	50's, male

Setting

Various locations around Charlotte, North Carolina, USA, present day

SCENE ONE

Lights up on the office of the Charlotte Adoption Counseling facility, a particularly soul-sucking room with drab office furniture and sallow lighting. DELLA YOUNG and her husband JIM YOUNG are seated in two of the chairs. They have a few moments of awkward business, DELLA taking out her phone to check the time, JIM flipping through a magazine or checking his phone. They don't speak to each other. After a few moments of silence, DELLA stands.

DELLA. This is pointless. We should just go.

JIM. Sweetheart, please don't—we have an appointment and we need to speak to the woman. Even if things don't— [*He breaks off, changing tactics*] She might be able to help us look at other alternatives! And we don't know for sure what she's going to say—

DELLA [*overlapping*]. She's going to say our application was denied. Again.

JIM. We don't know that for sure. Okay? Please sit down.

DELLA [*allowing him to pull her gently back into the chair*]. This is just insane. We keep trying and trying and...I don't know why I thought this time would be any different.

JIM. I have a really good feeling about things this time. Our home visit went so well, even you thought it went well, remember?

DELLA. Yes.

JIM. And the doctor said you've been in total remission for two years, which is really close to being considered in full remission, which is practically cancer free. So we've got that going for us this time. And I got that bonus at my new job has put us in a much stronger financial position than the last time we applied so—

DELLA. I know.

JIM. So, I think the important thing here is to stay positive. I know that's asking a lot, given, well, everything.

DELLA. I'm so sorry, Jim.

JIM. What? Why are you sorry? Don't say that.

DELLA. I want us to have a baby. It's all I can think about, all we've been able to think about, for the last ten years. And the cancer, and fertility treatments, and everything…I just wanted it to work out this time.

JIM. Don't talk crazy. Of course it's going to work out. We are going to be amazing parents. We've got so much love to give and I know that no matter what happens—if we are able to have a baby that is biologically ours or if we're able to adopt or—we grab one left unattended for a moment at a bus station—

DELLA. Jim! Seriously, hush!

JIM. I'm kidding! [*loudly, looking around*] Kidding about the bus station, to any official that might be listening in! Totally kidding… [*He takes her hands, sincerely looking into her eyes*] Della, listen to me. We just need to trust that the adoption folks will approve us or this round of IVF treatments will take or the stars come into alignment and we open the door to find a baby in a basket on the porch—

DELLA. Ugh! Why do you have to make everything into a joke?

He doesn't answer but crosses to her and wraps her in his arms. The unspoken support and unwavering love between them is obvious. She softens against him, letting him hold her. It is a long embrace and she finally pulls away, looking at him.

JIM. It's you and me. Always, okay?

DELLA. Okay.

JIM. Okay. [*He kisses her cheek and walks her back to the office chairs. They settle back into their places when POLLY AMANTE enters with a thick file folder and her clipboard.*]

POLLY. Mr. and Mrs. Young?

JIM. Yes! That's us! We're here!

POLLY. Hello, how are you today? I'm Polly Amante, we spoke on the phone? So glad you could come in today. [*She crosses to them and shakes their hands. She is coolly efficient but not cold. She has bad news for them.*]

JIM. Well? Did you get the results of the home visit back? I think the social worker was very impressed by the set-up we have for the nursery and—

POLLY. Mr. Young, when you and your wife initially put in an application to be considered as adoptive parents, the agency had some concerns in terms of your respective ages and health issues—

JIM. We're in our 40s. Lots of people adopt children in their 40s.

DELLA. She means about the cancer, Jim.

POLLY. Yes. To put it plainly, it just doesn't seem right to place a child in an adoptive home where there is a significant risk for the death of one adoptive parent. It's a traumatic event that a child who has already lost both biological parents should be spared. Don't you agree?

JIM. Now wait—we submitted four years' worth of medical information. Della has been in remission for two years. Did you see that? How can she still be a risk? She's even continued to do the IVF treatments when her body was strong enough, between the chemo, and—I just don't understand how someone could think—

DELLA. How many years of full remission would it take to not be considered a health risk anymore?

POLLY. It will always be a part of the assessment, Mrs. Young. You're never *not* going to be a cancer survivor.

DELLA. So even if I go ten years without another incident, it would still be the thing that prevents us from adopting?

POLLY. Not necessarily. But there are a lot of factors that go into determining—

JIM [*overlapping*]. This can't be right! I thought surely—after the home visit? After all the forms and, and the MONEY! All the counselors and—

DELLA. Jim, calm down.

JIM. No this is ridiculous! We would be incredible parents to a child that needs them. Surely you can see that? Who the hell are you people to decide if someone is a health risk? Are you a doctor?

POLLY. Mr. Young, this is not a decision that I personally am making. I understand this information is disappointing but it's our agency's responsibility to do what is in the best interests of the children and it's the determination of the application board that you are not eligible at this time.

DELLA. Well. That's…That's it, then?

JIM. Wait, there's got to be something else we can do. Appeal the decision or—reapply in a year or—?

POLLY. Mr. Young, it's my personal recommendation that you and your wife, that you both maybe consider how…how you might enrich the lives of children or, or other people in your community without being "parents" in the traditional definition of the word.

JIM. I think you're completely out of line, Ms. Amante!

POLLY. My apologies. That wasn't my intention.

DELLA. We should go.

JIM. No, I want to speak to the supervisor or whoever made the determination that we were "unfit!"

DELLA. Please, don't. I want to go home.

JIM. I want that person to have to look in my face and tell me they think I'm not fit to be a father!

POLLY. Mr. Young, it doesn't work that way. Hundreds of couples apply to be adoptive parents every year and—

JIM. We have done everything the right way, every single step! And now you're telling me it wasn't enough? I just don't understand. We've tried everything. I thought for sure…I had such a good feeling—

DELLA. We need to go.

POLLY. Mrs. Young?

DELLA. Yes?

POLLY. I wish I had better news. I really do. I'm sorry.

DELLA. I know. It's not your fault. You're just doing your job.

She helps JIM stand and they exit together, DELLA supporting JIM as he moves numbly offstage. POLLY gathers up her papers and exits. Lights down.

SCENE TWO

Lights up on the exam room of Winchester Reproductive Health Services Center. ESTHER SALGADO enters with a tray of injection syringes prepped for the next appointment. She fusses with the arrangement for a moment and records the number in a patient chart. She exits and returns with DELLA dressed in a hospital robe.

DELLA. I missed seeing you last week!

ESTHER. Oh yes! Your last appointment must have been while I was on vacation. My husband and I went to Myrtle Beach.

DELLA. I bet that was nice!

ESTHER. It really was—a much needed break! I love just lying on the beach and reading. I don't hardly get in the water at all, really.

DELLA. I'm just like that too. I love the beach but I don't like the water, especially when I can't see the bottom.

ESTHER. Agree completely! [*DELLA settles onto the exam table, laying back.*] Your blood work indicated that you never had a strong window for implantation last month. Dr. Reilly adjusted the dosage for this month to hopefully increase that window. You haven't been experiencing spotting unexpectedly, have you?

DELLA. No. Nothing out of the ordinary.

ESTHER. How are you feeling?

DELLA [*brief pause*]. We...we got denied by the adoption agency last week.

ESTHER. Oh no! Oh, Mrs. Young, I'm so sorry to hear that. I'm so sorry.

DELLA. Thank you, Esther. It's...I think Jim took it much harder than I did. I was expecting it, I guess. But he is still devastated.

ESTHER. I understand. That poor man. I'm so sorry for both of you.

DELLA. I knew it was a long-shot...but now it's made me feel a lot more pressure to make this work. [*She gestures to the syringes.*]

ESTHER. You don't want to put yourself under additional pressure, Mrs. Young. There's plenty of evidence to suggest that extra stress makes implantation more difficult. It's important to try and stay calm and have a sense of...acceptance? If that makes sense?

DELLA. That's easier said than done. We've spent so much time and money, trying to have a baby, trying to get approved for adoption, trying, trying! I turned down a round of chemo during my first bout of cancer because I thought I *might* be pregnant!

ESTHER. Can I—Can I get you something? A drink of water or—?

DELLA. I think about that all the time! If I had gone through with the chemo, would the cancer not have come back the second time? Would they still have had a reason to deny our adoption application if I could have prevented the recurrence?

ESTHER. There's no way to know for sure—

DELLA. Every decision I make, I second-guess! I never make the right choice! I'm so sick of it! My entire life has been like that.

ESTHER brings a cup of water to DELLA and sits beside her, comforting her. The two women sit in silence for a moment. DELLA takes a sip of the water, calming down.

ESTHER. It's difficult to make sense of the chaos of life. I've seen so many women devote their entire lives to trying to have a child and they forget to live.

DELLA. That's not what I'm doing!

ESTHER. I didn't say it was. But you can't spend your life going back over every decision that you've made and wish that you'd chosen a different path, you know? That's no way to live either.

DELLA [*trying to hold back tears*]. I wish I could go back...I don't want to look back on things this time and wish that I'd done it differently. But I know in my heart this round of treatment isn't going to work either.

ESTHER. Oh no, Mrs. Young, please don't say things like that.

DELLA. No, it's true. I want to give up. Dr. Reilly doesn't really believe that increasing the dosage will change anything. I know he doesn't.

ESTHER [*carefully*]. Dr. Reilly is very...methodical. He looks at the numbers and makes adjustments based on that information. He wouldn't change your dosage if he didn't think it could have a positive impact.

DELLA. But I've done my research. I know the reality of what I'm up against.

ESTHER. It's moments like this that I encourage patients to try to find solace in a higher power.

DELLA. I'm not very religious.

ESTHER. I don't mean God, necessarily, although I personally find a lot of comfort in my church.

DELLA [*not unkindly*]. That's good for you. I'm glad you have something that helps—

ESTHER. But sometimes it's about trusting the forces in the universe to unfold for you—feeling open to the possibilities that solutions may lie outside of a normal...path?

DELLA. What do you mean?

ESTHER. I feel—okay, this is not something that I normally do, and I could get in a lot of trouble if Dr. Reilly found out—

DELLA. What?

ESTHER. I wouldn't suggest this to most women because there is a great amount of risk, but I feel so...compelled? I think God is trying to tell me to help you and I should listen...

DELLA. Esther, what on earth are you talking about?

ESTHER. There is a doctor in town who has helped women, women like you whose situations seemed...helpless. Hopeless. He doesn't have a practice anymore—He lost his license because some of his treatments are very experimental. He refused to follow the medical board's recommendations and he works, well, outside of traditional medicine now. But he cares about women, and it is his calling to help them become mothers.

DELLA. He sounds like a quack?

ESTHER [*insulted*]. Mrs. Young, I would never mention it if I thought he was dangerous.

DELLA. No, no, of course not. I'm sorry—that's not what I meant.

ESTHER. He has a success rate with high-risk cases like yours. Women who have struggled for years with infertility, with pregnancy post-cancer treatment, all sorts of tragic situations that he was able to bring a pregnancy to term. Those women have children—beautiful healthy babies! One woman had a set of triplets through his methods!

DELLA. What's the treatment?

ESTHER. It's drug-based. Daily pills and supplements. You test your blood yourself and when the numbers are right, you go to him for implantation of embryos.

DELLA. That sounds almost exactly like what Dr. Reilly does here.

ESTHER. Well, the drugs he prescribes are very strong. Much more intense than anything that is available under medical board approval. He has to import them from overseas. And he often has multiple drug regimens going on simultaneously so there can be some intense side effects. But most women feel it's a small price to pay—

DELLA [*interrupting*]. How do I get in touch with him?

ESTHER. I can give you his contact information. But you have to promise me that you won't mention my name or how you found out about him to anyone. Not your husband, not anyone! I could lose my nursing license!

DELLA. Esther, of course not. I won't say anything. I just—I'm ready to try something different. My current treatment isn't working and I—I can't look back on this as yet another opportunity I screwed up by being overly cautious. I need this. Please. You can trust me.

ESTHER [*looking up the number in her phone*]. I want all my patients to find the happiness they are seeking. That is my calling and why I got into this field in the first place. When I see women like you, I want to do everything I can to help. Here. [*She sets her cell phone on the exam table and DELLA types the number into her own phone. When she is finished, ESTHER picks her phone back up.*] Okay.

Let's get you set up for this round and then Dr. Reilly is going to come in and see you, okay?

She helps DELLA lay back on the exam table as the lights fade.

SCENE THREE

Lights up on a hotel bar. TRICIA MCDONALD is seated at a barstool, drinking a beer and waiting for someone. She checks her phone, then puts it in her purse and sips her drink. JIM enters cautiously, unsure of himself. He makes his way to the open barstool next to her and sits down. He is tentative and she smiles at him.

TRICIA. Hi there.

JIM. Hello…Umm…are you Tricia?

TRICIA. That's me. You must be Jim.

JIM. You don't look much like your picture.

TRICIA. It's an old picture. You don't look like your driver's license or passport picture either, if that makes you feel any better.

JIM. You looked up my passport picture?

TRICIA. Can't be too careful in this line of work. We want to know who we're dealing with right off the bat.

JIM. Oh…sure, sure. I get that.

TRICIA. You seem nervous. Are you okay?

JIM. Yeah—I just don't…I mean, I've never done anything like this before. I didn't even know what I was really…looking for? Or if such a thing even existed?

TRICIA. It's the internet age. If someone has thought of it, it exists for someone else to buy.

JIM. Even a baby?

TRICIA. Whoa my dude. Let's establish some ground rules before we go any further. Okay?

JIM. Oh—sorry, okay, sure.

TRICIA. Rule number one: open discussion of the terms of our agreement, should we come to such an agreement, is forbidden. Don't talk about it to your family, friends, or co-workers. As far as anyone else is concerned, you obtained the sought-after item through the standard channels. Period. The end.

JIM. Right. I understand.

TRICIA. My employer is well connected. Violation of this rule would be...problematic for you.

JIM. No, I understand. Scout's honor. Pinkie promise. Whatever.

TRICIA. Pinkie promise? What are you, eight?

JIM. Sorry. Lame joke.

TRICIA. Right. Okay, ground rule number two—

JIM. No more lame jokes.

TRICIA. Let's call that rule zero.

JIM. Right.

TRICIA. Rule number two: all transactions are in cash. No wire transfers. No credit cards. No cashier's checks. Cash only.

JIM. That makes sense.

TRICIA. This requires planning on your part—the amounts of cash we are talking about usually take a little bit of time to get together. You can't just walk up to your neighborhood ATM. However, in the course of checking your background, you were determined to be a viable candidate to manage this financial aspect of our arrangement. So. Well done, you.

JIM. You are very direct. I appreciate that.

TRICIA. I am discreet when I need to be. The final ground rule: when you get the call from me that your item is ready for pickup, you have to come immediately. This industry has a lot of risk, of course, but there is an incredible demand for the service. You aren't the only clients that I am talking to. And I don't always have a good read on when items become available. So when one does, you have to be ready to respond immediately. First come, first serve. Literally.

JIM. Do you...I mean, is it likely to be very soon? Because like you said, I'll need time to get the money together...

TRICIA [*checking her phone*]. I don't anticipate anything in the coming weeks. But your first payment is $50,000. Cash. You have my contact info and you can reach out when you get everything together. We can discuss a meeting location then.

JIM. First payment?

TRICIA. Yes. Three payments of $50,000 will get you in the pool of clients that are informed when an item becomes available. The last payment comes when the final exchange happens.

JIM. Ok…I mean…god. $200,000 total? That's…I mean, I knew we were talking about a lot of money but…

TRICIA. Jim, let me shoot straight with you for a second.

JIM. Ok—

TRICIA [*overlapping*]. When I was checking you out before setting up this meeting, my instincts said: "Don't bother with this guy. He's not prepared to take this step." I've been in this game a long time and I've seen a lot of people in your shoes. Turned down by the system, frustrated by biology and bureaucracy. Desperate for a solution. I'm offering you that solution. And you have the means to make it happen if you're willing to take the steps, but you might not have the constitution.

JIM. It's not that! This transaction would totally wipe us out. Between the cancer treatments and the IVF and the huge market downturn, our savings took a hit—

TRICIA. Of course, you've had a lot on your plate these past few years. Based on your current situation, I could understand if this is too much to take on right now. You're welcome to walk away, no questions asked. But this offer is a one-time thing—I don't have time to deal with people who can't make up their minds. If you say "no thanks" today, that's it.

JIM *stares at her, feeling torn and helpless. TRICIA watches him with a sense of professional distance, not trying to sway him one way or the other.*

JIM. When I think about everything that Della has suffered, how much she wants a ba—this item…I want more than anything in the world to make that happen for her.

TRICIA. You two have been through hell and back together. And I know you love your wife.

JIM. I do. I love her to the ends of the earth.

TRICIA. Then isn't $200,000 a small price to pay for bringing her the thing that will complete her happiness? And yours?

JIM. This is—I know this isn't exactly legal, is it?

TRICIA. Not in the strictest sense, no.

JIM. You're very casual about that.

TRICIA. I'm a broker. I help connect people who want to buy something with people who have something to sell. It's pretty straightforward.

JIM. Wow. That's weirdly blasé. How does one even get into this line of work?

TRICIA. Why do you ask? You looking to make a career transition?

JIM. What? No, no, just, uh, making conversation?

TRICIA. Huh. Feels like stalling to me. [*She shrugs, grinning at him*] What can I say? It's a family business.

JIM [*laughing louder than he means to*]. Ok, that's a good one!

TRICIA [*smiling*]. Thanks. Not everyone finds it funny when I say that.

JIM. No, it's great. Dark humor. Love it.

TRICIA. Yeah, you gotta laugh, right? I got into this business because I was already in another non-traditional brokerage market. This was a natural next step. But it's not for everyone. I've known a lot of folks, men mostly, who couldn't handle it.

JIM. Oh?

TRICIA. Yeah. There's a lot of raw human emotion that you have to confront. Occasionally dealing with desperate people on both ends of the transaction. It's too much for them. The guy I work with now though, he's great. My boss introduced us a few years ago and we've been a team ever since.

JIM. You look so young. How long have you been doing this?

TRICIA. Ten years.

JIM. How many—I mean, in that time, do you complete a lot of "transactions?"

TRICIA. Fifteen to twenty a year, on average.

JIM. Wow.

TRICIA. Yeah. I'm really lucky to be in a career where I have such a direct impact on people's happiness.

JIM. Right. I could see that. Fulfilling.

TRICIA. Yup. [*Pause*] So. Do we have a deal, Mr. Young?

JIM. I really have to make a decision right now?

TRICIA. Like I said, I don't have time to be involved with people who are back and forth on this. It's too risky. Either we enter into an agreement today or we don't and we part ways forever.

JIM. Ok.

TRICIA. Ok?

JIM. Yes. I want to move forward. I will be in touch when I have the first payment.

TRICIA. In cash.

JIM. Yes. $50,000. In cash.

TRICIA. Excellent. I look forward to hearing from you, Jim. [*She stands, shaking his hand firmly*] Pleasure doing business with you.

She exits and he exhales, sinking back into his barstool. Lights fade.

SCENE FOUR

Lights up on the living room of the YOUNG home. A modestly furnished room with a sofa and coffee table. DELLA is seated on the sofa, working on a laptop. JIM enters with two cups of coffee.

JIM. Good morning, sweetheart! How're you feeling?

DELLA. I'm good. [*taking the coffee*] Thanks. I didn't hear you come in last night.

JIM. Yeah, I had a meeting run late. I knew you were going to bed early so...

DELLA. Everything okay?

JIM. Yeah, yeah. Everything okay with you?

DELLA. Yes. Working from home today—everyone else in the office is in Phoenix so not much point in going in.

She turns her attention back to her work and JIM sits on the arm of the sofa, watching her. He almost speaks, then second-guesses himself. She interprets his discomfort as wanting to talk about the meeting at the adoption counselor and sighs heavily.

DELLA. Jim, I know you're still upset and angry about the adoption people. I wish you—

JIM [*overlapping*]. No, it's not—I mean, I am upset but—

DELLA. I know! And I am too, but we have to just let it go. We can't let it consume our lives. It's just…it wasn't meant to be.

JIM. I'm not ready to totally let go of the idea of having a child.

DELLA. I didn't say that! I'm not letting go of that idea either!

JIM. Okay, what are you "letting go of" then?

DELLA. I'm letting go of the idea that we are ever going to be able to adopt. That's clearly not in the cards. But we could still have a child ourselves.

JIM. Did something—did Dr. Reilly say things looked promising this month?

DELLA [*a long pause as she weighs her words carefully*]. It's… promising. Yes. I'm cautiously optimistic.

JIM. Really? Wait, what does that mean?

DELLA. I just have a good feeling. I'm a little more at ease, that's all.

JIM. I'm sorry I couldn't go with you to your last appointment. I wish I could have been there to hear what he said that's made you calmer.

DELLA. It wasn't anything Dr. Reilly said, exactly.

JIM. You seem more at peace about everything.

DELLA. I'm not like, totally Zen about it or anything but, yeah. I feel like I've got a plan and a path forward.

JIM [*carefully*]. Well, honey, I'm glad you feel that way. I think you're right—we have to be willing to let go of our preconceived version of what our path to becoming parents looks like.

DELLA. Right? I think that's been our problem all along. We were so stuck in a version of reality that only looked like one thing, we closed ourselves off to other opportunities. It had to be option A or option B. But we didn't consider—

JIM. Option Q?

DELLA [*laughing*]. I was going to say C, but sure. I guess we would be about at option Q at this point.

JIM. So what's changed? Did Dr. Reilly increase your dosage or change you to a different drug or—?

DELLA. Um, yes. It's a new drug. It's supposed to be more effective than what we've been doing in the past.

JIM. Oh! You didn't mention it to me?

DELLA. Well, it's...I mean, I didn't think you would know the difference, to be honest.

JIM. After all the research we've both done? What is it? Another HCG-style drug?

DELLA. It's not really on the traditional drug list.

JIM. What does that mean?

DELLA. It's new. Fairly new.

JIM. Like, how new? Is it experimental?

DELLA. Yes?

JIM. Are you in some kind of test group? Della! Did you sign up for some new drug?

DELLA. It's not like that Jim.

JIM. Wait, you can't just—you're taking a new, untested drug and you didn't think that was important news to share with me?

DELLA. I made an informed decision to try something that has not been totally approved by the medical board in America. But it's got a long track record of success in Europe and—yes. I decided to do it. Without talking to you about it. I'm sorry.

JIM. What are—I mean, have you looked at the risks? What are the side effects? How do you know if it's safe? I can't believe Dr. Reilly would suggest something like this— [*He looks at her, suddenly realizing*] Wait. Dr. Reilly isn't doing this, is he? Are you seeing another doctor?

DELLA. Look, I wanted to tell you but I just didn't want to risk getting your hopes up, especially after the last meeting with the adoption counselor. But I've been seeing another physician for two weeks. A doctor who specializes in very difficult cases like ours, and he's been really wonderful.

JIM. This is unbelievable! Why would you not say anything to me about changing doctors?

DELLA. I wasn't sure I was changing at first! I went to meet him and hear what he had to say and...he was convincing.

JIM. I'm so—I'm stunned that you would make a decision like this without consulting me!

DELLA. Jim, we're never going to be able to adopt and years of IVF and everything that Dr. Reilly has tried and none of it's worked! This feels different! Dr. Sturman is—

JIM. I don't like the idea of you putting your health on the line for some experimental treatment! You're not a guinea pig! Your body has been through so much already—

DELLA. Don't tell me what my body has been through! I'm *well* aware!

JIM. I'm sorry. You're right. I'm just so…I'm shocked you would take a step like this on your own. Della? Have you got all the information? Did this Dr. Herman—

DELLA. Sturman.

JIM. Whatever! Did he really tell you about the risks that are involved in being a test subject? And did he know about your full medical history as well?

DELLA. Of course he knows my medical history!

JIM. And where does an unlicensed infertility specialist even practice, anyway? A back alley? A basement?

DELLA. Stop it, Jim!

JIM. I'm serious! Where did you find out about this guy?

DELLA. That doesn't matter. I'm not telling you. I can't.

JIM. We've never kept secrets from each other before.

DELLA. What do you want me to do? Do you want me to stop the treatment? [*Long pause*]

JIM. Are you experiencing any side effects? Anything at all?

DELLA. It's still early but nothing so far. In fact, it's less painful than the stuff Dr. Reilly had me on so it's actually an improvement on that front.

JIM. And you promise that if something starts to feel off? Or if you feel like you're getting worse in any way, you'll stop? Okay? I know how badly you want to have a baby but I…I can't bear the thought of losing you. Promise me, Della. Please.

DELLA. I know my own body. I know when something feels wrong—and I feel fine. Okay? Please, trust me.

JIM. The thought of us having a child together…after all this time…Our baby…

DELLA. I know.

JIM *allows himself a moment of pleasure thinking about the possibility. DELLA, still cautious that he's upset, watches him for a moment before letting a smile burst across her face.*

JIM. I love you.

DELLA. I love you too. By this time next month, we'll be pregnant. I can feel it.

He embraces her as the lights fade.

SCENE FIVE

Lights up on the bar from Scene Three. TRICIA is seated on the same bar-stool from scene three, wearing a slightly different outfit. She is messing around on her phone when JIM comes in carrying a drawstring-style gym bag. He sits down next to her.

JIM. Okay. Here it is.

TRICIA. No hello? No small talk? "Hey Tricia, how's it hanging?" "Oh, I'm great, Jim, living the dream!" Man. You are no fun today!

JIM. I'm sorry. Carrying around this much money in cash makes me nauseous.

TRICIA. Nauseated. It makes you nauseated.

JIM. What?

TRICIA. The verb is nauseated. Carrying around fifty grand in cash will cause nausea. In some people.

JIM. Ok. Fine. Carrying around this much cash makes me nauseated. Keeping Della in the dark about this is also making me "nauseated." I spend the vast majority of my time recently feeling that way.

TRICIA. You still haven't told her? That's good, glad to hear that.

JIM. She's put herself under so much strain, I just—she would not understand this… [*He gestures to TRICIA and the gym bag vaguely*] this whole situation.

TRICIA. Well, [*she takes the bag and puts it in her oversized purse*] this completes your third installment. I've been impressed by both your promptness and your tenacity. My employer is impressed as well.

JIM. Yeah, well. I am going to have to work until I'm 97 to repay all the money I've "borrowed" from our retirement account.

TRICIA. Are you going to be able to get the last payment together?

JIM. How soon is a baby— [*He stops himself as she glares at him.*] Sorry—is an item going to become available sooner than you expected?

TRICIA. My employer has a line on something that could come available sooner. He likes you. I've informed him about your unique circumstances and he was very moved. His own wife died of ovarian cancer a few years ago, so he has a certain personal investment in seeing this transaction completed to everyone's satisfaction. A tribute to his late wife, her commitment to helping families, yada yada /

JIM [*overlapping*]. You told your boss about Della?

TRICIA. Yes. Is that a problem?

JIM. Uh. No. I guess not. I'm sorry about his wife.

TRICIA. I'll be sure to pass along your condolences. So. Let's get down to brass tacks here. Did you or Della have any preferences?

JIM. Sorry?

TRICIA. You know, preferences. Gender? Race? Hair color? Country of origin? Favorite sports teams?

JIM. No! No... [*Pause*] Well...I mean, isn't this where I'm supposed to say "Just healthy?" Right? That's what people always say when you ask them what they want?

TRICIA. People are liars. They always have preferences.

JIM. Okay. Well, I really do want just healthy.

She grins at him.

JIM. I do! Although, okay, gun to my head, I've always wanted a son.

TRICIA. See! Everyone has preferences.

JIM. You act like you've uncovered some deeply guarded secret. We all want things—you just don't always come right out and say it.

TRICIA. I find that life would be so much easier if people would just come right out and say what they want. Okay. So. If an item that lines up with your stated preferences becomes available, I will make sure you are among the first of my clients to receive the information.

JIM. Now wait, if a girl comes up first—

TRICIA [*holding her hand up to silence him*]. You wanna try that again?

JIM. I mean, if the other style of item becomes available first, I don't want to be left out of the loop. I want to be clear: I'm interested in the item itself. Either style.

TRICIA. I understand.

JIM. Okay.

TRICIA. Have you thought about how the endgame of this scenario plays out? Or you just gonna cross that bridge when you get to it?

JIM. I've thought about it, sure. Basically every minute of every day for the past five months.

TRICIA. And?

JIM. And what? I don't know what I'm going to do.

TRICIA. Well it's nice that you've given it some thought, at least.

JIM. It would be different if Della—

TRICIA. I know. I was sorry to hear about that. Truly, Jim.

JIM. She was so sure. We almost made it to ten weeks this time.

TRICIA. Did she stop going to see what's-his-face and go back to a normal doc?

JIM. Oh God no! Dr. Sturman is a genius! He is adjusting her treatment and this time her body won't reject the embryo. That's how he phrases it. Like...he thinks about it like an organ transplant that her body is not acclimating to properly.

TRICIA. Hm. Kind of makes sense to think about it that way, I guess.

JIM. Della is totally enamoured of this guy. If he told her to drink smoothies made of ground-up glass and rat poison, she would be chugging them down and posting on Instagram about her life changing journey!

TRICIA. Yikes.

JIM. Sorry. Sorry, I shouldn't say things like that.

TRICIA. Hey. Don't beat yourself up. You're under a lot of stress right now. It's a normal response.

JIM. Is it? Is any of this normal?

TRICIA. Okay, not in the traditional sense of the word, no. But in my experience, what you're feeling is standard. People handle stress in different ways, of course. But I'm sorry about Della. I wish there was something more I could do to help.

JIM. See if your boss would waive that final payment?

TRICIA. Yeah, not likely. His capacity for sympathy has a hard limit.

JIM. Right, I was just kidding.

TRICIA. Man. I hate hearing about this kind of stuff. Guys like this Sturman dude really grind my gears, you know?

JIM. What's the matter? Do they cut into your boss's bottom line?

TRICIA. Yuk it up, wise guy. No, I just can't stand these quacks with their snake oil and their promises. It's disgusting that they're taking advantage of desperate people—

JIM. People like Della.

TRICIA. Yeah.

JIM. Not to put too fine a point on things but—I'm also desperate. I'm here, basically in the same desperate boat. So…wouldn't that make you…?

TRICIA. I see the dots you're trying to connect, buster.

JIM. I wasn't really—

TRICIA [*good-naturedly plowing ahead*]. There is a key difference in our business models you're overlooking. I do not promise any "miracles." I don't say I can do something that I can't possibly deliver on. I deal in practicalities, in the here-and-now. I don't make people believe in the impossible, you know? False hope dealers—those assholes are the real monsters.

JIM. Yeah. I guess I see that.

TRICIA. So listen, if you wanted…I could ask around about this Dr. Sturman guy. I don't know of him myself, drugs are not my line, obviously, but you'd be surprised about the…community overlap. Someone might be able to give you some info if you wanted to…

JIM. To what?

TRICIA. I mean, if you are concerned that she is being hurt by this guy, we could look into other options—

JIM. Are you talking about…?

JIM makes a slashing motion across his throat and TRICIA cackles.

TRICIA. Oh my God, that's precious! No, no. I mean, if you wanted, but that option is kind of out of your current price range. But no, I was talking about maybe putting some pressure on him to decide that maybe he didn't want treat Della anymore…maybe if he decided it wasn't worth the risk of exposure for his business as a whole? You know? Something along those lines. A little less… [*She mimics his slashing motion but adds in a gagging, blood spurting sound effect.*]

JIM. I don't know…I mean, thank you for the offer, really. But I'm afraid that if she didn't have whatever snake oil Sturman is giving her, she might do something even more drastic. That's why—that's the main reason I've kept this going. If we can get a bab—if we can secure an item—

TRICIA. There you go! Getting better all the time!

JIM. —this way rather than watching her put herself through hell trying to get her body to maintain a pregnancy that it just…isn't made to do. She can let that go, you know? I'm afraid if I don't get this settled soon, she just won't stop until it kills her.

TRICIA. That's heavy.

JIM. Sorry.

TRICIA. You know your wife. I've never met the woman, but from everything you've told me she sounds like the type of person who commits fully. She sets her sights on something and she's like a bloodhound on the scent, right?

JIM. Basically.

TRICIA. Just spitballing here but, maybe she's afraid of who she'll be if she isn't trying her damndest to be a mother. She's survived so much, you know? Sacrificed so much? I know you want to be the one to make her happy.

JIM. That's it! That's all I want—and a little tiny part of me hopes that when I walk through the door, carrying our "item" that she will take it in her arms and finally feel peace. She can live a full life instead of this emotional purgatory she's put herself in.

TRICIA. That's beautiful…and a little messed up. But I hope that happens for you. I really do. You both deserve this happiness.

JIM. Yeah…

TRICIA [*after a brief pause*]. She's not going to react like that, though. You need to just prepare yourself. She's going to freak.

JIM. Wait, what?

TRICIA. Just saying. The type of woman that would visit an unlicensed fertility specialist and take experimental drugs is not the type of person to melt away into a cloud of powder and lullabies the minute you come home with your item. She's going to want answers.

JIM. So what do I say?

TRICIA. I couldn't begin to tell you. But understand that confidentiality remains a priority even after the conclusion of our last exchange. As much as my employer has been impressed by your expeditious and professional manner, he can utilize his more ruthless nature when necessary.

JIM. You've mentioned that—

TRICIA. This is a multimillion-dollar enterprise. He will protect it.

JIM. I understand. I will figure something out. It won't be an issue.

TRICIA. Glad to hear it!

JIM stands to go.

TRICIA. Hey! I wanted to tell you—I enjoyed getting to know you. I don't get to meet a lot of people that I'd like to hang out with outside of work. You're really funny. After things get settled with your transaction, you think you'd be interested in, like, grabbing a drink or going to catch a ball game or something? You ever been to the roller derby?

JIM. Um…I don't—I mean, maybe?

TRICIA. Ah, never mind. No, forget it! Forget I said that, sorry. [*She pauses, suddenly overcome with a sense of intense loneliness*] Okay. Thanks for the gym bag. I'll be in touch when things become available.

JIM. Okay. Thanks Tricia. I mean it.

He exits. Lights fade as she turns back to her phone.

SCENE SIX

Lights up on the exam room of Winchester Reproductive Health Services Center. ESTHER SALGADO is making some notes on a patient chart when there is a soft knock on the door. She opens it, surprised.

ESTHER. Yes? Can I help—oh! Mrs. Young!

She steps back as a very disheveled looking DELLA enters, carrying a large handbag. She is nervous.

DELLA. Esther! I'm so glad to see you—I was afraid everyone would be gone—

ESTHER. You caught me just as I was about to lock up. You didn't have an appointment, right?

DELLA. No, no. I—this isn't an official visit…

ESTHER. I was hoping, when I didn't hear from you in a few months, that—

DELLA. Yes! It's come so close. But I didn't stay pregnant—

ESTHER. Oh, Mrs. Young…I'm so sorry. Has Dr. S been—I mean, have you gotten in touch with him?

DELLA. Yes. He's wonderful, just like you said. I think he's working miracles. He just put me on a new regimen of drugs.

ESTHER. That's wonderful news!

DELLA. I am on the highest dosage he's willing to give me—and the combination of things has kept me very, well, it's a strain on my body.

ESTHER. Of course.

DELLA. I was—I feel terrible about admitting this—I haven't said anything to Jim yet about some of the side effects I've been experiencing recently.

ESTHER. Oh? Why not?

DELLA. I'm afraid he wouldn't understand. Or he'd try to talk me out of it. He's…well, he's cautious, you know? About medical things. He took my cancer diagnosis almost harder than I did, if that makes sense? But lately I've been having a harder time—coping—

ESTHER *nods, bringing DELLA into the exam room and letting her sit on the table. DELLA allows ESTHER to casually check her pulse, who seems to take note of her overall medical condition without concern—it is a medical professional and patient relationship she is familiar with. It's almost comforting to DELLA and she relaxes a little, continuing to talk.*

DELLA. My heart feels like it's racing all the time. Not sleeping like, at all. I can't even be in the same room with food smells—anything stronger than crackers makes me gag. I'm not sure what's in the latest round of drugs. I brought them [*she fishes around in her bag and brings out a handful of orange pill bottles*] and I was wondering if you—well, if you knew anything about these particular drugs. If there was something else I should be taking to alleviate side effects—

ESTHER. Did Dr. S not answer these questions?

DELLA. That is the one thing, and it's such a minor complaint, really, but he's not very forthcoming with details. He's old fashioned, in that way, I guess. He doesn't want me to concern myself with those things. He says my only concern should be "Bringing—

ESTHER [*overlapping, recognizing his motto*]. —"healthy life into the world!" Yes, I know he says that.

DELLA. Right, and I do trust his expertise of course, but…

ESTHER. It can take some getting used to. His methods are a little, yes, old-fashioned is a nice way to put it. He comes from a generation of doctors who had a very "Trust us, we're the degreed professionals" attitude. [*She takes one of the bottles and looks at the label.*] Hmm. Well, I don't read Russian but I think this might be a follicle stimulator, similar to Follistem or Gonal-F, like Dr. Reilly uses here in the office. But this one is obviously a little different. For one thing, the dosage is very high. How many milligrams did you say you were taking?

DELLA. 200. It's four of the pills a day.

ESTHER [*visibly surprised*]. Oh! Goodness. That's...well, if that's what Dr. S said to take, then he must have a reason. But that's an awful lot of the hormone for your body to process at one time. 200 mg a DAY? You're sure?

DELLA. Yes.

ESTHER. Have you had bleeding or cramping?

DELLA. Not too bad.

ESTHER. Well...make sure that you talk to Dr. S if that starts to happen regularly. You need to know this class of drugs is very powerful. Your body can get um, dependent on it? So you have to be very careful when you are scaling back—once you become pregnant.

DELLA. He didn't mention that. We haven't—I mean, I've been pretty intense about taking everything he suggested at the maximum level. He recommended that way.

ESTHER. Of course. [*Pause. ESTHER hands the bottle back to DELLA.*] Mrs. Young, may I say something that...might be a little out of line?

DELLA. Yes?

ESTHER. I think you should talk to your husband about what you're experiencing while on these drugs. Make sure that he is aware of what you're taking and why and the potential risks...but also the potential reward. You said you did have a successful implantation at least once already?

DELLA. Yes. I made it to ten weeks.

ESTHER. That's promising! The treatment is having a positive effect so perhaps next time—

DELLA. I appreciate what you're saying, Esther, and I don't think you were out of line to say it. But I'm not going to tell Jim. He is under a tremendous amount of strain at work, so many late nights, and I...I want to solve this problem on my own. Dr. Sturman is so supportive and we're so close to success! I hope my coming here doesn't make you think I don't trust him—

ESTHER. Of course not!

DELLA. —but you have to understand how Jim is. If he knew, then worrying about my health or the details of what's going on would consume his life.

ESTHER. I see.

DELLA. You still think I should tell him?

ESTHER. I do. You and your husband have been through so much—why do you think he'd stop supporting you now?

DELLA. If I told him what I was experiencing now, he'd pressure me to stop the treatment. He's terrified that I'm doing permanent harm to myself. But I'm so close, I know I am! I just need him to trust me when I say it will be worth it in the end.

ESTHER. You should give him a chance. I think he will surprise you.

DELLA. Maybe...

ESTHER [*taking her hands*]. Mrs. Young, I have a wonderful feeling about you and your husband. You will get the child you both desire so deeply. It will complete your happiness and you will know the joy of bringing a life into this world.

DELLA starts to cry, and ESTHER hugs her tightly.

DELLA. Thank you. Thank you. I—ugh, I'm sorry. I don't know what's wrong with me, bursting in on you like this. I need to let you go. Thank you for talking with me. You're right. I'll tell him. I feel—yes, that's the right thing to do.

ESTHER. God bless you, Della.

DELLA. You too, Esther.

DELLA gets down off of the exam table and exits. ESTHER watches her go, then pulls out her cellphone and searches for a number. She puts the phone to her ear and we hear faint ringing until an automated voicemail picks up.

ESTHER [*on phone*]. Dr. Sturman, it's Esther Salgado. Give me a call back as soon as you get this message. A mutual friend of ours is starting to exhibit early warning signs. You need to reach out to her and adjust her dosage. You know how to reach me.

She hangs up the phone, her face tight with worry. Lights fade.

INTERMISSION (IF DESIRED)

SCENE SEVEN

Lights up on the YOUNG family living room. DELLA is fitfully asleep on the sofa, wearing sweatpants and a t-shirt. She is wrapped in a blanket and her hair is up in a messy bun. She looks sickly, pale and weak. Her phone is on the coffee table, along with a cup of tea and an assortment of pill bottles in a Crown Royal bag. Her phone rings and she reaches out to see who it is. She lifts herself up enough to answer it, trying to rally and not sound as weak as she feels.

DELLA. Hello, Dr. Sturman! Yes, good morning to you too! [*Pause as she untwists the blanket from around her legs, struggling to sit up*] Umm, yes, feeling pretty good. No more—or, at least, very little nausea. [*Pause, reaching for the Crown Royal bag*] Wait, let me get my pills— [*She dumps the entire contents of the bag on the coffee table, sorting through the canisters quickly*] Yeah, okay...so you want to change from the Clomid three times daily to the...wait, repeat that please? Letrozole—200 mg? I don't think I have that dosage. [*She chases a pill bottle that rolled away*] But I thought—No. Of course. And the maca supplements? Okay. So changing that to the yellow dock root powder? Oh, both? [*She grimaces, setting the bottles up like little soldiers in a line in front of her*] No, that's fine. I just had terrible headaches last time—Right, I can definitely drink more water.

JIM enters, carrying his briefcase. He sees DELLA on the phone and rolls his eyes, inferring she is talking to Dr. Sturman. He exits through to the kitchen, then re-enters carrying another coffee cup. He sits down on the sofa as DELLA tries to get off the phone, anxious at being overheard.

JIM. Dell...seriously?

DELLA [*shushing him, then back to the phone call*]. Shh, Jim. Yes, Dr. Sturman, I'm still here. [*Pause*] Uh huh. Absolutely. I am tracking calories—1,200 a day. Definitely. I promise.

JIM. When! When was the last day you ate that much!

DELLA. Shh, Jim!

JIM [*referencing the collection of pill bottles*]. What are these, anyway? I've never heard of most of these drugs. [*He picks up a bottle as she tries to get it back from him*] Where are these even coming from? The writing on the bottle isn't in English, Della. Do you have any idea what you're taking?

DELLA [*covering the phone with her hand*]. Yes! I'm taking the pills that Dr. Sturman tells me to take! In the order that he tells me. Everything is looking really good for this month—

JIM. Everything but your health—God, even when you were going through chemo you looked—

DELLA. Do not finish that sentence.

JIM. This is nuts! I want you to stop taking all this stuff!

DELLA [*on the phone*]. Sorry about this, Dr. Sturman, what's the last thing? We have a rough connection. Hmm? Yes, okay, I—right, but doesn't that cause a difficult interaction between—No, no, I understand. [*She pauses, listening intently, hearing something she did not expect to hear*] Wait…really? Oh. Okay. I—yes. Okay. Yes. I won't. I understand.

JIM. What's he saying?

DELLA [*covering the phone again*]. Nothing—Jim don't!

JIM stands up, extremely frustrated and exits without another word. DELLA looks after him, then once she is sure he is out of earshot she continues.

DELLA. Dr. Sturman? I'm experiencing several intense side effects that I wanted to mention— [*She pauses, listening and nodding*] Right, of course. I'm tracking my dreams, journaling and all that. [*Pause*] No. Nothing like that. Should that be a concern? [*Pause*] No. I haven't had suicidal thoughts…I mean, more than the normal amount, right? Sorry. Sorry. That was a joke. Bad joke. My husband makes jokes like that and—No, of course. I get what you're saying about the importance of taking the regimen and following the dosages religiously. I didn't know it was that serious but I promise, I won't stop until you— [*She sighs, sweeping the bottles back into the Crown Royal bag and standing up slowly*] Of course. I can come in tomorrow. I'll have to see if Jim is able to drive me because I can't—yes,

I've had dizziness before so I won't drive myself. Yes. Yes. See you soon. Thank you, bye bye.

JIM reenters, bringing her a plate with apple slices and peanut butter on them.

JIM. Hey Dell. I'm sorry. I didn't mean to snap at you. Made you a snack.

DELLA. Oh. Thank you...I'm not really hungry though.

JIM. When was the last time you ate something? Don't say coffee.

DELLA. Last night. I'm just a little nauseous.

JIM. Nauseated.

DELLA. What?

JIM. Nothing. Never mind, forget it. Della, I'm so worried about you. All these different pills, this doctor—do you think it's possible that maybe he's not—that this isn't working out?

DELLA. What? No, don't say that!

JIM. Why? Are you worried he's going to overhear you?

DELLA. I made it to ten weeks! That's longer than any time before and I'm not giving up now. I trust Dr. Sturman and I need you to support me on this. We are so close, Jim!

JIM. Have you seen yourself? You don't sleep, you don't eat, you stumble around this house like a zombie and for what? To make it to ten weeks instead of five?

DELLA pulls back as if he struck her.

JIM. God, Della, I'm sorry. I'm so sorry, that wasn't—please—

She begins gathering up her pill bottles, shoving them back in the bag.

JIM. No, stop, I'm sorry! I'm sorry—I just can't stand watching you put yourself through this. I want you! I want my wife and I'm losing you...

She allows him to get close to her, to take the Crown Royal bag from her hands and set it on the coffee table.

JIM. You don't have to do this, okay? Please, sweetheart, I'm begging.

DELLA. Jim.

JIM. I'm so scared seeing you like this. I'm sorry.

DELLA. I know. I'm scared too, sometimes, okay? It's... normal? Right?

She considers telling him more but stops and just holds him close to her. They embrace for a long time, each considering their own secrets.

JIM. Will you just promise me that you'll be honest with me and with yourself? If things continue to get any worse—I mean it, Della, if anything else comes up or if he suggests another newer, different set of drugs or whatever—you'll stop. Okay? I can't go through life alone.

DELLA. I promise that if anything changes from what's happening now, I will tell Dr. Sturman I want to stop. I can do that.

JIM. Okay. Okay, good.

He goes to pick up the bag of pills from the coffee table but she reaches them first and clutches them to her chest.

DELLA. I'm going to bed—I think I'll be able to get some sleep tonight.

JIM. Do you want to take this? [*Gestures to the plate with apples and peanut butter. She shakes her head, her face registering disgust, but then she regains control and takes the plate.*]

DELLA. Yes. You're right. I need to eat something. Thank you.

She exits to the bedroom and he watches her, waiting for her to go out of earshot. He pulls out his cellphone and finds a number in his contacts. They answer on the second ring.

JIM [*hushed tone*]. Hey. I can't talk long but I need a favor. I'm getting the final payment together tonight—yes, all of it, don't worry, I'm handling it—but I have to close this transaction soon. I want to meet you for the drop-off tonight—I know you don't have one available now, but Della needs to stop what she's doing but she won't listen to reason so— [*Pause*] No, leave him out of it. I can't deal with that on top of anything else, okay? Look, I think if I can just finish what I started then she won't— [*Pause*] Really? Okay. God... That's—okay. Text me the address. Thank you. Yes. I can do that. Yes. Good-bye. [*He pockets the phone*] Hey! Della, I've got to run back to the office—Gary just called and he needs me to let him in, he left his laptop and keys there—I'll be right back! Love you, sweetheart!

JIM exits. Lights fade.

SCENE EIGHT

Lights up on a very dingy motel room. TRICIA is sitting on the edge of the bed next to an empty bassinet. She is wearing gym clothes and sneakers. She keeps checking her phone and is clearly agitated. JIM knocks offstage and she goes to let him in.

TRICIA. That was fast.

JIM. I want this to be over, okay? I need to get back to Della.

TRICIA. Hey, hey! Settle down, big fella. I have some really, really exciting news for you.

JIM [*noticing the bassinet, then that it's empty*]. Tricia, what's going on? Is that—Oh my God, really?

TRICIA. Should be here in a few minutes. You have your final deposit?

JIM hands her the duffle bag. She opens it and inspects the bundles quickly, expertly assessing their value by weight.

TRICIA. Okay. We're good. Are you ready?

JIM. This is it? Like, it's happening tonight?

TRICIA. You sounded so desperate on the phone just now and it hit me right in the feels, you know? I knew I had to help you both. I reached out to my colleague and he brought his client here and— [*She sends a quick text and sets her phone down on the bed.*] Now. You need to practice the story you're going to tell people. Get the details straight now. Come up with dates, locations, research agency names or hospitals in Texas or somewhere in the South.

JIM. Why the South?

TRICIA. More restrictive abortion laws lead to more babies being given up for adoption. Which is what happened in your case. You adopted this baby.

JIM. Right. Of course.

TRICIA. Practice it. Let me hear you say the words: "We adopted this baby…"

JIM. We adopted this baby.

TRICIA. "Through an agency."

JIM. Through an agency.

TRICIA. "In Arkansas."

JIM. I thought it was Texas?

TRICIA. Just messing with you. Texas.

JIM. But, like, where did it really come from?

TRICIA. We don't have to get into that right now. Have you told Della anything?

JIM. No. Nothing.

TRICIA. What did you tell her about where you were going tonight?

JIM. You have the money—when can I see the baby?

TRICIA. Let's not get ahead of ourselves, Jim. What are you planning to say to Della?

JIM. What difference does it make at that point? It's done!

TRICIA. It makes all the difference in the world. There are rules that you agreed to. This exchange happens only if you continue to abide by those rules.

JIM. How would you even know if I told her?

TRICIA. That's a really big move on your part, Jim. Think very carefully about what you say next.

JIM. What does that mean?

TRICIA [*picking up her phone, nonchalant*]. Your wife is still seeing Dr. Sturman? Still utilizing his treatments?

JIM. Y-yes...?

TRICIA. Dr. Sturman's suppliers are international. They have a carefully controlled pipeline of materials to come into the United States.

JIM. Yes. The labels look Russian? But what has that got to do with—

TRICIA. Has she discussed with you about the importance of tapering? With this particular group of drugs, it's very important not to go cold turkey. It can have really disastrous effects.

JIM. What?

TRICIA. Dr. Sturman has to scale down the drugs gradually or the withdrawal can kill. Surely she's mentioned that?

JIM. It hasn't come up.

TRICIA. Hm. Odd. Well, I'm not a marriage expert but it seems like something she would have mentioned.

JIM. I'm sure she will follow his directions exactly. She's very methodical about things like that.

TRICIA. Sure. But things sometimes happen that are outside of her control—or even Dr. Sturman's control. Things to upset a delicate supply chain of illegal pharmaceuticals. Things that could impair her ability to scale down appropriately.

JIM. Are you for real?

TRICIA. We know each other better than that, come on. Don't ask stupid questions. I'm just trying to stress the importance of your adherence to our agreement, that's all.

There is a knock offstage. TRICIA wiggles her eyebrows a la Groucho Marx at JIM and exits. She returns a few moments later with JAMIE, a tall, wiry older man holding a baby carrier, on her heels. He nods briefly to JIM and stands by the door, awaiting instructions from TRICIA.

JIM. Who's that?

TRICIA. This is my colleague I was telling you about. Jamie. Jamie, Jim.

JAMIE. Hey.

JIM. Okay...

TRICIA. Jamie helps with collection and he sometimes helps supervise exchanges. Great guy.

JAMIE. Thanks.

JAMIE kneels next to the baby carrier, watching TRICIA. She looks at him and he shakes his head meaningfully. JIM is transfixed by the baby in the carrier and doesn't pay a lot of attention to the following exchange.

TRICIA. Hm. Okay, that's not great news. [*to JAMIE*] How did you handle it?

JAMIE. Usual way.

TRICIA. Clean up?

JAMIE. When we're finished here.

TRICIA [*rolling her eyes*]. Seriously?

JAMIE. Not much. Won't take long.

JIM. May I...?

He holds his hands out to take the baby carrier. JAMIE looks at him, then to TRICIA. She nods and JAMIE hands over the baby carrier. JIM takes it and sits down on the bed, overcome as he looks at his son for the first time. The sound of baby whimpers becoming slightly louder cries emits from the baby carrier.

JIM. Do you have—I didn't think to bring any formula or bottle or—

JAMIE. Here you go. [*JAMIE hands JIM a newborn formula bottle with a screw-top nipple like they give you in the hospital.*]

JIM [*to the baby, unsure and awkward*]. Here you go, baby. Shhh... here you go...Uh, Tricia?

TRICIA. Yep?

JIM. How...um, how old is this baby?

TRICIA. Why do you ask?

JIM. He just—I mean, it is a "he" right?

TRICIA [*glances to JAMIE, who nods before she answers*]. Yes. Your stated preference, if I recall correctly.

JIM. Okay, great, right, how old is he?

TRICIA. Fairly new.

JIM. Fairly?

TRICIA. Like, brand new. Like...less than a day.

JIM. Where is his—I mean, what happened to his—

TRICIA. I don't know that we want to get into all that.

JIM. No, I want to know. [*JIM picks up the baby carrier and sets it on the bed next to him, holding the bottle for the baby to drink.*]

TRICIA. I told you at the bar. I'm a broker. I connect people who have something to sell with people who have money to buy.

JIM. She sold her baby?

TRICIA. That's, yeah, that's the easiest way to think about it.

JIM. What the hell does that mean? Is she okay? Did she want to give up her child?

TRICIA [*falsely chipper*]. Jim, I don't think you need to go down this road, okay? You've been under a tremendous amount of stress but now look! Look at that sweet little face! You're so good with him already!

JAMIE. Do you have a car seat?

JIM. What?

TRICIA. You didn't think to bring a car seat? Uh-oh! Dad of the Year here, folks!

JIM. Oh, no I didn't—what do I do?

TRICIA. I guess we'll have to take him back to his mother!

JIM. No!

TRICIA. Kidding! Totally kidding.

JIM. Can I see her?

JAMIE and TRICIA exchange a look. JAMIE doesn't move but TRICIA reads it loud and clear.

TRICIA. No. That's not a good idea.

JIM. Did she die giving birth?

JAMIE. Mr....

TRICIA [*helpfully*]. Young.

JAMIE. Young. Look, you really don't need to worry about her. She was a willing and eager participant in the whole process. But this was still a difficult decision for her and seeing you would be more painful. Surely you don't want that?

JIM. No, but I—I don't like this. What's going on with her? Why did she agree to—Is she in the motel now? Is she okay?

JAMIE [*with a glance to TRICIA*]. She agreed to the terms and was fairly compensated.

TRICIA. See? There you go. Straight from the horse's mouth. Everything cool?

JIM. That's—that didn't answer my question.

TRICIA. Yeah. Well, that's all you're going to get from us.

JIM. I hate the idea that I was...I caused this—

TRICIA. Oh, buck up, Jim. You are the reason this industry exists. Don't try to absolve yourself of any involvement now.

JAMIE. Mr. Young, this child's mother was in a really unique situation. But now she is happy and healthy and ready to start the next chapter of her life.

JIM. That's total bullshit, isn't it?

TRICIA. If it makes you feel better and you're able to walk out of here and feel good about what's happened—

JIM. How can I feel good? I am part of this seedy world that this poor woman—

TRICIA. Stop with the liberal guilt, Jim.

JIM. She's dead because you made her give birth in this shitty motel instead of a hospital?

JAMIE. These folks tend to avoid hospitals anyway—

TRICIA. Not now, Jamie.

JAMIE. You're right. Not helpful.

TRICIA. In any event, she was participating in a transaction, just like you are, with full faith and knowledge of the terms.

JIM. Did she give up her baby as payment for some debt?

TRICIA. Jim…

JIM. Just tell me. I need to know.

JAMIE. You really don't. It's best that you don't.

TRICIA. You need to trust us in all this, Jim. You need to listen to the experts, okay? Take your son. Name him. Tell people how you were able to adopt him and love him and how he's made your and Della's lives complete and you are happy beyond measure.

JIM. I…okay. You're right.

JAMIE and TRICIA are visibly relaxed at this admission. JIM prepares to leave.

JIM. I don't know what to do about the car seat situation—

JAMIE. Are you going far? In a pinch, the baby carrier can serve as a makeshift car seat for a short drive. But you're going to want a five-point harness, rear-facing car seat for your ultimate final purchase—

TRICIA. Jamie! We don't need a safety lecture. I'm sure Jim will get it all sorted out.

JIM. She's dead, isn't she?

There is a long pause. JIM stands, holding the baby carrier and watching them both. TRICIA and JAMIE exchange glances, then she groans.

TRICIA. What do you want from me, man? If I tell you the sordid details, you will just get all weird and wrapped up in your morality about it. And it will poison this [*gestures to the baby carrier*] and you have worked so hard—

JIM. No! Tricia, I—God—I don't know—

JAMIE. Tell yourself a safe story, Mr. Young. Please.

TRICIA. Listen to Jamie. He knows what he's talking about.

JIM. No. Tell me about her. The truth. Someday, my son will look at me and want to know and I want to be able to tell him…at least something that is close to the truth.

TRICIA. You can't tell him either.

JIM. Tricia.

He looks at her and she relents after a long pause.

TRICIA. Fine.

JAMIE. Tricia?

TRICIA. No, it's cool. [*To JIM*] She's originally from El Salvador. So you can tell him that, although it will probably be obvious that he has Central American origins anyway. She came to us last year.

JIM. Us?

TRICIA. My employer has wide and varied business interests.

JIM. Was she a prostitute?

TRICIA. Why would you assume that?

JIM. Sorry. Ok. She's from El Salvador. What's her name—her first name?

TRICIA [*looks to JAMIE and nods*]. Well?

JAMIE. Maria.

JIM. Seriously?

TRICIA [*overlapping*]. Very original.

JAMIE. Yes. Maria.

JIM. Okay. What did she look like—

TRICIA. Jim, this is—

JIM. No! I need to be able to tell him! I need to know!

JAMIE. Her name was Maria. She was 15. She was a victim of domestic abuse. She ran away and got mixed up with sex trafficking. She got away—with our employer's help, actually—but she couldn't keep this baby, so he was able to connect him with you, and she is glad her child will have a loving, stable home to grow up in. You can tell your son that, truthfully. She wanted him to have the best chance at the best life she could offer.

JIM. She wasn't coerced? She wasn't forced to give him away at gunpoint or anything?

TRICIA. God Jim! No! You make us sound like monsters.

JIM. No, no, sorry.

TRICIA. There. You happy? You have a nice story to be able to tell Jim Jr. when he's old enough to ask about it.

JIM. Yes.

TRICIA. Okay. Jamie, go ahead and start clean up, okay?

JAMIE nods and he goes past JIM to exit. JIM stops him, grabbing his arm with his free hand.

JIM. Look at me. You did everything you could to prevent her death? You offered to take her to a hospital and she refused?

TRICIA. Jamie—

JAMIE. Yes—she passed away from totally natural causes.

JIM. I don't believe you! You killed her? You killed her!

JAMIE. I'm not interested in getting into two clean-up situations, Tricia.

TRICIA. Yeah, well, neither am I! Jim, you need to stop this right now. Go. Go back to Della and you need to start this new chapter. Stop asking messy questions.

JIM [*setting the baby carrier down, the full weight of what's happened pressing down on him*]. Oh my God…Oh my God…Oh my God…

JAMIE. Tricia! This is spiraling.

TRICIA. Handling it, Jamie! [*to JIM*] Look, you need to get yourself together! Stop acting like you're some innocent victim and own the inevitable consequences of your decisions!

JIM. You know what this means to me! I'm saving Della's life with this child! I didn't know what else was at stake—

JAMIE. Tricia, maybe you should—

TRICIA. Okay, no, no, you're right. I spoke in anger. I'm just floored at this response from you. You're getting what you wanted!

JIM. I didn't want someone to die for me to have a son.

TRICIA. What did you think was going to happen? Someone would happily skip in, pop out a baby for you and Della, and exit stage left, never to be seen again?

JAMIE. Mr. Young, I think you should go. You should go back to your wife now. For your own safety.

TRICIA. Remember our agreement, Jim. Okay?

JIM. I know! I know!

TRICIA. I know you know. Have your story, and stick to it.

JIM. I know. I will.

JAMIE. Good luck, Mr. Young.

TRICIA. Did you name him yet?

JIM. What?

TRICIA. You should think of a name for him.

JAMIE [*there is a long pause before JAMIE offers helpfully*]. His mother called him Henry. That was his grandfather's name, apparently.

JIM. Fine. Henry. Yes. That's good. [*He takes the baby carrier off-stage, leaving TRICIA and JAMIE alone.*]

TRICIA. Ugh. Don't give me that look! Okay, not one of our smoothest transactions. Sorry about that. I got a little too invested. Too close. Won't happen again. Always room for improvement, right? *JAMIE shrugs.*

TRICIA. How bad is clean up?

JAMIE. Bad. Pretty bad. [*Shrugs*] 7 out of 10.

TRICIA. Lead the way, kemo sabe.

They exit. Lights fade.

SCENE NINE

Lights up on the YOUNG family living room. DELLA is in a very anxious state, checking her phone and sitting on the sofa, tense as she waits for any communication from JIM. She opens one of the many pill bottles that litter the coffee table, pouring some tablets into her hand. She counts them out, takes three and a long drink from the glass on the table. Her stomach cramps painfully and she doubles over, groaning. Her phone rings and she scrambles to answer it.

DELLA. Jim? Oh—Dr. Sturman, hello—no, I'm sorry I couldn't come, I left a message that my husband wasn't able to drive me and—no, I tried to but I was too afraid to get behind the wheel. [*Pause*] It's mainly the dizziness—yes, and some spotting. Nothing heavy but—Right. Yes, I've been drinking the red tea. Yes. I'm—I understand you're concerned but I don't know where my husband is right now and— [*She winces, lurching to a standing position*] Okay, I'll see if I can make it in to see you. No, I understand. No hospitals. I won't—yes, thank you, Dr. Sturman. I know. [*Pause*] Yes, I trust you. See you soon. [*She hangs up the phone, making her way unsteadily offstage. She comes back with her purse and car keys, stopping to kneel by the coffee table to gather up the pills and toss them into her purse. She white-knuckles her way back to standing, a recognition that she is having another miscarriage registers on her face. She is doubled over, the pain finally forcing her to the floor. She manages to get her phone from the table and dials JIM's number.*] Jim. Please pick up—goddamn it, pick up the phone! [*A brief sob escapes her lips as the voicemail picks up.*] Jim, I need to you to come home. It's an emergency…I can't get to Dr. Sturman and—I need to—please, whatever you're doing, it's got to wait. I need you. [*She hangs up the phone, groaning again and crawling back to pull herself up on the sofa where she curls into a fetal position.*]
Nothing changes for a long moment. DELLA may moan softly, unable to do anything to assuage her pain. After a minute, we hear a car door slam and JIM comes onstage, carrying the baby carrier.
JIM. Della! Della, are you awake?
DELLA. Jim…
JIM. Hey—oh my god, honey?
DELLA. Where have you been? Why didn't you answer your phone?
JIM. I couldn't—Della, I have—this is our son. Henry.
DELLA [*staring at him in complete disbelief*]. What the hell have you done?
JIM. What's going on? Do you need to go to the hospital or—?
DELLA. No! No hospitals. Tell me what you've done!

JIM. Please, Della, just try to understand—this is a solution to our problem and…he's so wonderful. Just look at him, please.

DELLA. What? No, no, no…

DELLA tries to get off the sofa to get away from JIM and not look at the baby in the baby carrier. JIM is dumbfounded.

JIM. Take it easy, don't— [*He crosses with the baby to sit on the sofa.*]

DELLA. Get away from me! I don't want it—I didn't ask for you to do this, Jim!

JIM. Please just look at him! Hold him for a moment, Della, he's ours and—

DELLA. No! He's not ours! You BOUGHT him! Like a washing machine!

JIM. How is what I did any different from us going to the adoption agency? I found an agency that wouldn't turn us down.

DELLA. Because—it's different! The people giving up their babies for adoption aren't victims of God only knows what kind of—Jim, what will we tell people who ask how we suddenly got a baby?

JIM. Okay, I have that part all worked out already.

He unbuckles the baby from the carrier but DELLA reacts viscerally, the cramping of the miscarriage she is still in the throes of as they are talking overwhelming her.

DELLA. I don't want to hold him! You need to take him back where he came from—this isn't how I wanted to have a child!

JIM. I can't take him back! That's insane! And besides, his mother died. There's nowhere for him to go.

DELLA. Did those criminals tell you she was dead? To make you feel better about what you were doing?

JIM. Why are you being this way? This is what we wanted—and I think I did the right thing! For us! You can stop trying, taking these crazy pills and killing yourself!

DELLA. HOW! How could you have kept something like this from me?

She finally is able to stand and JIM tries to reach out to her but she pushes him away.

DELLA. Don't touch me! Oh…

She doubles over, now the blood is visible on her clothes and she presses into it, trying to stem the worst of it. JIM cries out and she wavers as he catches her.

JIM. Della! Oh my god, Della—what's—we need to call 911!

DELLA. No no no—call Dr. Sturman—

JIM. I am not calling that lunatic! He's the one that did this to you—

DELLA. I can't go to a hospital!

JIM. Here, sit...

He leads her back to the sofa, blood soaking through, covering her hands.

DELLA. We can't call 911. Just take me to Dr. Sturman—

She swoons, losing consciousness from the pain. The baby starts to cry.

JIM. Della! No no no, please... [*The baby's crying becomes more pronounced and he picks the child up, cradling the newborn while he tries to find his cell phone.*] Shhhh, shhh, it's all right. It's all right. I will fix this—Shhh, Henry, just give me a second— [*He finds her phone and dials the number, rocking the baby who is still crying.*] Hello? Dr. Sturman? This is—no, shut up! This is Jim Young, Della's husband. We need you to come here and—No! You heard me! You. Come. Here! Della's bleeding and she won't let me call 911 because she said YOU told her not to! So you get your unlicensed ass over here— [*The baby cries louder*] What?! No! [*Pause*] Yes, that's a baby! It's none of your goddamn business! You get over here because— because I know people—if she dies, you will be held responsible, and I will make you pay for it.

He hangs up the phone, cradling the baby and kneeling next to DELLA, still unconscious. He manages to find a towel and presses it to DELLA, the blood getting on his hands. As he readjusts his position, he switches the baby to his other side, getting the blood all over the blanket wrapping around the baby. Lights fade as he begins to sob along with the baby.

SCENE TEN

Lights up on the adoption agency office from SCENE ONE. The office is closed. There is a long time where there is no action on the stage. Phone rings. No one picks it up. POLLY enters from the front of the office, followed closely by JIM carrying the baby carrier. He has changed shirts and put a new blanket around the baby.

POLLY. This is really—I mean, incredible—and highly irregular! I'm not sure I understand—

JIM. No, I know. But thank you for…talking with me on such short notice. [*The baby starts to cry. He sets the baby carrier down and rummages through a bag, producing a pre-made formula bottle. He lifts the baby from the baby carrier and proceeds to feed him throughout the following*] Look. I can't go into the details so please don't ask—but my wife…she passed away. I can't—the thought of raising a child, our child, on my own—

POLLY. I'm so sorry to hear that! Please, accept my condolences—

JIM. Yes, thank you.

POLLY. Was it complications from childbirth?

JIM. What? No. Well…Maybe.

POLLY. How long ago did she pass?

JIM. Ah—yesterday? [*He glances at his watch*] Yes. Yesterday.

POLLY. Oh my God! I'm so sorry! Mr. Young, you're very upset, which is totally understandable, but I'm not sure you're in the best place to be making these major life decisions. Is there a family member or friend I could try to reach for you—?

JIM. No there's no one. It was just me and Della.

POLLY. Your wife wanted this child so badly—I know it's hard to see this now, but try to think about the love that you both held for this child before he was born—

JIM. She didn't want *this* child—she never even held him.

POLLY. What? Where did this baby come from?

JIM. I can't tell you that.

POLLY [*suddenly understanding*]. Oh…Oh, Mr. Young…this is—I can't be a part of this.

JIM. I cannot raise this child—I'm not fit. The only possible thing I can do is to try to give Henry the best chance. You've got to know some family that could be that chance for him.

POLLY. This isn't how things are done, Mr. Young! We have policies and procedures to ensure that children—

JIM. What do I have to say? Do I have to say that I'm going to hurt him? Do you need to hear me to say something like that?

POLLY. You've gotten involved with very dangerous people. Are you being threatened now? [*She has a moment of panic*] Are they here? Were you followed here?

JIM. No! I am trying to— [*His voice catches and he struggles to maintain control over his emotions. He buys himself some time by putting the baby back in the carrier.*] All of this, everything, was for Della. I wanted to make her happy and I would move heaven and earth to give her what she wanted. I thought that's what I was doing. I have nothing left. All our savings, retirement, everything, I used all of it to pay for him. I can't afford to keep the lights on this month and I have this baby. But no Della. I can't bear to look at him. Please. I'm begging you to take him.

POLLY. You should have never—These people are monsters! This is a level of evil that you have willingly participated in and by coming here—

JIM. My wife is dead! She died taking some extreme, unregulated fertility treatment pushed on her by some quack! I didn't know the extent of it and now she's gone...it's my fault. This is all my fault.

POLLY [*POLLY sighs, exasperated. She crosses to him, looking at the baby in the baby carrier*]. My official recommendation is that you find the closest Safe Haven and drop the child off there. There's no criminal prosecution if the child is dropped off unharmed at a Safe Haven. He will go into emergency foster care and be adopted by a qualified and approved family soon. If I take him from you now, there will be too many questions that you don't need to answer—for all our sakes. Okay? Can you do that?

JIM. I don't know—

POLLY. You need to pull your head out of your ass and figure it out! They will kill you and resell this baby to the next highest bidder. Which could be another desperate family that would love him or to a wealthy person with unimaginably evil intentions. They don't care.

It's a business. Listen to me, Mr. Young, okay? Do you understand what I'm telling you?

JIM. Yes.

POLLY. Can you do what I said? Can you take him home tonight and go to a Safe Haven in the morning?

JIM. Yes.

POLLY. Good. Okay. [*Pause*] I'm very sorry about your wife. She was a good woman—I think she would have been a wonderful mother.

JIM. Yes. She would have.

He picks up the baby carrier, exiting. POLLY sits down on one of the waiting room chairs, shaken and sad. Lights fade.

SCENE ELEVEN

Lights up on the living room of the YOUNG home. DELLA's body is gone but the sofa is still a mess. Bloody towels where JIM attempted to clean up cover the sofa and coffee table. TRICIA and JAMIE are standing on either side of the room when the lights come up, surveying the damage.

JAMIE. Good lord, would you look at all this?

TRICIA. This is why you don't mess with unlicensed doctors, Jamie. This right here. God this pisses me off!

JAMIE. I know.

TRICIA. This poor woman trusted that idiot. God, poor Jim. [*TRICIA paces, her frustration bubbling out of her.*] I know there's a ton of money in the illegal pill racket, but I hate it! It's this kind of— I mean, look at this mess! She's…she's dead, don't you think?

JAMIE [*noncommittal*]. It looks like she lost a lot of blood…

TRICIA. Why didn't Jim put a stop to this? You know? He had a plan, the plan was working, why didn't he tell her she had to taper off the drugs? So stupid! Stupid! Stupid!

JAMIE. Hey!

TRICIA. What?!

JAMIE. You need to focus, Tricia. You got too invested, you said so yourself, but you know what's at stake here and you are a professional. Okay? [*She doesn't respond.*] Say it.

TRICIA. I'm a professional.

JAMIE. We're expected to… [*He waits for her to finish the sentence. She glares at him.*]

TRICIA. To handle the shit.

JAMIE. Exactly. Now. Where'd he go? We know no 911 or ambulance came here so…

TRICIA. My money's on a Safe Haven. You can drop kids off there, no questions asked.

JAMIE. There would be some questions.

TRICIA. I mean, not the kind of "get you in trouble" questions.

JAMIE. Okay but that's not "no questions." That's a few questions. There's still a risk we need to access.

TRICIA. Look, Mr. Literal, we don't have to—

The sound of a car pulling up stops further conversation. The car door opens and the sound of a baby's crying is heard offstage. Car door shuts. TRICIA motions to JAMIE to go off stage out of sight, and she perches on the arm of the sofa to avoid the worst of the mess. JIM enters, holding the baby carrier.

JIM [*almost dropping the baby carrier*]. Oh shit! What are you doing here? How'd you—

TRICIA. Hey! Calm down! It's okay, it's cool. Just a check-in. Just a follow up. Careful there, Dad. [*She takes the baby carrier from him and sets it on the coffee table. JIM is still speechless and terrified to see her in his home.*] So…looks like things got kind of crazy here… Is everything okay? I mean, clearly not…Did you take Della to the hospital? Is that where she is now?

JIM. No. She…she wouldn't let me call 911 and when Dr. Sturman got here she'd lost a lot of blood—

TRICIA [*overlapping*] Yeah, I see that—

JIM. —and I… [*The baby is still crying and JIM picks him up out of the baby carrier, rocking him gently. He is more comfortable with the action than he was before.*] How did you get in my house?

TRICIA. Not important. We need to talk. There's some concern that you're trying to abandon your fatherly responsibilities. Is that true?

JIM. She died on this sofa! Yesterday! I'm not—it was less than 24 hours ago! I can't take care of a baby on my own and—

TRICIA. I see.

JIM. Are you here to take him back?

TRICIA. We need to talk about some other things before we can get to that.

JIM. Are you going to sell him to some pedophile?

TRICIA. I don't know who you've been talking to but that's not the plan. More money in finding another family to adopt him. Plenty of desperate people around.

JIM. Am I able to get my money back?

TRICIA. You can't be serious right now. What happened to— [*Her voice catches*] where's her body?

JIM. Dr. Sturman took her away.

TRICIA. And you're worried about US being connected to shady people?

JIM. Don't, please.

TRICIA. Okay. Sorry. [*Pained pause*] God, Jim...You're really great with him. Are you sure you don't want to take a few more days, sleep on things? Before you make any rash decisions? I mean, you did pay $200,000 for the little guy.

JIM. This is completely insane.

TRICIA. Hey...I don't want to but I gotta ask. Did you say something to Dr. Sturman? About the baby? Where he came from?

JIM. No. We were a little busy trying to keep Della from dying to have a lot of chitchat.

TRICIA. Okay. I understand.

JIM. What else do you want me to say, Tricia? I need to change Henry and try to get him to sleep. I'm exhausted and— [*Everything bears down on him and he starts to weep. TRICIA is uncomfortable and she allows him to cry without speaking for a few moments. Finally, she sighs and sits down next to him on the sofa.*]

TRICIA. Do you want us to take him back? I can't give you your money back but I don't want you to suffer needlessly.

JIM. Can you promise me that he'll go to a good family?

TRICIA. Does that affect your decision?

JIM. I—of course! Christ, I'm not going to give him to you to hand over to some child predator.

TRICIA [*evenly*]. Do you think I'd let that happen?

JIM. After everything I've seen the past 48 hours, I'm not sure what anyone is capable of doing anymore. [*Pause*] Did your boss mess with Della's fertility drugs?

TRICIA. That was only on the table if you told her about us. To my knowledge, that didn't occur yet.

JIM. So her death…it wasn't because you thought I'd—

TRICIA. I'm impressed you think that we're as fast—acting as that, but no. We had nothing to do with your wife's death.

JIM. If I had told her, if I had said from the beginning what I was planning to do—do you think she would have stopped taking the drugs?

TRICIA. That's a catch-22 of a question, Jim-bo.

JIM [*Long, hard silence. JIM stares at the baby in his arms, his expression blank and unreadable*]. I want you to take him. I think… yes, that's the best thing.

TRICIA. All right. [*Calling offstage*] Jamie?

JAMIE emerges, JIM is shaken by his sudden presence.

JAMIE. Hello Mr. Young.

JIM. Where did you come from?

TRICIA. He came in with me. Didn't know for sure what we were going to be walking into over here so—he's good in a crisis, aren't you Jamie?

JAMIE. That's what I hear. I'm sorry about Mrs. Young.

JIM. Yes…I can't…

JAMIE [*expertly taking the baby from JIM's arms*]. I understand. [*to TRICIA*] I'm going to change him before we get back in the car.

TRICIA. Sounds good.

JAMIE exits back into the kitchen, carrying the baby. JIM watches him go, numb and empty.

TRICIA. I don't—Look, I'm not good with—goodbyes. Emotions. Whatnot. And to be honest, I'm a little afraid that you're going to blow your brains out when we leave.

JIM. No guns in the house.

TRICIA. Okay, cool. Guess everything's hunky-dory then!

JIM. What do you care if I do it? You got my money. You got the "item" back to resell. It's a big win-win for you and your asshole boss.

TRICIA. Yep. Everything's coming up my way. [*Her joke falls so flat.*] This is the opposite of what I wanted. I wanted you and Della to be happy—to have your perfect family! I wanted that as much as you did! This is breaking me, Jim. I can't—Ugh! [*She stands*] So you are going to...what? Sit in the garage with the car running? Rope over the rafter? Toaster in the bathtub? Not telling you how to live your life but taking a bunch of pills seems a little "On the nose."

JIM. I don't know what I'm going to do.

TRICIA. Well I'm not really an ideal advisor in this capacity.

JIM. I'm not asking for a how-to manual.

TRICIA. No, I know. [*She makes an awkward attempt at a side-hug, very uncomfortable with feeling guilty*] I'm sorry. I wish things had worked out.

JAMIE re-enters and puts the baby into the baby carrier while JIM and TRICIA watch silently. When he is finished, he stands up and goes to the exit but stops when TRICIA speaks.

TRICIA. Jim! Jim, this is final—you can't take it back, okay? So you are really, truly sure this is what you want to do? No take-backs! No redos! I think you're making a mistake.

JIM. No. I *made* a mistake. This is a correction.

TRICIA stares at him, then shrugs off the sudden display of emotion. She is crisp and businesslike again.

TRICIA. Okay.

JIM. Please make sure he goes to a good family. I'm begging you, Tricia.

TRICIA. I know. I will.

JIM. Say the words.

TRICIA. I promise. [*Pause*] I really do. Take care, Jim.

JIM. Okay. You too.

TRICIA and JAMIE exit, leaving JIM alone on the sofa. Lights fade.

END OF PLAY

O

THE FOOL .

PART II

The Risk
Theatre Essays

CHAPTER 4
Faces of Chance in Shakespeare's Tragedies: Othello's Handkerchief and Macbeth's Moving Grove

THE FOOL.

Playwrights explore chance in its many guises. To create a play, playwrights collide want, will, and intention with accident, chance, and fortune. In the no-man's land between accident and intention, drama arises. Where accident intensifies the protagonist's will, comedy results. Where accident eclipses the protagonist's will, tragedy results. Chance is a playwright's plaything because uncertainty, being unknown, is inherently dramatic.

In the tragedy *Othello*, Shakespeare explores chance by asking: "How high a degree of probability must one attain to have a sufficient basis for judgment?" Shakespeare sets the backdrop by crafting characters who are not what they seem. Their actions, reputations, and speech belie their being. When seeming and being are at odds, certainty goes out the window. Only the uncertain parts and probable fragments are left behind. In this world, there is no knowing, only thinking:

> IAGO. My lord, you **know** I love you.
> OTHELLO. I **think** thou dost. (3.3.119–20, emphasis
> added: Honigmann edition)[1]

The play follows Othello as he pieces together broken probabilities, looking for the chance event so convincing that it rules out every doubt. He looks for a tattered proof known as moral certainty.

In *Othello*, Shakespeare casts Othello as the star and makes chance the theme. The moving form of chance lies ancillary to the star: by chance the handkerchief drops but it is the star who decides whether there is a basis for action. In *Macbeth*, however, Shakespeare casts chance as the true star and makes the theme Macbeth's reaction to it. When chance brings Birnam Wood to Dunsinane Hill, it is a sign that the witches' prophecy has already taken place. All that is left is for Macbeth to react. Because chance is the prime mover, Shakespeare uses *Macbeth* to ask: "How do highly improbable events affect us?" To this end, he incorporates chance into the action through a series of low-probability, high-consequence events. By observing Macbeth's reaction to these improbable events, we see what happens when more things happen than what we thought would happen happens. In this essay, I will contrast Shakespeare's different approaches to chance by looking first at *Othello*, then at *Macbeth*.

Je Est Un Autre or "I is Another"

> Come on, come on, you are pictures out of doors,
> Bells in your parlours, wild-cats in your kitchens,
> Saints in your injuries, devils being offended,
> Players in your housewifery, and housewives in …
> Your beds! (2.1.109–13)

"Men should be what they seem," says Iago, "Or those that be not, would they might seem none" (3.3.129–30). But that is not the case here. By cleaving apart seeming and being, Shakespeare creates a setting to explore chance. In *Othello*—to take poet Arthur Rimbaud's memorable idea, *Je est un autre* ("I is another")—each character is also "another" (250). Appearances deceive. When characters seem to be such, but are, in reality, another, understanding and certainty become best guesses. By cleaving seeming and being, Shakespeare takes the audience into a world of probability, a world where there is a chance of being correct and a chance of being incorrect. In this indeterminate world, characters weigh probabilities, form plans "probal to thinking" (2.3.333), and search for moral certainty, the probability that is so high that, even though uncertain, is called by the name of certainty. The tragedy is that even moral certainty is less than certain. Like bells in the parlours or men who might seem none, moral certainty only seems to be the real thing.

Iago seems honest. His epithet is "Honest Iago." "Honest Iago," says Othello, "My Desdemona I must leave to thee" (1.3.295–96). Roderigo entrusts him with his wealth and fastens each hope to him (1.3.363–80). Desdemona confides in him (3.4.133–41). "I never knew," says Cassio, "A Florentine more kind and honest" (3.1.40–41).[2] Iago's seeming, however, belies his being. "I am not what I am," he says, "but seeming so" (1.1.59 and 64).

Desdemona seems dishonest. "I do beguile," she says, "The thing I am by seeming otherwise" (2.1.122–23). "Look to her, Moor, if thou has eyes to see," warns her father Brabantio, "She has deceived her father, and may thee" (1.3.293–94). "Swear thou art honest," demands Othello, "Heaven truly knows that thou art false as hell" (4.2.39–40). Her seeming, however, belies her being. She is a true heart.

Emilia seems bawdy. "She's a simple bawd," says Othello (4.2.20). In between Cassio's kiss and his suspicions of her infidelity, Iago remarks her services are for the common use:

> EMILIA. I have a thing for you.
> IAGO. You have a thing for me? it is a
> common thing—
> EMILIA. Ha? (3.3.305-07)

Though seen as a bawd who would sell great vice for a small price, she ends up buying virtue at the cost of her own life, at the last standing between Iago's maleficence, Othello's rage, and Desdemona's help-lessness, exposing the wickedness of both her husband and Othello. Not even Othello's sword can silence her virtue:

> EMILIA. Thou hast done a deed [*He threatens her with his sword.*]
> —I care not for thy sword, I'll make thee known
> Though I lost twenty lives. Help, help, ho,
> help! (5.2.160–62)

Her surface appearances belie her core values. By judging her by her surface appearances, Iago, who knew her best, seals his doom.

Othello seems a man for all seasons. The assembled Venetian senate regales him as "all-in-all sufficient," "a nature whom passion could not shake," and one whose virtue lay beyond "the shot of accident" (4.1.264–68). He is of such steadfast repute that, when Emilia inquires whether he is jealous, Desdemona replies: "Who, he? I think the sun where he was born / Drew all such humours from him" (3.4.30–31). His seeming, however, belies his being. In reality, he proves insufficient, full of passion, and most susceptible to accident and chance.

So too, in the play's macrocosm, the invading Turkish fleet seems sometimes smaller, sometimes larger. And, whether larger or smaller, sometimes it seems to bend for Rhodes, and sometimes for Cyprus. Its size and trajectory belie its intentions (1.3.1–45). Though the senate would rather act on certain – rather than probable – intelligence, because the enemy projects a false gaze more full of seeming than being, the senate must act on probabilities. So too, Othello, Roderigo, Desdemona, and the other characters looking on at the grand pageant must hazard the probability of being caught on the wrong side of seeming and being.

In this play populated by topsy-turvy *Je est un autre* types, Iago presses the confusion forwards. Iago is an obsequious go-getter. His primary weapon is dissimulation. To enrichen himself, he plays panderer to Roderigo, though he panders nothing. To rise up the chain of command, he devises a way to cashier Cassio, Othello's lieutenant.

He will persuade Othello that Cassio cuckolds him. To this end, he employs a series of strategies. When convenient, he spreads rumours that Cassio is having an affair with Desdemona, Othello's younger wife. He starts with Roderigo:

> IAGO. Lechery, by this hand: an index and obscure
> prologue to the history of lust and foul thoughts.
> They met so near with their lips that their breaths
> embraced together. Villainous thoughts, Roderigo:
> when these mutualities so marshal the way, hard
> at hand comes the master and main exercise,
> th'incorporate conclusion. (2.1.255–61)

and then moves to Othello:

> IAGO. I lay with Cassio lately
> And being troubled with a raging tooth
> I could not sleep. There are a kind of men
> So loose of soul that in their sleeps will mutter
> Their affairs—one of this kind is Cassio.
> In sleep I heard him say 'Sweet Desdemona,
> Let us be wary, let us hide our loves,'
> And then, sir, would he gripe and wring my hand,
> Cry 'O sweet creature!' and then kiss me hard
> As if he plucked up kisses by the roots
> That grew upon my lips, lay his leg o'er my thigh,
> And sigh, and kiss, and then cry 'Cursed fate
> That gave thee to the Moor!' (3.3.416–28)

If there is a kernel of truth Iago can explode into reckless speculation, he will do so:

> IAGO. She did deceive her father, marrying you,
> And when she seemed to shake, and fear your looks,
> She loved them most.
> OTHELLO.   And so she did.
> IAGO.   Why, go to, then:

She that so young could give out such a seeming
To seel her father's eyes up, close as oak—
He thought 'twas witchcraft. But I am much
to blame,
I humbly do beseech you of your pardon
For too much loving you.
OTHELLO. I am bound to thee for
ever. (3.3.209–17)

When all else fails, Iago practices psychological warfare. Through insinuation, he gets Othello to convince himself. Conclusions drawn when one convinces oneself root more firmly than persuaded proofs:

IAGO. Did Michael Cassio, when you wooed
my lady,
Know of your love?
OTHELLO.   He did, from first to last.
Why dost thou ask?
IAGO. But for a satisfaction of my thought,
No further harm.
OTHELLO.   Why of thy thought, Iago?
IAGO. I did not think he had been acquainted
with her.
OTHELLO. O, yes, and went between us very oft.
IAGO. Indeed?
OTHELLO. Indeed? Ay, indeed. Discern'st thou
aught in that?
Is he not honest?
IAGO. Honest, my lord?
OTHELLO. Honest? Ay, honest.
IAGO. My lord, for aught I know.
OTHELLO. What dost thou think?
IAGO. Think, my lord?
OTHELLO. Think, my lord! By heaven thou
echo'st me
As if there were some monster in thy thought

Too hideous to be shown. (3.3.94–111)

Despite the rumours, speculations, and insinuations, Othello sees, or believes he sees, Desdemona's true heart:

> OTHELLO. What sense had I of her stolen hours
> of lust?
> I saw't not, thought it not, it harmed not me,
> I slept the next night well, fed well, was free
> and merry;
> I found not Cassio's kisses on her lips. (3.3.341–44)

Beginning to suspect foul play, he retains enough good sense to demand proof from Iago, telling Iago to provide proof, or his life:

> OTHELLO. Villain, be sure thou prove my love
> a whore,
> Be sure of it, give me the ocular proof, [*Catching*
> *hold of him*]
> Or by the worth of man's eternal soul
> Thou hadst been better have been born a dog
> Than answer my waked wrath! (3.3.362–66)

Nothing improper has transpired, and, as a result, Iago has no proof, cannot come up with a proof. He reaches an aporia. But, in a twist of fate, chance provides Iago proof.

A Handkerchief, Spotted with Strawberries

Desdemona has on her person a handkerchief, spotted with strawberries. It is of an unusual provenance. Artifact-like, it was sewn by an ancient sibyl during moments of inspiration. Hallowed worms spun its threads and maidens' hearts stained its cloth. It was given to Othello's mother to charm his father, and damnation to her if she lost it. She, however, saw it in her safekeeping until she died, at which time she gave it to her son. He, in turn, gave the handkerchief, spotted with strawberries to Desdemona (3.4.57–77).

Halfway through the play, Desdemona takes out the kerchief to wrap Othello's head. He has a headache. It falls off. In their haste to meet dinner guests, they forget the napkin. Emilia, having been asked by her husband many times to steal it, chances upon it. She gives it to Iago, unaware of why he should want it (3.3.288–332). Through the accident of the dropped napkin, Iago has an opportunity to bolster his flagging argument.

Once he has the handkerchief, Iago can produce the wicked proofs required by Othello. He begins by planting the handkerchief in Cassio's bedroom. Next, he tells Othello he has seen Cassio wiping his beard with it. This, in turn, prompts Othello to ask Desdemona for the napkin. She cannot produce it, and, fatally misjudging the gravity of the situation, asks Othello to reinstate Cassio. This drives Othello into a huff, who is incredulous that Desdemona not only has the appetite for another man, but also has the appetite to demand from him his favour.

At this point, Othello is getting a bit run down. His epileptic attack as he visualizes the intertwined lovers is a physical analogue of his broken internal state. Even now, however, standing in his mellow-fading glory like a black Caesar, he demands proofs. As he recovers from the epileptic attack, Iago provides verbal and ocular proofs, one by cunning, and the other by another stroke of chance.

Iago arranges for Othello to overhear his conversation with Cassio. While getting Othello to believe he is questioning Cassio about Desdemona, he actually asks Cassio about Bianca, a strumpet overfond of Cassio. In hearing Cassio tell Iago of his extracurricular activities with Bianca, Othello believes Cassio refers to Desdemona. Then, in a second twist, as Othello eavesdrops, Bianca comes out of nowhere to rebuke Cassio. Cassio had found the handkerchief in his chamber, and, appreciating the design, had asked Bianca to make a copy. Bianca agreed, but, on second thought, believing the handkerchief to be a gift from a rival, now finds it beneath her dignity to do any such thing. That Bianca appears at this moment surprises Iago, who had planned many things, but not this godsend. When she rebukes Cassio, Othello draws the conclusion that, first of all,

Desdemona was in Cassio's chamber, and, second of all, Desdemona has given Cassio the handkerchief as a token of her affection. Though Bianca does not mention Desdemona, it is a short leap for Othello, a general accustomed to making snap judgements on the field of battle, to conclude that Cassio's hobby-horse is none other than Desdemona:

> BIANCA. Let the devil and his dam haunt you! What
> did you mean by that same handkerchief you gave
> me even now? I was a fine fool to take it—I must
> take out the work! A likely piece of work, that you
> should find it in your chamber and know not who
> left it there! This is some minx's token, and I must
> take out the work? There, give it your hobby-horse;
> wheresoever you had it, I'll take out no work on't!
> CASSIO. How now, my sweet Bianca, how now,
> how now?
> OTHELLO. By heaven, that should be my handker-
> chief! (4.1.147–56)

Who else but Desdemona could have left the napkin there? The scene with Bianca and Cassio convinces Othello. He resolves to kill them both. He has proof. Or so he thinks.

If Emilia had—as Iago requested—stolen the napkin, the tragedy would have taken on a more ominous tone: the sound of good and evil clashing. But that is not what happens. The sound of good and evil clashing is dull. Emilia, rather, finds the napkin by chance. Chance is more interesting. That she finds it by chance leaves the audience with a sense of wonder and awe: wonder at how impartial chance should have become Iago's partisan and awe over the extraordinary consequences that follow.

At one moment chance saves, sending a storm to drown the Turkish fleet. But in the next moment, chance casts down, putting the napkin into the wrong hands. Chance's fantastic nature makes it a wonderful dramatic pivot. Othello himself, a crack storyteller, engages chance to woo Desdemona by telling her the stories of "battles, sieges, fortunes," "most disastrous chances," and of "moving accidents by flood and field" (1.3.131–36). These accidents he lives to tell, but the tale of the dropped napkin another will tell.

Chance fascinates because every eventuality lies within its grasp, given enough time. But even given its myriad combinations and permutations, some eventualities are more probable, some, less so, and others implausible unto impossible. This feature of chance—that some probabilities are more likely and others less so—allows Othello to draw fatal proofs.

Five-Sigma Events, Significance Tests, Moral Certainty, and Iago's Gambit

In the character Othello, Shakespeare has created a sceptic to rival Sextus Empiricus. For Othello, it was not enough that Iago was the most honest of Venetians. Nor was it enough that Iago had stood shoulder to shoulder with him, comrades-in-arms on the front lines. It was not even enough that Desdemona's own father warned him to be wary. Othello, after all, had heard the wise Duke rebuking Brabantio for acting on circumstantial evidence:

> DUKE. To vouch this is no proof,
> Without more certain and more overt test
> Than these thin habits and poor likelihoods
> Of modern seeming do prefer against
> him. (1.3.107–10)

Othello will not be a brash Brabantio. He will demand a certain and more overt test:

> OTHELLO. Make me to see't, or at the least so prove it
> That the probation bear no hinge nor loop
> To hang a doubt on, or woe upon thy life!
> (3.3.367–69)

Now Iago is in a jam. Othello demands proof, or his life. Iago cannot make Othello see it, as there is nothing to see. Othello himself, likewise, is in a jam. He must judge a covert crime, and, having judged, kill. He can count on neither Desdemona nor Cassio to fess up: unchaste mouths must never name the things unchaste hearts cannot do without. When Iago proposes the test of the napkin, however, Othello has a path forward:

> IAGO. But if I give my wife a handkerchief—
> OTHELLO. What then?
> IAGO. Why, then 'tis hers, my lord, and being hers
> She may, I think, bestow't on any man.
> OTHELLO. She is protectress of her honour too:
> May she give that? (4.1.10–15)

In Iago's gambit, the napkin will stand in for her honour. Since Desdemona is honourable, the likelihood that she gives away the token of her honour is low. Because it would be an outlier event to see the napkin in the hands of another man, if it is seen, the likelihood is high that the observation is significant. The test of the napkin—coupled with both Iago and Brabantio's warnings—may constitute, therefore, a sort of proof that, while not absolute, demonstrates infidelity beyond a reasonable doubt. This probabilistic proof that "the probation bear no hinge nor loop / To hang a doubt on" is the best proof available in the indeterminate world of the play. The idea that random chance may—or may not—engender absolute truth is the powerful idea Shakespeare plays with.

Though it was not until 1668 that philosopher and mathematician Gottfried Wilhelm Leibniz formally associated probability with certainty by arguing that, given a sufficient probability, a degree of moral certainty could be achieved, it is clear that Shakespeare was already thinking along these lines in the opening years of the seventeenth century. Probability is in the air. Mathematician Jacob Bernoulli in the late seventeenth century would quantify these thresholds: something possessing 1/1000 a fraction of certainty (0.1%) would be morally impossible, whereas something possessing

999/1000 a portion of certainty (99.9%) would be morally certain. The standard is flexible. Modern statisticians use anywhere from one to five percent significance tests to establish certainty.[3] Different fields likewise require different levels of certainty. When physicists used a sensitivity of three sigma to validate discoveries (corresponding to a 99.7% chance that the result is real and not by the action of chance), they found that, because their work involved a multitude of data points, they would arrive at many discoveries which would be later proved spurious. Accordingly, when searching for the Higgs boson, they adapted a five-sigma threshold.[4] This threshold translates to a 99.99994% confidence level: the chance that the discovery is an anomaly is roughly 1 in 3.5 million. Even with a five-sigma sensitivity, however, the chance that the observation is a fluke and not the real thing remains. Moral certainty is a subjective and pragmatic standard. Too low a threshold results in false discoveries and too high a threshold results in no discoveries. The question is: does Othello achieve moral certainty and, if so, to what degree?

The first great critic of *Othello*, Thomas Rymer, found the proof of the handkerchief so implausible as to be risible. To Rymer, Othello was acting without any kind of certainty, let alone moral certainty. In 1693, he voiced his misgivings in a jingling couplet: "Before their Jealousie be Tragical, the proof may be Mathematical (132)." Everyone knows that Michael Cassio is the great arithmetician of the play, not Othello. Perhaps Othello had miscalculated the odds?

What Iago wants is for Othello to assemble all the information— the warning from Brabantio, the accusations from Iago, Cassio's frequent associations with Desdemona, Desdemona's importuning, and so on—so that the napkin "speaks against her **with** the other proofs" (3.3.444, emphasis added). Probability theory in the time of Shakespeare and Rymer was in its infancy. That is not to say, however, that Othello could not intuit conditional odds: that is, in effect, what he does. So too, without formal probability theory, Iago well knows that many less plausible proofs may add up into one great proof, saying: "This may help to thicken other proofs / That do demonstrate thinly" (3.3.432–33).

The formal calculation of conditional probabilities lay in the future. That future arrived in 1763 when Bayes' theorem was posthumously published. Thomas Bayes was a mathematician and Presbyterian minister. His contribution to probability theory was a formula to calculate conditional probabilities, a way to revise probability estimates as new information comes to light. With Bayes' theorem, it is possible to test Iago's hypothesis that many lesser proofs constitute one great proof. With Bayes' theorem, it is possible to test Rymer's couplet, to see whether Othello's proof be mathematical, and, if so, to what extent.

To determine the posterior probability—that is to say, the revised probability that Othello has been cuckolded after the test of the napkin—we require four probability values. The first two values are $P(C)$, the initial or prior probability that he has been cuckolded, and $P(\sim C)$, the initial or prior probability that he has not been cuckolded. Before Iago's gambit, Othello's opinion on whether he has been cuckolded appears evenly divided:

> OTHELLO. By the world,
> I think my wife be honest, and think she is not,
> I think that thou [Iago] art just, and think thou art
> not. (3.3.386–88)

Given what he says, we can assign a value of 0.50 (with 0 representing an impossibility and 1 representing a certainty) to $P(C)$ and a similar value, 0.50, to $P(\sim C)$. The odds he has been cuckolded are 50:50.

The third probability value is P(H | C), and it represents the chance that Cassio should have his handkerchief given that Othello has been cuckolded. The dialogue suggests Othello believes that, next to catching the lovers in the act, the test of the handkerchief is a great proof. The value of P(H | C), while not 1 (which is an absolute certainty), must approach 1: perhaps 0.90, representing a 90% chance, is reasonable.

The final probability value is $P(H \mid \sim C)$, and it represents the chance that Cassio should have his handkerchief given that Othello has not been cuckolded. Although Iago suggests true hearts give away telltale tokens all the time, Othello's reaction suggests he strongly disagrees. As a result, the likelihood of $P(H \mid \sim C)$ is quite low, having an order of magnitude of 0.01, or a 1% chance.

Here is what Bayes' theorem looks like when solving for $P(C \mid H)$ or the posterior probability that Othello is a cuckold, should he see his napkin with Cassio. The formula takes into account his initial, or prior belief, and revises it to take into account the test of the napkin:

$$P(C \mid H) = P(C) \times \frac{P(H \mid C)}{\{P(H \mid C) \times P(C)\} + \{P(H \mid \sim C) \times P(\sim C)\}}$$

Putting it all together yields this result:

$$0.989 = (0.50) \times \frac{0.90}{\{0.90 \times 0.50\} + \{0.01 \times 0.50\}}$$

Othello can be now 98.9% certain that he has been cuckolded. While this falls short of the five-sigma standard (99.99994%) used in high energy physics, its significance falls within the one to five percent tests used by modern statisticians. The napkin brings him to a point of moral certainty, the degree of probability one must attain to act. The jealousy was tragical because the proof was mathematical.

Is Othello correct to believe that he has caught the lovers in his mousetrap? That, I think, is the question Shakespeare invites us to ask. The answer—like many answers in the great plays—is fluid. Some may argue that $P(H \mid \sim C)$—the odds that Desdemona gives away the napkin and is true—is too low at 1%. People with the truest hearts, may, some of the time, give away treasured tokens as though trifles. Changing $P(H \mid \sim C)$ from 0.01 to 0.10 (from 1% to 10%) would decrease Othello's confidence level from 98.9% to 90%. There is now a 10% probability that what he sees is a pageant of chance rather than a proof of infidelity. Others, however, would argue that starting from a 50% prior probability of being a cuckold is egregiously low. Given the constant goings-on between Cassio and Desdemona as well as warnings from both Desdemona's father himself and the most honest person in the room, Othello's initial belief, or the prior probability $P(C)$, that he has been cuckolded should be much higher, perhaps closer to 80%. Now, even with $P(H \mid \sim C)$ at 0.10, Othello can still be 97.3% certain he is a cuckold. If $P(H \mid \sim C)$ stays at the original 0.01 and the prior probability Othello is cuckold rises from 50% to 80%, the posterior probability of being a cuckold after a positive napkin test rises to a confidence-inspiring 99.7%, equivalent to the three-sigma threshold used by physicists until rather recently.

By cleaving seeming and being in twain, Shakespeare invites the audience to explore probability and its ramifications. Would different ages, ethnicities, and sexes input different values into Bayes' theorem? How high a degree of confidence must we have to act? Those who contend Othello achieved moral certainty must also contend that, in the final examination, he was wrong. Those who contend Othello failed to achieve moral certainty would do well to wonder how yesterday and today's insurance, medical, and consumer safety industries—not to mention courts—often hang matters of life and death on less stringent significance tests. *Othello* makes us wonder: should graver actions demand higher levels of certainty? Not only that, it also makes us wonder if our interpretations of *Othello* reveal something about ourselves. Do we allow Othello to judge after receiving a tip from an honest source and catching the culprit in the mousetrap? And would these same people who say no to Othello allow Hamlet to judge after receiving a tip from a possibly dishonest (and diabolical) source and catching the culprit in another sort of a mousetrap?

The intersection between probability theory and theatre is one of the richest crossroads in interpretation today. Through a twist of chance, Shakespeare takes *Othello* from good to great: since chance is indeterminate, interpreters of the play will forever debate whether

Othello achieves moral certainty, and to what degree. *Othello* makes us think on the role of chance in theatre and in life.

In *Othello*, Othello stars and the theme is chance. Chance, represented by an errant napkin, provides the great pivot. A few years after *Othello*, chance was on Shakespeare's mind again, but this time, he gave chance the leading role.

Chance as a Low-Probability, High-Consequence Event in *Macbeth*

The true star of *Macbeth* is the low-probability, high-consequence event. And the true story of *Macbeth* is the hero's reaction to it. In this tragedy, a man is transformed by a series of low-probability, high-consequence events, in the beginning raised up by chance, and, in the end, cast down by the same power he hoped to harness. *Macbeth* is the story of how low-probability, high-consequence events encouraged a man to wager all-in, thinking that he was bound for glory, and of how the random element fooled him.

For the dreamers who believe that low-probability, high-consequence events could be tamed through progress, the play warns of evil's allure and the follies of ambition and confidence. For others, whose powers of recognition are clearer, and who perceive the random element working at each existential juncture in life and in history, the hypotheses of other-worldly powers, ambition, and confidence were redundant. To them, *Macbeth* tells an all-too-human story of how, because of our innate predilection to scorn chance, having always satisfied our intellectual biases by seeking any other explanation than one which involved the random element, we thought ourselves lords of chance and became, instead, the fools of chance.

The definition of a low-probability, high-consequence event is one in which, before it happens, is considered improbable. Sometimes the possibility it can even happen cannot be imagined, such is its remoteness. Examples include the Gutenberg Press, the rise of the personal computer, or the Gunpowder Plot. We can know that a low-probability, high-consequence action has occurred by watching the reactions. Sometimes, it prompts the one who has seen it to alert others. "From the spring," says the dying Captain, "whence comfort seemed to come / Discomfort swells: mark, King of Scotland, mark" (1.2.27–28: Clark and Mason edition). Other times it elicits disbelief. "Nothing is," says Macbeth, "but what is not" (1.3.144). Sometimes, one takes one's own life: this was the case of the "farmer that hanged / himself on th'expectation of plenty" (2.3.4–5). Having bet all-in on a bumper crop, when waylaid by the low-probability event, out of rent, out of food, and out of luck, he hangs himself. The danger these events present is that, though they were impossible to predict beforehand, after they happen, we retrospectively invent simplistic explanations of how they arose. In doing so, our sense of comfort is misguided, as we fail to give chance its due. This danger extends to the criticism of *Macbeth*.

In *Macbeth*, the action pivots around four low-probability, high-consequence events. The first is when, contrary to expectation, Macbeth becomes Thane of Cawdor. The second is when, against all hope, he becomes king. The third is when Birnam Wood, impossibly, comes to Dunsinane Hill. The last is when, beyond nature's permutations, he meets a man not of woman born. That each of these events will happen is foreshadowed by the Witches—Shakespeare's agents of improbability—to Macbeth. He, in turn, rejects each as being out of hand. By dramatizing the path from prediction to rejection to fulfillment, Shakespeare makes probability the play's true theme: what happens when more things happen than what we thought would happen happens?

To most people, the Witches are not agents of improbability, but rather supernatural agents. Like the oracles of old in Greek tragedies, the Witches would prophesy to Macbeth his fate, fate being the antinomy of chance and probability. But, the funny thing is, to dramatize fate—to bring fate onto the stage—fate had to be cast into the play as a random event that takes place against all odds. That such an event could have taken place against overwhelming odds is then *attributed back* onto the powerful action of fate. The feeling of surprise that a miracle has occurred is the proof that fate exists. But really, there was no fate, only the fulfilment of a low-probability, high-consequence event that the audience appreciates to represent fate. Fate in tragedy is a literary artifact, is probability dressed up as fate. In this way, *Macbeth,* by exploring fate, became a venue to explore the impact of the highly improbable. Wherever there is fate, there is also chance: the way fate manifests itself in literature is by overcoming the random element. At last, fate and chance are synonymous, two sides of the same coin.

Macbeth begins with Scotland in alarm. The first crisis sees the rebel Macdonald leading Irish soldiers into Forres. King Duncan sends in Macbeth and Banquo. But, in the act of dispatching Macdonald, a second crisis strikes. Seeing Scotland convulsed by civil war, Sweno, Norway's king, seizes the moment. He allies with another Scottish rebel, the Thane of Cawdor. With covert support from the thane and fresh Norwegian troops, they open a second front at Fife. Macbeth and Banquo remobilize to win the day. The opening action sets the scene for the first two of the four low-probability, high-consequence events.

After the battle, Macbeth and Banquo, on the road to Forres, encounter the Witches:

> MACBETH. Speak, if you can: what are you?
> 1 WITCH. All hail Macbeth, hail to thee, Thane of Glamis.
> 2 WITCH. All hail Macbeth, hail to thee, Thane of Cawdor.
> 3 WITCH. All hail Macbeth, that shalt be king hereafter. (1.3.47–50)

The first Witch accosts Macbeth by name and title. This draws his attention: when his father died, he had become Thane of Glamis. The second Witch teases him with a present tense pronouncement, calling him Thane of Cawdor. Macbeth finds this both disturbing and unlikely. The news that Duncan has executed the traitor and given his title to Macbeth is still in transit. Then, the third Witch goes in hook, line, and sinker, hailing Macbeth as tomorrow's king. Macbeth finds this impossible:

> MACBETH. Stay, you imperfect speakers, tell
> me more.
> By Finel's death, I know I am Thane of Glamis,
> But how of Cawdor? The Thane of Cawdor lives
> A prosperous gentleman: and to be king
> Stands not within the prospect of belief,
> No more than to be Cawdor. Say from whence
> You owe this strange intelligence, or why
> Upon this blasted heath you stop our way
> With such prophetic greeting? Speak, I charge
> you. (1.3.70–78)

The Witches vanish. At that moment, Angus and Ross enter. Acting as the mouthpiece of chance, Ross hails Macbeth the Thane of Cawdor:

> ANGUS. We are sent
> To give thee from our royal master thanks,
> Only to herald thee into his sight
> Not pay thee.
> ROSS. And for an earnest of a greater honour,
> He bade me, from him, call thee Thane of Cawdor:
> In which addition, hail most worthy thane,
> For it is thine.
> BANQUO. What, can the devil speak true?
> MACBETH. The Thane of Cawdor lives. Why do you
> dress me
> In borrowed robes?
> ANGUS. Who was the Thane lives yet,
> But under heavy judgement bears that life
> Which he deserves to lose.
> Whether he was combined with those of Norway,
> Or did line the rebel with hidden help
> And vantage, or that with both he laboured

In his country's wrack, I know not,
But treasons capital, confessed and proved,
Have overthrown him. (1.3.101–118)

Macbeth's surprise—"Why do you dress me in borrowed robes?"—relays to the audience the improbability of what is happening. Banquo too, stunned, says: "What, can devil speak true?" a little too loud.

As the true star of the show, not only do low-probability events change our perceptions of how many things there are in heaven and earth, they also change the plot's trajectory. Macbeth, previously fighting traitors, turns traitor. With the low-probability event, Shakespeare boldly pivots the trajectory of the play. The imperial theme begins.

Shakespeare's Swans

Part of the good interpreter's task is to sound out yesterday's iambs on today's instruments. For yesterday's plays to jingle and jangle to modern ears, new approaches are required, approaches which resonate with today's preoccupations. Today, there is a preoccupation with low-probability, high-consequence events: 9/11, the Great Recession, the fall of the Berlin Wall, Deepwater Horizon, and other events give us reason to reflect on how nothing is impossible, once it happens. In the last decade, a new term has arisen to describe these events: today, we call them "black swans."

The term "black swan" comes from Roman antiquity, and its journey to the present day has been itself swan buffeted. In the beginning, it meant something entirely different. The Roman poet Juvenal coined the term in the *Satires* where he likened a wife, perfect in all her virtues, to "a rare bird on this earth, exactly like a black swan" (6.165). Since it was believed that the perfect wife does not exist, the black swan became a byword for the impossible. This was the term's first meaning.

In 1697, European explorers sighted black swans off the coast of Australia. With one sighting, the improbable overcame the probable and a belief system—that all swans are white—fell. As a result, the term was orphaned. In 1843, however, John Stuart Mill reinvented it. In *A System of Logic*, Mill transformed the term from an expression of impossibility (which it could no longer denote) into a visual representation of the power of the unexpected (379). In Mill, the black swan is the empiricists' bogeyman. It symbolizes the philosophers' horror of how one observation can wreck any number of inferences based on any number of observations made over any immemorial period of time. In philosophical circles, the black swan came to symbolize the danger of formulating general principles from particular observations, otherwise known as the problem of induction. Another swan event, however, was required for the term to enter the public consciousness.

In 2007, mathematician, options trader, and philosopher Nassim Nicholas Taleb released *The Black Swan*. He argued that Wall Street's risk management models, far from containing risk, exacerbated risk and endangered the financial system. Being rooted in the idea of past as prologue, these models gave traders false assurances that they could wager all-in: every swan will be white and events progress forwards, inexorably, quiescently, in a predictable steady state. But, if history were a punctuated equilibrium and arrived in fits and starts like ketchup out a glass bottle, full of revolution, a world of hurt awaits. Taking the cue from Mill, Taleb called these unforeseen, unexpected, and catastrophic events black swans. Mainstream financial pundits, busy riding the boom, disregarded Taleb, whom they regarded as an eccentric voice crying out in the wilderness. But, without warning, the Great Recession broke out in 2008 to break each one of the world's oldest and most decorated financial institutions. The timing of Taleb's book—having come out the previous year— seemed prescient.

Though experts disavowed that such a catastrophe could be ascribed to as fleeting a notion as chance, Taleb's ideas were backed by a badass image (a sinister swan) and hardcore math (attacking the venerable bell curve). When the media suggested that the Great Recession could be understood as a swan event, a low-probability, high-consequence event precipitated by, of all things, chance, a firestorm of controversy ensued. It was at this time that the term "black swan" to denote the impact of the highly improbable entered the popular consciousness.

Before there was Taleb, there was Shakespeare. Only *Macbeth* was not taken as a warning of the highly improbable, but rather, a warning of the dangers of confidence, ambition, and evil. Perhaps that was because people did not associate Shakespeare with probability theory, which, having been recently founded in the sixteenth century, was still in its infancy. Shakespeare, however, grasped with his playwright's intuition the inordinate impact of the highly improbable. Consider his use of the improbable elsewhere to generate fantastic outcomes: Desdemona, in *Othello*, dropping the handkerchief, spotted with strawberries, or the letter-carrier, in *Romeo and Juliet*, being caught in the wrong house at the wrong time. Hamlet's injunction to Horatio—"There are more things in heaven and earth, / Than are dreamt of in your philosophy"—also warns of the impact of the highly improbable (*Hamlet* 1.5.167–68: Thompson and Taylor edition). Shakespeare's tragedies are full of curious improbabilities and now, when they are all the rage, is the time to talk about Shakespeare's swans.

The Imperial Theme

Shakespeare's understanding of the highly improbable and its dramatic applications can be illustrated through Macbeth's interaction with Angus and Ross. Macbeth's question: "Why do you dress me / In borrowed robes?" is spoken from the viewpoint of his initial reality. In this reality, Duncan is his cousin and king. He will lay his life on the line fighting foreign kings and native rebels to defend this reality. In this reality, all swans are white. But the moment Angus and Ross confirm the second Witch's pronouncement, Macbeth sights the black swan. A new reality opens, one in which he is king. It is the improbable that draws him to the existential fulcrum. In this reality, having seen the swan, he knows the impossible is possible. The plot pivots into the imperial theme.

Finding himself, unexpectedly, Thane of Cawdor, Macbeth muses: "Glamis and Thane of Cawdor: / The greatest is behind" (1.3.118–19). The greatest that lies behind is to be king. Not only have the Witches prophesied thus, but Ross, in his fruitfully ambiguous phrase that the new thaneship is "an earnest of greater honour," intimates that Macbeth could be named heir apparent, a declaration consonant with the system of tanistry used in medieval Scotland where the crown, not yet bound by primogeniture, would revolve between collateral branches of the leading families.

Why would the greatest lie behind? We perceive the past, not the future, as that which lies behind. "Leave the past behind," we say. We perceive the future as that which lies ahead. "Look to the future," we say. The future is something we see approaching. Our expressions reflect our biases. Since we fear uncertainty, we disarm it by putting it in plain view. To highlight the role of the unexpected, Shakespeare turns convention on its head by placing the future behind, rather than before Macbeth. The future now steals up to Macbeth with the result that, when it catches him, it takes him by surprise. The image highlights the elusiveness of chance: not only does it lie in the future, sometimes we cannot even see it coming.

The improbable event has so unseated Macbeth that he allows himself to consider murder. But the thought of murder is so abhorrent to his previous beliefs that his hair stands on end and his heart knocks against his chest (1.3.137–44). His last recourse to preserve his previous reality is, ironically, to trust chance: "If chance will have me king, why chance may crown me, / Without my stir" (1.3.146–47). As soon as he considers it, however, Duncan names his son heir. Crushed by having the prospect of the crown presented and ripped away, Macbeth moves further towards murder with his "Stars, hide your fires" soliloquy (1.4.50). Within a day, Duncan will be dead, clearing the path for Macbeth to be invested at Scone. The imperial theme is complete.

The Engine of Suspense

After the first two swan events take place, two remain: Birnam Wood and the man not of woman born. When Macbeth faces his first setbacks, he seeks a fresh start and goes back to where it all began. He will seek the Witches. All they presaged has come to pass. They said he is Thane of Cawdor, and it was confirmed. They said he will be king, and he became king. They said Fleance would found the Stuart line, and Fleance proved hard to kill.

To show Macbeth the path forward, the Witches conjure three Apparitions. The first Apparition tells Macbeth to beware Macduff. Even without the Apparition, Macbeth knew Macduff would be trouble: Macduff had declined to attend both the coronation and the state dinner. The second and third Apparitions prove more helpful, setting in motion the last two low-probability, high-consequence events:

> 2 APPARITION. Be bloody, bold and resolute: laugh
> to scorn
> The power of man, for none of woman born
> Shall harm Macbeth. *Descends.*
> MACBETH. Then live, Macduff: what need I fear
> of thee?
> But yet I'll make assurance double sure,
> And take a bond of fate: thou shalt not live,
> That I may tell pale-hearted fear it lies
> And sleep in spite of thunder. *Thunder*
> [*Enter*]: *a child crowned, with a tree in his hand.*
> What is this,
> That rises like the issue of a king
> And wears upon his baby-brow the round
> And top of sovereignty?
> ALL.   Listen, but speak not to't.
> 3 APPARITION. Be lion-mettled, proud, and take
> no care

Who chafes, who frets, or where conspirers are.
Macbeth shall never vanquished be, until
Great Birnam Wood to high Dunsinane Hill
Shall come against him. *Descend*[*s*].
MACBETH.   That will never be.
Who can impress the forest, bid the tree
Unfix his earth-bound root? Sweet bodements, good.
Rebellious dead, rise never till the Wood
Of Birnam rise, and our high-placed Macbeth
Shall live the lease of nature, pay his breath
To time, and mortal custom. (4.1.78–99)

Like the prospects of becoming thane and king, Macbeth finds the
likelihood of either eventuality so low as to approach nil. His courage
swells with apodictic certainty:

MACBETH. Bring me no more reports, let them
fly all;
Till Birnam Wood remove to Dunsinane,
I cannot taint with fear. What's the boy Malcolm?
Was he not born of woman? (5.3.1–4)

Exactly as Hecate predicts, Macbeth, consumed by certainty, begins
reciting the Apparitions' words like a novel mantra:

HECATE. He shall spurn fate, scorn death, and bear
His hopes 'bove wisdom, grace and fear;
And you all know, security
Is mortals' chiefest enemy. (3.5.30–4)

He repeats it to the Doctor: "I will not be afraid of death and bane,"
he says, "Till Birnam forest come to Dunsinane" (5.3.59–60). "Thou
wast born of woman," he says, gloating over Young Siward's corpse
(5.7.12). He is becoming chance's fool.

   In addition to all the functions mentioned earlier—driving the
action forwards, exploding and reshaping worldviews, and pivoting
the plot—black swan events also fire drama's engine of suspense.

They are part of a metatheatrical game played between dramatists and audiences.

A funny thing is that low-probability events, while low-probability to the characters (who are invariably blindsided by them), are, from the audience's perspective, high-probability events. When the second Apparition tells Macbeth that "none of woman born / Shall harm Macbeth," Macbeth understands that, chances are, it will not happen. The audience, however, is of the opposing belief. They understand that a man not of woman born will certainly strike Macbeth down.

Similarly, when the third Apparition tells Macbeth that "until / Great Birnam Wood to Dunsinane Hill / Shall come against him," Macbeth understands that, chances are, it will not happen. The audience, however, is of another belief. They understand that, like a Houdini or a David Copperfield—Shakespeare will wow them by pulling off the impossible in plain sight. The moment the Apparitions speak, the theatregoers start trying to figure out how Shakespeare will accomplish the impossible. On the one hand, the playwright telegraphs cues to the audience, and, on the other hand, the audience tries to figure out these cues. This metatheatrical game between playwrights and audiences is drama's engine of suspense. With a few cues, the dramatist stokes the fires of a thousand imaginations.

When the Apparition tells Macbeth that he will never be vanquished until Birnam Wood comes to Dunsinane Hill, Shakespeare is telegraphing to the theatregoers that it will happen. Since it is not immediately obvious how Shakespeare can accomplish this, the theatregoers try to figure it out. As they try to figure it out, they feel the thrill of suspense. "Am I on the right track?" thinks one. "This is how he will do it," thinks another. In these thoughts is the magic of suspense, and its magic increases with improbability. To bring about a probable event only requires the skills of a probable dramatist. To bring about the improbable event requires the skills of a most improbable dramatist. In this way, when Macbeth responds to the Apparition by saying, incredulous: "That will never be," the audience understands it two ways. On the one hand, Macbeth is saying that it cannot happen. On the other hand, it is Shakespeare saying to the audience through Macbeth: "If I pull this off, you will admit I am a dramatist of the most improbable skill." And so, this game of suspense between dramatist and audience plays out.

As the endgame approaches, Malcolm closes on Inverness with the English forces to revenge his father. Shakespeare has a chance to locate the action. The English, being unfamiliar with the terrain, request a bearing:

> SIWARD. What wood is this before us?
> MENTEITH. The Wood of Birnam.
> MALCOLM. Let every soldier hew him down
> a bough
> And bear't before him; thereby shall we shadow
> The number of our host, and make discovery
> Err in report of us. (5.4.4–7)

In the cat and mouse game of suspense, this is the moment the audience has been anticipating. Shakespeare satisfies the audience in the following scene where the Messenger arrives, breathless:

> MACBETH. Thou com'st to use thy tongue: thy
> story, quickly.
> MESSENGER. Gracious my lord,
> I should report that which I say I saw,
> But know not how to do't.
> MACBETH. Well, say, sir.
> MESSENGER. As I did stand my watch upon the hill,
> I looked toward Birnam, and anon methought
> The wood began to move.
> MACBETH. Liar and slave.
> MESSENGER. Let me endure your wrath, if't be
> not so.
> Within this three mile may you see it coming.
> I say, a moving grove. (5.5.28–37)

From two scenes earlier, they know that ten thousand march on Inverness. In any other play, the Messenger would have simply reported that troops approach under camouflage. In this play, however, Shakespeare plays up the improbability of the commonest of tactics to place the audience in check. He has brought Birnam Wood to Dunsinane Hill. The copse are coming.[5]

Though the improbable has, once again, happened, Shakespeare reminds the audience through Macbeth that their game is not done. The man not of woman born still lurks, undiscovered:

> MACBETH. They have tied me to a stake; I
> cannot fly,
> But bear-like I must fight the course. What's he
> That was not born of woman? Such a one
> Am I to fear, or none. (5.7.11–14)

The probable, most of the time, prevails over the improbable. The improbable, however, has one decisive advantage. The probable can occur many times, and that is all that it can be: probable. The improbable, however, only needs to happen once. So it was with the black swan and so it is with Macbeth. As the end approaches, Macduff finds Macbeth:

> MACDUFF.   Turn, hell-hound, turn.
> MACBETH. Of all men else I have avoided thee.
> But get back, my soul is too much charged
> With blood of thine already.
> MACDUFF.   I have no words.
> My voice is in my sword, thou bloodier villain
> Than terms can give thee out. *Fight. Alarum.*
> MACBETH.   Thou losest labour;
> As easy mayst thou the intrenchant air
> With thy keen sword impress, as make me bleed.
> Let fall thy blade on vulnerable crests;
> I bear a charmed life, which must not yield
> To one of woman born.

MACDUFF.   Despair thy charm,
And let the angel whom thou still hast served
Tell thee, Macduff was from his mother's womb
Untimely ripped. (5.8.3–16)

Checkmate. The improbable man is the man born from caesarean section. The suspense, building since the second sabbath, resolves. The audience feels entertained, having seen how Shakespeare brings to pass the highly improbable, and many times.

Tragedy is a compact between dramatist and playwright. Its structure consists of a series of low-probability, high-consequence events, foreshadowed and fulfilled. Tragedy showcases the playwright's ingenuity in bringing about the highly improbable. Minor feats of improbability for minor playwrights and major feats of improbability for major playwrights. Such a reading interests us, who are today most interested in finding new ways to explore the unexpected, as more and more, we see that in life as in tragedy, the more improbable it is, the harder it hits.

Not Intended Consequences, but Unintended Consequences

Tragedy dramatizes low-probability, high-consequence events to remind us how good actions can have bad consequences. Unintended consequences arise when the swan event happens because the world has been changed: though no one knows what to do, everyone must act quickly. When Sweno and the Thane of Cawdor see Macdonald revolting, they must act at once, risking all: there is a tide in the affairs of men. This all-in risk, in turn, further antagonizes the unintended consequences: the greater the risk, the further the risk-taker's resources are stretched beyond what the risk-taker can cover. The risk-taker stands naked in the rain. Actions made in the new world, made in haste and multiplied by risk, tend towards unintended consequences.

Macbeth's quest for the crown is set against the backdrop of all the failed attempts on the crown. Macdonald and the Thane of Cawdor dared, and lost their lives. Sweno dared, and was out ten thousand dollars. The opening action establishes that, in the world of this play, the highest risk enterprise is to reach for the crown. Despite the risks, however, the play also establishes Macbeth's competency to fulfil the task. *He* was the one who thwarted the ingrates and upstarts, who, by all accounts, had been within a hair's breadth. If they had been close, Macbeth, who was by far greater than them, could entertain higher hopes. Duncan, an armchair king, hardly stands in his way. From the outset, to kill a king is, paradoxically, presented as both the riskiest *and* the most assured task: riskiest because the others had failed and most assured because Macbeth is like no other. The deed needs to be fraught with risk to cement Macbeth's daring. But the deed also needs to be most assured so that when the unintended consequences occur, the audience is surprised. This is the pleasure of tragedy.

Having seen what happened to Macdonald and the Thane of Cawdor, Macbeth knows the risk of "Vaulting ambition, which o'er-leaps itself, / And falls on th'other" (1.7.27–28). In awe of risk, he changes his mind, telling Lady Macbeth they will go no further. "I dare do all that may become a man," he says, "Who dares do more is none" (1.7.38–39). Despite his ample resources and insider knowledge, Macbeth remains circumspect. He refuses to act unless every question mark is removed.

At this point, Lady Macbeth offers the failsafe of failsafes. In addition to the assurances they already possess, she proposes to frame Duncan's chamberlains for the murder. She will ply them with wine so that they can access Duncan. Once murdered, she will smear them with royal blood and set their weapons—now the instruments of murder—next to them. Everyone will be in a deep sleep after the long day. When the murder is discovered, Macbeth will, in a fit of rage, murder the chamberlains. The truth will die with them. None will know. Her plan, being foolproof, convinces Macbeth. Every question mark disappears. "I am settled," he says, "and bend up / Each corporal agent to this terrible feat" (2.1.80–81).

They put the plan into action. As expected, it works perfectly. Macbeth becomes king. Duncan's sons, Malcolm and Donalbain flee, drawing suspicion of murder on themselves. No one knows better. The play shows them controlling, taming, and mitigating the foreseen risks. But then the play turns to the unseen risks in the unintended consequences of their actions, cascading one after another in a beautiful sequence of mischance.

Macbeth had wanted to become king. But he cannot become the type of king he had expected. The best he can do is to become a tyrant, a degraded form of a king. This is the first of the unintended consequences. Now he begins consorting with murderers. Friends must die, and Fleance too. But when he marks them with death, further unintended consequences result. To be sure, ghosts can be found in Shakespeare's other plays. In the world of this play, however, ghosts are like Juvenal's black swans: they do not exist. Now, for the first time, the undead rise:

> MACBETH. Blood hath been shed ere now,
> i'th'olden time,
> Ere humane statute purged the gentle weal;
> Ay, and since too, murders have been performed
> Too terrible for the ear. The times have been
> That when the brains were out, the man would die,
> And there an end. But now they rise again
> With twenty mortal murders on their crowns,
> And push us from our stools. This is more strange
> Than such a murder is. (3.4.73–81)

Macbeth, too, could not have foreseen how Lady Macbeth, entrenched within her iron will, would crack under pressure. Nor could he have foreseen that the moment he masters stoicism, hardening himself to all perils, is the moment Seyton breaks the news:

> MACBETH. I have supped full of horrors;
> Direness familiar to my slaughterous thoughts
> Cannot once start me. Wherefore was that cry?

SEYTON. The Queen, my lord, is dead. (5.5.13–16)

Lady Macbeth, too, generates unintended consequences. She had wanted to become queen. But she can only be a posthumous queen, a degraded form of queen: Seyton, as she dies, first addresses her thus.

How did Macbeth fall, Macbeth who removed every last question mark? Some say he fell because of overconfidence. If you believe he was overconfident, ask yourself if Shakespeare could have done any more than what he did to justify Macbeth's confidence. He gave Macbeth the competence. He gave him insider knowledge. He gave him the best-laid plan. Why should Macbeth not have been confident? His confidence is grounded. He was confident, but did not fall as a result of confidence.

Others say Macbeth fell through uxoriousness. He should not have listened to Lady Macbeth. Lady Macbeth, however, had the foolproof plan. Her plan is shown to be successful. The suspicion of the murder falls on Malcolm and Donalbain. He was swayed by Lady Macbeth, but did not fall through uxoriousness.

Then, there are those who say he fell because of his ambition. The world of the play, however, encourages ambition. The throne is ready for a shaking. Macdonald, the Thane of Cawdor, and Sweno all sense a changing of the guard. Later Banquo—and perhaps Donalbain—entertain their own imperial themes. The king is a poor judge of character, easily deceived, and cannot take it to the field. God had already deserted him: he can only send his wounded to the surgeons, other kings heal their subjects by a divine touch. Macbeth was ambitious, but his ambition was justified.

If not confidence, uxoriousness, or ambition, why did he fall? I think he fell through chance, the unexpected, more things happening than what he thought would happen, black swans, uncertainty, unknown unknowns, and low-probability, high-consequence events, the effects of all of which were compounded by risk. While indiscriminate evil cannot explain why Malcolm should ask the troops to cut down the boughs of Birnam Wood, chance multiplied by risk can. By chance, Macbeth meets a man not of woman born. By risk, he dies. Had he not put so much on the line by killing Macduff's wife, babes, and lord, the encounter may have been less grievous.

Chance and the unexpected appear to the mind as a gap in nature, as a vacuum where there should have been knowledge. The intellect is poorly designed to comprehend the dark night of chance: though the math to comprehend chance was available from antiquity, it was not until the Italian Renaissance that probability theory laid down its footings. The intellect strives at all times to prove that everything happens for a reason. Thought finds a world where the random element runs amok false and impenetrable. Thought abhors empty space, rails against wild things.

When the world confronts timid natures with accident and uncertainty, they feel pity and fear. Pity for the tolling of the bell and fear that they too are exposed. These natures, who needed to reassure themselves from chance, sought to contain it, some by devising simplistic explanations (overconfidence, uxoriousness, ambition, etc.,) and others by devising complex metaphysics (the forces of darkness and evil). With these objectively questionable and subjectively comforting explanations, they allayed their fears, saying to one another: "Be more modest in your ambitions," "Do good," and other like refrains, thinking that with a change in behavior, next time they could stop Birnam Wood. Their explanations are from the point of view that the mischance of men's ambitions are caused by man, and not by chance.

When the world, however, confronts more ambitious and confident natures with accident and uncertainty, far from pity and fear, they feel wonder and awe, wonder at how an individual, so full of fire and the seed of greatness, could be struck down by chance, and awe for the smallness of man drowning in the boundlessness of randomness. They see that the killing risks are not the risks they see, but the ones that cannot be seen until after. They see that greatness is not without risk, and that there is a price to live dangerously. These fiery natures Macbeth marshals forwards, into the unknown, into risk, into the dark night of thought, as though saying to them: "Friend, dare to live dangerously, and you too shall die. Why the fuss? I also died, who was better by far than you."

To these souls on fire, the highest honour is to join Macbeth and the pageant of tragic heroes who, having climbed past every ladder, found a way to climb on top of their heads, ever higher, higher than Ida's peaks and Icarus' flight. For them, to live is to dare. But it may be that there are other readings, and that there are as many truths to *Macbeth* as there are hearts, some circumspect, some like fire, some obsequious, some firing out their chests like cannons, some lily-livered, some cold as iron, hard as rock.

Littlewood's Law

Some find the concatenation of low-probability, high-consequence events in *Macbeth* beyond belief. How could one individual become thane, then king, fall into tyranny, lose his lady to madness, see the wood come up the hill, and then meet a man not of woman born? That this too is part of an all-too-human heuristic that shuns chance and uncertainty can be demonstrated through Littlewood's Law.

J. E. Littlewood, a twentieth century Cambridge mathematician, believed that exceedingly improbable events happen more often than we anticipate. To demonstrate his hypothesis, he devised a thought experiment. First, he called these unanticipated events *miracles*. Next, he defined miracles as events a million to one against. Through the observation that we experience many events each day, he demonstrated that we encounter the highly improbable monthly:

> Littlewood's Law of Miracles states that in the course of any normal person's life, miracles happen at a rate of roughly one per month. The proof of the law is simple. During the time that we are awake and actively engaged in living our lives, roughly for eight hours each day, we see and hear things happening at a rate of about one per second. So the total number of events that happen to us is about thirty-thousand per day, or about a million

per month. With few exceptions, these events are
not miracles because they are insignificant. The
chance of a miracle is about one per million events.
Therefore we should expect one miracle to happen,
on the average, every month.[6]

In life, it is thought that we experience a handful of defining
moments, moments full of miracle and wonder such as comings of
age, marriage, and convalescence. The implication of Littlewood's
Law, however, is that these existential fulcra whereon life hangs in
balance happen more often than we anticipate. Life, far from being a
steady state with gradual change, is in a constant state of revolution.
The moments of respite are as infrequent as the major upheavals
are frequent. In this probabilistic existence, we find ourselves often
standing, like Macbeth, outside the safety of circumscribed beliefs.

Macbeth, in dramatizing the crossroad between probability and
life, not only illustrates that more things can happen than what we
think will happen, but also that these more things happen more frequently than we allow. These strange concatenations of events in the
play may be more emblematic of life than critics have allowed. Even
in a world of pure good, and one in which the drives of ambition and
confidence are constantly held in check, we should expect to see a
Birnam Wood event, by chance alone, on the average, every month.

The Old Master

Part of the reason so few have based their readings of *Macbeth* around
low-probability, high-consequence events is that such readings are
inherently paradoxical. The low-probability event is only improbable to Macbeth. To the audience, it is a high-probability event. This
paradox drives critics to look elsewhere for the play's keys. Many
have done exactly this, basing their reading around ambition, hubris,
error, uxoriousness, or the insidious action of evil. It need not be
so, as the paradox is easily resolved: it exists to generate suspense.
Another reason, however, why so few have tried this reading is that
it flies in the face of the old master, Aristotle.

Just as the intellect abjures the role of chance as a causal factor in life, it is perhaps fitting that the greatest of intellects would abjure the role of chance from the construction of the best of plots. Aristotle declares in the *Poetics* that tragedy dramatizes the sorts of thing that could happen. Tragedy deals with probable events:

> It is also evident from what has been said that it is not the poet's function to relate actual events, but the *kinds* of things that might occur and are possible in terms of probability or necessity. (1451a)

Not only should tragedy deal with the probable, he goes on to say that chance events, being signs of inferior plot construction, are to be avoided (1454a–b). The net effect of his condoning the probable and condemning the improbable was to preclude chance and the highly improbable from the discussion of tragedy. What a shame.

Aristotle had reasons for banishing the improbable. He was trying to rehabilitate tragedy. His teacher, Plato, had found tragedy to be degenerate and unceremoniously banned it from his ideal city-state.[7] To rehabilitate tragedy, Aristotle gave it a social function. To Aristotle, theatregoers seeing the consequences of characters' actions onstage would better understand the consequences of their own actions off-stage. For this stage-to-street transference to work, however, actions had to be repeatable. For actions to be repeatable, they had to be probable. If a flaw onstage would lead to a similar fall offstage, nine or ten times out of ten, then tragedy could fulfil its social function.

In rehabilitating tragedy, Aristotle turned tragedy into a distant early warning of poor character. For the next two thousand years we would talk about how irascibility led to the fall. The fall was precipitated by confidence, stubbornness, ambition, and other behavioral factors that the agent could change, and by changing, escape tragedy. By neutering the improbable, Aristotle rehabilitated tragedy.

Aristotle has ruled the roost for two thousand years. In new millenniums, however, we seek new truths. In this age of the unexpected, we seek and find, through *Macbeth*, a new truth for tragedy that speaks to the pervasiveness of the random element. From its dramatization of black swans, *Macbeth* gains its overwhelming impetus. By affirming how the unthinkable happens again and again, *Macbeth* touches all the themes of our day. What is more, tragedy is once more dangerous. When it is dangerous, it is exciting and fit entertainment for the highest natures.

Whether Heads or Tails, Chance Always Prevails

In this essay, I have argued that chance and probability form a basis of interpretation. In *Othello*, Shakespeare represents chance in the form of a handkerchief, spotted with strawberries. The action pivots around the errant handkerchief because its journey gives Othello the proof that Iago could not provide. Chance supplies the proof because it is made up of probabilities, some common, some uncommon, and others so uncommon as to stand outside the prospect of belief. For Othello, it stood outside the prospect of belief that the handkerchief could have gone from Desdemona, to Cassio, and then to Bianca, unless Desdemona were untrue. To Othello, Iago's extraordinary claim required extraordinary evidence, and, through chance, he witnessed an extraordinary proof. Whether or not this proof achieves a point of moral certainty, however, will be a point of debate forever, as chance is, in the last examination, subject to uncertainty. *Othello*, read through the lens of chance, makes for great reading for pollsters, jurors, insurers, high-energy physicists, ethicists, medical researchers, and anyone else corroborating theories based on many observations: there is always a risk that what appears certain is only a statistical anomaly that has the seeming of truth.

In *Macbeth*, Shakespeare concentrates an even greater emphasis on chance and probability by pivoting the action around a series of low-probability, high-consequence events. The machine of chance is now the true star of the play. By the advantage conferred by this force-multiplying machine, with the lightest touch Shakespeare provokes Macbeth and Lady Macbeth to abandon belief systems and risk certain comfort on uncertain hopes. Risk unbound, in turn, leaves them susceptible to the unintended consequences of their actions:

the more risk they assume, the more susceptible they become to each tremor. All the meanwhile, Shakespeare plays a metatheatrical game with the audience, creating suspense by dangling before the audience the prospect that he will bring about an event so rare and wild that any lesser dramatist would cringe at the attempt.

From the page to the stage, tragedy is a theatre of risk. And what better for today's days of risk than to look at tragedy as a theatre of risk?[8] When life gives you lemons, make all of theatre a theatre of risk and you will see not only the play, but all of life, through new eyes. "O vain boast, / Who can control his fate? 'Tis not so now," says the one who has seen the power of chance in all its guises, sometimes raising up, and other times casting down (*Othello* 5.2.262–63).

Despite different approaches to chance in *Othello* and *Macbeth*, Shakespeare unifies them by dramatizing in both the empire of chance in its limitless power. When want, will, and intention collide with accident, chance, and fortune, no matter how strong want, will, and intention are and how unlikely accident, chance, and fortune were, chance finds a way. Some thought that the gods were fate. Others thought that politics or character was fate. But, really, chance is the rebel fate. Certain proof of this lies in the great mystery of tragedy, the mystery of how, whether heads or tails, chance always prevails.

Notes

1. Thank you to Robert C. Evans for his encouragement to write this essay. Anton Brakhage and Kara Flanagan offered much appreciated feedback for which I am most thankful.
2. On Iago's reputation for honesty—which he himself cultivates—see also: 1.3.285, 2.1.199, 2.3.6, 2.3.173, 2.3.243, 2.3.262, 2.3.330, 2.3.332, 3.3.5, 3.3.121, 3.3.246, 3.3.262, 3.3.384, 5.1.31, and 5.2.150.
3. On the development of the idea of moral certainty from Leibniz and Bernoulli to today's statisticians, see Hacking, 143–53.

4. On the adoption of a five-sigma rather than a three- or four-sigma significance test in high-energy physics, see Louis Lyons, "Statistical Issues in Searches for New Physics."
5. Thank you to David Konstan for this joke.
6. Littlewood's Law, as explained by Freeman Dyson, one of Littlewood's pupils at Cambridge; see Dyson 273.
7. See, for example, Plato *Laws* 817a–e and *Republic* 607b.
8. For a discussion of tragedy as a theatre of risk, see: Wong, *The Risk Theatre Model of Tragedy*. On the role of chance in ancient drama, see: Wong "Greek Tragedy, Black Swans, and the Coronavirus: The Consolation of Theatre."

Works Cited

Aristotle. *Poetics*. Translated and edited by Stephen Halliwell. In *Aristotle: Poetics, Longinus: On the Sublime, Demetrius: On Style*. Loeb Classical Library 199. Harvard UP, 1995.

Dyson, Freeman. *The Scientist as Rebel*. New York: The New York Review of Books, 2006.

Hacking, Ian. *The Emergence of Probability*. 2nd ed. Cambridge UP, 2006.

Juvenal and Persius. *Juvenal and Persius*. Translated and edited by Susanna Morton Braund. Loeb Classical Library 91. Harvard UP, 2004.

Lyons, Louis. "Statistical Issues in Searches for New Physics." Paper presented at the Second Annual Conference on Large Hadron Collider Physics, New York, NY, June 2014. arXiv:1409.1903v1.

Mill, John Stuart. *A System of Logic*. Vol. 1. Harrison and Co., 1743.

Plato. *Complete Works*. Edited by John M. Cooper and D.S. Hutchinson. Hackett, 1997.

Rimbaud, Arthur. *Oeuvres complètes*. Edited by André Guyaux and Aurélia Cervoni. Bibliothéque de la Pléiade, 2009.

Rymer, Thomas. *The Critical Works of Thomas Rymer*. Edited by Curt Zimansky. Yale UP, 1956.

Shakespeare, William. *Hamlet*. Edited by Ann Thompson and Neil Taylor. The Arden Shakespeare, 2014.

_____. *Macbeth*. Edited by Sandra Clark and Pamela Mason. The Arden Shakespeare, 2015.

_____. *Othello*. Edited by E. A. J. Honigmann. Rev. ed. The Arden Shakespeare, 2016.

Taleb, Nassim Nicholas. *The Black Swan*. Random House, 2007.

Wong, Edwin. "Greek Tragedy, Black Swans, and the Coronavirus: The Consolation of Theatre." In *Literature in Times of Crisis*. Edited by Robert C. Evans. Salem Press, 2021, pp. 46–60.

_____. *The Risk Theatre Model of Tragedy: Gambling, Drama, and the Unexpected*. Friesen Press, 2019.

CHAPTER 5
Greek Tragedy, Black Swans, and the Coronavirus: The Consolation of Theatre

THE FOOL.

We unravel, and to whom should we turn? Many of us—even the older ones—have never experienced a pandemic of these proportions. For direction, let us turn to an unlikely art form that has collected over two and a half millennia of experience in risk management: the dramatic art of tragedy.[1]

There are many ways of looking at tragedy. If we look at tragedy as a theatre of pity and fear, as Aristotle described it, doing so will not help us deal with our current situation. If we look at tragedy as a genre invested in death and destruction, as did Geoffrey Chaucer's Monk, that claim also will not help. If we adopt Howard Barker's view of tragedy as a theatre of catastrophe, doing so, once again, will not help in these circumstances (55–60). Finally, if we look at tragedy as a collision of ethical positions, as Georg Wilhelm Friedrich Hegel called it, that view will not help. But, if we look at tragedy as a theatre of risk that dramatizes the impact of low-probability, high-consequence "black swan" events, tragedy will be our Muse during times of crisis such as the Great Quarantine of early 2020 when the coronavirus pandemic spread fear across the globe.

The coronavirus pandemic: It came out of nowhere, yes? It has a large impact, yes? And its impact on life, society, and civilization was impossible to model before the event, yes? This, by definition, is a "black swan" event—a term I will discuss more fully later. First, I will argue that tragedy is the art that explores these low-probability, high-consequence occurrences. Next, I will show how we trigger these types of events in tragedy and in life. Then, I will show you the path forward and the consolation of tragedy.

Place Your Bets in Three Greek Tragedies

Let's start with Euripides's *The Bacchae*. The play, a masterpiece of Euripides's final period, is named after the chorus of Lydian women who accompany Dionysus. In this play, Euripides dramatizes the arrival of a new god and the king's response to the dangerous stranger. Dionysus, the god of the vine, the god of dreams, intoxication, and ecstasy, having established his cult in Asia, now comes to Greece. His first stop is the city-state of Thebes.

As in many tragedies, a family dynamic plays out. Dionysus is the son of Zeus and Semele, a mortal princess and daughter of Cadmus, the former king of Thebes. Semele, however, never lived to see her son. Hera, jealous of Zeus's infidelities, made him promise her a favor. When he complied, she asked him to appear to Semele in his elemental form. Semele died, but Zeus was able to save Dionysus by sewing him into his thigh. Though Semele's house still smolders from the divine blast, the townsfolk deny that Zeus loved Semele. They say instead that Zeus blasted her for claiming so much (lines 30–31). This sets the stage for the play: Dionysus is angered by the rumors. He has returned to set the record right.

As the play begins, Dionysus, to punish Thebes, has struck the Theban women with madness, driving them into the woods to conduct Bacchic rites. Thebes's ruler Pentheus, Cadmus's grandson, confronts the upstart stranger. Pentheus wonders whether the stranger bringing a new cult is god or a charlatan.

Pentheus bets on what happens most of the time. I think that most of the time, when a child is born out of wedlock, there is a more plausible explanation than "I was having an affair with the king of the gods." Notice, however, that Euripides doesn't dramatize what happens most of the time. He dramatizes the instance where Zeus *is* the father. What is more, most of the time the long-haired stranger waltzing into town proselytizing a new cult is a charlatan, not a god. Notice, however, that Euripides doesn't dramatize what happens most of the time. He dramatizes the instance where the stranger *is* a god. Most of the time, Pentheus would have booted the stranger out of town. But this time, Pentheus is torn apart limb by limb because he's mistaken.

The birth of a new god, the arrival of an effeminate stranger, and the sparagmos of a powerful king: is Euripides dramatizing the impact of low-probability, high-consequence events in *The Bacchae?* In works of literature, closing lines are critical. They deserve rereading. Consider *The Bacchae*'s closing lines, spoken by the chorus:

> What heaven sends has many shapes, and many
> things the gods accomplish **against our expectation**.
> What men look for is not brought to pass, but a god
> finds a way to achieve **the unexpected**. Such was
> the outcome of this story. (lines 1388–92, empha-
> sis added)

What does the action consist of? It consists of "many things the gods accomplish against our expectation." "A god," says the chorus, "finds a way to achieve the unexpected." Point blank, the text says that tragedy dramatizes the impact of the highly improbable. This isn't a coincidence, either: Euripides concludes *Helen* and *Andromache* with the same lines and *Medea* with a similar refrain.[2] Tragedy, according to these closing lines, dramatizes the impact of the highly improbable.

Next, let's consider how Sophocles's *Oedipus the King* drives home the impact of the highly improbable. How often does the detective on the trail of murder find out that he himself is the killer? Not often. It's a low-probability, high-consequence event, and that is precisely what Sophocles dramatizes.

Next, let's consider how Aeschylus's *Seven against Thebes* brings to life the impact of the highly improbable. You're in the middle of a civil war. You and six other captains will be posted to each of Thebes's seven gates. Outside, six captains—with your insolent brother as the seventh—will be posted to attack each of Thebes's gates. All the assignments are random, drawn by lot (lines 375–76).[3] You're trying to figure out if the gods are on your side.

In the stylized violence of the play, each captain bears a shield. In this proxy battle, the shields clash, and not the combatants themselves. You can see whether the gods are on your side by interpreting the clash of blazons on the combatants' shields. If your guy bears the device of Zeus and the other guy bears the device of the fire-breathing monster Typhon, that's the gods telling you they're on your side: just as Zeus tamed Typhon in mythology, your guy will prevail. Through the crack of probability and chance, heaven reveals its will.

Besides seeing whether the gods are on your side, you're also trying to avoid the worst-case scenario: being posted to the same gate as your brother. There are rituals to purify spilt blood, but no rituals to purify spilt kindred blood (lines 734–41). What are the chances that, just as you've established that the gods are on your side, you find out that they call you to die? In other words, what are the chances that the matchups favor you from gates one to six, but you find out your brother awaits you at the final gate?[4] In this game of death, you have one specific captain who is able to nullify the shield device of each of the belligerent attackers.

Seven captains can arrange themselves into factorial seven (7 * 6 * 5 * 4 * 3 * 2 * 1), or 5,040 unique arrangements at seven gates. Only one out of these 5,040 permutations yields the sequence of attackers we see: Tydeus at gate one, Capaneus at gate two, all the way up to

Polyneices at gate seven. The same goes for the defending captains. They too can arrange themselves into 5,040 different permutations, but only one out of these 5,040 outcomes sees Melannipus at gate one, Polyphontes at gate two, all the way up to Eteocles at the highest gate.

To find all the possible permutations with seven attacking and seven defending captains, we multiply 5,040 by 5,040: 25,401,600 different matchups are possible. Now we can answer the question: What were the chances that the matchups from gates one to six favored you so that, just as you were certain of victory, you are cast down at the seventh gate? The odds of that happening were 25,401,599:1 against. Most of the time, it doesn't happen. But Aeschylus doesn't dramatize "most of the time." He dramatizes how the two sons fulfil their father's curse against overwhelming odds.

I like to think of tragedy as a risk simulator that dramatizes the impact of the highly improbable. Tragedy looked at in this way becomes of topical interest, a mirror into which we can see reflections of the Great Quarantine of 2020, or of some future low-probability, high-consequence scenario you may find yourself up against in the days to come.

Black Swans on Stage and in Life

The arrival of a new god, the detective on his own trail, and two brothers called to the highest gate: There's a name for these events. Like the day JFK died, or when Chernobyl melted, or when the Challenger rocket ship lit up the skies, or when the Berlin Wall fell, we call these events "black swans."

The term "black swan" originates from the Roman satirist Juvenal, who likens the perfect wife to "a prodigy as rare upon the earth as a black swan" (*Sat.* 6.165). Since it was thought that the perfect wife does not exist, the black swan became a byword for objects and ideas that lie outside the realm of belief. When, in the seventeenth century, black swans were sighted in Australia, the long-standing belief that black swans did not exist went out the window. The term "black swan" could then take on a novel meaning. Because the sighting of black swans was a low-probability event (Europeans had been looking at swans for millennia without seeing one) and the sighting of one had high consequences (millennia of data were falsified), the black swan could become a visual representation of unexpected low-probability, high-consequence events.

It was mathematician, philosopher, and options trader Nassim Nicholas Taleb who popularized the modern term "black swan." Taleb argues that we are blind to the impact of low-probability, high-consequence events. Both our cognitive and mathematical models underestimate the frequency of the highly improbable.[5] The timing of his 2007 book, *The Black Swan*, was impeccable. The Great Recession, a swan event, broke out the following year. As a result, the term "black swan" to denote outlier events with profound implications would enter the popular consciousness.

After the Great Recession, there was a rush to understand the role of chance and uncertainty in life and in the markets. Experts mumbled and fumbled and charlatans spoke out. It seemed to me, however, that there was a ready-made art form to explore how things that pop out of the blue could leave an enduring legacy. That art form was tragedy. Euripides, after all, tells us through the chorus that tragedy explores how game-changing events happen out of the blue. Aeschylus too dramatizes how life is impacted by events that are 25,401,599:1 against. If we wanted to understand the role of chance and uncertainty in life, all we needed to do was to give tragedy a chance. For over twenty-five hundred years, tragedy has been exploring the origins and impact of swan events.

In tragedy and in life risk triggers black swan events. By taking risks, Oedipus triggers the black swan event: He discovers that he is the regicide he is searching for. In another famous tragedy, *Macbeth*, by taking inordinate risks, triggers the swan event: Birnam Wood coming to Dunsinane Hill. In a more modern instance, Willy Loman, by betting all-in on the American Dream, triggers the swan event: he finds out that he is worth more dead than alive: "Funny, y'know? After all the highways, and the trains, and the appointments, and the years, you end up worth more dead than alive" (Miller 76). In life, speculators, by taking too much risk, triggered the Great Recession. Risk provokes unintended consequences because it multiplies the risk-taker's position many times beyond what the risk-taker is able to cover. The more concentrated the bet, the more precarious the position.

The function of drama is to explore risk. That's why there are two types of drama: comedy and tragedy. Comedy dramatizes upside risk. The gods are on your side. "Coincidence must really be a divinity," says Demeas in Menander's comedy *The Girl from Samos*; "She looks after many of the things we cannot see" (lines 163–64). If you're in a comedy, you should take risks, as you'll be rewarded. If you're in a tragedy, however, you should be wary of risk. The gods are not on your side. Risk skews to the downside. Tragedy dramatizes downside risk. Let's see how we trigger black swan events in tragedy and in life.

I believe that confidence triggers black swan events. Take Oedipus. The black swan event didn't have to happen. He makes it happen with his incessant question-asking. Tiresias, Jocasta, and the shepherd all plead for him to stop asking questions. But, like a bull in a china shop, he keeps going because he's sure he can crack the case.

Just as in the tragedy, I think confidence played a role in the black swan event called the Great Recession. Speculators, confident that property prices would continue to climb, leveraged their positions. Old timers who had seen this movie before pleaded for them to stop. But, like bulls in a china shop, the speculators charged onwards. Then the bottom fell out. It always does. Not only did the speculators lose their own capital, because they used leverage to multiply their bets, they lost the capital of others.[6] Many faced ruin, lenders and borrowers alike.

I believe that idealism triggers unintended consequences. Take Creon in Sophocles's *Antigone*. The unexpected event is that, in defending his homeland, he destroys his family. The unexpected happens because he's a zealot. His zealotry rises to such a pitch that when his niece gives her brother—who was a traitor in the recent civil war—burial rites, he sentences her to death. Her death, in turn, triggers a ruinous sequence of unanticipated events that destroys his family.

Just as in the tragedy, I think idealism and zealotry played a role in the black swan event called 9/11. Bin Laden appropriated religion to launch a holy war that saw four planes flying where no planes were expected to fly: two into the World Trade Center, one into the Pentagon, and one—were it not for the intervention of brave men and women—into the White House. In an afternoon, the world changed.

I believe that a concentration of capital and resources triggers low-probability, high-consequence events. Aeschylus says: "God's sharp lightnings fly to stagger mountains" (*Agamemnon* p. 59). Shakespeare, many years later, echoes the sentiment: "When beggars die, there are no comets seen; / The heavens themselves blaze forth the death of princes" (*Caesar* 2.2.30–31). When you start a venture, and a low-probability event happens, the consequences are not necessarily astounding. If you start up a venture and have access to the wealth of nations, when the low-probability event happens, the consequences may be much higher. "The heavens blaze forth the death of princes" because princes have the means to change the course of history. Consider Xerxes in Aeschylus's *Persians*. If he had been a minor king, death would not have undone so many.

Just as in the tragedy, if you have capital and resources—say half a billion dollars burning a hole in your pocket—when the low-probability event happens, the consequences may be staggering. Half a billion dollars is the sticker price for one Deepwater Horizon, a powerful oil rig (Boebert and Blossom 5). It can drill deeper and further than ever before. But, if things go awry and the rig explodes and the blowout preventer fails and the blind shear ram fails, then it will spill 600,000 tons of crude into the Gulf of Mexico. If, however, your capital and resources had been less, the consequences would have been less grievous.[7]

I believe that when we devise elaborate schemes around probabilities that only have the appearance of certainty, we trigger black swan events. Prophecy is a good example. Here's a well-known example from Herodotus, the father of history. When Croesus, King of Lydia, asks the Delphic oracle whether he should attack Persia, the oracle says: "If Croesus attacked the Persians, he would destroy a great empire" (1.53). Croesus proceeded to devise grand plans of conquest around the oracular utterance. He would only understand afterwards that the oracle meant the destruction of his own empire, a catastrophic event.

An echo of how the misinterpretation of prophecy leads to unintended consequences occurs in Sophocles's tragedy *Women of Trachis*. In prophetic words, a dying centaur tells Deianeira that he will leave her a love charm:

> Thus shalt thou have a charm to bind the heart
> Of Heracles, and never shall he look
> On wife or maid to love her more than thee.
> (lines 574–76)

When she uses the charm, however, she finds out that it kills her husband. The charm works, but not in the way she intended.

Just as in the tragedy, I think when we devise elaborate schemes around probabilities that have the seeming of certainty, we trigger black swan events. Financial algorithms are today's equivalent to yesterday's prophecies. While yesterday's prophecies spoke with oracular certainty, today's algorithms speak with mathematical certainty. Whether yesterday or today, however, when misunderstandings arise, the results devastate. A case in point is Long-Term Capital Management, a hedge fund founded by two Nobel Prize winners.[8] Their formulas identified irrationally priced bonds. As the prices of these bonds returned to their expected value, they would profit.

The traders at Long-Term Capital Management trusted their financial models. They put their trust on display when they borrowed over $100 billion to leverage their bets: in 1995, with $3.6 billion of equity, they controlled over $100 billion in assets. They did this by leveraging 28:1 (Lowenstein 78). It turns out that, like the oracles of old, their algorithms were correct. But what they also found out was that the market could remain irrational longer than they could remain solvent. When their trades went awry in 1998, their lenders issued a margin call. With only $2.28 billion of their own equity remaining, they could hardly repay the $128 billion in loans (Lowenstein 159). Their lenders, a consortium of international financial institutions, lacked the equity themselves to cover the losses and the global financial system fell to its knees. Alan Greenspan and the Federal Reserve, playing the role of the deus ex machina, were forced to intervene.

I believe that extraordinary situations increase the likelihood of black swan events. Such situations force you to act with abandon. You have to throw the Hail Mary. When you do so, you throw risk to the winds. Take *Oedipus the King*. There's a plague. Oedipus must continue the investigation or else all Thebes perishes. He has no choice. But, by continuing, he triggers the risk event.

Just as in the tragedy, today we also experience the extraordinary: COVID-19, the coronavirus pandemic. To find a solution, we're developing cures at a breakneck pace. Vaccines are going from the lab to human trials without the usual step of animal testing: on March 16, 2020, Moderna began testing a vaccine on human subjects in Seattle (Moderna). In a Hail Mary attempt, drugs designed to remedy an assortment of unrelated remedies (e.g. remdesivir and chloroquine) are being fed to coronavirus patients (Wang et al.). In a shot in the dark, convalescent plasma from patients who have recovered is being injected into sick individuals (Chen et al.). What could go wrong as we start tinkering with the genetic sequence of viruses and antibodies? Our real-life setting, like the dramatic setting in Sophocles's *Oedipus the King*, encourages us to throw risk to the winds. When we do so, we invite the black swan.

Tragedy's Consolation: Antifragility

In conclusion, I've asked you to reimagine tragedy as a theatre of risk. I do so because tragedy, as the art that dramatizes downside risk, may be a source of wisdom. Because tragedy simulates swan events, it raises our sensibility of how highly improbable events impact life.

I began with Euripides, who emphasizes in the closing refrain of many plays how tragedy dramatizes swan events. I went on to Sophocles, and pointed out how *Oedipus the King* dramatizes a low-probability, high-consequence outcome: a man who damns himself. Then, I demonstrated with math that the outcome of *Seven against Thebes* takes place against overwhelming odds. I chose these examples to encourage us to reimagine tragedy as a theatre where risk runs riot.[9]

Then I told the tale of how heroes trigger devastating risk events. I talked of their confidence and idealism. I talked of tragedy's other commonplaces: kings and queens with capital burning a hole in their pockets. I talked of the fool's gold of oracles and algorithms. And I talked of how dire straits compel us to close our eyes, say "Hail Mary," and throw the long desperation pass deep into the end zone.

What's the takeaway? Well, there's no magic bullet. Black swans are impossible to predict: They're not known knowns or known unknowns, but rather, unknown unknowns. They're the arrival of a new god, the invention of the Gutenberg press, or Birnam Wood coming to Dunsinane Hill. Such events lie beyond prediction because they illustrate the problem of induction, the problem of ascribing to the unknown future the features of a known past. But there is something we can do. We can, to borrow another of Taleb's terms, become "antifragile" (*Antifragile* 23–27).

Look at these heroes of tragedy. Despite having the strength of Heracles, the charisma of Richard, and the cunning of Macbeth, they're wonderfully fragile. When they make a plan, there's no plan B. They wager all-in: "Go big or go home," they say as they go off to hunt the white whale. Fragility is absolute conviction that the oracle is true, that the algorithm is right, that past is prelude, and that all swans are white.

What is antifragility? Antifragility is the essence of the tragic hero turned upside down. Antifragility is a plan B. It is redundancy. Antifragility is keeping some powder dry. It is putting eggs into different baskets. Antifragility is fluidity, taking the shape of water. Antifragility is skepticism: This time may be different. Antifragility is not strength of conviction, but the greater strength that calls into question one's own convictions, the courage to ask: "What is the downside if I'm wrong?" Instead of clever equations and oracular authority, antifragility is time-tested folk wisdoms such as: "Don't go for a home run when you can get by with a hit" and "A bird in hand is worth two in the bush."

From my childhood to my maturity—I'm forty-five now—there have been two trends: urbanization and globalization. Urbanization packs more and more people into downtown cores. Pandemics love crowded spaces. As Thucydides realized long ago, overcrowding exacerbates the risk of contagion: Shortly before the plague of 430 BC, the countryfolk had been crammed into the city to protect them from the Peloponnesian invasion. When the plague hit Athens, it hit with greater intensity. Then there's globalization. Globalization connects all the world's cities in a tight embrace: Wuhan is connected to Milan, is connected to New York, is connected to Tehran. When Wuhan sneezes, the world catches cold.

If we were to overlay the art form of tragedy onto today's pandemic, we would discover that, in the theatre of life, we are the heroes who have wagered all-in on the benefits of urbanization and globalization. While we were toasting each other, the coronavirus stole up to us like a thief in the night. A few months ago, we stood at the sixth gate, standing in the same place Eteocles once stood as he began planning the day of celebration. Funny how it is, how we're in the gravest danger when we're the most confident. This is tragedy's legacy.

What's the takeaway? Let us be antifragile. Let us have a plan B. Let us have redundancy in our social networks and bank balances. Let us keep some powder dry. Let us diversify rather than intensify our positions. Let us be more a Renaissance jack-of-all-trades rather than a twenty-first century master of one. Let us urbanize and globalize, but let us also challenge urbanization and globalization. Let us listen to the oral tradition of folk wisdom. That is the prudent course. But, if we do not want to be antifragile, then let us go all-in like the wonderfully fragile heroes of tragedy. There is glory in that as well. And there is a comfort in knowing that, when we are struck down, we will join the parade of heroes—Oedipus, Joan of Arc, Faustus, Antigone, and the many others—who drank in life from the brim to the dregs. Although they bit off more than they could chew, when they perished, the world seemed a smaller place.

Whichever way we go—whether we choose circumspect antifragility or fragile heroism—if we invoke Melpomene, tragedy's Muse, we will go in with a greater awareness of how it isn't the decades that will define our lives, but the unexpected moments, few and far between. If you're a bike rider, it isn't the tens of thousands of kilometers you ride that will define you, but that one meter. If you tweet, it's not the tens of thousands of tweets that will define you, but that one tweet that, contrary to all expectation, goes viral. We will not be defined by what we will, but by that stray moment that steals up to us like a thief in the night. None of us will be where we plan on being in five years or ten years. But, ever onwards, we will keep going. And one day, the historians of the future will tell us what we should have done on the day Birnam Wood came to Dunsinane Hill. But that is another story, the tragedy of which is that it cannot be written now, when we most want it.

Notes

1. This essay is adapted from an online presentation given at Memorial University on April 3, 2020, while under quarantine. I am indebted to Luke Roman for the invitation to speak on this timely topic and the attendees for their enthusiastic feedback. Thank you to Robert C. Evans for his guidance and suggestions in transforming the talk into the present essay.
2. See *Helen* lines 1688–92 and *Andromache* lines 1284–88. See also the ending of *Medea*: "Zeus on Olympus has many things in his treasure house, and many are the things the gods accomplish against our expectation. What men look for is not brought to pass, but a god finds a way to achieve the unexpected. Such is the outcome of this story" (lines 1415–19).

3. The scout informs Eteocles that the attackers draw lots to determine their gate assignations. How Eteocles chooses the defender assignations is a subject of debate. Here I follow Hermann's brilliant solution that a stage instruction has been lost in transmission: As the scout names the attacker, Eteocles also draws a lot to determine the defender (58–62). Regardless of whether Hermann's conjecture is correct, Eteocles's selection may as well be random, as he names the defender in response to the attacking captain, which the scout informs us most definitely is random. For a discussion of how Aeschylus weaves together the underlying design of randomness to bring about the fated yet unexpected outcome, see Wong *Risk Theatre Model* 181–89.

4. The view that the dramatic potential of the play relies on Eteocles being emboldened by the overwhelmingly favorable matchups from gates one to six only to be cast down at gate seven is stated most succinctly by Gilbert Murray: "Eteocles with six chosen champions is prepared to meet them one by one; and has a cheerful retort to all their blazons" (139). On how poets entertain audiences by pulling fated outcomes seemingly out of the blue, see Wong "Harmony of Fixed Fate" 11–14.

5. See Taleb *Fooled by Randomness* "Why Don't Statisticians Detect Rare Events?" 112–13.

6. On the role of leverage in stock market bubbles, see Galbraith.

7. For a discussion of the Deepwater Horizon disaster, see Boebert and Blossom.

8. In a display of dramatic irony, if ever there was one, Robert Merton and Myron Scholes received their Nobel Prizes as the first cracks in Long-Term Capital Management started to appear. See Lowenstein chapter 6 "A Nobel Prize."

9. It is possible to construct an exciting new twenty-first century theory of tragedy around this exact theme, and that is what I have done in my book: *The Risk Theatre Model of Tragedy: Gambling, Drama, and the Unexpected*. In this book, I argue

that tragedy is a theatre of risk where risk is the dramatic fulcrum of the action. On the premise of risk theatre, see Wong *Risk Theatre Model* "Preface." In 2018, Langham Court Theatre launched an international playwriting competition "The Risk Theatre Modern Tragedy Competition" inviting playwrights to create new tragedies to explore the impact of the highly improbable. At the time of writing, the competition is in its third year, see risktheatre.com.

Works Cited

Aeschylus. *The Oresteian Trilogy (Agamemnon / The Choephori / The Eumenides)*. Translated by Philip Vellacott, Penguin, 1959.

_____. *Suppliant Maidens, Persians, Prometheus, Seven Against Thebes*. Translated by Herbert Weir Smyth, Loeb-Harvard UP, 1922.

Barker, Howard. *Arguments for a Theatre*. 2nd ed., Manchester UP, 1993.

Boebert, Earl, and James M. Blossom. *Deepwater Horizon: A Systems Analysis of the Macondo Disaster*. Harvard UP, 2016.

Chen, Long, et al. "Convalescent Plasma as a Potential Therapy for COVID-19." *The Lancet*, vol. 20, no. 4, 1 Apr. 2020, pp. 398–400, doi.org/10.1016/S1473-3099(20)30141-9.

Euripides. *Children of Heracles, Hippolytus, Andromache, Hecuba*. Translated by David Kovacs, vol. 2, Loeb-Harvard UP, 1995.

_____. *Helen, Phoenician Women, Orestes*. Translated by David Kovacs, vol. 5, Loeb-Harvard UP, 2002.

_____. *Bacchae, Iphigenia at Aulis, Rhesus*. Translated by David Kovacs, vol. 6, Loeb-Harvard UP, 2002.

Galbraith, John Kenneth. *A Short History of Financial Euphoria*. Penguin, 1993.

Hermann, Fritz-Gregor. "Eteocles' Decision in Aeschylus' *Seven against Thebes*." *Tragedy and Archaic Greek Thought*, edited by Douglas Cairns, Classical P of Wales, 2013, pp. 39–80.

Herodotus. *The Histories*. Translated by Aubrey de Sélincourt, revised by John M. Marincola, Penguin, 1972.

Juvenal. "Satire 6." *Juvenal and Persius*. Translated by G. G. Ramsay, Loeb-Heinemann, 1918.

Lowenstein, Roger. *When Genius Failed: The Rise and Fall of Long-Term Capital Management*. Rev. ed., Random House, 2011.

Menander. *Plays and Fragments*. Translated by Norma Miller, Penguin, 1987.

Miller, Arthur. *Death of a Salesman*. Penguin, 1998.

Moderna. "Moderna's Work on a Potential Vaccine Against COVID-19." *Moderna*, www.modernatx.com/modernas-work-potential-vaccine-against-covid-19.

Murray, Gilbert. *Aeschylus: The Creator of Tragedy*. Oxford UP, 1940.

Shakespeare. *The Riverside Shakespeare*, edited by G. Blakemore Evans, Houghton Mifflin, 1974.

Sophocles. *The Three Theban Plays: Antigone, Oedipus the King, Oedipus at Colonus*. Translated by Robert Fagles, Penguin, 1982.

——. *Ajax, Electra, Trachiniae, Philoctetes*. Translated by F. Storr, vol. 2, Loeb-Heinemann, 1913.

Taleb, Nassim Nicholas. *Fooled by Randomness: The Hidden Role of Chance in Life and in the Markets*. 2nd ed., Random House, 2005.

——. *The Black Swan: The Impact of the Highly Improbable*. Random House, 2007.

_____. *Antifragile: Things That Gain from Disorder*. Random House, 2012.

Thucydides. *History of the Peloponnesian War*. Translated by Rex Warner, rev. ed., Penguin, 1972.

Wang, Manli, et al. "Remdesivir and Chloroquine Effectively Inhibit the Recently Emerged Novel Coronavirus (2019-nCoV) In Vitro." *Cell Research*, vol. 30, 4 Feb. 2020, pp. 269–71, doi.org/10.1038/s41422-020-0282-0.

Wong, Edwin. *The Risk Theatre Model of Tragedy: Gambling, Drama, and the Unexpected*. Friesen P, 2019.

_____. "The Harmony of Fixed Fate and Free Will in the *Iliad*." *Antichthon*, vol. 36, 2002, pp. 1–18, doi.org/10.1017/S0066477400001295.

_____. *The Risk Theatre Modern Tragedy Competition*. Langham Court Theatre, Apr. 2018, risktheatre.com.

CHAPTER 6
The Price of Patriotism: Opportunity Cost and the American Dream in Arthur Miller's *All My Sons*

THE FOOL.

> I don't know why it is, but every time I reach out for something I want, I have to pull back because other people will suffer. (16)[1]

In the mid-1940s, the American century was dawning. The daybreak of Pax Americana had arrived. From January to November 1947, *All My Sons* ran for 328 performances.[2] Arthur Miller went from being a famous person nobody knew, to being a famous person everybody knew. In dramatizing the possibilities and problems of an upstart world order, Miller became an overnight sensation.

Pax Americana brought peace to the conquered by releasing the animal spirits of the economy, long bottled up in wartime rationing and a decade of depression and dust bowl. No more gloom. Opportunity and prosperity lay on every horizon line. Amidst the go-fever of a new superpower firing on all cylinders, one voice dissented. It was the voice of Miller asking whether the American dream was a zero-sum game.

In *All My Sons*, money is the measure of success. Money is everywhere. It represents the American dream. The choice to make money, however, comes at a cost. When one chooses to make money, one loses the next best alternative that one could have pursued, had one chosen otherwise. The negative part of choice is known as opportunity cost. Opportunity cost illustrates the cost of choice because it presents choice as an either/or rather than a both/and proposition.

All My Sons dramatizes the cost of the American dream, its entry fee, the yearly dues, and the ongoing expenses. It does so by following characters as they make choices in pursuit of the dream. By making, through opportunity cost, the characters pay for their decisions, Miller exposes the true price of Pax Americana.

The minor characters understand opportunity cost. Having chosen, they reflect on the forsaken alternatives, and are left with "a wisp of sadness" (6). Their tragedy anticipates, augments, and amplifies the tragedy of the Keller family—Joe Keller, or simply Keller, Kate Keller, otherwise known as Mother, and Chris Keller. The Kellers fail to understand opportunity cost. They are the sort of people who think that they can have their cake and eat it too. In the end, however, Miller destroys them. In their destruction, they pay for their devotion to the ideals of the American century.

For the orthodox interpreters who consider that the fall of heroes through hubris brings about a catharsis of pity and fear through pity and fear, or, that the tragic arises when irreconcilable ethical positions collide, *All My Sons* could take a position of pride alongside the tragedies of old. But, for the young guns who understand the opportunity cost concept, who seek farsighted interpretations for the new century, tragedy is, first and foremost, a valuing mechanism. To the rebel interpreters, patriotism goes through a price discovery process. It is on sale. Its price is measured in terms of the opportunity cost of all the things that are left behind in choosing it. The emotional effect of tragedy is wonder and awe. Wonder at how much Keller pays. And awe over how faraway, so close he was to pulling off a fast one. To the new interpreters, pity and fear were barbaric relics left over from past ages.

Show Me the Money

The Second World War is over. America has won. In the postwar boom, new industries, professions, and opportunities rise up:

> KELLER [*shakes his head*]. All the kind of business
> goin' on. In my day, either you were a lawyer, or a
> doctor, or you worked in a shop. Now…
> FRANK. Well, I was going to be a forester once.
> KELLER. Well, that shows you; in my day, there was
> no such thing. (7)

It is a time of rapid urbanization and rising social mobility. The young move to the new metropolises of Cleveland and New York to stake their claims. On stage right, the baby boom that will redefine demographics and drive demand for the next century is taking place: in the space of three years, Frank and Lydia Lubey have three babies. In the postwar boom, the business of America is business. To partake in this world of business, money is the currency of exchange, the symbol of the dream, the projection of Pax Americana.

In *All My Sons*, money is ubiquitous. Money seals the deal between men and women: "Oh Annie, Annie," says Chris to his fiancée, "I'm going to make a fortune for you!" (36). "You wanted money," says Keller to Mother, "so I made money" (76). Money is the sign of social approval. "He's got money," says Sue to Ann when she finds out Ann is engaged to Chris (44). Money makes all the difference. When she met Jim, her future husband, his wallet was threadbare. She was, however, already a nurse. Money laid the groundwork for future strife:

> SUE. It makes all the difference. I married an interne.
> On my salary. And that was bad, because as soon as
> a woman supports a man he owes her something.

> You can never owe somebody without resenting
> them. (44)

Money is how fathers demonstrate their love to sons. "What the hell did I work for?" Keller asks his son Chris. "That's only for you, Chris," says Keller, referring to his factory where everything from aircraft cylinder heads to pressure cookers and washing machines are built, "the whole shootin'-match is for you!" (17).

In the postwar boom, money is the new measure. Net worth is the measure of an individual and gross domestic product the measure of a nation. How much has one contributed to society? The answer lies in the bankbook. The bigger the better. Public projections of the bankbook start with the family house. In the opening description of the set, Miller describes the monetary attributes of the Keller house alongside its physical attributes: it is a two-storey, seven-room structure hedged in with tall poplars and a porch that extends into the yard six feet. To build it cost fifteen thousand (5). Like the height of the poplars and the porch that extends six feet, money has a dimension. It is measured in dollar units. In addition to the family house, secondary projections of the bankbook include the new cars and fridges (36). To own a house with a driveway, a new car, and fridge is the sign of a made man.

To comport oneself to life in the new dream, one must understand how money works. Besides the obvious material applications, money can buy human, all-too-human values. It can buy allegiances. Keller finds out that, not only has Ann returned after a three-and-a-half-year absence, but that her brother George is unexpectedly also on the way. George could be a danger: Keller had ruined his father. To win his allegiance, he proposes to fast-track George on the road to riches. George, having just joined the bar, is a new lawyer. He is in the beginning stages of building a clientele. Keller can help:

> KELLER. You say he's not well. George, I been
> thinkin', why should he knock himself out in New
> York with that cut-throat competition, when I got so

many friends here; I'm very friendly with some big
lawyers in town. I could set George up here. (48)

The allure of money may entice even Steve Deever, Ann and
George's father, the man Keller ruined:

> KELLER. I like you and George to go to him in
> prison and tell him… "Dad, Joe wants to bring you
> into the business when you get out."
> ANN [*surprised, even shocked*]. You'd have him
> as partner?
> KELLER. No, no partner. A good job. [*Pause. He sees
> she is shocked, a little mystified. He gets up, speaks
> more nervously.*] I want him to know, Annie … while
> he's sitting there I want him to know that when he
> gets out he's got a place waitin' for him. It'll take
> his bitterness away. To know you have a place … it
> sweetens you. (49)

Relationships are defined by money, and Keller has figured out how
to create winning relationships.

A fundamental relationship is the one between husband and wife.
Here, too, the successful relationship is grounded in an understanding
of money. Jim, learning that Ann is engaged, offers monetary advice:

> JIM [*To* ANN]. I've only met you Ann, but if I may
> offer you a piece of advice—When you marry,
> never—even in your mind—never count your
> husband's money. (25)

Those who understand the advantages of money in the postwar
world are lauded and those who fail to understand censored. Money
is the basis of a new morality:

> KELLER. Goddam, if Larry was alive he wouldn't act
> like this. He understood the way the world is made.
> He listened to me. To him the world had a forty-
> foot front, it ended at the building line. This one,

everything bothers him. You make a deal, overcharge two cents, and his hair falls out. He don't understand money. Too easy, it came too easy. Yes sir. Larry. That was a boy we lost. (77)

The goal of this new morality is to have children and pay off the mortgage. "That big dope next door," says Mother, "who never reads anything but Andy Gump has three children and his house paid off" (61). Social causes, politics, and standing up for one's beliefs are impediments, unwanted distractions to the patriotic goal of making money and babies:

> MOTHER [*reading his thoughts*]. She got pretty, heh?
> GEORGE [*sadly*]. Very pretty.
> MOTHER [*as a reprimand*]. She's beautiful, you damned fool!
> GEORGE [*looks around longingly; and softly, with a catch in his throat*]. She makes it seem so nice around here.
> MOTHER [*shaking her finger at him*]. Look what happened to you because you wouldn't listen to me! I told you to marry that girl and stay out of the war!
> GEORGE [*laughs at himself*]. She used to laugh too much.
> MOTHER. And you didn't laugh enough. While you were getting mad about Fascism Frank was getting into her bed. (61)

Against the monetization of all values is a competing ideal. But it lies offshore on the distant fronts. Chris saw a fleeting glimpse while he commanded a company in the war:

> CHRIS. Everything was being destroyed, see, but it seemed to me that one new thing was made. A kind of … responsibility. Man for man. You understand me?—To show that, to bring that on to the earth again like some kind of monument and everyone

would feel it standing there, behind him, and it
would make a difference to him. (36)

But, as Chris adds, back at home there was no place for the things that come "out of a love a man can have for a man" (36). Before his company could come back from the war, they were already all dead. They had not been selfish enough. When, on the distant fronts, the dream of the brotherhood of man died, the American dream lost its last adversary.

The American dream is the dream of prosperity. It is the dream that tames the proud. It channels the grief of the widows and orphans, the frustrations of the veterans, and the energy of the emerging nation to create the wealth of nations. It is transacted in greenback dollars. It recorded its successes privately in bankbooks and publicly in the proliferation of factories, stone houses, automobiles, refrigerators. It sees material abundance as its highest good, and, in doing so, eschews brotherhood, the "love a man can have for a man." Instead, it elevates self-interest as its new good.

Self-interest became the new creed because it creates prosperity. So argues the Scottish economist and philosopher Adam Smith. "It is not," says Smith, "from the benevolence of the butcher, the brewer, or the baker that we expect our dinner, but from their regard to their own interest" (1.2.2). In Smith's economic philosophy, the formula to maximize national prosperity in the aggregate is for each individual to maximize individual prosperity. The greater good of a unit is dependent on all the butchers, brewers, and bakers thinking about themselves first. When individuals put others' interests before their own, frictional losses diminish the aggregate potential of the unit. So the air mask procedure on an airplane: individuals maximize the group's welfare by putting on their own masks first. So the zipper merge in traffic: when two lanes coalesce into one, the whole queue moves faster if each driver, in an act of self-interest, advances to the head before merging. In crucial applications, self-interest draws a line between life and death:

CHRIS. You remember, overseas, I was in command
of a company?
ANN. Yeah, sure.
CHRIS. Well, I lost them.
ANN. How many?
CHRIS. Just about all.
ANN. Oh, gee!
CHRIS. It takes a little time to toss that off. Because
they weren't just men. For instance, one time it'd
been raining several days and this kid came up to
me, and gave me his last pair of dry socks. Put them
in my pocket. That's only a little thing ... but ...
that's the kind of guys I had. They didn't die;
they killed themselves for each other. I mean that
exactly; a little more selfish and they'd've been here
today. (35)

While Chris's company died because they put self-interest second,
Keller takes the opposite approach. He champions self-interest.
While others wind one another up like tinker toys, Keller gets ahead
by considering his own interests. When, for example, Ann expresses
her appreciation to Keller for offering to help set George on his feet,
Keller corrects her:

ANN. That's awfully nice of you Joe.
KELLER. No, kid, it ain't nice of me. I want you to
understand me. I'm thinking of Chris. [*Slight pause*]
See ... this is what I mean. You get older, you want
to feel that you ... accomplished something. My
only accomplishment is my son. I ain't brainy. That's
all I accomplished. Now a year, eighteen months,
your father'll be a free man. Who is he going to
come home to, Annie? His baby. You. He'll come,
old, mad, into your house.
ANN. That can't matter any more, Joe.

KELLER. I don't want that hate to come between us.
[*Gestures between* CHRIS *and himself*] (48–49)

Keller thinks of his self-interest first and foremost. He is the ideal citizen, the new model patriot showing the others how to live the dream. Or is he? That is the question Miller considers.

The Opportunity Cost of Choice

Opportunity cost is the notion that choice involves a negative component. The negative component is that, when the best alternative is chosen, the next best alternative is forsaken. Choice is decision, and embedded in the etymology of the term *decision* is the opportunity cost concept. The English term comes from the Latin verb *decidere*, itself a combination of the prefix *de-* in its privative sense of "removal" and the verb *caedere* "to cut."[3] When one decides one literally "cuts off" or "cuts away" the flotsam of competing alternatives.

Economists, in examining the problem of scarcity, have formulated the clearest exposition of the opportunity cost concept. Economics is called the dismal science because it sees an impoverished world, a world where there are too many mouths, and too little to eat. There are too many sick, and too few cures. There are too many kings, and too few crowns. The task of economists is to manage resources that are in a perpetual short supply. To do this, they developed opportunity cost as the basis of an economic theory of choice to allocate inadequate resources.

Smith proposes opportunity cost as a basis for decision making in his 1776 treatise *The Wealth of Nations*. To find the underlying framework for decision making, he peels away the complexities of developed economies by reconstructing the primitive economy of early hunter-gatherers. Exchange, he finds, is informed by the opportunity cost of production. He illustrates the concept by the example of the one beaver and the two deer:

> In that early and rude state of society which
> precedes both the accumulation of stock and the

appropriation of land, the proportion between the
quantities of labour necessary for acquiring different
objects seems to be the only circumstance which
can afford any rule for exchanging them for one
another. If among a nation of hunters, for example, it
usually costs twice the labour to kill a beaver which
it does to kill a deer, one beaver should naturally
exchange for or be worth two deer. It is natural
that what is usually the produce of two days' or
two hours' labour, should be worth double of what
is usually the produce of one day's or one hour's
labour. (1.6.1)

When a hunter prepares a beaver, the hunter has lost the opportunity to prepare two deer. The opportunity cost of preparing a beaver is the loss of two deer. Conversely, should the hunter prepare two deer, the hunter loses the opportunity to prepare one beaver. With this simple example where there is one input (labor) and two outputs (beaver and deer), cost enters into the theory of choice: with a given input, it is either one beaver or two deer. In the real world, the inputs are more, the outputs are more, and the costs more grievous than animal skins. But the results are the same: you cannot have your cake and eat it too.

If economics is the dismal science, then tragedy is the dismal art. Tragedy, like economics, sees a world of privation where, to gain *x*, one gives up *y*. In *All My Sons*, the characters confront opportunity cost. Take Ann. In the prehistory of the play, she had been engaged to Larry Keller, an army pilot. He died in the war. At the same time, her father, Steve, and Larry's father, Keller, were tried for selling cracked airplane cylinder heads to the Army Air Force. They were accused of welding over hairline fractures and passing off the heads as good. Twenty-one pilots died. Keller was exonerated. Steve, however, was convicted. Ann is incredulous that her father should have been so base:

> KELLER. Annie, the day the news came about Larry
> he was in the cell next to mine ... Dad. And he
> cried, Annie ... he cried half the night.
> ANN. [*touched*]. He shoulda cried all night. (33)

She disowns him:

> KELLER [*to* ANN]. The next time you write Dad ...
> ANN. I don't write him.
> KELLER [*struck*]. Well every now and again you ...
> ANN. [*a little ashamed, but determined*]. No, I've
> *never* written to him. Neither has my brother. (31)

Her indignation comes at a cost, the cost of her shame. Her awkward interaction with Frank, who enquires about her father, highlights the price she pays. She cannot answer his simple question: she has no idea how he is (28–29). Polite society questions one who has disowned one's own. She buys her indignation at the cost of her shame.

Economists use opportunity cost to price out goods and services. In the primitive economy, the cost of a beaver is two deer because two deer represent the opportunity cost of one beaver. In the developed economy, the cost of a house call is ten dollars because it compensates Jim for the next best thing he could have done, had he passed on the house call, which, in a moment of levity, would have been to drive Sue to the beach. While economists use opportunity cost to price out goods and services, Miller uses opportunity cost to price out the human. In the mad money world of *All My Sons*, it is either your money or your life.

From the perspective of opportunity cost, the case of Jim is illuminating. He is an early prototype of Willy Loman in *Death of a Salesman*, a play that would come out two years later. Willy, after getting lost in the dream, exposes the brutal paradox of opportunity cost in complex economies. In a brutal insight as he chats about life insurance with Charley, Willy realizes that it is his money or his life:

> CHARLEY. I've got some work to do. Take care of
> yourself. And pay your insurance.

WILLY. Funny, y'know? After all the highways, and
the trains, and the appointments, and the years, you
end up worth more dead than alive. (74)

Willy can have the dream, but at the cost of his life. Jim is not there
yet, but he is getting there. In *All My Sons*, Jim wants to be a good
husband. He also wants to follow his calling. He discovers that his
wants present him with an either/or proposition:

JIM. One year I simply took off, went to New
Orleans; for two months I lived on bananas and
milk, and studied a certain disease. It was beautiful.
And then she came, and she cried. And I went back
home with her. And now I live in the usual darkness; I can't find myself; it's even hard sometimes to
remember the kind of man I wanted to be. I am a
good husband. (74–5)

When Jim reflects on his choice, he realizes the value of all he left
behind. In this way, Miller makes opportunity cost the dramatic
pivot through which characters pay the price.

Miller specifies the price Jim pays. From Sue, we learn that medical
researchers make twenty-five dollars a week and doctors ten dollars
per house call (10 and 44). During the course of the play (which
takes place on a Sunday), Jim calls on at least three patients—Mrs.
Adams, Mr. Hubbard, and an unnamed patient with a headache. He
has made, at minimum, thirty dollars. In one day, Jim makes more
than he would have in a week as a researcher. At this rate, he could
make $210 a week, over eight times the amount of a researcher.

From an opportunity cost perspective, an inference may be
drawn: $185 per week—the difference in pay between a researcher
and a doctor—is the remuneration Jim receives each week for having
given up his dreams. Put another way, $185 per week is the price
he pays to be a good husband. To add insult to injury, it appears
that his services as a doctor are superfluous. His patients—who think
they are dying—are, in fact, well. "Money," says Jim in a moment of
resignation, "Money-money-money-money. You say it long enough it

doesn't mean anything" (73). In complex economies, it is no longer the opportunity costs of beavers and deer, but rather those of dollars, cents, and dreams.

Jim's domestic tragedy sets the scene for Keller's tragedy. One evening during the war, Steve—Keller's erstwhile partner—rang, frantic. They were manufacturing aircraft cylinder heads. There was a fault in the process. A batch came out with hairline fractures. To Keller, it was either his business or his integrity. He has a choice: disclose that the process is faulty or weld the fractures. The former could put them out of business. The latter could endanger lives. He instructs Steve to pull out his tools.

The next morning, Keller calls in sick. But he does not have the flu. He is sick with the enormity of his decision. He is worried. When worried, he sleeps (41). By the time he returns to work, the heads have shipped. He thinks that the army quality control will catch the defect. By that time, he will have corrected the process. Before he can blink, however, 121 heads have gone in and 21 Curtiss P-40 Warhawks have crashed. The defect is traced back to the shop. Keller and Steve are arrested.

If Keller is convicted, he will lose his business. If he is exonerated, he will save his business. In his mind, he has done wrong by instructing Steve to cover up the cracks. But he knows a loophole: the evidence of telephone conversations is inadmissible in court:

> GEORGE. Dad was afraid. He wanted Joe there if he was going to do it. But Joe can't come down … he's sick. Sick! He suddenly gets the flu! Suddenly! But he promised to take responsibility. Do you understand what I'm saying? On the telephone, you can't have responsibility! In a court you can always deny a phone call and that's exactly what he did. They knew he was a liar the first time, but in the appeal they believed that rotten lie and now Joe is a big shot and your father is the patsy. (54–55)

Keller is confronted with a choice. The opportunity cost of his business is forsaking the next best alternative, the ties that bind him to his neighbor and business partner. For the sake of his sons, he chooses the business.

Whereas Ann and Jim make their choices and pay, Keller thinks that he can have both his money and his integrity. He believes that, without repercussions, he can ship out the heads. He believes, that, without repercussions, he can make Steve the fall guy. For some time, he succeeds. After his exoneration, he comes back into town the cock of the walk, with the result that "fourteen months later I had one of the best shops in the state again, a respected man again; bigger than ever" (30). He brags of his bravado to Ann: "Every Saturday night the whole gang is playin' poker in this arbor. All the ones who yelled murderer takin' my money now" (30).

In the world of tragedy, it is a crime against the natural law of opportunity cost to have your cake and eat it too. There may be free lunches in comedy, a world of abundance.[4] But this is no comedy Keller is in. He is in a tragedy, the dismal art regulated by the dismal science. In the ancient world, the gods would ensure that the price is paid. In the modern world, the new gods are the forces of economic science. Opportunity cost is the avenging god. With bravado, Joe "McGuts" Keller can delay nemesis, but, like the tragedies of old, only for so long.

Masters of Reality

The Kellers are the masters of reality, manipulating reality to avoid paying their existential dues. Each of the Kellers—Mother, Chris, and Keller—pursues a complementary strategy that, while cunning, falls short. Opportunity cost is there lurking, biding its time, like the neighborhood kids:

> KELLER [*laughs*]. I got all the kids crazy!
> CHRIS. One of these days they'll all come in here
> and beat your brains out. (13–14)

Mother knows the truth, knows that Keller ordered Steve to ship the cracked heads, knows that Keller framed Steve. She knows that, for his choices, there is a price to be paid. Three years ago, her son Larry flew on a mission. He never returned. Even though he never flew a P-40—the airframe into which the heads were mounted—in her calculus, if Larry were dead, Keller is the murderer. But no. God is on her side. God would not allow it. "God does not," she says, "let a son be killed by his father" (68). God will lift the burden of opportunity cost from her.

If God exists, Larry will return. That is a mother's faith. Until his homecoming, she devises alternate means to sustain her faith. Her neighbor, Frank, is an astrologer. In astrology, there is a prodigy known as a "favorable day." On one's favorable day, death looks away. "The odds are a million to one," says Frank, "that a man won't die on his favorable day" (66). Larry had gone down on November 25. To find out if November 25 was Larry's day, Mother has Frank cast his horoscope. It turns out that it was his day. The chances are 999,999:1 that he is alive. The apple tree further validates her. The morning of the play, it was blasted down by the wind. It was blasted down because it was an abomination. Memorials are for the dead.

But Mother only buys time. She is fooled by randomness, confusing the static in the star ways and the blasts of wind for a signal. God is not on her side. The universe feels no sense of obligation. In a show of dramatic irony, it is her insistence that Larry is alive that forces Ann to produce Larry's suicide note. It is this note that undoes the Kellers' mastery of reality.

Chris, unlike Mother, does not know the truth, does not know Keller ordered Steve to ship the heads, does not know Keller framed Steve. He is a dreamer, has not reached the jaded age. He weighs reality in the scales of his inexperience. In his inexperience, the only measure he knows is that of the responsibility of "man for man," and so he judges all hearts (36). Into his heart will not enter that Jim could choose a bigger bankbook over being a better benefactor to humanity. Into his heart will not enter that Keller could choose the business over his responsibility to fellow human beings.

With his depth of conviction, Chris is persuasive. Every few years, he tells Jim he would be happier helping the sick by being an under-paid researcher rather than an overrated doctor. His persuasiveness alarms Sue, who, worrying about the size of Jim's bankbook, asks Ann to move away with Chris (44). His persuasiveness also convinces George to disown his own father:

> CHRIS [*sits facing* GEORGE]. Tell me, George. What
> happened? The court record was good enough for
> you all these years, why isn't it good now? Why did
> you believe it all these years?
> GEORGE [*after a slight pause*]. Because you believed
> it … That's the truth, Chris. I believed everything,
> because I thought you did.

His conviction casts a reality distortion field. Keller cannot be guilty because he is the best of fathers. If he were guilty, the court would have determined so. But he is fooled by his goodness. The depth of his conviction never penetrated below the surface simplicity of his inexperience.

Now Keller: not only does he know the truth, he has fabricated the truth. He is the interior dramatist. If the neighborhood kids have heard disturbing rumors, he will create a spin:

> KELLER. Actually what happened was that when I
> got home from the penitentiary, the kids got very
> interested in me. You know kids. I was [*Laughs*] like
> the expert on the jail situation. And as time passed
> they got it confused and … I ended up a detec-
> tive [*Laughs.*]
> MOTHER. Except that *they* didn't get it confused.
> [*To* ANN] He hands out badges from the Post
> Toasties boxes. [*They laugh.*] (29)

What federal penitentiary? Nothing is amiss. He manipulates reality: he is a detective, the cellar his jail.

So too, when George questions Keller's innocence, Keller distorts reality. He reiterates how Steve was a small man who "never learned how to take the blame" and reinforces his position with a litany of examples (63). There was the time Steve almost burned down the shop and blamed the mechanic. There was the time Steve lost money on an oil stock and blamed Frank (64). There is a pattern here, argues Keller: Steve did wrong in shipping the heads and, because he was a small man, blamed Keller. Though Keller can win over some of the people most of the time, he cannot win over the iron law of opportunity cost.

Opportunity cost rears up in the explosive conclusion to Act 2 when the Kellers' contrasting realities collide. Chris finally tells Mother that, come hell or high water, he will marry Ann, Larry's fiancée. Mother, however, cannot accept Larry's death. Cornered, she says things to Chris it were better not to say:

> MOTHER. Your brother's alive, darling, because if
> he's dead, your father killed him. Do you understand
> me now? As long as you live, that boy is alive. God
> does not let a son be killed by his father. Now you
> see, don't you? (68)

She draws her line in the sand. If she loses hope, she will kill herself (22). Her last-ditch gambit, however, comes at a tremendous cost. She preserves her hope by admitting, in so many words, that Keller has been guilty all along.

After her burst, she exits, leaving Chris to confront Keller. Keller confesses. He was responsible for the heads. He knew lives were at risk. But he did it for Chris, did it to save the business. Chris rebukes him and, having surfeited his rage, exits in despair.

Keller and Mother regroup. She suggests that it is time for him to pay. Between the horoscopes and revisionist narratives, the past is catching up:

> MOTHER. I think if you sit him down and you ...
> explain yourself. I mean you ought to make it clear
> to him that you know you did a terrible thing.

> [*Not looking into his eyes*] I mean if he saw that you
> realize what you did. You see?
> KELLER. What ice does that cut?
> MOTHER [*a little forcefully*]. I mean if you told him
> that you want to pay for what you did.
> KELLER [*sensing ... quietly*]. How can I pay?
> MOTHER. Tell him ... you're willing to go to prison.
> [*Pause.*] (76)

Keller will have none of it. Chris will forgive him. "I'm his father and he's my son," he says, "and if there's something bigger than that I'll put a bullet in my head" (77). Family will lift the burden of opportunity cost from him.

As Mother draws her line in the sand, Ann will not stand by idle. She has come 700 miles to marry Chris. She will prove to Mother that Larry is dead. She has a letter, a letter from Larry, his suicide letter. It is the atom bomb of letters. In it, Larry tells Ann not to wait. Larry has heard Keller and Steve have been charged. "Every day three or four men never come back," he says, "and he sits back there doing business." "I could kill him," writes Larry (83). But instead of killing Keller, he kills himself, flying into the void.

After Chris reads the letter to Keller, Keller realizes the game is up. Keller had been put out when he was ten years old. He had lived through the Great Depression and the Dust Bowl. To ensure his sons would have an easier life, he has avoided paying his opportunity costs. He avoided the cost by framing Steve, by perjuring himself, and by distorting reality. He tried to get around the cost by making money, passing the business on to Chris, helping George set up, and welcoming Steve back into the business. He came so close to having his cake and eating it too.

When it started unravelling, Keller could still count on the support of his good son, his dead son, the younger, more perfect son who understood the cost of a buck. But the letter strips him of his final hope. After he reads the letter, Mother, with a dark premonition, cuts in:

MOTHER. Larry was your son too, wasn't he? You
know he'd never tell you to do this.
KELLER [*looking at letter in his hand*]. Then what is
this if it isn't telling me? Sure, he was my son. But I
think to him they were all my sons. And I guess they
were, I guess they were. (83)

The letter brings the masters of reality back down to Earth. The
Kellers thought they could dream the dream and live it too. But they
could only delay the day of reckoning. Mother loses her religion. Her
faith that Larry would return was bought at the cost of God and the
stars. For her, the stars will forevermore wander random pathways,
silent, dumb. Chris, on the other hand, buys experience at the cost of
his worldview where the money is clean, the courts are just, and the
fathers are like Jesus. Then, there is Keller. He buys a better future
for his family at the cost of his integrity. In the dog-eat-dog world
of tragedy, it is either responsibility to family or responsibility to
humanity, but not both. The Kellers were only mortal gods, building
houses of cards.

The Dismal Art

Tragedy, like economics, is a dismal art. Tragedy is an economics of
the final resort that examines the opportunity cost of being alive.
While participants in hunters' markets, farmers' markets, and stock
markets come together to value beavers and deer, fruits and veg-
etables, and stocks and bonds by the opportunity cost concept of
one beaver for two deer, patriots come together on the marketplace
of the tragic stage to value their devotion to the new ideals of Pax
Americana. Economists price goods. Dramatists price dreams. To
define the price, both identify what is given up in exchange.

To price out intangible assets, one turns to tragedy because tragedy
is a valuing mechanism for human assets. Economists can tell you a
gallon of milk is worth $4.99, but not how much the milk of human
kindness costs.[5] To find out how much the milk of human kindness
is worth, one turns to tragedy. In a world of privation, where the

shortfalls are perpetual, there are no free lunches, only opportunity costs. Because of the opportunity cost mechanism, tragedy establishes the price of the all-too-human as the next best alternative that is given up in exchange.

The function of drama as a valuing mechanism is unique to tragedy. Miller could not, for example, have priced out the cost of the dream if he had set the action in a comedy. Comedy is a world of plenty. There is no opportunity cost in comedy: it is a world of free lunches. Compare the father Micio in *The Brothers*, by Roman comedian Terence, to Keller:

> MICIO. He dines and wines and reeks of scent: I pay
> for it all. He keeps a mistress: I shall pay up as long
> as it suits me, and when it doesn't, maybe she will
> shut his door on him. He has a broken door-lock; I'll
> have it mended. He has torn someone's clothes; they
> can be repaired. (344)

Both Micio and Keller provide for their sons. In the world of comedy, the limit of Micio's largesse is whether "it suits me." Micio, flush with cash, effortlessly provides for his son. For Keller, however, to provide for his sons in the world of tragedy, he must feign illness, lie, perjure himself, put his reputation on the line, throw his neighbors to the wolves, and endanger the lives of others' sons. The brutality of tragedy is what makes it a great valuing mechanism.

As a valuing mechanism, Miller uses it to explore the price patriots pay to live the American dream. What is the cost of being a good husband? To become a good husband, one gives up the dream of true research. What is the inverse cost, the cost of being a researcher? That cost works out to be the additional income of $185 per week that is lost when one gives up the general practice. What is the cost of a mother waiting for her son? Her other son picks up the tab. "We're like at a railroad station," says her other son, "waiting for a train that never comes in" (21). What is the cost of solidarity with fellow human beings? The cost of solidarity is life; the war kills those not greedy enough of their lives. What is the cost of standing up for justice? The cost is the ties that bind together families. What is the cost of saving an engagement? The cost is turning a blind eye to a father-in-law's crimes. What is the cost of becoming practical? The cost of practical society life is to watch "the star of one's honesty" go out (74). What is the cost of money? Money, in *All My Sons*, comes at the price of integrity. What is the cost of being a good father? The cost is your life, all your sons will spit you out.

In *All My Sons*, each time the subsidiary characters are confronted with several alternatives, they choose one, eliminate the others, and are left with a certain "wisp of sadness" (6). The wisp of sadness is the surface manifestation of the invisible hand of opportunity cost at work. Keller, however, wants it all, choosing—simultaneously—the best of every alternative. Every time the future proliferates and forks, he is there having his cake and eating it too. But opportunity cost is an iron law. It will find a way through the sliding door of chance.

By the efficient mechanism of opportunity cost, Miller asks how much runaway patriotism costs. Uncle Sam had made it the patriotic duty of each American to make money. *All My Sons*, however, steps back and dramatizes how, behind every beautiful thing—the smiles and the "attaboys," the long driveways and the mansions on the hill, the new fridges and the fast cars—lay some kind of pain. In dramatizing the cost so beautifully, it caught the imagination of a new generation of theatergoers and created, in the process, the uncreated conscience of American patriotism.

Notes

1. Arthur Miller, *All My Sons* (Penguin, 2000). Text references are to page numbers of this edition. Thank you to Robert C. Evans for his encouragement to write this essay.
2. Christopher Bigsby, Introduction to *All My Sons*, by Arthur Miller. Penguin, 2000, p. xxiv.
3. *Oxford Latin Dictionary*, 1st ed., s.v. "*decido*."

4. On comedy as a world of plenty, see Edwin Wong, *The Risk Theatre Model of Tragedy: Gambling, Drama, and the Unexpected.* Friesen Press, 2019, pp. 234–36.
5. On tragedy as a valuing mechanism, see Wong, *The Risk Theatre Model of Tragedy* pp. 79–110.

Works Cited

Bigsby, Christopher. Introduction to *All My Sons*, by Arthur Miller, vii–xxvi. Penguin, 2000.

Miller, Arthur. *All My Sons*. Penguin, 2000.

———. *Death of a Salesman*. 50th anniversary ed. Penguin, 1999.

Smith, Adam. *The Wealth of Nations: Books I–III*. Edited by Andrew Skinner, Penguin, 1999.

Terence. *The Comedies*. Translated by Betty Radice, Penguin, 1976.

Wong, Edwin. *The Risk Theatre Model of Tragedy: Gambling, Drama, and the Unexpected*. Friesen Press, 2019.

CHAPTER 7
Aeschylus's *Seven against Thebes*: A Patriot's Portrait of a Patriot

THE FOOL.

Aeschylus's tragedy *Seven against Thebes*, winner of the Dionysia in 467 BCE, separates the impulse of patriotism into its constituent ideologies, emotions, and behaviors. In *Seven*, the spark of patriotism is kindled by the opening flourish of bugle calls. When, through the pathetic fallacy, homeland becomes motherland, the spark becomes a flame. Then, calling the gods and the fervor of religion under its banner, the flame becomes a fire. Finally, by drawing a line between "us" and "them," the fire becomes a blaze. Individuality is seared away, revealing the archetypes behind the human mask, the ancient compulsions that speak through the heraldic devices emblazoned on the warriors' arms. Aeschylus, by dramatizing a city besieged, presents a perfect prism that refracts the intense blaze of patriotism into a scintillating rainbow of ideologies, emotions, and behaviors that, while touching every facet of the human experience, is bound together by the biological imperatives underlying human nature.

Although remembered today as the father of tragedy and the eldest of the big three of Aeschylus, Sophocles, and Euripides, Aeschylus was a soldier and a patriot. He fought in the four major engagements of the Persian Wars, where a motley consortium of bickering city-states checked the Persian Empire. In 490 BCE, he distinguished himself in the hoplite ranks at Marathon, where his brother, Cynegirus, perished. He fought in 480 at Artemisium and Salamis, and at Plataea in 479 when freedom came to Greece (Herodotus 6.114).

In the second century CE, the travel writer Pausanias visited Athens. He was surprised to learn that Aeschylus's patriotism took such pride of place that the poet neglected to recollect his other achievements on his epitaph:

> Aeschylus, who had won such renown for his
> poetry and for his share in the naval battles before
> Artemisium and at Salamis, recorded at the prospect
> of death nothing else, and merely wrote his name,
> his father's name, and the name of his city, and
> added that he had witnesses to his valor in the
> grove at Marathon and in the Persians who landed
> there. (1.14.5)

The Athenians, however, remembered him as a poet and a patriot. The fifth century had been the Athenian century, the century where backwoods Athens had risen against empire only to itself become an empire. Towards the end of the century, however, Athens was fighting for survival, exhausted by plague, stasis, and the Peloponnesian War. In 405 BCE, Aristophanes's comedy *Frogs* was produced. The nostalgic play reflects on Athens's heyday, when civic poets promoted civic virtues, taking the city from peak to peak. In its reflections, it intertwines Aeschylus's poetry with his patriotism.

In *Frogs*—which is named after the chorus of frogs that inhabit the lake at the entrance to the underworld—all the great tragic poets are dead. The tragic poets were the ones who had inculcated the Athenians with a sense of virtue and responsibility by holding the reflecting mirror of Achilles, Patroclus, and the role models of myth before the youth. In the logic of *Frogs*, Athens could be saved if a poet-saviour could be brought back from the dead. Dionysus, the god of tragedy, goes to the underworld where he judges a poetic agon between the two leading candidates: Aeschylus and Euripides. He will bring the winner back to life. Though a comedy, *Frogs* implies a real urgency for a saviour. Athens stood on the brink. If it seems strange to ask a poet to save the city, remember that then, the division of labor was less pronounced. If moderns lived like the ancients, singer-songwriter Lucinda Williams would also be a field commander, four-star general Colin Powell would write Broadway hits, and playwright Caridad Svich would be Pope. Those were different times.

In their contest, Euripides's ghost establishes the qualities that poets bring to the table. They offer "skill and good council" and "make people better members of their communities" (1009–10). Aeschylus responds with *Seven*:

> EURIPIDES. And just how did you train them to be
> so noble?
> DIONYSUS. Speak up, Aeschylus, and don't be
> purposefully prideful and difficult.
> AESCHYLUS. By composing a play chock-full
> of Ares.
> DIONYSUS. Namely?
> AESCHYLUS. My *Seven Against Thebes*; every
> single man who watched it was hot to be
> warlike. (1019–22)

When *Frogs* was produced, the real Euripides had been dead a year and Aeschylus fifty. Sixty-two years separated *Seven* from *Frogs*. Despite the recency bias in Euripides's favour, Aeschylus prevails. In real life, however, Aeschylus was not coming back. Six months after *Frogs*, Athens fell. That, in the fantasy of *Frogs*, Aeschylus could be imagined as such a saviour, however, testifies to the enduring vision of nobility in *Seven*, a play that set fire to the flames of patriotism, the most patriotic of plays by the most patriotic of poets. In the character of Eteocles, Aeschylus gives us a patriot's portrait of a patriot.

Eteocles's State of the Union Address

Seven begins with Thebes, the city of seven gates, under siege. After an initial ranging of powers, the enemy mounts a final, all-in assault. In his war room atop the acropolis, Eteocles coordinates the defense. His is a master class in statecraft.

In his opening address to the Thebans, Eteocles delivers his vision of patriotism. Patriotism begins with a contradiction. While god is responsible for success, Eteocles himself is responsible for failure:

> ETEOCLES. For if we win success, the God is
> the cause
> but if—may it not chance so—there is disaster,
> throughout the town, voiced by its citizens,
> a multitudinous swelling prelude
> cries on one name "Eteocles" with groans. (4–8:
> Grene translation)

Eteocles's "heads the god wins; tails Eteocles loses" heuristic defies logic. His statement appears lopsided because Eteocles is pursuing two strategies that, considered singly, are at odds, but, considered together, amplify one another. His first strategy is to motivate the Thebans by rousing their blind and irrational hopes. Hope, as Aeschylus notes in another play, is one of the sapiens's two greatest possessions:

> CHORUS. Did you perhaps go further than you have
> told us?
> PROMETHEUS. I caused mortals to cease foresee-
> ing doom.
> CHORUS. What cure did you provide them with
> against that sickness?
> PROMETHEUS. I placed in them blind hopes.

CHORUS. That was a great gift you gave men.
PROMETHEUS. Besides this, I gave them fire.
(*Prometheus Bound* 249–54)

Though despair whispers the day is lost, blind hope never surrenders. What is more, by invoking "god" and "success" together, Eteocles amplifies blind hope with the sum of his compatriots' faith, their religiosity, and all their beliefs in providence. This is no longer blind hope, but a seeing hope kindled by religious fervor. They are on the acropolis. They see the temples, monumental projections of power. The emotion of hope coupled with the human predisposition to belief is a winning combination.

If the gods take credit for success, it stands that they should take the blame for failure. Anthropologist James George Frazer records many such instances of divine failure in *The Golden Bough*. In one example, during a six-month drought, the Sicilians abused the statue of Saint Angelo, their patron rainmaker. They stripped him, reviled him, put him in irons, and threatened him with drowning and hanging (86). In another example, he records how the Chinese would alternately praise or censure their gods. Compliant gods were raised to a higher level of divinity by imperial decree. Recalcitrant gods, however, were deposed and stripped of the rank of deity (85). Eteocles, however, takes an asymmetric approach to the assignment of praise and blame. Why?

Eteocles recognizes that an effective leader cannot transfer the risk of failure to others. Leaders who transfer risk are perceived by their constituents to lack skin in the game. Agamemnon in Homer's *Iliad* illustrates the shortcomings of a skinless leader. Although Agamemnon apologizes to Achilles for inciting their ruinous quarrel, he transfers the underlying blame to Zeus, Fate, and the Erinys (19.87). "They made me do it," he says. What a daft apology. So too, Agamemnon points the finger at Zeus when, facing mounting losses, he proposes to evacuate Troy. Though god was responsible for their setbacks, this is not something he can say. He is immediately rebuked by a junior commander, and to the resounding assent of his joint chiefs of staff (9.17–51). Unlike Agamemnon, Eteocles recognizes that leaders who wish to unify their peoples must bear responsibility. His second strategy, therefore, involves shouldering the blame.

By holding himself accountable, Eteocles aligns his interests with his constituents' interests. He has skin in the game. The principle of skin in the game finds that, the higher the personal cost of failure, the more one is incentivized to perform. Knowing that, if their ship of state goes down, Eteocles goes down with them, is a great reassurance to his constituents.[1] They expect that Eteocles, in saving his own skin, will save them all.

In the final examination, Eteocles's "heads the god wins; tails Eteocles loses" heuristic, while lopsided, works in real life. It activates the emotion of hope, engages the mind's predisposition to religious belief, and unifies leaders and constituents by giving leaders skin in the game. Patriotism is the mood of an animal under stress, the outpourings of a human nature for which reason is a last resort. Patriotism prefers blind hopes, fast heuristics, deep-seated beliefs, and other strategies predating novel reason, which is, from the perspective of evolution, one of the mind's newer tools.

In the second half of his state of the union address, Eteocles states the motherland doctrine. For a patriot, the concept of homeland is too small to fire hearts. It must be amplified by the pathetic fallacy. The pathetic fallacy is a literary device that attributes human qualities to inanimate nature. By personifying the land into a motherland, Eteocles adds urgency to the defensive effort. They fight for Mother Earth, the original mother:

> ETEOCLES. Help Earth your Mother.
> She reared you, on her kindly surface, crawling
> babies, welcomed all the trouble of your nurture,
> reared you to live in her, to carry a shield
> in her defense, loyally, against such needs as
> this. (16–20)

Filial devotion due to a biological mother is transferred onto the home range. The land is alive, suckling its babes. Every Theban who has drank her milk is her debtor. By turning mother's milk into an intoxicating wine, Eteocles takes kinship, the most fundamental of relationships for sapiens and other social animals, and appropriates it for homeland security.

Patriotism is one of the most dynamic and encompassing forces of the human mind. By vesting human hopes onto the gods, the quality of patriotism engages the human predisposition towards religious belief, itself a primal calling going back at least sixty thousand years to the Neanderthals, who buried their dead in elaborate funerary rites (Rendu et al. 81–86). Likewise, by transforming the home range into the myth of the motherland, patriotism repurposes for its own objectives the behavior of altruism and fundamental notions of kinship and family. Social organization, emotions, behaviors, cult, and mythology, however, are only the starting points of patriotism, which is so much more. There is still to consider in- and out-groups, the higher ideologies, self-sacrifice, and monumental art, of which *Seven* itself is a bright example.

Us and Them

In *Seven*, there are two sets of us and them, one inside the gates, one at the gates. The first set of us and them are represented by Eteocles and the defenders of Thebes, on the one hand, and the chorus, on the other hand. The second set of us and them are represented by the two sets of seven captains: one defending and the other besieging Thebes. Eteocles's goal is to unify "us" inside the gates and destroy "them" outside the gates. After his opening speech, he encounters the first "them": the chorus of Theban women. They are making their way to the temples on the acropolis.

The chorus are terrified. They have seen "the wave of warriors, with waving plumes," the "Horse of the White Shield / well equipped, hastening upon our city," and "the jagged rocks they hurl / upon our citizens" (89–90, 112, 299–300). They have heard trampling hoofs, whirring spears, and screeching axles bruiting impending rapine, rape, and ruin (84, 153, 155). They come to prostrate themselves:

CHORUS. Shall I kneel at the images of the Gods?

O Blessed Ones, throned in peace,
It is time to cling to your images.
We delay and wail too much. (96–99)

Frazzled, the chorus say their raggedy prayers. Some turn to Zeus. "Zeus, Father Omnipotent! all fulfilling!" says one, "Let us not fall into the hands of the foeman!" (118–19). "Cypris, who are our ancestress," says another, "turn destruction away" (140–41). After addressing the deities individually, they address the divine collective:

CHORUS. O Gods all sufficient,
O Gods and Goddesses, Perfecters,
Protectors of our country's forts,
do not betray this city, spear-won,
to a foreign-tongued enemy. (166–70)

As the chorus say their broken prayers, Eteocles falls on them, rebuking them with strong words. To Eteocles, the chorus are either with him or against him:

ETEOCLES. You insupportable creatures, I ask you,
is this the best, is this for the city's safety,
is this enheartening for our beleaguered army,
to have you falling at the images
of the city's gods crying and howling,
an object of hatred for all temperate souls? (181–86)

The chorus protest: they were afraid; they ran to the gods; their actions fall in line with custom (211–16). Eteocles and the chorus engage in a stichomythic, back and forth exchange:

CHORUS. I am afraid: the din at the gates
grows louder.
ETEOCLES. Silence! Do not speak of this throughout the city.
CHORUS. O Blessed Band, do not betray this fort.
ETEOCLES. Damnation! Can you not endure
in silence?

CHORUS. Fellow-citizen Gods, grant me not to be
a slave.
ETEOCLES. It is you who enslave yourselves, and all
the city. (249–54)

Many years later, the great magician Faustus, having achieved
world dominion, perhaps at too great a price, was looking for another
way. He calls on God. "I do repent," he says, "and yet I do despair"
(Marlowe, *Doctor Faustus* 5.1.69). His is a negative prayer filled with
self-doubt, spoken from the point of view of the damned. God spits it
out. Eteocles's quarrel with the chorus is precisely this: their prayers
are negative prayers, spoken from the loser point of view. "Grant me
not to be a slave" and "do not betray this city," though prayers, lack
skin in the game. Vanquishers have their prayers and the vanquished
theirs. The chorus' prayers are those of the vanquished.

Eteocles gives them a better prayer, one with skin in the game, one
that partakes and has a share of victory. It begins by invoking the gods
as the city's allies, a joyous paean of thanksgiving promising them
hearths flowing with the blood of sacrificed sheep and slaughtered
bulls, their altars adorned with the foe's spoils (264–79). Although
they need time to adjust, the chorus rejoin Eteocles's in-group.

The exchange between Eteocles and the chorus illustrates how
patriotism overwhelms reason. Patriotism is like the instinct that
jumps back from the snake even before the higher mental processes
establish the nature of the serpent threat. So, too, the chorus's initial
position may have been innocuous, and Eteocles's binary arguments
fallacious. But first survival: there will be time for logic after, if they
live. In crises, instinct comes before reason and morale before logic.
Eteocles, by unifying the city, checks off another box on the patriot's
rulebook. But there is still another "them": the barbarians at the gates.

Patriotism strips humans of their personality and individuality.
Once patriotism separates a man from his multitudes, what is left
behind is a type, a caricature, a sign and representation of the raw
biological forces animating the man. In the sequence leading up to
the play, Eteocles had sent a Messenger to spy on the Argive camp.
The Messenger, having learned the identities of the seven attacking

captains, returns. As he relays the information to Eteocles, he systematically deindividuates the foe until all that is left of the man is his shield device, the proud advertisement blazoned on his shield. Deindividuation is part and parcel of patriotism's process.

Stripped of his humanity, a man becomes an abstract representation. Polyneices becomes the idea of justice, advertising on his shield a woman identifying herself as Justice leading a man—ostensibly himself—home (642–49). Others expose their animality. Tydeus stands ready to strike like a serpent (381). In Hippomedon and Parthenopaeus, the madness of the chthonian powers, hateful to civilization and the bright gods, breaks out. One has the fire-breathing monster Typhon blazoned on his shield, the other the Sphinx (493, 541). Through their devices, the two captains are reduced into savage personifications of madness and unreason. Others become caricatures of blasphemy. At the third gate, Eteoclus carries a shield on which:

> A man in armor mounts a ladder's steps
> to the enemy's town to sack it. Loud
> cries also this man in his written legend
> "Ares himself shall not cast me from the
> tower." (466–69)

Capaneus goes further. He will sack the city "with the Gods' good will or ill" (425–29). Parthenopaeus vaunts that he will sack Thebes "in despite of Zeus" (532). In this deindividuated world of patriotism where the abstract symbolic device stands in for the person, even a blank shield is a sign. Amphiaraus's lack of a shield device signifies how "He is best not at seeming to be such / but being so" (591–92).

Patriotism loves mental frugality, and typology is a sign of frugality. One is never oneself, but a sign, a sign of justice, a sign of animality, a sign of darkness and evil. Shield devices, vaunts, and even names are signs. Parthenopaeus, whose name means "the maiden one," represents war's rite of passage where a boy becomes a killer (532–38). Once people have become types, it is easier to categorize them into in- and out-groups, the former bent on multiplying its seed and the latter on destroying it. Binary mentalities are a survival heuristic, practiced not only by the sapiens, but also by their animal precursors from ant colonies to baboon troops. Patriotism is not such a new thing. Patriotism started long ago.

Patriotism also demands that the defending captains become types. One defender is a sentry "hostile to strangers" ("*Echthroxenos*"; 621). Patriotism has distilled Lasthenes into that one quality. It is sufficient. Such is also the fate of Melanippus and Polyphontes, who are reduced into their elemental qualities. The former hates "insolent words" and the latter is "a man of fiery spirit" (410, 447). Other defenders are likewise stripped down. In a roll call of sons, one defender is the "son of Astacus," another "Creon's son," and a third the "son of Oenops" (408, 474, 505). By emphasizing genealogy, Eteocles gives his troops skin in the game: sons must equal fathers. When even skin in the game is insufficient, he gives them land in the game: two defenders—Melanippus and Megareus—are born from the race of sown men, the original founders of Thebes who sprang up autochthonous, from the soil itself.

In the narrative of us and them, not only human reason, but human madness breaks out. The invaders, though Argives speaking a common language, are called "a foreign-tongued enemy" (170). The unreason of patriotism in bending the truth may be motivated by hidden biological prime movers. Anthropologists have identified in early hunter-gatherers evidence of a binary mentality cleaving sapiens into in- and out-group members. The Nyae Nyae, for example, a group of !Kung hunter-gatherers living in the Kalahari Desert "speak of themselves as perfect and clean and other !Kung people as alien murderers who use deadly poisons" (Wilson 92).

Patriotism may be, speculates biologist Edward O. Wilson, a behavior encoded into our genes through eons of evolution, allowing the sapiens who exhibited such impulses to multiply. In this light, patriotism is a hypertrophy and cultural outgrowth of an innate tribalism that unites kin groups into bands (82–92). Too little patriotism, and Thebes falls. Too much patriotism, and nationalism and racism rise, stalling the spread of culture and information. Patriotism, like so many other all-too-human impulses, is "on the spectrum." Lasthenes, with his Stone Age xenophobia, makes a good sentry. His value in peacetime, however, may be debatable. The limitation of biology is one of the issues with building a space age society from genes adapted to Stone and Heroic Age environments.

A Delivery Mechanism

Like a megaton bomb, the dramatic payload of *Seven* sits idle until Aeschylus devises an appropriate vehicle with which to target his audience. The outcome of *Seven* is part of myth. Myth is a great spoiler: the theatergoers know myth through and through. To make the theatergoers "hot to be warlike," Aeschylus needed a powerful delivery system to sidestep the audience's knowledge. In chance and the random element, Aeschylus found a far-shooting ballistic rocket whereby he could take an outcome, known to all the theatergoers, and explode it in the face of the play's unsuspecting characters.

By making chance responsible for the fated outcome and by sub-jectively and objectively suppressing the odds of the fated outcome happening, Aeschylus brings myth to life. The audience, until the last second, sits in thrall, wondering how to reconcile what they know must happen with the contradictory data presented on stage. The greatness of drama lies in the dramatic sleight of hand in making the inevitable seem to have been impossible.

The fated outcome is that Eteocles and Polyneices will die by one another's hands. This is civil war. Polyneices returns to reclaim the throne. The play is structured so that the fated outcome takes place only if both brothers are assigned the seventh gate. Chance enters the play through the gate assignations. The seven attacking captains—one of whom is Polyneices—and the seven defending cap-tains—one of whom is Eteocles—are all assigned their gates by lot.[2]

Mathematically, the likelihood of a compound event happening is the product of its constituent probabilities. The odds of rolling snake eyes, or two ones on a pair of six-sided dice are 1:36 (1:6 * 1:6). On that analogy, the likelihood of the fated outcome happening is 1:49, as each of the brothers has a 1:7 chance of being assigned the seventh gate. The probability, therefore, of the fated outcome happening is exceedingly low. In random simulations with seven attackers, seven defenders, and seven gates, 48 out of 49 times the fated outcome will be averted.

Aeschylus begins his suppression of the fated outcome by dealing the captains their assignations by random lot. Though his audience lacked access to modern probability theory (which arose in the Italian Renaissance with the work of gambler-mathematician Gerolamo Cardano), they grasped the fundamental notion of intuitive probability.[3] Ancient Greek had a term *eikos* that denoted *probability* or *likelihood* in the modern sense ("*Eikos*"). "To succeed in many things, or many times, is difficult," writes Aristotle, "for instance, to repeat the same throw ten thousand times with dice would be impossible, whereas to make it once or twice is comparatively easy" (*On the Heavens* 292a).

Aeschylus's audience would have understood that, from the randomness built into the gate selection process, the fated outcome would have been implausible. That Aeschylus encourages his audience to think about probability can be seen in the play's aleatory references. Hermes is invoked in his capacity as the god of lots who brings captains together for mortal combat (508).[4] Ares throws dice to single out the quick from the dead (414). Even specific throws are alluded to. "I will take six men, myself to make a seventh," says Eteocles as he initiates the defense. "The number 6 + 1," notes Hanna Roisman, "was considered an unlucky throw in the six sided dice" (22). *Seven* is a most probabilistic play, aleatory and ludic, a game of chance and a game of death.

Through the lottery device, Aeschylus begins to suppress the fated outcome. Then, in a wonderful, marvelous masterstroke, he discounts the odds of the fated outcome from 48:1 against to 25,401,599:1 against. Never did the waters of artistic imagination rise so high as when he painted the inevitable as nigh impossible. To dam back possibility's flood, he engineered an architectural marvel: the monumental shield scene.

The shield scene consists of seven matched speeches between Eteocles and the Messenger, each separated by an intervening prayer from the chorus. The Messenger has been collecting intelligence. He has seen the seven hostile captains draw lots to determine their gate assignations, has seen their shield devices, has heard their vaunts. He informs Eteocles of the threats. As the Messenger identifies each captain, Eteocles draws a lot to assign a defender. Having assigned the defender, like a commentator at a boxing match, he analyzes the tale of the tape.

In this peculiar battle, men do not fight. Because patriotism has reduced men into types and abstractions, it becomes a proxy battle where signs and representations clash. By examining the clash of representations, Eteocles can see whether the gods are on his side. Chance has brought the combatants together, but chance is not random. The casting of lots was a means of divination. Through the crack of chance, the gods reveal their will.

The tale of the tape at the first six gates favours Eteocles beyond any reasonable doubt. If the enemy has Typhon blazoned on his shield, he is, through a strange synchronicity, paired against a defender sporting the image of Zeus (511–20). In mythology, Zeus tamed Typhon. If the enemy is a blasphemer, he just happens to be paired against a defender "honoring the throne of Modesty" (409). If the enemy appears to be sprung from the race of giants, he is, against all odds, paired with a defender who has the "favor of Artemis / and of the other Gods" (449–50). As the giants fell, so too, in this new Gigantomachy, the gods will prevail.

In addition to the overwhelming objective indications of victory, every subjective indication also points away from the fated outcome: enemy morale is such that they have already sent home memorial tokens (49–50); the enemy's sacrifices are unfavourable (379); infighting plagues the enemy ranks (382–84). While every Theban—from Eteocles to the soldiers, women, old men, and young boys—stand united, the enemy stands divided. The certainty that the foe is doomed rises to a pitch when the Messenger announces that, at the sixth gate, the best of the Argives—the prophet-warrior

Amphiaraus—lays into Polyneices, telling him that his leading a foreign army home is an abomination to the gods. What is more, Amphiaraus says that he expects to be struck dead, such is the sacrilege of their expedition (571–89).

At this moment, time stands still. The odds of the fated outcome were unlikely. The pairings at each of the gates portend victory. The enemy is divided. Eteocles basks in the moral certainty of victory. It is almost a foregone conclusion. The chorus capture the moment of jubilation. In the beginning of the shield scene, the chorus, although undergoing rehabilitation, were still singing the fall of Thebes. Their prayers at the initial gates talk of success, but also of dying friends, ravishment, and fear (420–22, 455–56, 565). In other words, negative prayers. At the sixth gate, however, they find their stride in a devastating triumphant prayer calling on Zeus to "strike down and slay" the foe (629–30). The halcyon moment, however, is brief. The Messenger proceeds to the seventh gate, telling Eteocles his brother awaits. Eteocles, having dispatched the other captains, suddenly realizes the gods call him to die.

What are the odds that Eteocles would be encouraged by six perfect pairings only to be cast down in the end? In other words, what are the odds that Melanippus confronts Tydeus at the first gate, Polyphontes confronts Capaneus at the second gate, and that all the pairings took place as they did up to Lasthenes confronting Amphiaraus at the sixth gate? According to the law of permutations, the formula for the number of unique arrangements possible with seven captains at seven gates is seven factorial 7! (7 * 6 * 5 * 4 * 3 * 2 * 1) or 5,040. Since there are seven attackers and defenders, to find out how many permutations exist at seven gates, multiply 5,040 by 5,040. With seven gates, seven attackers, and seven defenders, 25,401,600 permutations are possible. The odds, therefore, of Eteocles being raised up from gates one to six only to be struck down at gate seven are 25,401,599:1 against. By suppressing the odds of the fated outcome to a nonce quantity, Aeschylus animates the myth. Never again in the millenniums afterwards, neither in Greece nor in the lands that practice the art of playwriting, has a playwright dared to dramatize a deed so explosively blowing apart the possible and the probable.

Though Aeschylus's audience lacked a working theory of combinations and permutations, the Greeks did have a term *sumplokē* "intertwining, complication, or combination" to denote this sort of combinatorial analysis ("*Sumplokē*"). "Xenocrates asserted," says Plutarch, "that the number of syllables which the letters will make in combinations is 1,002,000,000,000" (*Moralia* 733a). Plutarch also records that the Stoic philosopher Chrysippus, postulating the number of illnesses that arise from the different combinations of food and drink on the body, turned to a combinatorial analysis. Through an analogy, Chrysippus calculated that, from ten simple propositions (representing different foods and drink), over a million compound combinations (representing different ailments) were possible (732f). Chrysippus and Xenocrates's attempts demonstrate that Aeschylus's audience would have been able to infer the enormous range of possibilities in seven gates, seven attackers, and seven defenders. If their calculations are indicative, Aeschylus's audience, if anything, would have grossly overestimated the possible permutations, making the play even more dramatic in its rebel probability.

The thrill of drama, is not, as Aristotle claimed, to bring about the probable outcome, but, is rather the opposite, to bring about the most improbable outcome, the one that is 25,401,599:1 against (*Poetics* 1451a; Wong 206–17). Here is no pity and fear, but rather wonder and awe, wonder at how, each time a pair of captains who are not the brothers goes to the gates, the fated outcome seems subjectively further away, but is objectively closer—although 25,401,600 permutations had been available at gate one, only four permutations remain at gate six—and awe for how Eteocles—like Caesar at the Capitol or Myron Scholes and Robert C. Merton at the Nobel Prize ceremony—stood highest when closest to the fall.[5] As Aeschylus brings the hammer down on Eteocles, however, he also exalts him. The highest form of patriotism is self-sacrifice: it separates run-of-the-mill from purple-hearted patriots. Though Eteocles dies, in dying Aeschylus vouchsafes him patriotism's crowning glory.

The Ancient Quarrel between Poetry and Philosophy

In the closing decades of the fifth century, poetry, tragedy, and myth were under attack. "There is an ancient quarrel," says Plato, drawing up the lines of battle, "between poetry and philosophy" (*Republic* 607b). With the rise of rationalism, it was time for the old poets to make way for the new educators of Greece, the philosophers. The fallible heroes of the old myths would make way for Socrates, Plato's new and improved hero. The time had come for the sword of reason to shine:

> [Socrates speaking] And so, Glaucon, when you happen to meet those who praise Homer and say that he's the poet who educated Greece, that it's worth taking up his works in order to learn how to manage and educate people, and that one should arrange one's whole life in accordance with his teachings, you should welcome these people and treat them as friends, since they're as good as they're capable of being, and you should agree that Homer is the most poetic of the tragedians and the first among them. But you should also know that **hymns to the gods and eulogies to good people are the only poetry we can admit into our city. If you admit the pleasure-giving Muse,** whether in lyric or epic poetry, **pleasure and pain will be kings in your city instead of law or the thing that everyone has always believed to be best, namely reason.** (*Republic* 606e–607a, emphasis added)

As Plato mobilized philosophy, others, seeing a chance to make their mark, joined the assault. The historians, led by Thucydides, attacked the stories used by the tragedians as fake myth. While the poets "exaggerate the importance of their themes" and teach by using examples from the distant and unverifiable past, the historian would instruct by providing examples filtered through the rational apparatus of the historical method (1.21–22). Gods, oracles, and omens—so often the prime movers in tragedy—are replaced with the scientific apparatus of cause and effect, eyewitness testimony of what really happened, and the careful consideration, corroboration, and weighing of evidence. At the end of the fifth century, the winds of change were blowing wild.

Whenever myth engaged with the forces of rationalism, myth was driven back. In myth, the Trojan War was the greatest of wars. Thucydides examines it with the historical method (1.10). It emerges diminished. It may well have been fought by village peoples. Rationalism advanced and myth fell back. Thucydides has Pericles, his new world hero, say that Homer is redundant (2.41). Rationalism advanced and myth fell back. Ion, a professional reciter of poetry, considers himself an educator, educating his audience on health, war, and the many other themes sung by rhapsodes. Ion, however, runs into the hero-philosopher Socrates in Plato's dialogue *Ion*. Using the Socratic method, Socrates deconstructs his expertise. It turns out that neither Ion nor the poets know anything. They have nothing to teach. Rationalism advanced and myth fell back.

Rationalism invaded the prerogative of poetry as the teacher of Greece, and poetry fell back. Rationalism pooh-poohed poetry's fake myth, its tall tales and childish gods, and poetry fell back. Poetry had made too many concessions, was in a full retreat, smarting from the sword of reason. But it had one advantage. Poetry charges the thunders of the heart. It gives its admirers something to believe in, a proof. Rationalism here falls short. It may explain *how* we came to be, but not *why*. It is silent on our ultimate purpose. Knowing this secret, Aristophanes mounted a powerful rearguard action in *Frogs*, calling on art and the author of *Seven* rather than the new rationalists to save the city.

The crowning moment of *Seven*, the moment that makes patriots "hot to be warlike," is Eteocles's reaction to learning that his brother is at the seventh gate. He is out of captains. He sees the writing on the wall. "I'll go myself," he says, "bring me my greaves" (673, 675). Though he realizes the gods call him to die, he wants for himself "no crying and no lamentation" (656). The chorus, knowing that neither brother can hope to emerge from the confrontation alive, reason with him, telling him to save himself:

> CHORUS. Go not you, go not, to the seventh gate.
> ETEOCLES. No words of yours will blunt my
> whetted purpose.
> CHORUS. Yet even bad victory the Gods hold
> in honor.
> ETEOCLES. No soldier may endure to hear
> such words.
> CHORUS. Do you wish to reap as harvest a broth-
> er's blood?
> ETEOCLES. If Gods give ill, no man may shun their
> giving. (714–19)

In his final words, he tells the chorus that he feels the "whetted purpose" thundering in his heart. This is proof enough. He will fulfil his duty by making the highest sacrifice, the "admirable offering" gods and mortals alike will envy:

> ETEOCLES. We are already past the care of Gods.
> For them our death is the admirable offering.
> Why then delay, fawning upon our doom? (703–05)

Patriotism gives patriots something that the logicians and rationalists never could: something greater than life to live and die for. Patriotism takes the raw biological basis of human nature, hidden from plain view by the mediating apparatus of consciousness, and codifies it in its strictures. It takes the primordial murmurings of tribalism and the irrational emotions of gentle altruism and hateful aggression and unites them under a common banner. It then harnesses the myriad impulses that draw the sapiens into ever higher levels of social organization—from nomadic life to life in hamlets, cities, and megalopolises—to give the patriot something to believe in.

The patriot, with his tribalism, hears the murmuring song singing new syllogisms, singing of the beauty of kinsfolk and the ugliness of those who dwell beyond the gates. With these new syllogisms, the patriot lays down patriotism's doctrine, beginning with in- and out-membership groups. To draw himself up to a higher perfection, the patriot takes the other, and turns the other into a sign and representation of all that he must, in his highest moment, overcome. In his fever, the patriot desires no mediocre other, but rather the highest type of other, the most gargantuan other against which he can assay his rising strength. He transforms the other into a bogeyman adorned with blasphemy, the dark images of the night, the eye of the full moon, the serpent's hiss, and all the other trappings inimical to kin and civilization. Against this error of nature, the patriot girds his kin together in a tight embrace. To withstand such a powerful foe, the patriot himself enlists higher powers, builds shrines to the gods and talks of motherland and fatherland, talks of how the land and the folk are bound by ancient, inviolable, and reciprocal bonds.

Surrounded by powerful and holy monuments, spires reaching up into heaven like the arms of god, the patriot begins to see that he himself is part of the proof, is the son of a line of heroes in a patrilineal and matrilineal succession going back to the crack of time. He himself dissolves into a symbol and representation, the mortal instrument of an immortal purpose. Armed now with high ideology, the patriot now has proof of his goodness, of how his people were meant to persevere, the chosen ones tilling the chosen soil. Heeding the higher calling of country, god, and people, the patriot validates the desultory dross of life and drinks in the sense of belonging and purpose so foreign to the logicians and the rationalists who could only see the wisdom of the sapiens, but not the underlying biology firing the human fuse.

Now, eternally justified, the patriot is himself life's proof. Having reached this exalted state, there is left but one act whereby he perfects life. To the rationalist who talked of virtue, there was no difference between virtue in theory and in practice. To the patriot, there is. Talk is cheap, insufficient skin. To die performing great heroic deeds is to have the highest skin in the game. It is the patriot's finest hour, the hour of the affirmation of the highest existence.

In this curious battle, the outcome is exactly as Eteocles predicted. The city is saved. In fact, on the Theban side, there is only a single casualty. In the closing scene the Herald makes a proclamation:

> HERALD. Our Lord Eteocles for his loyalty
> it is determined to bury in the earth
> that he so loved. Fighting its enemies
> he found his death here. In the sight
> of his ancestral shrines he is pure and blameless
> and died where young men die right honor-
> ably. (1006–11)

In his burial, in the dirges and the wailing, it is accomplished. Eteocles's sepulchres and monuments stand as inviolable proofs of his patriotic apotheosis. Though dead, he is born posthumously in *Seven* to light the way for all tomorrow's standard-bearers. Patriotism, having enlisted human emotions and behaviors into its service, now calls out to one of the highest constructs of the human mind—art—to justify its eternal claim.

To rational minds, *Seven* dramatized the clash between the magic of the opposing shield devices. Eteocles, like a seer, interprets the combatants' vaunts and shield devices. By the science of hermeneutics, he deciphers—and perhaps even manipulates—the hidden signs animating the cosmos. For these reasonable interpreters, Eteocles came close to mastering hermeneutics. To them, *Seven* is a tragedy of Eteocles's discourtesy to the chorus and his hubris in thinking he could master the gates. To the interpreters, however, who feel the comprehensiveness of the human experience, for those whom not only the higher and evolved sensibilities, but also the lower and primal drives of the triune brain declare themselves, *Seven* dramatizes the myriad impulses that together constitute patriotism, hot to endure all time's slings and arrows. To these other interpreters, *Seven* is a kaleidoscope of patriotism, reflecting all its changing patterns and colors, from its animal origins to its highest expressions in art, architecture, and culture. Gate by gate, Eteocles is stripped of his personality until, at the seventh gate, all his individual qualities have withdrawn behind patriotism's mask. He is no longer man, but an incarnation of duty, the great intoxicated patriot, drunk on the valor of the ages. *Seven*, in this more unified view, is a tragedy of the paradox of patriotism, the mystery of how one becomes greatest when one becomes nothing. We do not, perhaps, exist for our own sake, but for the sake of perpetuating the generations of leaves on the tree of life.

In this comprehensive view, patriotism is greater than either the philosophers or the mythographers have imagined. Patriotism is a human expression of the animal behavior of territoriality, practiced by each of the social animals from ants and hyenas to baboons and chimpanzees. As animals mark their home range in elaborate rituals, so, too, the sapiens mark their territories with doors, locks, gates, gatekeepers, walls, and banners in the sky. Patriotism in this last examination is a biological imperative, is the will to power driving natural selection. To ensure the survival of the species, it will mingle reason with unreason, self-preservation with self-sacrifice, and base ideologies with the highest of the arts and sciences. In the art of *Seven*, a patriot's portrait of patriotism, the ancient calling calls out.

Seven reminds us that you can take the individual out of the country, but not the country out of the individual. Though part of our highest ideologies and mental constructs, patriotism is also felt in the blood. Nowhere is this more evident than in the legacy of *Seven*, where generations of youths, ardent for desperate glory, fulfilled biology's gnarled imperative: *dulce et decorum est pro patria mori*.

Notes

1. For examples of negative incentives, see Taleb 12–15. Parts of this essay were presented at the 2018 Society for Classical Studies and 2020 Classical Association of the Middle West and South annual meetings, as well as a 2018 lecture at the University of Victoria. I would like to thank Laurel Bowman, Robert C. Evans, Helene Foley, David Konstan, Sophie Mills,

John P. Oleson, Gregory Rowe, and Terry Scarborough for their insights, advice, and encouragement.

2. That the attackers draw lots to determine their gate assignations is confirmed by the Messenger (56–57, 377, 424, and 456–59). How Eteocles assigns the defenders' assignations is unclear. When assigning the defenders, Eteocles uses the future tense three times ("I will station," 408, 621, 672), the perfect tense two times ("he has been sent," 448, 472), the aorist passive once ("he was chosen," 505), and the present tense once ("here is the man," 554). Previous conjectures that have arisen to explain the tenses fall into three broad categories: (1) Eteocles had decided all the assignations prior to meeting the Messenger, (2) Eteocles decides the assignations on the spot, after hearing the Messenger's reports, and (3) Eteocles decided some assignations before and some during his meeting with the Messenger. I follow Herrmann 58–62. In his bold conjecture, Herrmann argues that an important stage direction has been lost: each time the Messenger relays the assailant at the gate, Eteocles draws a lot to determine the defender. Not only does Herrmann's conjecture solve the problem of the tenses (he can draw the lot and easily switch between tenses), it also adds dramatic vitality to the action.

3. On why the ancients failed to develop a theory of probability, see Kidd 1–25. Kidd argues convincingly that probability theory failed to develop because ancient games of chance involved communal probabilities: probability theory does not grant the ancient gambler any advantage. Only when games of chance individualized risk did the first mathematician-gamblers begin exploring probability in earnest.

4. On Hermes as the god of lots, see Apollodorus 3.10.2 and Aristophanes, *Peace* 364–66.

5. Scholes and Merton received their Nobel Prizes as their hedge fund, Long-Term Capital Management, began its collapse. Its fall triggered one of the largest financial meltdowns of the modern era. See Lowenstein 96–120.

Works Cited

Aeschylus. *The Persians, Seven against Thebes, The Suppliant Maidens, Prometheus Bound.* Edited by David Grene, et al., U of Chicago P, 1959.

Apollodorus. *The Library of Greek Mythology.* Translated by Robin Hard, Oxford UP, 1997.

Aristophanes. *Clouds, Wasps, Peace.* Translated by Jeffrey Henderson, Loeb-Harvard UP, 1998.

_____. *Frogs, Assemblywomen, Wealth.* Translated by Jeffrey Henderson, Loeb-Harvard UP, 2002.

Aristotle. *On the Heavens.* Translated by W. K. C. Guthrie, Loeb-Harvard UP, 1939.

Aristotle, et al. *Poetics, On the Sublime, On Style.* Translated by Stephen Halliwell, W. H. Fyfe, and Doreen C. Innes., Loeb-Harvard UP, 1995.

"Echthroxenos." *A Greek-English Lexicon,* compiled by Liddell, Scott, and Jones, 9th ed., Oxford UP, 1996.

"Eikos." *A Greek-English Lexicon,* compiled by Liddell, Scott, and Jones, 9th ed., Oxford UP, 1996.

Frazer, James George. *The Golden Bough: A Study in Magic and Religion.* Abridged ed., Macmillan, 1922.

Herodotus. *The Histories.* Translated by Aubrey de Sélincourt, revised by John M. Marincola, Penguin, 1996.

Herrmann, Fritz-Gregor. "Eteocles' Decision in Aeschylus' *Seven against Thebes.*" *Tragedy and Archaic Greek Thought.* Edited by Douglas Cairns, Classical P of Wales, 2013, pp. 39–80.

Homer. *The Iliad of Homer.* Translated by Richmond Lattimore, U of Chicago P, 1951.

Kidd, Stephen. "Why Mathematical Probability Failed to Emerge from Ancient Gambling." *Apeiron*, vol. 53, no. 1, 2020, pp. 1–25.

Lowenstein, Roger. *When Genius Failed: The Rise and Fall of Long-Term Capital Management.* 2000, Random House, 2011.

Marlowe, Christopher. *The Complete Plays.* Edited by J. B. Steane, Penguin, 1969.

Pausanias. *Description of Greece: Books 1–2.* Translated by W. H. S. Jones, Loeb-Harvard UP, 1918.

Plato. *Complete Works.* Edited by John M. Cooper, Hackett, 1997.

Plutarch. *Moralia.* Translated by Edwin L. Minar, Jr., F. H. Sandbach, and W. C. Helmbold, vol. 9, Loeb-Harvard UP, 1961.

Rendu, William, et al. "Evidence Supporting an Intentional Neandertal Burial at La Chapelle-aux-Saints." *Proceedings of the National Academy of Sciences of the United States of America*, vol. 111, no. 1, Jan. 2014, pp. 81–86.

Roisman, Hanna M. "The Messenger and Eteocles in the *Seven against Thebes*." *L'Antiquité Classique*, vol. 59, 1990, pp. 17–36.

"*Sumplokē*." *A Greek-English Lexicon*, compiled by Liddell, Scott, and Jones, 9th ed., Oxford UP, 1996.

Taleb, Nassim Nicholas. *Skin in the Game: Hidden Asymmetries in Daily Life.* Random House, 2018.

Thucydides. *History of the Peloponnesian War.* Translated by Rex Warner, Penguin, 1972.

Wilson, Edward O. *On Human Nature.* 25th anniversary ed., Harvard UP, 2004.

Wong, Edwin. *The Risk Theatre Model of Tragedy: Gambling, Drama, and the Unexpected.* Friesen, 2019.

CHAPTER 8
But Who Does Caesar Render Unto? Three Faces of Risk in Shakespeare's *Julius Caesar*

THE FOOL.

O n 12 June 1599, *Julius Caesar* premiered at the grand opening of the new Bankside Globe, a three-thousand-seat, custombuilt theatre (Sohmer 3–16). As Shakespeare had taken personal and financial risks to build and become a stakeholder in the Globe, it is fitting that he made risk the dramatic fulcrum of the action. In *Julius Caesar*, Shakespeare explores risk in all its guises: first, as danger; second, as exposure to danger; and finally, as the trigger of devastating low-probability, high-consequence events.

It is 44 BC.[1] History has arrived at a crossroads between the old and the new, the Republic and the Empire, the last of the Romans and the first of the Caesars. On one fork lies dignity, uncomfortable liberty, and the rule of the unhappy many. On the other fork lies new things, comfortable servitude, and the rule of the one. Though history's wheel inclines towards empire, the furrows, four-and-a-half centuries deep, follow the familiar ways. Risk is the dramatic fulcrum of the action because the wheels are flying off the tracks. It is a time of risk and a time to take risks: at stake is the soul of Rome.

Four risk-takers—Caesar, Antony, Brutus, and Cassius—will clash as they wager all-in on the fate of the Eternal City. This daredevil quartet will trigger the improbable acts, accidental judgments, and unintended consequences that ensure *Julius Caesar* will be acted in new Globes many ages hence. As freedom is to the soul of Rome, so is risk to the soul of tragedy.

Risk as Hazard – An Improbability unto Truth

Polysemous risk has many faces. The first face of risk is its most familiar: risk is "danger" and "the possibility of loss, injury, or other adverse or unwelcome circumstance" ("Risk," *n.* 1, 4b). From the get-go, warnings, prophecies, prodigies, omens, thunderstorms, and supernatural events, the shadows of unhappened things, simultaneously flash danger. It begins with the Soothsayer telling Caesar to "Beware the Ides of March" (1.2.23). Casca's amazed "never till tonight, never till now" declaration quickly follows, amplifying the Soothsayer's forebodings:

> *Thunder and lightning. Enter* CASCA, *with sword drawn, and* CICERO, *meeting*
> CICERO. Good even, Casca. Brought you
> Caesar home?
> Why are you breathless, and why stare you so?
> CASCA. Are not you moved, when all the sway
> of earth
> Shakes like a thing unfirm? O Cicero,
> I have seen tempests when the scolding winds
> Have rived the knotty oaks, and I have seen
> Th'ambitious ocean swell, and rage, and foam,
> To be exalted with the threat'ning clouds;
> But never till tonight, never till now,
> Did I go through a tempest dropping fire. (1.3.1–10:
> Oxford edition)

To impart upon the audience the singularity of the moment, Casca adds to his litany of prodigies: a lion fascinating Romans, a slave impervious to fire, men on fire, the bird of night calling during day (1.3.15–28).

To Casca, the prodigies are illegible signs. Cassius, however, can see that the portents are physical manifestations of nature's consternation that one man should wear the crown. Caesar had recently been proclaimed dictator for life (Plutarch *Caesar* 57). Now he would be king. Nature retches.

Brutus also sees nature's goings-on: "The exhalations whizzing in the air," he says, "Give so much light that I may read by them" (2.1.44–45). The prodigies, blazing across the sky, ensure that 14 March is a night to remember. As the scene shifts to Caesar and Calpurnia's on the morning of the ides, the portent sensory overload continues. "Thrice hath Calpurnia," says Caesar, "in her sleep cried out 'Help, ho! They murder Caesar'" (2.2.2–3). She sees a dream where Caesar's statue "with an hundred spouts, / Did run pure blood" (2.2.76–77). He asks the haruspices for insight. The priests cut open the sacrificial animal to discover that, though lacking a heart, it had lived, breathed, and ran. Even the omens about the other omens cry nature's revolt.

Calpurnia continues reciting litanies of prodigies, recounting how the watch has witnessed a whelping lioness, graves yielding their dead, warriors fighting in the clouds, blood raining on the Capitol, neighing horses, the groans of the dying, and shrieking ghosts (2.2.15–24). The portents connect the Capitol, the noises of battle, and the forms of war. It so happens that Caesar is heading to the Capitol to prepare for war. He will go east to recover the standards Marcus Crassus carelessly lost. At the Capitol, the senators will declare him "King of all the provinces outside Italy with the right of wearing a diadem in any other place except Italy" (Plutarch *Caesar* 64; 1.3.85–88, 2.2.93–94). Their declaration would fulfil an oracle in the Sibylline books that Rome could only conquer Parthia if led by a king (Plutarch *Caesar* 60). Calpurnia recognizes the portents presage ill. She tells him to stay home.

The portents heighten, increase, and augment the suspense. They activate our intuitions and speculations on the probable, the improbable, and the impossible. A black cat or comet is commonplace. So many cats are black. Every few years, a comet visits. It is probable, therefore, that, every so often, one sees a prodigy. To see a flurry of prodigies, however, is improbable: a prodigy, by definition, is unusual and, therefore, unlikely. Calpurnia argues from probability to persuade Caesar:

> CALPURNIA. Caesar, I never stood on ceremonies,
> Yet now they fright me. There is one within,
> Besides the things we have heard and seen,
> Recounts most horrid sights seen by the
> watch. (2.2.13–16)

While unsuperstitious ("I never stood on ceremonies"), she argues that the flurry of portents are overwhelming ("these things are beyond all use," 2.2.25). In a stroke of dramatic economy, we are never told "the things we have heard and seen." By tacit accord, however, unspoken things quicken beating hearts. To see so many prodigies is improbable, and, being improbable, likely presages catastrophe: in these portents are no rainbows and halcyon beaks, but the shapes of apocalypse now.

Calpurnia's probabilistic argument echoes that of Casca, who says to Cicero:

> CASCA. When these prodigies
> Do so conjointly meet, let not men say
> 'These are their reasons, they are natural';
> For I believe they are portentous things
> Unto the climate they point upon. (1.3.28–32)

Casca drives home the point, that, while natural explanations may account for scattered prodigies, they fall flat when so many prodigies "conjointly meet." Although Shakespeare's Cicero downplays Casca (1.3.34–35), the historical Cicero may well have agreed. In his treatise on divination, Cicero classifies the highly improbable in a category outside chance:

> Can anything be an 'accident' which bears upon itself every mark of truth? Four dice are cast and a Venus throw [where each of the four four-sided dice displays a different value] results—that is chance; but do you think it would be chance, too, if in one hundred casts you made one hundred Venus throws? (*On Divination* 1.23)

Each prodigy is like a Venus throw. A Venus throw results: that is chance. If the dice were fair (and not the rectangular knuckle-bones of livestock), the probability of rolling a Venus throw is 1:256 (the outcome of four independent rolls being the product of their individual probabilities: 4 * 4 * 4 * 4). Two Venus throws result in succession: the probability is 1:65,536 ($1:256^2$). This, too, chance will produce. But, should a hundred Venus throws happen in succession, it is no longer chance, as the odds—$1:256^{100}$—are beyond all use. The number lies beyond nature's ken. In powers of ten, you could scale the universe from Planck's infinitesimal length to the broadest expanses of its outermost limits, and never encounter such an abomination.

Through a superabundance of prodigies, Shakespeare fills *Julius Caesar* with such abominations of probabilities that, whatever it is, it is no longer chance. It is something greater than chance. Nature, imbued with hylozoism, the idea that all matter is somehow alive, is partaking in history's grand march. Improbability can supply the proof.

In the old days, they discovered that improbability could be the basis of something to believe in. Centuries before French philosopher and mathematician Blaise Pascal was credited with putting belief on a probabilistic footing by making his famous wager (known as "Pascal's Wager"), an obscure theologian writing on the shores of North Africa found a way.[2] Sometime in the early third century,

Tertullian, an early Christian apologist, demonstrated that the higher the improbability, the greater the cause for belief:

> The Son of God was crucified; I am not ashamed because men must needs be ashamed *of it*. And the Son of God died; it is by all means to be believed, because it is absurd. And He was buried, and rose again; the fact is certain, because it is impossible. (*On the Flesh of Christ* 5)

Over the centuries, his conclusion *certum est, quia impossibile* ("the fact is certain, because it is impossible") led to the anti-rationalist declaration *credo quia absurdum* ("I believe because it is absurd"). Improbability, by being unlikely, becomes the highest of signs and the most assured of proofs. It is a proof that dumbfounds naysayers because the unlikelihood of it being mistaken can be stated in figures which are overwhelming.

I know not whether people today still believe it is impossible for the dead to rise. It is likely that some do. It is, however, my belief that Shakespeare uses improbability to announce that the Ides of March is a moment like no other. Revolution is in the air. The world will never be the same because the odds of so many wonders happening at once transcend reason. That the prodigies signify imminent historical metamorphosis is certain, because they are impossible. This is the improbability unto truth. Probability, the familiar stranger, is truly one of the least understood yet most potent of devices, whether on the stage of theatre or on the stage of life.

Risk as Opportunity – Caesarism's Paradox

The contact point between the bicycle and the road is all but two square inches of rubber, one square inch per tire. Upon two rubber inches, riders ride. To hobby riders, harrowing alpine descents, hairpin corners, poor visibility, slick roads, and raging crosswinds are signs to ease off. Risk unnerves. To riders riding the Tour de France, however, these are signs to attack. Some attack to help teammates, some attack out of envy and spite, some from principle, and some for the thrill of it all. Descending the Col de Vars, a high alpine pass with gradients of twelve percent, at 80kph is pedestrian; go into the supertuck and scream down over 100kph. Attack them at the switchbacks on the world's edge. Attack them where the road is slick or the visibility poor. Carve a line and drop them on the S-curves. If two square inches suffice, you will wear the coveted *maillot jaune*, the yellow jersey. Down they go on history's slopes into time's valleys, the Cassiuses, Brutuses, Antonys, and Caesars, blazing into glory or riding into ruin–it is uncertain whither.

This brings us to the second face of risk. Risk as a noun denotes hazard. As a verb, however, risk paradoxically denotes the exposure to danger ("Risk," *v*. 1). Risk refers to both danger and its exposure because it derives from the early Italian *risicare* meaning "to dare" (Bernstein 8). To those reckless of danger, risk is opportunity. In *Julius Caesar*, many opportunities arise.

In the daredevil quartet, Caesar speaks least: he has 1,126 words to Brutus's 5,394, Cassius's 3,709, and Antony's 2,540 (Rowe 152–53).[3] His words, however, fascinate: with each utterance he is, curiously, assessing, defining, and saying out loud his relationship with risk. The Soothsayer warns him of grievous danger. Caesar looks him straight in the eye. "He is a dreamer," says Caesar, "Let us leave him. Pass" (1.2.24). In a perfect pentameter line, he reveals his DNA. "Pure gold," says Granville-Barker (374). "A line of magisterial finality," says Humphreys (1.2.24). Though it is the holiday of the Lupercalia, Caesar is ever the general, his ear (the one that works) ever attentive. Like a general on the field, he is constantly identifying, evaluating, and negotiating risks. Risk affords Caesar an existential opportunity to be Caesar. Caesar becomes Caesar by walking the line.

Now, contrast Brutus's attitude to risk-taking. As soon as Caesar's Lupercalia train exits, Brutus finds himself alone with Cassius. Now, it is Brutus's turn to confront risk. Cassius warns him of grievous danger. Brutus looks away ("If I have veiled my look," 1.2.38). Cassius presses on, prompting Brutus to ask: "Into what dangers would you lead me, Cassius / That you would have me seek into myself / For that which is not in me?" (1.2.63–65). Brutus's dithering reply, full of question marks, is a far cry from Caesar's "pure gold." Another fifteen lines later, they arrive at the elephant in the room: Caesar is fast becoming a god. Brutus awakens:

> BRUTUS. What means this shouting? I do fear the people
> Choose Caesar for their king.
> CASSIUS.   Ay, do you fear it?
> Then must I think you would not have it so.
> BRUTUS. I would not, Cassius, yet I love him well.
> But wherefore do you hold me here so long?
> What is it that you would impart to me?
> If it be aught toward the general good,
> Set honour in one eye, and death i'th'other,
> And I will look on both indifferently;
> For let the gods so speed me as I love
> The name of honour more than I fear
> death. (1.2.78–89)

Risk presents him with an ethical-political opportunity to demonstrate his ancestry: he is descended from Lucius Junius Brutus, expeller of kings. For the good of Rome, he would die.

Like Caesar, Brutus sees risk as opportunity. But, unlike Caesar, Brutus is slow on the uptake. "For the present," he says, "I would not, so with love I might entreat you, / Be any further moved. What you have said / I will consider" (1.2.165–67). He retrenches into endless musings. It is not until the beginning of act two that he finds his magisterial line: "It must be by his death" (2.1.10). Caesar found his gold in one line and Brutus his after tens and hundreds. Their appetite for risk lies powers of ten apart because risk encapsulates the idea of both opportunity *and* loss.

Brutus appears to lack nerve. It is an illusion. Shakespeare has him hesitate for another reason: to show that Brutus has more to lose than Caesar. Once Brutus commits, he puts at risk his friend and benefactor Caesar (who, rumour has it, is his father, see Plutarch

Brutus 5.2; Shakespeare *2 Henry VI* 4.1.136–37), his wife Portia, his boy Lucius, and the safety of many Romans. Caesar, on the other hand, gives the impression that he has too little to lose.

Brutus and Caesar's differences are encapsulated in another work of art: the sculptor Auguste Rodin's *The Burghers of Calais*. Rodin's monumental six-figure bronze sculpture depicts a tragic moment in Calais's history. In AD 1347, Calais falls after a difficult siege. The English victor, Edward III, will tame the conquered: if six of Calais's leaders voluntarily give up their lives, he will spare the people. The sculpture depicts the six volunteers walking to the gallows. Three burst out. The next three, with wandering steps and slow, stumble out. One interpretation is that, while the former are bona fide heroes, the latter deserve less commendation. Rodin rejects this interpretation:

> While these three men of Calais may be less
> brave than the three first, they do not deserve
> less admiration. For their devotion is even more
> meritorious, because it costs them more. (Rodin
> *Conversations* 36)

The case between Caesar and Brutus is analogous: Brutus is held back not by a lack of nerve, but by a higher estimation of all he leaves behind. Shakespeare captures the beauty of all Brutus leaves behind in his final scene with Portia. He loves her more than he dares to tell:

> BRUTUS. O ye gods
> Render me worthy of this noble wife!
> *Knocking heard*
> Hark, hark! One knocks. Portia, go in awhile
> And by and by thy bosom shall partake
> The secrets of my heart.
> All my engagements I will construe to thee,
> All the charactery of my sad brows. (2.1.303–09)

Adding credence to this view is his reaction to her death. Although he is a philosopher, his philosophy fails: "I am sick of many griefs," he says (4.3.142).

Caesar's final scene with Calpurnia lies in stark contrast. He chides Calpurnia, who rolls her eyes as she hands him his death robe:

> CAESAR. How foolish do your fears seem
> now, Calpurnia!
> I am ashamèd I did yield to them.
> Give me my robe, for I will go. (2.2.105–07)

She recognizes in this terrible moment her perceived smallness—and indeed, the smallness of all the world—when set against Caesarism's immensity. This is the horrible contradiction of Caesarism, that, because everything must be on the line, and all the time, nothing can be worth much. It is easy come and easy go. That is the price Caesar pays to create the Caesar myth.

Risk speaks differently to Cassius. It presents him with an opportunity to reclaim his dignity. Cassius is a person we all know: the smartest kid in school, the valedictorian who was marked for celebrity. But somewhere along the line, he lost his way. Now you can find him in the taverns talking about his glory days: his 8.93 GPA, how he was recruited like a rock star, how he used to do things no one else was doing, and easily. Cassius is a has-been.

When Brutus and Cassius squabble, Brutus, in a fit of rage, takes a swipe at his dignity:

> CASSIUS. Urge me no more, I shall forget myself.
> Have mind, upon your health. Tempt me no further.
> BRUTUS. Away, slight man!
> CASSIUS. Is't possible? (4.2.86–89)

Brutus's "Away, slight man!" stops Cassius because the truth hurts. Back in the day, Cassius and Caesar would campaign together, colleagues in arms (1.1.119–121). At home, they would swim together in the Tiber's flood (1.2.100–15). They grew up together, went to the same schools. Now Caesar has overleapt him. Now Caesar favours others (1.2.310). Now Caesar no longer returns his calls. They were equals. Now, when Caesar lifts his legs, Cassius, like a cur, stoops down. Cassius is envious.

Envy drives Cassius to distraction. On the night of the prodigies, he walks the streets, raving:

> CASCA. Who ever knew the heavens menace so?
> CASSIUS. Those that have known the earth so full
> of faults.
> For my part, I have walked about the streets,
> Submitting me unto the perilous night,
> And thus unbracèd, Casca, as you see,
> Have bared my bosom to the thunder-stone;
> And when the cross blue lightning seemed to open
> The breast of heaven, I did present myself
> Even in the aim and very flash of it.
> CASCA. But wherefore did you so much tempt
> the heavens?
> It is the part of men to fear and tremble
> When the most mighty gods by tokens send
> Such dreadful heralds to astonish us. (1.3.44–56)

Not only is his shirt undone, but he also taunts the thunderclouds. Envy emboldens him. Recent events, however, are handing him an opportunity to regain his mojo. Although Caesar has not gone all the way, Cassius can convince others that Caesar will go all the way. That will be the basis of his sham conspiracy to liberate Rome. Once Caesar is dead he will walk his streets again, again the cock of the walk. That is his opportunity and his risk.

As Brutus and Caesar reflect one another's genius—the former with too much to lose and the latter with too little—so too are Cassius and Antony mirrors. While envy prompts Cassius, the opposite emotion—friendship—moves Antony. Antony is "beloved of Caesar," is the one who walks on Caesar's right hand (1.2.213, 2.1.157). Caesar's assassination affords Antony the opportunity to demonstrate the ties that bind. To memorialize Caesar, Antony, like a proper friend, will do cosmic terrors:

> ANTONY. A curse shall light upon the limbs of men.
> Domestic fury and fierce civil strife
> Shall cumber all the parts of Italy.
> Blood and destruction shall be so in use,
> And dreadful objects so familiar,
> That mothers shall but smile when they behold
> Their infants quartered with the hands of war,
> All pity choked with custom of fell deeds.
> And Caesar's spirit, ranging for revenge,
> With Ate by his side, come hot from hell,
> Shall in these confines, with a monarch's voice,
> Cry 'Havoc!' and let slip the dogs of war,
> That this foul deed shall smell above the earth
> With carrion men, groaning for burial. (3.1.262–75)

To do cosmic terrors, however, is easier said than done. It involves risk.

Caesar is dead. A void opens. Antony steps up to fill the void. That he does so is unexpected. Antony is the Roman Hal. Like Hal from Shakespeare's Henriad plays (which were written concurrently in the century's last lustrum), Antony is perceived as "gamesome" (1.2.28), a lover of plays (1.2.204), "given / To sports, to wildness, and much company" (2.1.189–90), one who "revels long a-nights" (2.2.116), and "a coward or a flatterer" (3.1.193). He is "but a limb of Caesar," incapable of grand politics (2.1.166). Like Hal becoming Henry V, Antony surprises all. The surprises begin with Antony pledging allegiance to Brutus (3.1.133–34). If the conspirators look him askance, he offers his life (3.1.159–63). So far so good: he is welcomed by Brutus. Then, in tragedy's white heat, he takes their hands, dripping purple gore:

> ANTONY. Let each man render me his bloody hand.
> First, Marcus Brutus, will I shake with you;
> Next Caius Cassius, do I take your hand;

Now, Decius Brutus, yours; now yours, Metellus;
Yours, Cinna; and, my valiant Casca, yours;
Though last, not least in love, yours, good
Trebonius. (3.1.184–89)

Perhaps Homer's *Iliad*—an ancient Greek epic that Shakespeare alludes to in the next act (4.2.180–82)—was on his mind here as well. In the crowning moment of the *Iliad*, Priam takes the hand of the man who has murdered his son [Priam to Achilles]:

"I have borne what no man
Who has walked this earth has ever yet borne.
I have kissed the hand of the man who killed my
son." (24.535–43)

Shakespeare exploits the full dramatic potential of Homer's narrative by investing Antony with Priam's lines; as Priam's words awed Achilles, Antony's actions awe the conspirators. Awestruck, they allow him to speak at Caesar's funeral. Antony, in making the most of his opportunity, pulls off a coup.

Antony's transformation into the man of the hour highlights the face of risk as opportunity. When dangers proliferate, the hero may be who you least expect. In AD 1415 at the Battle of Agincourt, it was the transfigured Hal, now Henry V. In 44 BC at the Battle of Philippi, it will be Antony. To do tales of glory is different than talking about tales of glory. The difference is risk. Talk is cheap. Doing involves exposing yourself to risk, kissing the hand of the murderer. Risk, though it denotes "danger," is not all on the downside. Sometimes, when one takes risks, things swing to the upside. Risk opens doors. "Fortune is merry," says Antony after his coup, "And in this mood will give us anything" (3.3.259–60). This brings us to the third, and final face of risk: risk as uncertainty, and even as destiny. Risk is truly a familiar stranger, one with the power to transfigure either a person or an entire world.

Risk as Uncertainty and Destiny
– Crossing the Rubicon

> But when at last the fatal die is thrown,
> The hollow mask no longer serves, they fall
> Into the mighty hands of nature, of
> The spirit that obeys none but itself,
> Knows of no treaties, and will deal with them
> Not on their terms, but on its own alone. (Schiller
> *Wallenstein's Death* 343)

When one confronts risk, whether by throwing Schiller's "fatal die" or by crossing Caesar's stream, one opens the uncertain doors behind which peer snake eyes, black swans, unsolved mysteries, unintended consequences, unknown unknowns, and many things that were—before they happened—unthinkable. Risk, in this guise, is "uncertainty" ("Risk," *n.* 2a, 2b). Uncertainty arises because risk-takers, having spread themselves too thin, can no longer cover their positions. Containing chance involves keeping some powder dry. Keeping powder dry, however, is the last thing on risk-takers' minds. Risk-takers prefer to light up the stage with the fireworks of their all-in bets. When risk-takers leverage and multiply their positions beyond what they can cover, chance is in the ascendant.

In Schiller's memorable phrase, when players play with risk, they fall into "the mighty hands of nature." In this sense, the term "risk" recalls its derivation from the Arabic "rizq" denoting "fortune, luck, destiny, chance, and lot" ("Risk," etymology). Risk becomes destiny. We think we master destiny, but chance is the true master. How we encounter and provoke chance is through risk. Risk is a gateway from a place where events occur in terms of probability or necessity into a place where wild improbabilities play.

Antony throws the fatal die by approaching the conspirators alone and unarmed. He pledges allegiance; he bares his neck; he takes their hands. It may turn out poorly. Instead, Brutus allows him to speak last at Caesar's funeral (3.1.251). It is a boon he could hardly have anticipated. He will attain his finest hour in his funeral oration by inciting the mob to riot, lynch, set fire to the conspirators' houses, and drive them running from Rome (3.2.246–52). Having thrown himself into the hands of nature, he feels a rising tailwind. Chance has his back.

After the funeral oration, the second half begins. It will culminate in the final confrontation at Philippi where they decide the fate of Rome. Brutus and Cassius have applied the tyrant's emergency brakes, have activated powerful kill and dead man's switches in a last-ditch attempt to save the Roman machine. But Caesar's spirit, ranging for revenge, will have none of it, knows of no fail-safes, having now shed the mortal form of risk to take on risk's incorporeal form. Risk is becoming destiny.

Brutus throws the fatal die when he decides Caesar must die. Caesar's death opens a can of worms. First, Brutus discovers that, to do God's work, he must conspire with the devil: "O conspiracy," he says, "Sham'st thou to show thy dang'rous brow by night, / When evils are most free?" (2.1.77–79). Next, he discovers that, by pre-emptively striking, Caesarism grows stronger, not weaker. Ere Caesar's blood cools, Caesarism grows warm. Ere he finishes his funeral oration, Caesarism stirs:

> BRUTUS. With this I depart, that as I slew my best
> lover for the good of Rome, I have the same dagger
> for myself, when it shall please my country to need
> my death.
> ALL THE PLEBEIANS. Live, Brutus! Live! Live!
> *BRUTUS comes down*
> FIRST PLEBEIAN. Bring him with triumph home
> unto his house.
> FOURTH PLEBEIAN. Give him a statue with
> his ancestors.
> THIRD PLEBEIAN. Let him be Caesar.
> FOURTH PLEBEIAN. Caesar's better parts
> Shall be crowned in Brutus. (3.2.43–51)

As Caesar triumphed over Roman friends instead of foreign enemies, the plebs will bring Brutus home with triumph. Brutus will be a new Caesar, crowned their new king. Brutus had little idea the precariousness and power of risk.

Brutus preferred liberty because he had the luxury to ponder the constitution, the history of Rome, and the nature of freedom. It had not occurred to him that the tired plebeians, working nine-to-five, would prefer comfortable servitude to uncomfortable liberty. Though he dies, Shakespeare vouchsafes him the deeper understanding that comes with death: he will see the new direction the world turns. "O Julius Caesar," says Brutus in his apotheosis of Caesar, "thou art mighty yet!" (5.3.94). As his day sets, Brutus understands how, in saving the Republic, he destroys the Republic.

Cassius likewise plays with the fates. He has assembled the right conspirators to access and assassinate Caesar. His band, however, is short on nobility and long on "youth and wildness" (2.1.148). They lack the cachet to usher in the new world order. To gain respectability, Cassius enrolls Brutus. By doing so, Cassius brings into the conspiracy the ineptitude of the good. The train wreck of unintended consequences quickly follows.

Cassius foresees division among the conspirators. To forestall division, he would have them swear an oath (2.1.113). Brutus, in his ineptitude of goodness, vetoes Cassius (2.1.114–40). Cassius foresees the benefits of inviting Cicero into the conspiracy (2.1.141–42). Brutus vetoes Cassius (2.1.156–62). Cassius, foreseeing the cunning of Mark Antony, proposes to kill him. Brutus, in his ineptitude of goodness, vetoes Cassius (2.1.163–84). Cassius, foreseeing mischief, opposes Antony's request to speak at Caesar's funeral (3.1.231–35). Brutus, by the ineptitude of goodness, overrules Cassius (3.1.235–42). Cassius, foreseeing the advantage of rested troops, proposes to wait for the enemy. Brutus, thinking fortune favours the good, marches to Philippi. Cassius had little idea the ruinousness of virtue.

Like the others, Caesar triggers unintended consequences. The unintended consequence of Caesar's daring is that it makes him hated and a hazard to the Republic. He can see how some are envious of his person, but he fails to see his threat to the Republic. He thinks the risks he takes benefit the Republic. "What touches us ourself," says Caesar, "shall be last served" (3.1.8). He is there to guide the Republic: "What is now amiss," he asks, "That Caesar and his Senate must redress?" (3.1.31–32). Like Brutus, Shakespeare vouchsafes Caesar the higher understanding that comes with death. Even after so many wounds, he would have lived, but when Brutus strikes, he realizes how odious he has become:

> CAESAR. Doth not Brutus bootless kneel?
> CASCA. Speak, hands, for me!
> > *They stab CAESAR, CASCA first, BRUTUS last*
> CAESAR. *Et tu, Brute?*—Then fall, Caesar! *He*
> *dies.* (3.1.76–77)

He conveys his astonishment at how hated he has become by speaking Latin. Ever the Caesar, he commands himself to die for Rome's sake.

Each character, by taking inordinate risks, triggers indeterminate, out of control anarchy. Risk is the dramatic mechanism animating *Julius Caesar.* The more risk they take, the more they expose themselves to chance, the principle of which may be illustrated through the bicycle analogy. If you eschew risk, descending the Col de Vars on the brakes and black winds batter you, you will have a fright, falling like Gloucester in *King Lear* (Shakespeare 4.5.41). If you embrace risk, however, descending at terminal velocity where the wild winds blow, you will, with Brutus, say: "Fates, we will know your pleasures" (3.1.98). Risk makes a difference.

When players stretch their means beyond what their means will allow, they expose themselves to "incertain affairs," "fortune," "the tide in the affairs of men," and "hateful Error" (5.1.96, 5.3.110, 4.2.268, 5.3.67). Because he has set too much at stake, a trick of the light compels Cassius to kill himself: he thinks Titinius has been taken when, in reality, Titinius is hastening back to crown him in laurel (5.3.78–90). So, too, Caesar, Antony, and Brutus are, like

Cassius, desperadoes on history's verge, leveraging their mortal positions many times beyond their mortal prowess.

Wong *contra* Aristotle – Risk *contra* Hamartia

Ever since Aristotle, there has been a tendency for armchair quarterbacks to see personal fault, mistake, or error—otherwise known as hamartia—as the dramatic pivot in tragedy. The change from "prosperity to adversity," says Aristotle, is brought about "by a great error [*hamartia*] of a character" (*Poetics* 1453a). If only the characters had been listening to the armchair quarterbacks shouting from their couches, they would have avoided the fall. From their couches, the armchair quarterbacks shouted: "Antony, do not party so hard, Caesar needs you to be sharp." From their couches, they shouted: "Brutus, less principle and more ruthlessness, please." From their couches, they shouted: "Cassius, be not so envious, accept your lot." From their couches, they shouted: "Caesar, why go for a home run, when you can get by with a hit?" Many believed, and perhaps some still do, that these critics expressed high literary theory's most profound truths.

The reason why Aristotle focused on agency in bringing about the fall was to rehabilitate tragedy. His teacher, Plato, had labeled the art "degenerate," banning it from his ideal city-state (*Laws* 817a–e; *Republic* 607b). By theorizing that: 1) the fall results from error, and 2) the sequence of events follows a probable course (*eikos*, *Poetics* 1454a), Aristotle could argue that the events in tragedy, because they are "the *kinds* of things that might occur and are possible in terms of probability or necessity," are replicable in life (*Poetics* 1451a; Wong "Faces of Chance" 98–99). Being replicable, the audience, by seeing the mistake on the stage, would avoid it in life. It is a brilliant argument, and one that restores tragedy's social function. But it is wrong. While it is highly questionable whether the great error could so easily be subtracted from the individual, it is patently false that hamartia is the dramatic pivot of tragedy.

To Aristotle and the armchair critics, if Brutus had been more ruthless, he would have carried the day. If Caesar was not always hitting home runs, he would have lived, and so on. To others, however, Caesar's confidence and Brutus's goodness, far from being errors, were written in their DNA. Without confidence, Caesar would not be Caesar. Without goodness, Brutus would not be noble. Each great error is written into the DNA of a character's blended humors. Aristotle's "You would have scored had you not fumbled the ball" is irrelevant and quarrelsome. The good and evil geniuses are bound together by the Gordion knot of human nature.

In this essay, I have offered you another reading, one in which the pivot of hamartia was unnecessary. Instead of error, risk is the dramatic fulcrum of the action. Instead of straight-line runs of predictable and probable events following a tidy cause-and-effect causality, improbable events abound. "*Et tu, Brute?*" says Caesar (3.1.77). "O Julius Caesar, thou art mighty yet!" says Brutus (5.3.94). To Aristotle and the armchair critics, these words signify the characters' reactions to the culmination of a sequence of events that followed a necessary or probable course. With their last words, the characters offer helpful advice to playgoers by recanting their errors. To keener critics, however, these words signify the characters' utter surprise over the complete disproportion of their *improbable* losses in the face of the *probable* risks they took. Hamartia was the old dramatic fulcrum. Risk is the new dramatic fulcrum. The probable and the necessary were the old mechanisms: make mistake *x* and *y* will certainly occur. Improbability and risk are the new mechanisms: wager *everything* and *anything* can happen. When anything can happen, actions are no longer replicable. Risk falsifies the hamartia hypothesis.

Risk is the basis of my new theory of tragedy called risk theatre (Wong *Risk*). Risk theatre is, in turn, the basis of the world's largest competition for the writing of tragedy, now in its fourth year (Wong *Competition*). Risk theatre is my *daring* attempt to restore tragedy's legacy of audacity. Once upon a time, the greatest poet, inaugurating his new theatre, elected tragedy.

If tragedy is not about avoiding the same mistakes, then what is it about? These days we concern ourselves with statistics and awards, honors and accolades. The Pulitzer Prize is the measure of a writer. The best basketballer is the one with the most rings. The boxer dreams of going 50–0. Conversely, the self-published writer is scorned, the street-corner basketballer is a nobody, and the defeated boxer yesterday's headlines. What a shame. I think the sensibility Shakespeare presents is that, whether 50–0 or 0–50, the final record of victories, losses, awards, and accolades is inconsequential. What is important is how we comport ourselves on life's journey.

In *Julius Caesar*, there are no "bad guys." Cassius, Brutus, Antony, and Caesar shine. I think they are bright because they dared to overcome the smallness of their existence by the greatness of their daring: Caesar by daring majesty, Brutus nobility, Cassius choleric envy, and Antony friendship. In *Julius Caesar*, Shakespeare administers a concoction of ancient Roman values as an antidote to American virtue with its base preoccupation with statistics, accolades, and awards. Some win all and others lose all. That is inconsequential. What is important is how greatly one dares. The agon is for a moment; the beauty is forever.

If, in future ages, theatregoers exiting the theatres say: "I should be less envious; I saw what happened to Cassius" or "I should be less ambitious; I may die for my ambition," then Aristotle will be proved correct: we can learn, in life, to foresee the things that the characters could not even imagine. Tradition vouches for Aristotle: for a long time teachers taught and students learned by pointing fingers, remonstrations, and assigning blame. If, however, risk is the trigger and do-gooders keep doing themselves in and politicians keep blowing up, then, perhaps, the dawn of the new day breaks here. On this new and blameless day, teachers and students, imbued with a higher sensibility than the rod, will insist that—instead of hamartia—risk is the great pivot because the soul of drama is less about fault-finding and more about entertaining. Risk, being danger, opportunity, uncertainty, and fate, entertains in a way hamartia never could.

While we render unto Caesar what is due to Caesar, Caesar renders unto risk what is due to risk. What is due to risk are the entertaining and unintended consequences of "incertain affairs," "fortune," "the tide in the affairs of men," and "hateful Error." Risk entertains because what they thought would happen did not happen, and in a way they least expected.

The year is 2021. Wonders and signs return. History has arrived at a crossroads between the old and the new, the poetics of the probable and the poetics of risk. On one fork lies Aristotle, hamartia, and didactic theatre. On the other fork lies risk theatre, a magic gateway into the world of clouds, dews, and dangers. At stake is the soul of drama. Whither, Roman, will you choose?

Notes

1. In an act of dramatic compression, Shakespeare binds three years of events (from Caesar's triumph over the sons of Pompey in October 45 BC to the festival of the Lupercalia on 15 February and the Battle of Philippi in October 42 BC) tightly around the centrepiece of Caesar's assassination on 15 March 44 BC. I would like to thank Robert C. Evans for encouraging and giving me the opportunity to write this essay.

2. In the game of chance known as Pascal's Wager, Pascal sets the existence of God on a probabilistic footing by arguing for God's existence based on the expected future value of the belief in God:

    Let us examine this point, and say, "God is, or He is not." But to which side shall we incline? Reason can decide nothing here. There is an infinite chaos which separated us. A game is being played at the extremity of this infinite distance where heads or tails will turn up. What will you wager? According to reason, you can do neither the one thing nor the other; according to reason, you can defend neither of the propositions....

> Let us weigh the gain and the loss in wagering
> that God is. Let us estimate these two chances. If
> you gain, you gain all; if you lose, you lose nothing.
> Wager, then, without hesitation that He is. (81)

For a discussion of the wager—which is more complex than it appears on a first examination—see Ian Hacking 63–72.

3. In terms of line numbers, Brutus speaks 738 lines, Cassius 513, Antony 361, and Caesar 155 (King 199).

Works Cited

Aristotle, et al. *Poetics. On the Sublime. On Style.* Translated by Stephen Halliwell, W. H. Fyfe, and Doreen C. Innes, Loeb-Harvard UP, 1995.

Bernstein, Peter L. *Against the Gods: The Remarkable Story of Risk.* John Wiley & Sons, 1996.

Cicero. *On Old Age. On Friendship. On Divination.* Translated by W. A. Falconer, Loeb-Harvard UP, 1923

Granville-Barker, Harley. *Prefaces to Shakespeare.* 1930. Vol. 2, B. T. Batsford, 1958.

Hacking, Ian. *The Emergence of Probability: A Philosophical Study of Early Ideas about Probability, Induction and Statistical Inference (Cambridge Series on Statistical & Probabilistic Mathematics).* 2nd ed., Cambridge UP, 2006.

Homer. *Iliad.* Translated by Stanley Lombardo, Hackett, 1997.

Humphreys, Arthur, editor. *Julius Caesar,* by William Shakespeare, The Oxford Shakespeare, 1984.

King, T. J. *Casting Shakespeare's Plays: London Actors and Their Roles 1590–1642.* Cambridge UP, 1992.

Pascal, Blaise. *Pensées. The Provincial Letters.* Translated by W. F. Trotter and Thomas M'Crie, Random House, 1941.

Plato. *Complete Works*. Edited by John M. Cooper and D. S. Hutchinson, Hackett, 1997.

Plutarch. *Fall of the Roman Republic*. Translated by Rex Warner, rev. ed., Penguin, 1972.

_____. *Plutarch Lives, VI: Dion and Brutus. Timoleon and Aemilius Paulus*. Translated by Bernadotte Perrin, Loeb-Harvard UP, 1918.

"Risk." *Oxford English Dictionary*. 3rd ed., 2010.

Rodin, Auguste. *The Burghers of Calais*. 1895, Town Hall, Calais.

_____. *Rodin on Art and Artists: Conversations with Paul Gsell*. Translated by Romilly Fedden, Dover, 1983.

Rowe, Nicholas. "List of Roles." *Julius Caesar*. Edited by David Daniell, The Arden Shakespeare, 1998, 152–54.

Schiller, Friedrich. *The Robbers and Wallenstein*. Translated by F. J. Lamport, Penguin, 1979.

Shakespeare, William. *Henry VI Part One. Henry VI Part Two. Henry VI Part Three*. Edited by Lawrence V. Ryan, Arthur Freeman, and Milton Crane, The Signet Classics Shakespeare, 2005.

_____. *Julius Caesar*. Edited by Arthur Humphreys, The Oxford Shakespeare, 1984.

_____. *The Tragedy of King Lear*. Edited by Jay L. Halio, The New Cambridge Shakespeare, 1992.

Sohmer, Steve. *Shakespeare's Mystery Play: The Opening of the Globe Theatre 1599*. Manchester UP, 1999.

Tertullian. *On the Flesh of Christ. Ante-Nicene Fathers*. Translated by Peter Holmes, edited by A. Cleveland Coxe, vol. 3, New York, 1885.

Wong, Edwin. "Faces of Chance in Shakespeare's Tragedies: Othello's Handkerchief and Macbeth's Moving Grove."

Critical Insights: Othello, edited by Robert C. Evans, Salem Press 2021.

_____. *The Risk Theatre Model of Tragedy: Gambling, Drama, and the Unexpected.* Friesen, 2019.

_____. *The Risk Theatre Modern Tragedy Playwriting Competition.* Risk Theatre, 12 Apr. 2018, www.risktheatre.com.

CHAPTER 9
Tragedy, Comedy, and Chance in Hardy's *Far from the Madding Crowd*

THE FOOL .

In 1874, Thomas Hardy was thirty-four and moonlighting as a writer. His day job as an architect paid the bills. *Far from the Madding Crowd*, his fourth published novel, was being anonymously serialized in the popular London magazine *Cornhill*. Rumor had it that it was George Eliot's new novel.[1] It was a hit. Its success allowed Hardy to become a full-time writer. Like the fictional events in the novel, the real-life events that led to his breakthrough were full of chance, risk, and the random element.

The coincidences that led to Hardy's rise began in 1862 when he started working for Arthur Blomfield, a London architect located at 9 St. Martin's Place (Millgate 74). In the same building, at 8 St. Martin's Place, was the Alpine Club (Halperin 740). Its president was Leslie Stephen. In 1862, Stephen published *Peaks, Passes, and Glaciers* recounting his ascent—the first—of the Schreckhorn, a 4078-meter alpine peak. Hardy was familiar with Stephen's book (Halperin 740–1). His familiarity was unsurprising: it was the golden age of mountaineering. What is surprising, however, is that years later, Stephen would be the one to give Hardy his golden opportunity.

By chance their paths had crossed and by chance their paths would keep crossing.

Flash forward ten years. Hardy has moved to Dorset, where he was working on his third novel, *A Pair of Blue Eyes*. In November 1872, he picked up a copy of *Fraser's Magazine*. One of the pieces was Stephen's fictional short story, "A Bad Five Minutes in the Alps," about a fall that leaves a mountaineer two hundred feet above a torrent hanging by a rhododendron stem. Hardy, captivated, rewrites Stephen's story into his own (literal) cliffhanger scene in *A Pair of Blue Eyes* (Halperin 742–4).[2] Their paths were crossing again.

That same year, Stephen became editor of *Cornhill*. He came across Hardy's second novel, *Under the Greenwood Tree*. He must have been captivated, because he wrote Hardy asking for a novel. His letter, however, was dropped in the mud on a Dorsetshire lane. If a laborer had not seen it, the winter rain and wind would have carried it away (Hardy *Life* 98). Hardy received the letter in late November, even as he was rewriting "A Bad Five Minutes in the Alps." He wrote back. Yes, he had a novel in mind. Its name would be *Far from the Madding Crowd*.

For over a decade, Hardy and Stephen's literal and literary paths—though they knew not why—had been crossing. Then, chance made something happen. For Stephen to have offered the little-known Hardy an opportunity to join the *Cornhill's* roster—which included heavy hitters Matthew Arnold, Charlotte Brontë, Wilkie Collins, George Eliot, Elizabeth Gaskell, Anne Thackeray Ritchie, John Ruskin, Alfred Lord Tennyson, and Anthony Trollope—was a godsend, and one that was lost and found, almost blown away by an errant gust.

Perhaps it was the impact of so many low-probability, high-consequence concatenations in life that led Hardy to foreground chance in his new novel. *Far from the Madding Crowd* entertains by flitting between tragedy and comedy. Chance is the narrative fulcrum between the two. The pastoral idyll, with its unchanging agricultural rhythms, highlights through contrast how accident, coincidence, and the unexpected rule life. Bathsheba Everdene, Gabriel Oak,

William Boldwood, and Francis Troy—like Hardy and Stephen in life—wander their desultory circuit. For a duration, the steady state prevails. Then chance romps through, changing all. Chance is the invisible hand of the new god writing life's text.

Between Tragedy and Comedy

Just as the architectural marvel of the great barn is built from arches, buttresses, and structures counterbalancing opposing forces, the narrative is built upon counterbalancing binary propositions. It is the work of an author-architect. On a macro level, the novel's title announces the opposing forces between town and country: *Far from the Madding Crowd* is how Londoners would describe rustics, not how rustics would themselves describe. On a micro level, binary propositions can be seen in the narrator's love of antithesis: "Deeds of endurance which seem ordinary in philosophy," says the narrator in one example, "are rare in conduct" (368).[3]

In chapter three, a crucial binary proposition emerges. In their first conversation, Gabriel unintentionally provokes Bathsheba's anger and embarrassment. She turns red. He turns away. When he turns back, she is gone. "With an air between that of Tragedy and Comedy," says the narrator, "Gabriel returned to work" (24). The air is comic insofar as the conversation kindles his interest and tragic insofar as she leaves. The proposition between tragedy and comedy provides the key to the novel's structure. As the suitors—Gabriel, the stalwart farmhand, Boldwood, the older gentleman-farmer, and Troy, the young and dashing libertine—vie for the hand of the independent and recalcitrant Bathsheba, the action veers between tragedy and comedy. *Far from the Madding Crowd*, as it counterbalances the ancient forces of comedy and tragedy, is, like the great barn, a marvel to behold and a work for all time.

The tension between tragedy and comedy is palpable when Troy tells Bathsheba that, while she means nothing to him, his previous lover, though dead, means everything. Distressed, Bathsheba barricades herself in the attic. To pass the time, she asks Liddy Smallbury, her servant-companion, for some books:

> "Bring up some books. Not new ones. I haven't heart to read anything new."
>
> "Some of your uncle's old ones ma'am?"
>
> "Yes: some of those we stowed away in boxes." A faint gleam of humour passed over her face as she said: "Bring Beaumont and Fletcher's *Maid's Tragedy*; and the *Mourning Bride*; and—let me see—*Night Thoughts*, and the *Vanity of Human Wishes*."
>
> "And that story of the black man who murdered his wife Desdemona? It is a nice dismal one that would suit you excellent just now."
>
> "Now Lidd–you've been looking into my books without telling me! And I said you were not to. How do you know it would suit me? It wouldn't suit me at all."
>
> "But if the others do—"
>
> "No they don't. And I won't read dismal books. Why should I read dismal books indeed? Bring me *Love in a Village*, and *The Maid of the Mill*, and *Doctor Syntax* and some volumes of the *Spectator*." (300)

Her initial choices assimilate her situation into tragedy. Francis Beaumont and John Fletcher's *The Maid's Tragedy* and William Congreve's *The Mourning Bride* are both tragedies of passion. *The Complaint: or, Night Thoughts on Life, Death & Immortality* by Edward Young is a didactic poem reflecting on loss, fortune's wheel, missed opportunities, and other tragic commonplaces. Samuel Johnson, in *The Vanity of Human Wishes*, likewise sets into poetry the follies preceding the fall.

Liddy picks up her mistress's cue, suggesting another tragedy of passion: Shakespeare's *Othello*. Then, as though to demonstrate life's mutability, Bathsheba requests four comic works: two comic operas (librettist Isaac Bickerstaff's *Love in a Village* and *The Maid of the Mill*), William Combe's comic poem, *Doctor Syntax*, and the *Spectator*, a periodical featuring comic essays and character sketches. She signifies through her choices that life pivots between tragic exhaustion and comic rejuvenation.

Tragedy and comedy can be conceptualized as life's two opposing poles. Such is the polarity the narrator presents when introducing Boldwood:

> He saw no absurd sides to the follies of life, and
> thus, though not quite companionable in the eyes
> of merry men and scoffers, and those to whom all
> things show life as a jest, he was not intolerable to
> the earnest and those acquainted with grief. Being a
> man who read all the dramas of life seriously, if he
> failed to please when they were comedies, there was
> no frivolous treatment to reproach him for when
> they chanced to end tragically. (122)

In the narrator's eyes, because life is a drama, it vacillates between drama's two classic forms: tragedy and comedy. In this synoptic view, while comedy is associated with folly and jest, tragedy is associated with seriousness and grief.

As the novel takes on the qualities of tragedy and comedy, theatrical references accumulate. While daydreaming, Bathsheba imagines her future romances would be "dramas in which men would play a part" (12). Unexpected announcements create an "intensely dramatic effect" (252). A pause in conversation is an "entr'acte," a French term for the interval between two acts of a play (106). The flames lighting the kiln at Warren's Malthouse are theatrical footlights throwing onto the ceiling the shadows of the assembled rustics, who are themselves likened to the theatre troupe *Her Majesty's Servants* (46: Penguin edition). In a serious turn, when Gabriel hands Fanny Robin a shilling, he can feel in her wrists the "throb of tragic intensity" (54). In a lighthearted moment, the narrator says that Bathsheba's face appears to Gabriel, who is admiring her, "as the uncertain glory of an

April day" (124). The passage draws from Shakespeare's comedy, *The Two Gentlemen of Verona*:

> PROTEUS. O, how this spring of love resembleth
> The uncertain glory of an April day,
> Which now shows all the beauty of the sun,
> And by and by a cloud takes all away. (1.3.84–87)

At that moment, as though on a cue, a cloud arrives as Boldwood takes Bathsheba away.

As theatrical references accumulate, Hardy transforms Shakespeare's well-loved characters into the rustics and farmhands that populate the novel. Shakespeare's characters strut out again, this time on the pastoral stage of Hardy's novel. While Shakespeare's Antony in *Julius Caesar* leads the plebs on, saying: "I am no orator, as Brutus is, / But, as you know me all, a plain blunt man," (3.2.210–1), Troy leads Bathsheba on, saying: "Because a plain blunt man, who has never been taught concealment, speaks out his mind" (169–70). In Laban Tall, a second Morton arises and a second tragedy unfolds: "Tall came into the enclosure, and leapt off—his face tragic as Morton's after the Battle of Shrewsbury" (139). Just as the messenger Morton announces the tragedy in *2 Henry IV* (1.1.70–1), so too, the mock-heroic Tall announces the pastoral iteration of the Battle of Shrewsbury: Bathsheba's flock is dying and help is wanting. In a lighter moment, the narrator likens Gabriel to Guildenstern, a source of comic relief in *Hamlet*. "Like Guildenstern," says the narrator, "Oak was happy in that he was not over happy" (145). Gabriel is happy, and, like Guildenstern, a step away from tragedy.

Hardy's references to theatrical conventions and works familiar to the madding crowd—the educated big-city readers of *Cornhill*—translate the Wessex countryside into the Londoners' idiom: a shepherd's loss of a flock is "a pastoral tragedy" (38); Joseph Poorgrass and the rustics, thinking the farm will be ruined, think they are living "in a tragedy" (105); Bathsheba, confronted with an errant husband, cannot decide if farm life is more like the comic *Love in a Village* or the tragic *A Maid's Tragedy*. Not only do the allusions draw cultivated city readers into the rustic country setting, once the novel has become a stage, Hardy has at his disposal all the elements of tragedy and comedy—such as tragic omens and stock comic characters—to use as narrative building blocks.

Tragic Omens and Stock Comic Characters

Omens precipitate negative turning points. A cat and dog presage Gabriel's initial, unsuccessful courting of Bathsheba: "just as he arrived by the garden gate," says the narrator, "he saw a cat inside, going into arched shapes and fiendish convulsions at the sight of his dog George" (31). A harbinger likewise attends Bathsheba's disastrous journey to Bath:

> "I hope nothing is wrong about mistress," said Maryann, who with some other women was tying the bundles (oats being always sheaved on this farm). "But a' unlucky token came to me int'house this morning. I went to unlock the door, and dropped the key, and it fell upon the stone floor and broke into two pieces. Breaking a key is a dreadful bodement. I wish mis'ess was home." (215)

So too, before Boldwood's fateful Christmas party, "a shadow seemed to rove about the rooms saying that the proceedings were unnatural" (348).

Omens, being chance events, amplify chance's dominion. Nature communicates through chance. When omens congregate together, it is, to those in the know, a "direct message from the Great Mother" (239). "I've had the news-bell ringing in my left ear quite bad enough for a murder, and I've seen a magpie all alone!" says Poorgrass the night Fanny goes missing and the rickyard fire breaks out (70). After Bathsheba fires her bailiff, the farmers worry about the impact of her inexperience upon their livelihoods. They begin seeing tell-tale signs:

> "Ay—there's some sorrow going to happen," said Matthew Moon. "I've had three very bad dreams

lately; and Sally put the bellows upon table twice
following last week."

"A sure sign that sommat wrong is coming," said
Joseph Poorgrass. "I had a white cat come in to me
yesterday breakfast-time. And there was a coffin-
handle upon my sister-law's candle last night."

"And I've seed the new moon two months following through glass. I was told, too, that Gammer Ball
dreamed of bees stinging her." (105)

The wicked storm is also presaged by signs: a toad crosses the path;
a slug goes indoors; spiders drop from the ceiling; sheep crowd
together. The sky itself, in a display of hylozoism, expresses solidarity
with the animal kingdom:

The night had a sinister aspect. A heated breeze
from the south slowly fanned the summits of lofty
objects, and in the sky, dashes of buoyant cloud
were sailing in a course at right angles to that of
another stratum, neither of them in the direction
of the breeze below. The moon as seen through
these films had a lurid metallic look. The fields were
sallow with the impure light, and all were tinged
in monochrome, as if beheld through stained glass.
The same evening the sheep had trailed homeward
head to tail, the behaviour of the rooks had been
confused, and the horses had moved with timidity
and caution. (236)

The portents are the pastoral equivalents to the tragic omen, a
commonplace in tragedy. In Shakespeare's *Julius Caesar*, for example,
wonders presage Caesar's doom:

CALPHURNIA. Caesar, I never stood on ceremonies,
Yet now they fright me. There is one within,
Besides the things that we have heard and seen,
Recounts most horrid sights seen by the watch.
A lioness hath whelped in the streets,

And graves have yawned and yielded up their dead.
Fierce fiery warriors fight upon the clouds,
In ranks and squadrons and right form of war,
Which drizzled blood upon the Capitol.
The noise of battle hurtled in the air,
Horses did neigh, and dying men did groan,
And ghosts did shriek and squeal about the
streets. (2.2.13–24)

So, too, in Shakespeare's *Macbeth*, omens anticipate the death of the king:

LENNOX. The night has been unruly: where we lay
Our chimneys were blown down and, as they say,
Lamentings heard i'th'air, strange screams of death,
And prophesying, with accents terrible,
Of dire combustion, and confused events
New hatched to th' woeful time. The obscure bird
Clamoured the livelong night. Some say the earth
Was feverous and did shake. (2.3.54–61)

Far from the Madding Crowd, like the art of tragedy, uses chance to anticipate what is to come.

If omens move the action towards tragedy, the likeness of Bathsheba's suitors to stock comic characters moves the narrative towards comedy. One of comedy's stock characters is the *adulescens amator*, the young man in love. The *adulescens amator* was such a standard fixture in Roman comedy, that, should he fail to appear, the playwright would be obliged to explain his absence (Plautus *Captives* 1032; *Casina* 64–5). The prototypical young man (such as Shakespeare's Proteus with whom Gabriel is explicitly identified) falls in love and asks for the hand of the first lady that comes his way. So too, it is love at first sight for Gabriel: he meets Bathsheba and is on his knees. Just as the *adulescens amator* in comedy has to overcome blocking characters, Gabriel will have to overcome Boldwood and Troy.

One species of blocking character is the old man in love, the *senex amator*. From Olympio in Plautus's *Casina* or Demenetus in his *Asinaria* to Chaucer's January in the *Merchant's Tale*, the *senex amator* is a common rival. Although the old man is wealthier and starts off from a position of power, he gives place, in the end, to his younger rival, and at a high cost to his dignity. Boldwood plays the old man in love. He is forty-one when he proposes to Bathsheba: twice her age and much older than the other suitors (127).[4]

As Boldwood plays the *senex amator*, his progression, mirroring that of Malvolio in Shakespeare's *Twelfth Night*, takes on further comic dimensions. Malvolio, deceived by a letter, woos a lady (2.3.151–57); Boldwood, deceived by a letter, woos a lady (98). Malvolio has a puritanical bent (2.3.142); Boldwood's house has the atmosphere of "a Puritan Sunday lasting all the week" (99). Malvolio is transformed into a fool as he woos an unwilling lady (3.4.17–60); Boldwood woos an unwilling lady and is made a fool by Troy (224–31). Malvolio rues his loss of dignity (5.1.338–39); Boldwood rues his loss of dignity (202–03, 252). Malvolio is sent to the madhouse (4.2.7–9); Boldwood is sent to the madhouse (373–75).

The braggart soldier, or *miles gloriosus*, is another stock character, and an audience favourite. He is a dashing rogue, a libertine whose tales are greater in the telling than the doing. Examples of the *miles gloriosus* include Plautus's bombastic Pyrgopolynices ("terrific tower-taker") in *The Braggart Soldier* and Shakespeare's Falstaff. Sergeant Troy plays the *miles gloriosus*. "Whilst he sometimes reached the brilliant in speech," says the narrator, "he fell below the commonplace in action" (167). "He could," says the narrator, "be eager to pay and intend to owe" (167). Troy would be at home in the tavern with Falstaff, Shakespeare's jolly knight. Like Troy, Falstaff is eager to pay, but intends to owe: if only his pockets had not been picked, he would pay his "four-and-twenty pound" tab to Mistress Quickly (*1 Henry IV* 3.3.73). Like the braggart soldier, Troy's daring is better suited to charming ladies and circus tricks than fighting. When it comes to blows, he is bested by Boldwood and, if we admit the brawl in the unpublished "Sheep-Rot Chapter," by Gabriel as well (228,

397). Like the comic soldier, Troy is the object of ridicule for those who see through his facade (193–94, 220–21).

Wessex is a stage. The malthouse kilns provide the theatrical footlights lighting the way for the new *adulescens amator*, *senex amator*, and *miles gloriosus* to walk the stage. When the action is grave, pulsing with disintegration, the countryside breaks out in strange omens presaging tragedy. But, when the action is gay and laughter-loving, when fortunes rise and marriage beckons, the novel approaches comedy.

Upside Risk and Downside Risk

In the *Canterbury Tales*, Chaucer's Monk connects tragedy with downside risk:

> I shall lament, and in the Tragic Mode,
> The sufferings of those who once stood high,
> Who fell from eminence, so that none could
> Deliver them out of adversity.
> For when Fortune makes up her mind to fly,
> Her course no man is able to withhold;
> Let no one trust in blind prosperity;
> Be warned by these examples true and old. (178)

The Monk makes it through seventeen tragedies before the Knight interrupts. "'Halt!' says the Knight. 'No more of this, good sir!'" (201). It is perhaps unsurprising that the Monk's stories of one-percenters being cut down annoys the Knight, who is himself one of the elites. Instead of downside risk, the Knight would rather hear of upside risk:

> And as for me, it is a real discomfort
> To hear of folk who live in wealth and comfort,
> And then, alas, learn of their sudden ruin.
> But on the other hand it's gratifying
> To hear about a man of low estate,
> How he climbs up and becomes fortunate,
> Thenceforth abiding in prosperity. (201)

From the quarrel between the Monk and the Knight a revelation flashes: tragedy is the art that dramatizes downside risk and comedy the art that dramatizes upside risk (Wong *Risk* 233–43).

In both comedy and tragedy, chance, coincidence, sliding doors, mysterious synchronicities, the unexpected, accidents, improbabilities, the random element, unintended consequences, and mischance are ubiquitous. In tragedy, chance waylays the hero. In comedy, chance helps the hero. "Coincidence must be a divinity," says Demeas in Menander's fourth century BCE comedy *The Girl from Samos*, "She looks after many of the things we cannot see" (163–4). Demeas has good reason to say this. Contrary to every expectation, accusations of fornication and adultery give way to a joyful wedding.

In comedy after comedy, chance brings the action home against a million to one odds. To end the internecine strife of the Peloponnesian War, the women of Sparta and Athens stage a sex strike. Their unlikely plan works (Aristophanes *Lysistrata*). In Greek New Comedy and its Roman emulators, the miser recovers the stolen gold (Plautus *The Pot of Gold*), kidnapped children are reunited with their family against all odds (Plautus *The Captives*), and young lovers marry in spite of cantankerous patriarchs (Menander *Old Cantankerous*). So, too, in Shakespeare's *The Comedy of Errors*, Egeon's execution is stayed when, a thousand miles away from home, he, his wife, his two sons, and their two sons' slaves "accidentally are met together" (5.1.352). Comedy is an agglomeration of the most improbable events that work to the upside. The conditions of comedy represent such an extreme that a character can say, in a metatheatrical turn: "If this were played upon a stage now, I could / condemn it as an improbable fiction" (*Twelfth Night* 3.4.125–26).

While chance, daring, and luck swing to the upside in comedy, the opposite happens in tragedy. In Shakespeare's *Othello*, Desdemona accidentally drops a handkerchief. Desdemona, Emilia, Othello, and Roderigo die. In Sophocles's *Oedipus the King*, the murder investigation reunites Oedipus with the Corinthian Messenger and the Shepherd, three characters long separated by both time and distance. Unlike the happy reunion of comedy, this reunion brings about a weeping and gnashing of teeth. In Aeschylus's *Seven against Thebes*, civil war rages at Thebes, the city of seven gates. With seven attackers, seven defenders, and seven gates, 25,401,600 permutations of attackers and defenders are possible. Against 1:25,401,599 odds, Aeschylus brings about the permutation most inimical to the hero's hopes, dreams, and ambitions (Wong "Aeschylus's *Seven*"). Comedy and tragedy both dramatize risk events. When chance skews to the upside, we call it comedy. When chance skews to the downside, we call it tragedy. Hardyan chance works similarly as it maneuvers the narrative between the two.

The language of chance pervades *Far from the Madding Crowd*. There are "whimsical coincidences" (20). Mischance is referred to as "a freak," something that happens "contretemps" (24, 119). Laborers "wait upon Chance" (43). Chance is capitalized, as though a god. Elsewhere, chance, as an active agent, can be seen to have "offered" something to someone (38). "Heartless circumstance" preys on unsuspecting characters (146). A "singular accident" ruins the best-laid plans (308). Eyes that "had been accidentally lifted at that moment" see things they ought not to (265). Comings are "sudden and unexpected" (89). A misunderstanding between All Saints' and All Souls' means the difference between life and death. The outcome of a marriage hangs on how much liquor the hired help drinks (276–83). Chance is everywhere.

The omnipotence of chance forces characters to make best guesses based on "reasonable probabilities" (317) and to warn one another "not to be *too sure*" even when the outcome seems certain (354). There is everywhere "many a slip" (354). Steeped in the world of chance, the characters gloomily admit that "nothing happens that we expect" (252). Chance is so pervasive that it fuels dramatic irony. At the shearing supper, Bathsheba sings "The Banks of Allan Water." "One of the verses," says the narrator, was "remembered for many months, even years, by more than a few of those who were gathered there:"

> For his bride a soldier sought her
> And a winning tongue had he:
> On the banks of Allan Water
> None was gay as she. (157)

In a few hours, she will meet Troy. So too, when Boldwood asks Bathsheba to marry him barring any "unexpected accidents," (343) the reader hears irony, hears echoes of tragedy, of King Duncan saying: "This castle hath a pleasant seat" as he approaches Inverness where he goes to die (*Macbeth* 1.6.1).

Chance pivots the action between tragedy and comedy. Having begun in low estate, Gabriel has saved for ten years to become an independent farmer. He begins the fortunate climb of Chaucer's Knight. A random act, however, triggers his pastoral tragedy (38–42). One morning, his overenthusiastic sheepdog drives his flock through the fence and down the precipice. Ten years of labor is lost. While Gabriel moves from comedy to tragedy, Bathsheba heads the other way. She begins in a state of destitution. Her uncle dies, however, and leaves her the Weatherbury Upper Farm. It is her turn to climb the ladder and grow fortunate.

After losing his livelihood, Gabriel hits the road looking for work. On his way to Shottsford, he passes a farm. A fire has broken out in the straw ricks. After putting it out, he asks for a job. Little does he know, he has stumbled onto Bathsheba's new farm. Bathsheba marvels at chance's power: "She scarcely knew," says the narrator, "whether most to be amused at the singularity of the meeting or to be concerned at its awkwardness. There was room for a little pity, also for a very little exultation; the former at his position, the latter at her own" (52). Like Hardy and Stephen in real life, Bathsheba and Gabriel's paths keep crossing. She hires him.

As is often the case between the sexes where feeling runs hot, Bathsheba, over a perceived impropriety, fires Gabriel. Or he leaves. Whatever the case, the day after he departs, she runs into her own pastoral tragedy: her sheep have gotten into the young clover. Blasted, they will die and are dying (136). Only Gabriel can save them. Through another coincidence, mistress and shepherd are reunited.

Chance also triggers the other two romantic interests. Bathsheba and Liddy toss a hymn book to see whether the anonymous Valentine sealed with the words "Marry Me" goes to Boldwood or Teddy Coggan (98). Chance selects Boldwood. The Valentine has an unanticipated and deleterious effect on him. He is transformed into the *senex amator* blocking Gabriel, the hapless *adulescens amator*. In a world mindful of class, he easily bests Gabriel, his social inferior.

It is likewise "by chance or by devilry" that Bathsheba meets Troy (165). While walking a dark path, Troy's spur and Bathsheba's dress become entangled. In extricating themselves, their hands touch "by accident or design" (163). Her beauty's flicker entices him. Their tragicomedy begins. If the novel had ended a few chapters earlier, Troy would have fulfilled his comedy by marrying Bathsheba. The novel, however continues. As it continues, chance works its strange ways, saving Troy from drowning only to kill him by a blast from Boldwood's shotgun.

With Boldwood in jail and Troy dead, laughter-loving Bathsheba "was beginning to know suffering" and turns into a "bust of Melpomene," the Muse of tragedy (270, 370). She marries Gabriel, the last suitor standing. The ending, perhaps, could have been foreseen: just as the *adulescens amator* prevails in comedy, Gabriel could have been expected to prevail. What *Far from the Madding Crowd* offers that is new, however, is an anastomosing path to the finish that is full of possibilities and rife with branches: this is not the unidirectional path of comedy or tragedy proper. "History," says Hardy, "is rather a stream than a tree. There is nothing organic in its shape, nothing systematic in its development. It flows on like a thunderstorm-rill by a road side; now a straw turns it this way, now a tiny barrier of sand that" (Hardy *Life* 179). Like history, the narrative flows from the highlands down to the sea. The topography of comedy and tragedy proper presents a single, deep channel. The topography of *Far from the Madding Crowd*, however, presents a myriad forking, complex, and anastomosing branches through valleys dividing once, twice, and thrice.

Works set in the meridian times of chance, of which *Far from the Madding Crowd* is a signal example, remind us of the limitations of the straight line of want, will, and intention. They show us how the unexpected happens not some of the time, but rather, all of the time. Trouble happens because everyone has a plan until they run into the unexpected. The unexpected prevails over the expected because, while expectation aims towards one eventuality, the unexpected takes the shape of any eventuality. A successful harvest, for example, depends on multiple factors from the availability of labor to the climate. Many events must occur in the desired sequence. Any one wayward event, however, could ruin the entire sequence. In short, expectation is fragile because one path leads to success and the unexpected is robust because many paths lead to failure.

The Eternal Pastoral

The perfection of the pastoral world highlights by contrast life's random walk. In contrast with the imprecision and instability of human affairs, the pastoral world is precise and self-regulating:

> The river would have been seen by day to be of
> that deep smooth sort which races middle and sides
> with the same gliding precision, any irregularities
> of speed being immediately corrected by a small
> whirlpool. (87)

Troy hopes "in the nature of things that matters would right themselves at some proper date and wind up well" (309). The possibility of self-regulating human mechanisms, Troy comes to realize, is illusory. While self-regulating systems occur in the pastoral world, randomness prevails in the human world.

Like the river, the pastoral sky is a portrait of precision:

> After placing the little creature with its mother he
> stood and carefully examined the sky to ascertain
> the time of night from the altitudes of the stars.
> The Dog-star and Aldebaran, pointing to the
> restless Pleiades, were half way up the southern
> sky, and between them hung Orion which gorgeous
> constellation never burnt more vividly than now
> as it soared forth above the rim of the landscape.
> Castor and Pollux with their quiet shine were almost

on the meridian: the barren and gloomy Square
of Pegasus was creeping round to the north-west:
far away through the plantation Vega sparkled
like a lamp suspended amid the leafless trees; and
Cassiopeia's Chair stood daintily poised on the
uppermost boughs.

    "One o' clock," said Gabriel. (18)

Perfection is for the heavens. The sky is the dial and the constellations the hands of the great clock. Human time, in contrast, is aleatory and subject to chance, breakdown, and malfunction. Gabriel's watch "had the peculiarity of going either too fast or not at all" (10). Bathsheba's watch stops on the night before her wedding (387). While Jan Coggan's pinchbeck repeater retains traces of the divine by speaking in the "still small tones" that recall the "still small voice" of God talking to Elijah, Coggan is already fuddled beyond hearing (279; 1 Kings 19.12). The pastoral timepiece of the sky, unlike human time, is perfect: its motions are the moving hands of time itself.

The pastoral calendar, insofar as it is linked to the celestial clock, is likewise robust. The hiring fair takes place in February on Candlemas (43). Lady Day in March sees the renewal of labor contracts (380). May is the month for sheep washing and June the month for shearing and the shearing supper (125, 142, 151). The harvest supper follows in August (236) and the sheep fair in September (331). The further away from the perfection of the seasons, however, the greater the dominion of chance. Lambing season ends some years in February, and other years goes past March (107). So too, the swarming of bees in a given month is a probability rather than a certainty (178). The helter-skelter lives of individual human beings lies at the far end of the range. Here, there is no certainty. Only probability remains. Certainty is reserved for the rivers, the sky, and the other furnishings belonging to the order of the eternal pastoral. Of these furnishings, the greatest is the great barn.

The Lindy Effect

A book that has been in print a hundred years can be expected to be in print a hundred more and a book in print for two hundred years can be expected to be in print another two hundred (Taleb *Antifragile* 318). Scientific theories, religions, and technologies that have stood the test of time for a thousand years can be expected to survive another thousand. This is the Lindy effect, the idea that the older something is, the longer its projected lifespan:

> Lindy is a deli in New York, now a tourist trap, that proudly claims to be famous for its cheesecake, but in fact has been known for fifty or so years by physicists and mathematicians thanks to the heuristic that developed there. Actors who hung out there gossiping about other actors discovered that Broadway shows that lasted for, say, one hundred days, had a future life expectancy of a hundred more. For those that lasted two hundred days, two hundred more. The heuristic became known as the Lindy effect. (Taleb *Skin* 141)

The oldest Wessex artifact is the great barn. An architectural design concept triumph, it exemplifies the Lindy effect. Like the unchanging constellations overlooking the countryside, the older the barn gets, the older it is likely to become:

> One could say about this barn, what could hardly be said of either the church or the castle, akin to it in age and style, that the purpose which had dictated its original erection was the same with that to which it was still applied. Unlike and superior to either of those two typical remnants of mediævalism, the old barn embodied practices which had suffered no mutilation at the hands of time. Here at least the spirit of the ancient builders was at one with the spirit of the modern beholder. Standing before this

abraded pile the eye regarded its present usage, the
mind dwelt upon its past history, with a satisfied
sense of functional continuity throughout, a feeling
almost of gratitude, and quite of pride, at the perma-
nence of the idea which had heaped it up. (143)

To measure change, one needs a point of reference from which
the change is measured. To see the gradual sweep of the heavens,
one needs to find a fixed point, as Gabriel does when he stands atop
Norcombe Hill: "To persons standing alone on a hill during a clear
midnight such as this, the roll of the world eastward is almost a palpable movement. The sensation may be caused by the panoramic
glide of the stars past earthly objects, which is perceptible in a few
minutes of stillness" (15). In the world of the novel, the great barn is
the fixed object past which mortal stars glide. From its vantage point,
one can reckon the palpable movement of human activity.

Two major episodes—the sheep shearing and the harvest dinner—
take place in the great barn. As the characters fuss, fret, flirt, and
flutter, the great barn, though itself unchanging in its pastoral per-
sistence, watches their changings of the guards, over and over. It had
stood while the Hundred Years' War raged. As the Tudors rose and
fell, it stood. It stood during the Interregnum and it stood during the
Restoration. As the Great Fire of London burned, it stood. When the
printing press came to England, it stood, and it stood when steam
engines arose. When Napoleon went on his wars of conquest, it was
there, and having gained four hundred years of momentum, it could
be expected to endure another four hundred: that is to say, to the
mid twenty-third century. That the tithe barn at Cerne Abbas—the
actual structure upon which Hardy modeled the great barn—stands
today in the twenty-first century, however, means that the prognosis
is to be moved upwards: by the Lindy effect, the great barn, having
stood nearly six centuries, can be expected to endure deep into the
twenty-sixth century (Bullen 35–38). Imagine that.

The pastoral world and, in particular, the great barn, highlight,
by way of contrast, the role of chance in the characters' lives. Time
changes humans because humans are perishable, but the more time

goes by, the more the great barn stays the same because the great barn represents another order of things: the eternal pastoral. As a survey marker of eternity, it provides a frame of reference against which human transience may be measured.

Littlewood's Law

Too often we ignore chance, relegating it into a footnote adorning the text of life. Chance in tragedy and comedy entertains, but the odds of an event a million to one against in life lay beyond the prospect of belief. We read *Far from a Madding Crowd* to experience the wildness of chance vicariously. That the real world is more stable than the fictional world, however, is a conjecture that, despite its appeal, is demonstrably false.

J. E. Littlewood, a Cambridge mathematician, demonstrated through the law that bears his name that, not only do improbable events happen more often than we expect, but that, when they happen, they impact us more than we expect: in fact, when they happen, they are called miracles. Beginning with the observation that we experience many events each day, Littlewood concludes that, by the action of chance, we should experience a miracle once per month:

> Littlewood's Law of Miracles states that in the course of any normal person's life, miracles happen at a rate of roughly one per month. The proof of the law is simple. During the time that we are awake and actively engaged in living our lives, roughly for eight hours each day, we see and hear things happening at a rate of about one per second. So the total number of events that happens to us is about thirty-thousand per day, or about a million per month. With few exceptions, these events are not miracles because they are insignificant. The chance of a miracle is about one per million events. Therefore we should expect one miracle to happen, on the average, every month. (Dyson 273)

In the span of the novel, it would not be far off the mark to say that Gabriel has seen, on the average, one miracle every month. Low-probability, high-consequence events in the novel are like low-probability, high-consequence events in life: though predictable in their unpredictability, when they happen, they overturn all things.

Far from the Madding Crowd, in acknowledging the dominion of chance, presents an order of existence where intention is the slave of want, and want is chance's fool. The ever-present eternal pastoral is like a rich, unexpected shadow over the narrative throwing in relief the indeterminacy of the all too human. Though the characters' lives are thrall to chance, the rural-idyllic novel offers a folk consolation. "You should take it careless-like," says one of the rustics, "and your time will come" (67). In a world chance has driven mad, it is best to keep going.

When we are "excessively hopeful and blithe," or, in other words, in the midst of comedy, we keep going because "a trouble is looming in the distance" (350). When we confront tragedy, we keep going because it is during these worst of times that our "malignant star was assuredly setting fast" (323). In both the novel and in life a "not frequent disregard of the probable in the chain of events" may be observed (Hardy *Preface* 437). Whether chance crowns us or sells us down the river, however, is beyond our control. What is in our control is to believe, hope, err, and strive. To some, this consolation may seem insufficient. But, in the face of chance, the upstart god, to rear ourselves up forthwith upright is all that may be said as a certainty. If you keep going, you just might receive the letter, the one dropped in the mud on a country lane.

Notes

1. An anonymous review from the January 1875 *Westminster Review* remarks how, when the novel was first anonymously serialized, "many good judges pronounced it to be a work of George Eliot's" (Cox 41–43). I would like to thank Robert

 C. Evans for the opportunity and encouragement in writing this essay.

2. Stephen's "A Bad Five Minutes in the Alps" is reprinted in Mallet 61–82. The cliffhanger episode in *A Pair of Blue Eyes* takes place in chapters 21 and 22.

3. Unless noted, quotations are from Falck-Yi's Oxford edition.

4. Bathsheba is "Sweet-and-twenty" in the first February (67: Penguin edition). When Boldwood proposes to her in May, she is twenty or twenty-one (birthdays being unstated). Although the narrator says in the closing pages of the novel she is "three or four and twenty," it is likelier that she is twenty-three—the novel covers three years and some odd months. In the first February, Boldwood is forty (76, 118). In May, when he proposes, he says that he is forty-one. At the end of the novel, he must be, therefore, forty-three. Troy dies on Christmas Eve two years after the novel begins (377). He is twenty-six. As the novel begins in December, he would have been twenty-four at that time, possibly twenty-three if his birthday is in December. In the first month of the novel, Gabriel is twenty-eight (11). By the end of the novel, Gabriel will be thirty-one and perhaps thirty-two if his birthday falls in the beginning of the year. It is difficult to square characters' stated ages with their relative ages. At one point during June in the first year, Gabriel tells Bathsheba that he is six years older than her and that Boldwood is ten years older than him (190). If we go by Boldwood's stated age of forty-one, this would make Gabriel thirty-one and Bathsheba twenty-five, considerably older than their stated ages. If we go by Gabriel's stated age of twenty-eight from the previous December and allow that he may be twenty-eight or twenty-nine at this point, Boldwood would be either thirty-eight or thirty-nine and Bathsheba either twenty-two or twenty-three. The stated ages, however, appear to be more accurate than their relative ages: in another passage that takes place around the second September, Gabriel tells Bathsheba that he is eight—and not six—years older than her

(345). Gabriel is either twenty-nine or, more likely, thirty at this point, making Bathsheba, in this reckoning, twenty-one or twenty-two.

Works Cited

Aristophanes. *Four Plays by Aristophanes: The Clouds, The Birds, Lysistrata, The Frogs*. Translated by William Arrowsmith, Richmond Lattimore, and Douglass Parker, Penguin, 1994.

Bullen, J. B. *Thomas Hardy: The World of His Novels*. Frances Lincoln, 2013.

Chaucer. *The Canterbury Tales*. Translated by David Wright, Oxford UP 1985.

Cox, R. G. *Thomas Hardy: The Critical Heritage*. Routledge, 1979.

Dyson, Freeman. *The Scientist as Rebel*. New York Review of Books, 2006.

Halperin, John. "Leslie Stephen, Thomas Hardy, and 'A Pair of Blue Eyes'." *The Modern Language Review*, vol. 75, no. 4, 1980, pp. 738–45.

Hardy, Thomas. *Under the Greenwood Tree*. London, 1872.

———. *Far from the Madding Crowd*. 1993. Edited by Suzanne B. Falck-Yi, Oxford UP, 2002.

———. *Far from the Madding Crowd*. Edited by Rosemarie Morgan and Shannon Russell, Penguin, 2000.

———. General Preface to the Wessex Edition of 1912. *Far from the Madding Crowd*, by Hardy, Alfred A. Knopf, 1991, pp. 437–42.

———. *The Life and Work of Thomas Hardy*. Edited by Michael Millgate, Palgrave Macmillan, 1984.

Holy Bible. King James Version. Thomas Nelson, 1976.

Mallett, Phillip. "Leslie Stephen's Bad Five Minutes in the Alps." *The Hardy Society Journal*, vol. 10, no. 2, 2014, pp. 58–84.

Menander. *Plays and Fragments*. Translated by Norma Miller, Penguin, 1987.

Millgate, Michael. *Thomas Hardy: A Biography Revised*. Oxford UP, 2004.

Plautus. *Amphitryon, The Comedy of Asses, The Pot of Gold, The Two Bacchises, The Captives*. Edited and translated by Wolfgang de Melo, Loeb-Harvard UP, 2011.

_____. *Casina, The Casket Comedy, Curculio, Epidicus, The Two Menaechmuses*. Edited and translated by Wolfgang de Melo, Loeb-Harvard UP, 2011.

Shakespeare, William. *The Comedy of Errors*. Edited by Charles Whitworth, The Oxford Shakespeare, 2002.

_____. *Four Histories: Richard II, Henry IV Part 1, Henry IV Part 2, Henry V*. Penguin, 1968.

_____. *Julius Caesar*. Edited by David Daniell, The Arden Shakespeare, 1998.

_____. *Macbeth*. Edited by Sandra Clark and Pamela Mason, The Arden Shakespeare, 2015.

_____. *Twelfth Night*. Edited by Andrew Worrall, The Heinemann Shakespeare, 1994.

_____. *The Two Gentlemen of Verona*. Edited by Clifford Leech, The Arden Shakespeare, 1969.

Sophocles. *The Three Theban Plays: Antigone, Oedipus the King, Oedipus at Colonus*. Translated by Robert Fagles, Penguin, 1984.

Taleb, Nassim Nicholas. *Antifragile: Things That Gain from Disorder*. Random House, 2012.

_____. *Skin in the Game: Hidden Asymmetries in Daily Life*. Random House, 2018.

Wong, Edwin. "Aeschylus's *Seven Against Thebes*: A Patriot's Portrait of a Patriot." *Critical Insights: Patriotism*, edited by Robert C. Evans, Salem Press, 2021.

_____. *The Risk Theatre Model of Tragedy: Gambling, Drama, and the Unexpected*. Friesen, 2019.

Maxims and Arrows

1. Risk theatre is the theory of drama that inspires us to overcome the smallness of our existence with the greatness of our daring.
2. Make risk the dramatic fulcrum of the action.
3. When risk drives action, we have two types of drama: comedy to dramatize upside risk and tragedy to dramatize downside risk.
4. Each dramatic act is a gambling act.
5. To find out how much a gallon of milk is worth, one goes to the market. To find out how much the milk of human kindness is worth, one goes to the theatre. Tragedy is a valuing mechanism.
6. The more heroes lose through daring, the more they become objects of veneration.
7. No risk, no reward. Nothing ventured, nothing gained.
8. Make risk palpable, and you have tragedy.
9. What do you get when probability theory and mathematics intersect with drama? You get risk theatre.
10. Do not confuse a playwright with a priest. Playwrights make risk the fulcrum of the action. Priests make morality the fulcrum of the action.
11. Do not confuse a playwright with an academic. Playwrights' points of views must be fruitfully ambiguous. Academics collapse these points of view into definitive for/against positions to support their standpoints.
12. Risk is primary. Suffering is secondary, a byproduct of risk. Focus on tragedy's primary instead of secondary attribute.

13. Some say art doesn't teach. I say, tragedy's lesson, and one learned at a premium price, is: "Nothing is free."

14. "How can I write a tragedy when I am living in a tragedy?" the inconsolable sufferer asks. While a plague struck Athens in 430 BC, wiping out a third of its population, Sophocles was writing his plague play, *Oedipus rex.*

15. The cobbler's children have no shoes. Everyone's in the photograph except the photographer. The comedian cries the tears of a clown. Perhaps tragedians enjoy benefits as well?

16. Sometimes the biggest risk is risk avoidance.

17. Read "The Monk's Tale" in Chaucer's *Canterbury Tales*: no one likes tragedy. Read Taleb's *The Black Swan*: everyone's fascinated with risk. Another reason to reimagine tragedy as risk theatre.

18. Unintended consequences attend the best intentions.

19. Risk isn't what happens most of the time. It's what happens some of the time. The young note what happens most of the time. The wise pay attention to what happens some of the time.

20. Who is the anti-Hamlet?—Caesar. Imagine what Hamlet would have done at the Rubicon?

21. Risk theatre is theatre for those who wonder what happens when want, will, and intention cross swords with chance.

22. Heroes believe in themselves as a fate. But the world had a different fate in store for them. And how this different fate happens is through chance. Such is fate's paradox: it needs chance.

23. Fate and chance are synonymous: how fate manifests itself in literature is through the random element.

24. Fate is only possible in literature; it is impossible in life. When it comes to fate, life cannot imitate art: life, unlike literature, life lacks a process by which fate can become.

25. In real life, fate is chance misinterpreted. When the mind revolts against chance, it calls the event "fate."

26. The highest virtue in risk theatre goes beyond good and evil. The highest virtue in risk theatre is daring and the most despised vice, cowardice.

27. In risk theatre, the more things are going your way, the more likely Fortune is to desert you.

28. Audiences love tragedy because it brings to life the hidden mechanisms which lead to the unexpected outcome.

29. How do you help a tragedian who has writer's block?—tell him your plans.

30. If, like Aristotle, you look at tragedy while sitting on the chesterfield, the hero is at fault, displays hubris. If you look at tragedy as a person of action, the hero's actions make perfect sense.

31. Risk theatre inspires those who have never danced to dance on the edge and it reminds those who have danced on the edge why they no longer dance.

32. Highly improbable events explode worldviews. Think of the first sighting of a black swan in Australia. In a second, two thousand years of convention—that a black swan is a byword for that which does not exist—is thrown out the window. Low-probability events are dramatic for this reason: they cleave time into a before and an after.

33. Live dangerously, carry on your crests, "*Sine audacia nihil* [Nothing without daring]."

34. Chance is destiny. Could it be?

35. When the world gives you risk, make risk theatre.

36. Artistic risk: no sanctuaries and shrines shelter artists on their never-ending road because these are theirs to build for others.

37. The higher the probability of failure, the more worthwhile the enterprise.

38. Risk theatre simulates life. Life without it is like a show without dress rehearsal.

39. Bend your bows for a multiplicity, rather than a singularity, of interpretations. Others will collapse your interpretations into a singularity for you; do not take their tasks from them.

40. Risk without loss is like freedom without opposition, a hill without a slope.
41. Whether heads or tails, chance always prevails.
42. Going with randomness is like pulling a rope; fighting randomness is like pushing a rope.
43. The path to tragedy is paved with good intentions.
44. Minor feats of improbability for minor playwrights; major feats of improbability for major playwrights.
45. They say: "Knowledge is power." But in tragedy, knowledge dooms.
46. Comedy is hilarious because the hero wins, despite the overwhelming odds against. Tragedy is sombre because the hero loses, despite the overwhelming odds for.
47. In comedy, zeroes becomes heroes. In tragedy, heroes turn into zeroes.
48. The cure for timidity is danger.
49. The white heat of white-knuckled risk cannot be taught, only experienced, and better in the theatre than on the street.
50. There are book smarts and there are street smarts. One learns of probability from the books and risk from the streets.
51. The transition between the books and the streets takes place in the theatre.
52. Finding risk is like finding grace—you don't find it: it finds you, unexpectedly.
53. Tragedy—even when it points to the future—seems in love with the past because it dwells on the incredible cost of every advance.
54. Everyone understands risk until the moment they experience it: by dramatizing this moment, tragedy captivates.
55. Mock fate by the greatness of daring.
56. Tragedy is a great marketplace where all the world is for sale. How much, hero, will you pay?
57. *Freefall* – Risk is like gravity. The only way to overcome it is to give in to it. With one fateful step, the heaviness of risk loses its weight.

58. In the old days, they talked of earth, water, air, and fire. I, too, have taken the shape of water, felt the weight of earth, and ran after the wind. But, of the elements, I think the greatest in this little life is to have the fire of daring to light up a legacy of audacity.

59. Of the mysteries contained in the old books, the most profound is how one can die once, yet live forever.

Acknowledgments

This volume is for all the creators, innovators, and theatremakers without whom risk theatre would be an empty stage. With you, risk theatre can become the greatest show on earth. Thank you for giving risk a shot. Keep going. The best is yet to come.

I would like to thank Luke Roman at Memorial University for inviting me to speak about tragedy and low-probability, high-consequence events. That talk would eventually become the essay: "Greek Tragedy, Black Swans, and the Coronavirus: The Consolation of Theatre." A debt of gratitude goes out to Robert C. Evans at Auburn University at Montgomery for encouraging me to write the essays in this volume. Without his encouragement, they would not exist.

The six essays were published in various volumes of the popular *Critical Insights* series edited by Robert C. Evans. They appear here by kind permission of Salem Press. The essay on *Othello* and *Macbeth* appeared in the *Othello* volume (2021); the essay on the consolation of tragedy in the volume *Literature in Times of Crisis* (2021); the essays on *All My Sons* and *Seven against Thebes* in the volume *Patriotism* (2021); the essay on *Julius Caesar* in the *Julius Caesar* volume (2022); and the *Far from the Madding Crowd* essay in the *Thomas Hardy* volume (2021). I am humbled to have contributed to these volumes alongside so many important scholars across a multitude of disciplines. I am grateful to the entire team at Salem Press and Grey House Publishing for their insightful comments, diligence, and enthusiasm.

Whether on Zoom or pounding the pavement, I appreciate every opportunity to talk about risk. I would like to thank new friends at new venues: Mark Bly and Gregg Henry at the Kennedy Center; Amber Bradshaw, Hank Kimmel, and Emily McClain at Working Title Playwrights; Timothy Wutrich and the Theater in Greece and Rome Committee (TIGR) at the Classical Association of the Middle West and South; Jess Hutchinson and Julie Felise Dubiner at the National New Play Network. In a world rife with risk, good company goes a long way.

A debt of gratitude goes out to everyone who has participated in making risk theatre come to life: Anton Brakhage and Kara Flanagan at Theatre Carpe Diem; Janet Munsil at The Canadian Play Thing; all the actors and volunteers at Langham Court Theatre who have lit up risk theatre's stage. It is a pleasure to team up again with editor Mark Grill at Sword Fern Communications and Kim Schacht, Julianne McCallum, and the team at FriesenPress.

Thank you to David Konstan for taking the time to read and comment on the essays. Thank you to Gord McLaren at PML Professional Mechanical for allowing me the flexible work schedule to pursue my dreams. To Gidi Nahshon for our conversations on the theory of tragedy—I turned to find you, but you were already gone. I will remember our friendship here. Finally, to the girl on the Salish Sea shore: I hope you found what it is you were looking for. But for me, the things that were hardest to find were the easiest to lose.

EDWIN WONG
Victoria, Canada

Index

About the Type

This book was set in Berling. Designed in 1951 by Karl Erik Forsberg for the Typefoundry Berlingska Stilgjuteri AB in Lund, Sweden, it was released the same year in foundry type by H. Berthold AG. A classic old-face design, its generous proportions and inclined serifs make it highly legible.

CPSIA information can be obtained
at www.ICGtesting.com
Printed in the USA
BVHW061604030522
635996BV00032B/2320